ROSARIO + VAMPIRE

Season II

13

AKIHISA IKEDA

ROSARIO+VAMPIRE Season II 13

Contents
& Story

Tsukune Aono accidentally enrolls in Yokai Academy, a high school for monsters! After befriending the school's cutest girl, Moka Akashiya, he decides to stay...even though Yokai has a zero-tolerance policy towards humans (a fatal policy). Tsukune survives with the help of his News Club friends—Moka (Vampire), Kurumu (Succubus), Yukari (Witch) and Mizore (Snow Fairy). Just as Tsukune and his friends begin contemplating their future after they graduate, they are attacked by Fairy Tale, an organization bent on destroying the world by reviving Alucard, the First Ancestor of the Vampires. When Fairy Tale kidnaps Moka, her friends train rigorously under Tohofuhai, one of the three Dark Lords, then infiltrate the Hanging Garden, the enemy's fortress.

Tsukune fights his way through the leaders of the branch offices of Fairy Tale down to the deepest level, where Alucard is awakening... Now Gyokuro, the leader of Fairy Tale, has taken control of Alacurd with Moka's Rosario. To access the power he needs to face Gyokuro, beyond the limit of his body, Tsukune begins to release the seals of his spirit lock—the only thing preventing him from turning into a ghoul...*forever!*

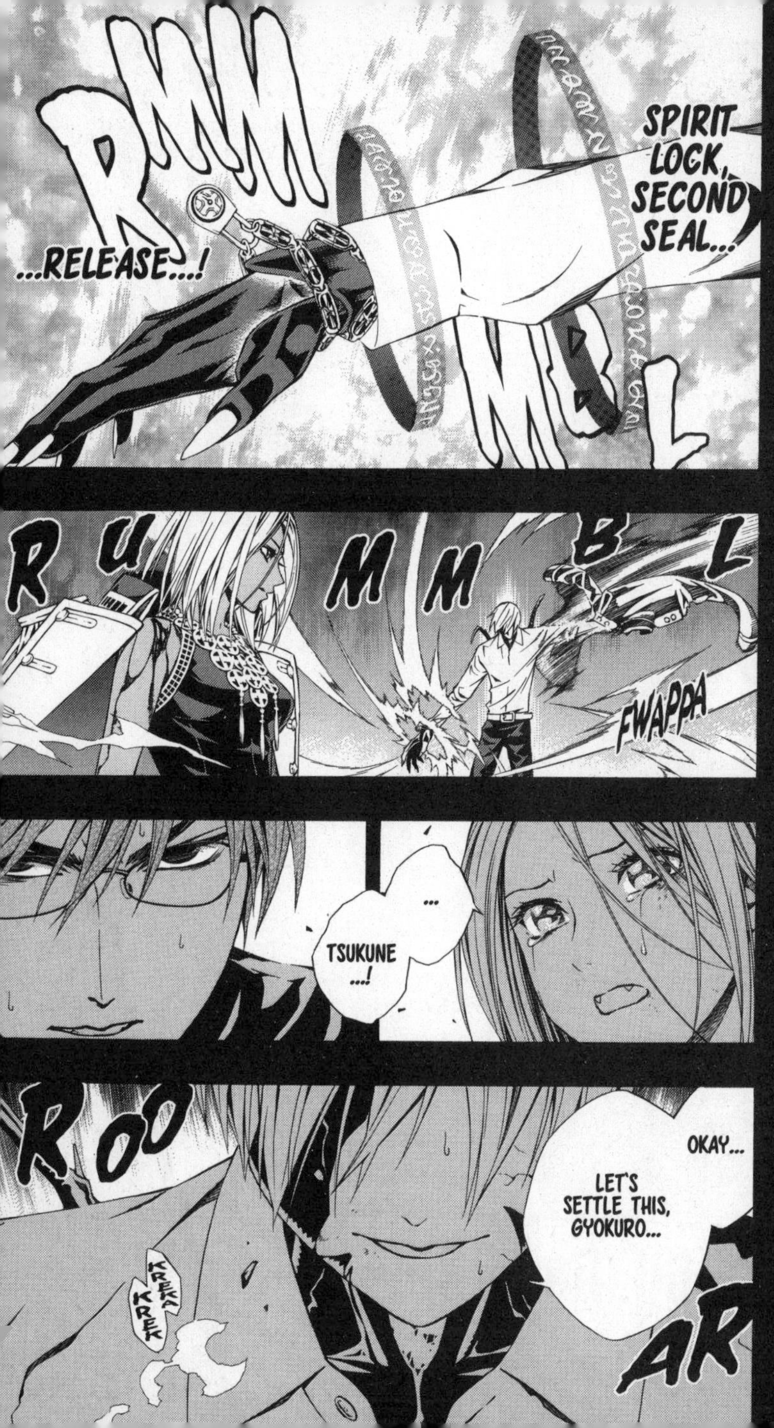
SPIRIT LOCK, SECOND SEAL...
...RELEASE...!
RMM
MBL
RUMMBL
FWAPPA
...
TSUKUNE ...!
OKAY...
LET'S SETTLE THIS, GYOKURO...
ROO
AR
KREKA KREK

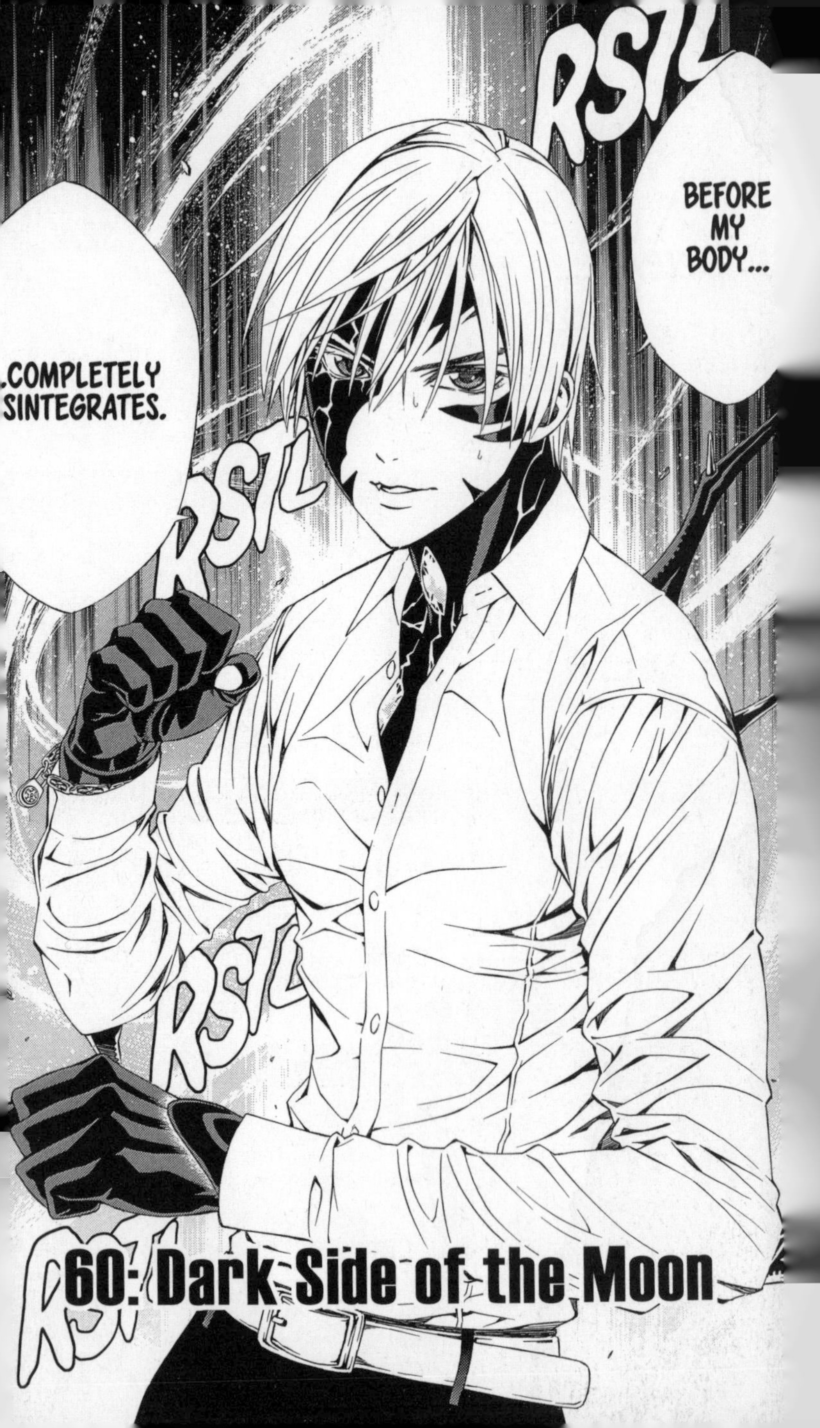
RSTL
BEFORE MY BODY...
.COMPLETELY SINTEGRATES.
RSTL
RSTL
RSTL

60: Dark Side of the Moon

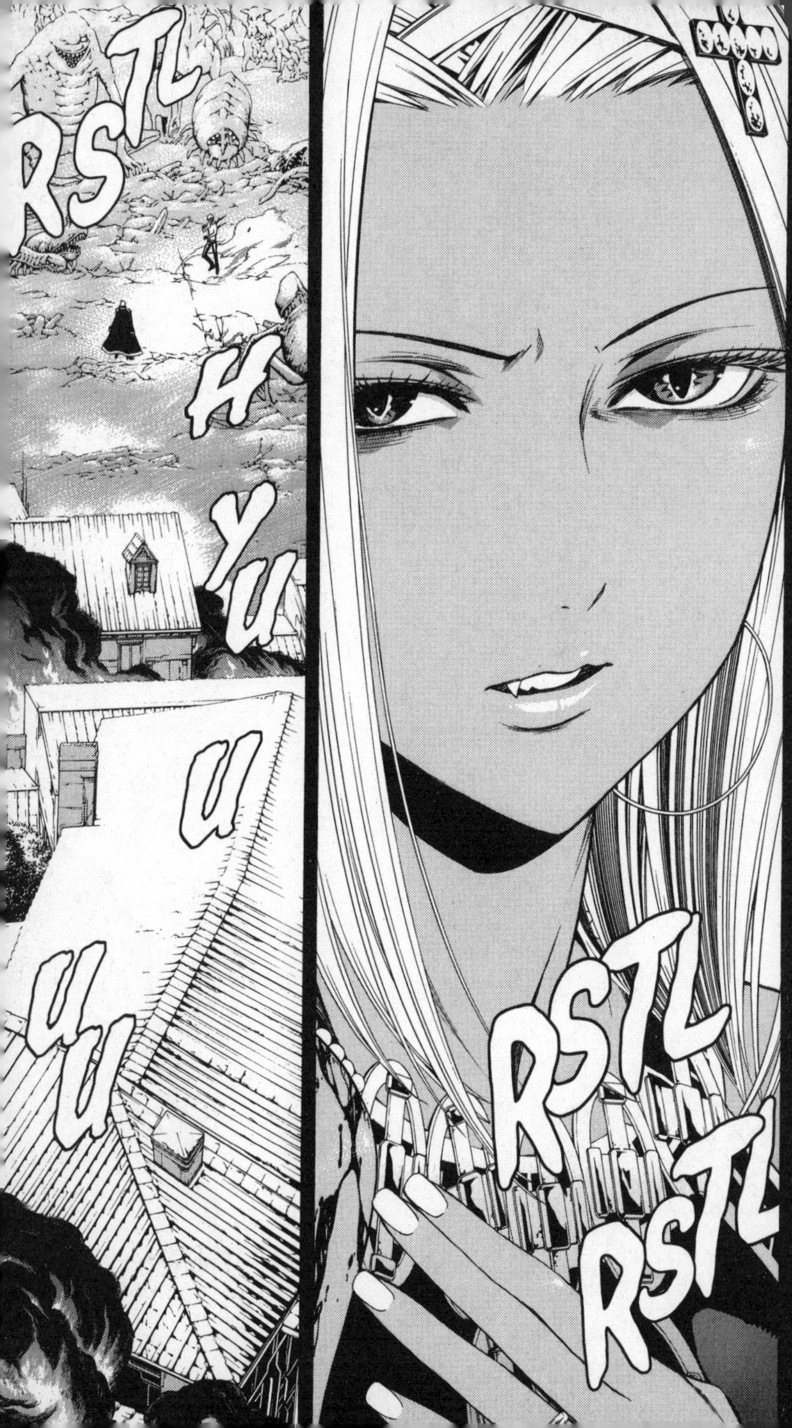
RSTL
RSTL
RSTL
RSTL
HYUUUU

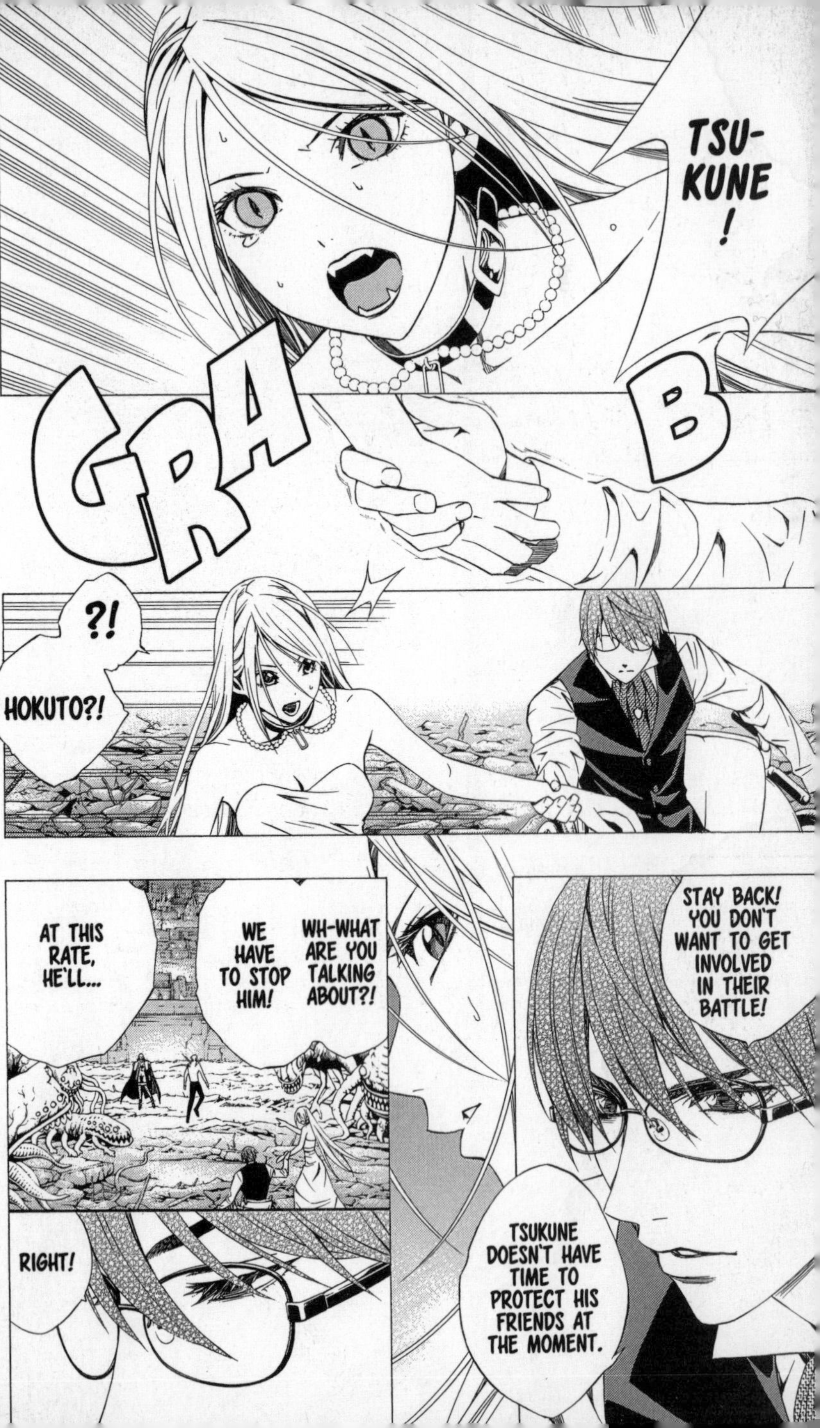
TSU-KUNE!
GRAB
?!
HOKUTO?!
STAY BACK! YOU DON'T WANT TO GET INVOLVED IN THEIR BATTLE!
TSUKUNE DOESN'T HAVE TIME TO PROTECT HIS FRIENDS AT THE MOMENT.
WH-WHAT ARE YOU TALKING ABOUT?!
WE HAVE TO STOP HIM!
AT THIS RATE, HE'LL...
RIGHT!

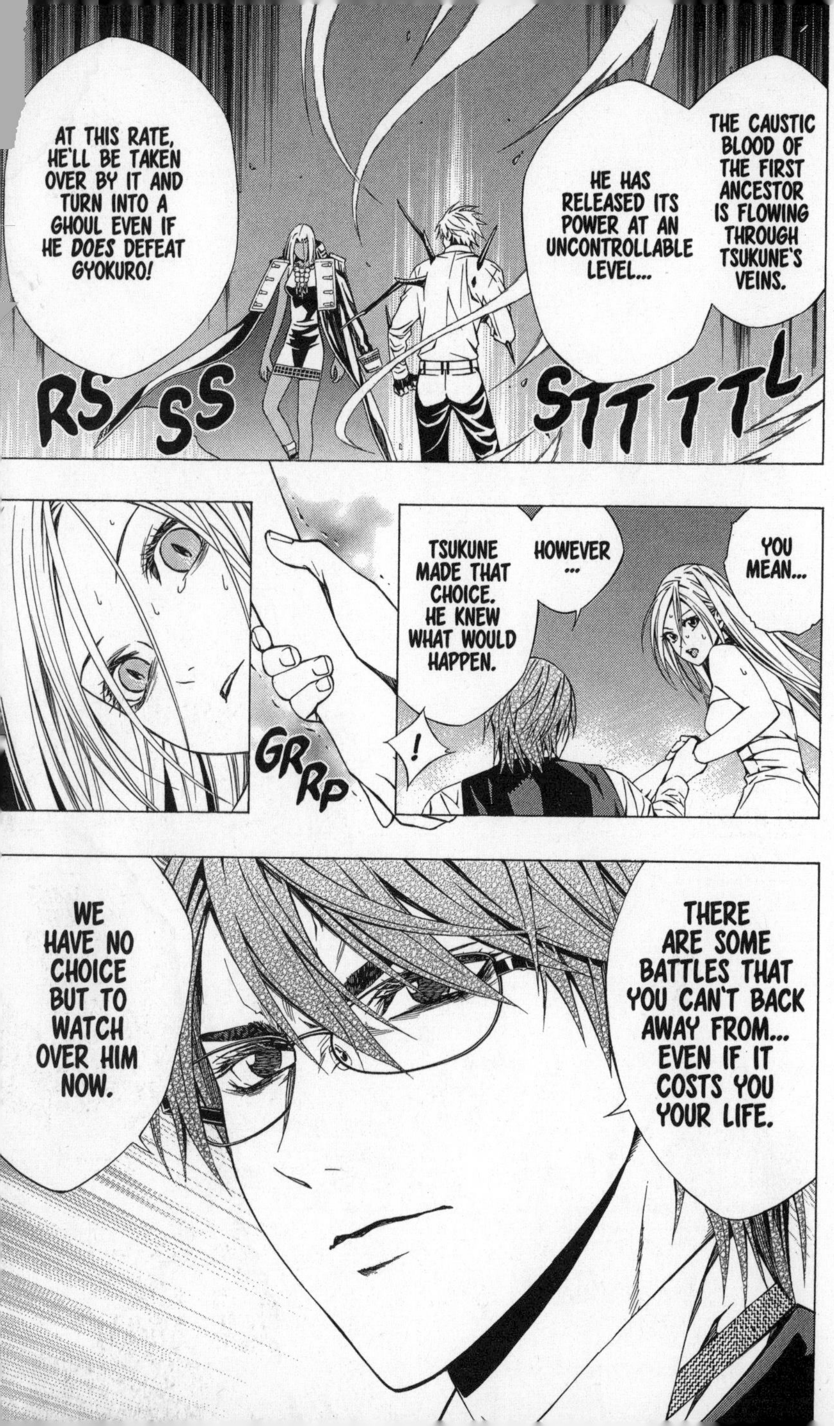
THE CAUSTIC BLOOD OF THE FIRST ANCESTOR IS FLOWING THROUGH TSUKUNE'S VEINS.
HE HAS RELEASED ITS POWER AT AN UNCONTROLLABLE LEVEL...
STTTTL
AT THIS RATE, HE'LL BE TAKEN OVER BY IT AND TURN INTO A GHOUL EVEN IF HE *DOES* DEFEAT GYOKURO!
RSSS
YOU MEAN...
HOWEVER...
TSUKUNE MADE THAT CHOICE. HE KNEW WHAT WOULD HAPPEN.
!
GRRP
THERE ARE SOME BATTLES THAT YOU CAN'T BACK AWAY FROM... EVEN IF IT COSTS YOU YOUR LIFE.
WE HAVE NO CHOICE BUT TO WATCH OVER HIM NOW.

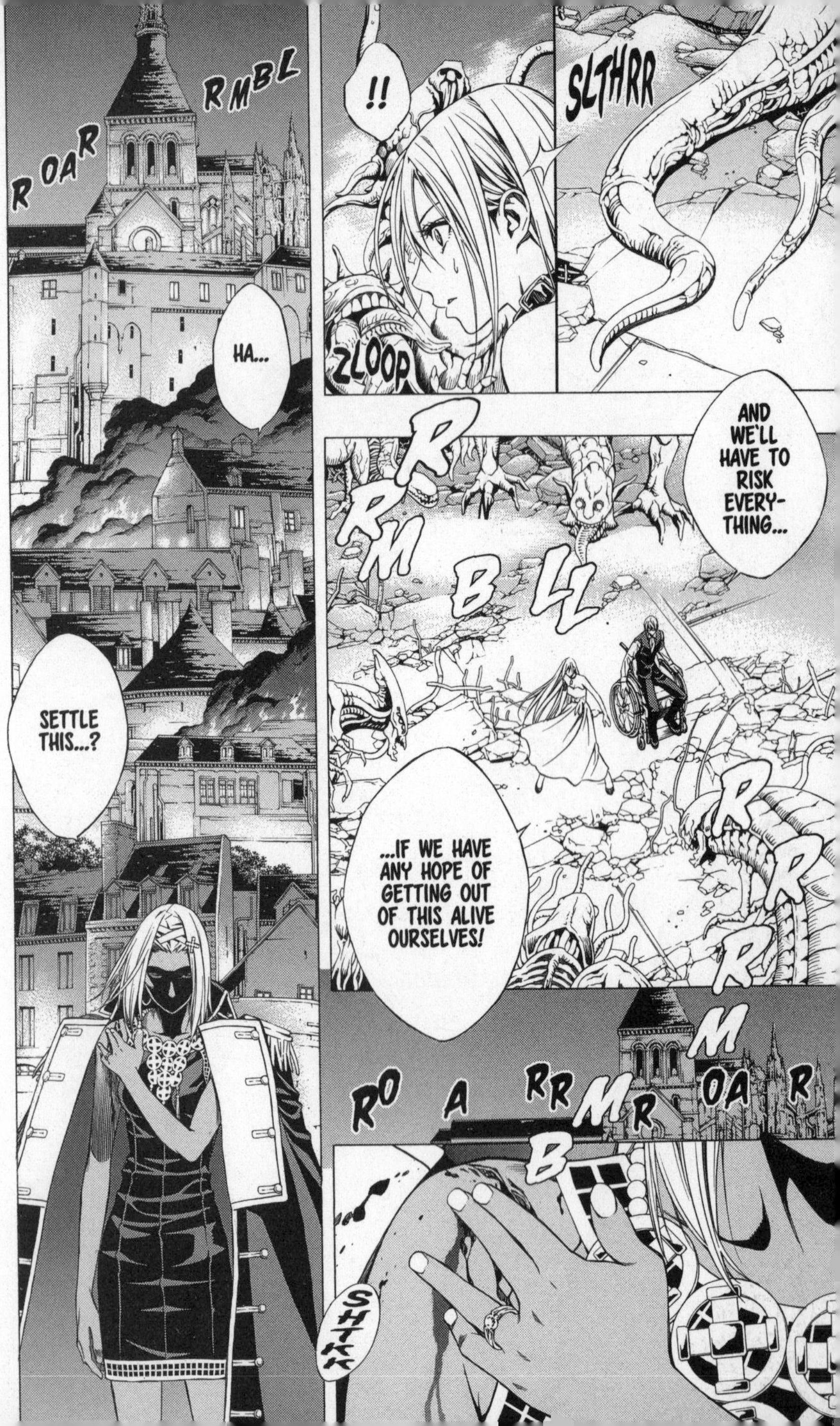
SLTHRR
!!
ZLOOP
AND WE'LL HAVE TO RISK EVERYTHING...
RRMBLL
RRRR
...IF WE HAVE ANY HOPE OF GETTING OUT OF THIS ALIVE OURSELVES!
RO A RR M R OA R
M B
SHTKK
R OAR
RMBL
HA...
SETTLE THIS...?

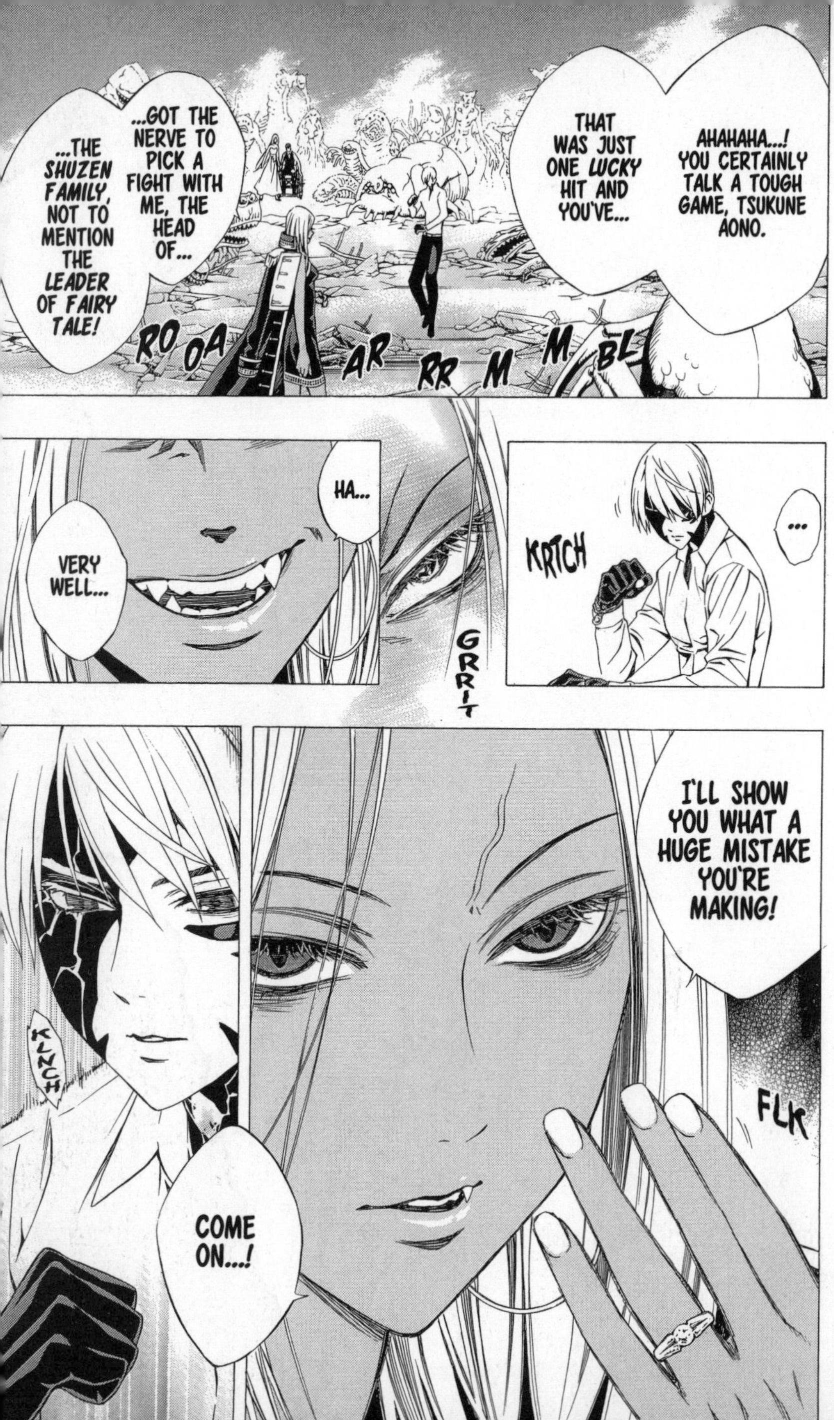
AHAHAHA...! YOU CERTAINLY TALK A TOUGH GAME, TSUKUNE AONO.
THAT WAS JUST ONE LUCKY HIT AND YOU'VE...
...GOT THE NERVE TO PICK A FIGHT WITH ME, THE HEAD OF...
...THE SHUZEN FAMILY, NOT TO MENTION THE LEADER OF FAIRY TALE!
RO OA AR RR M M BL
...
KRITCH
HA...
VERY WELL...
GRRIT
I'LL SHOW YOU WHAT A HUGE MISTAKE YOU'RE MAKING!
FLK
KLNCH
COME ON...!

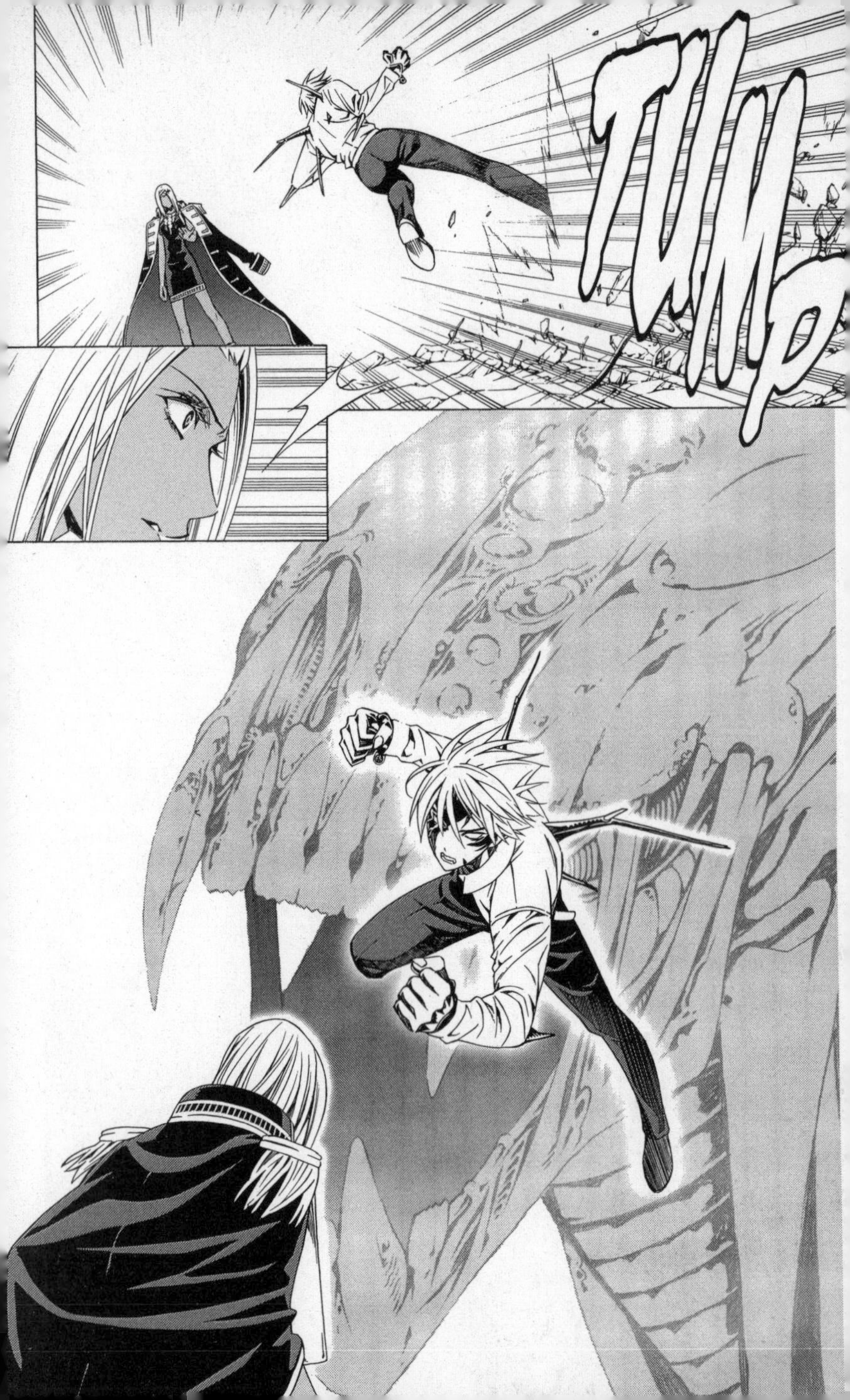
TUMP

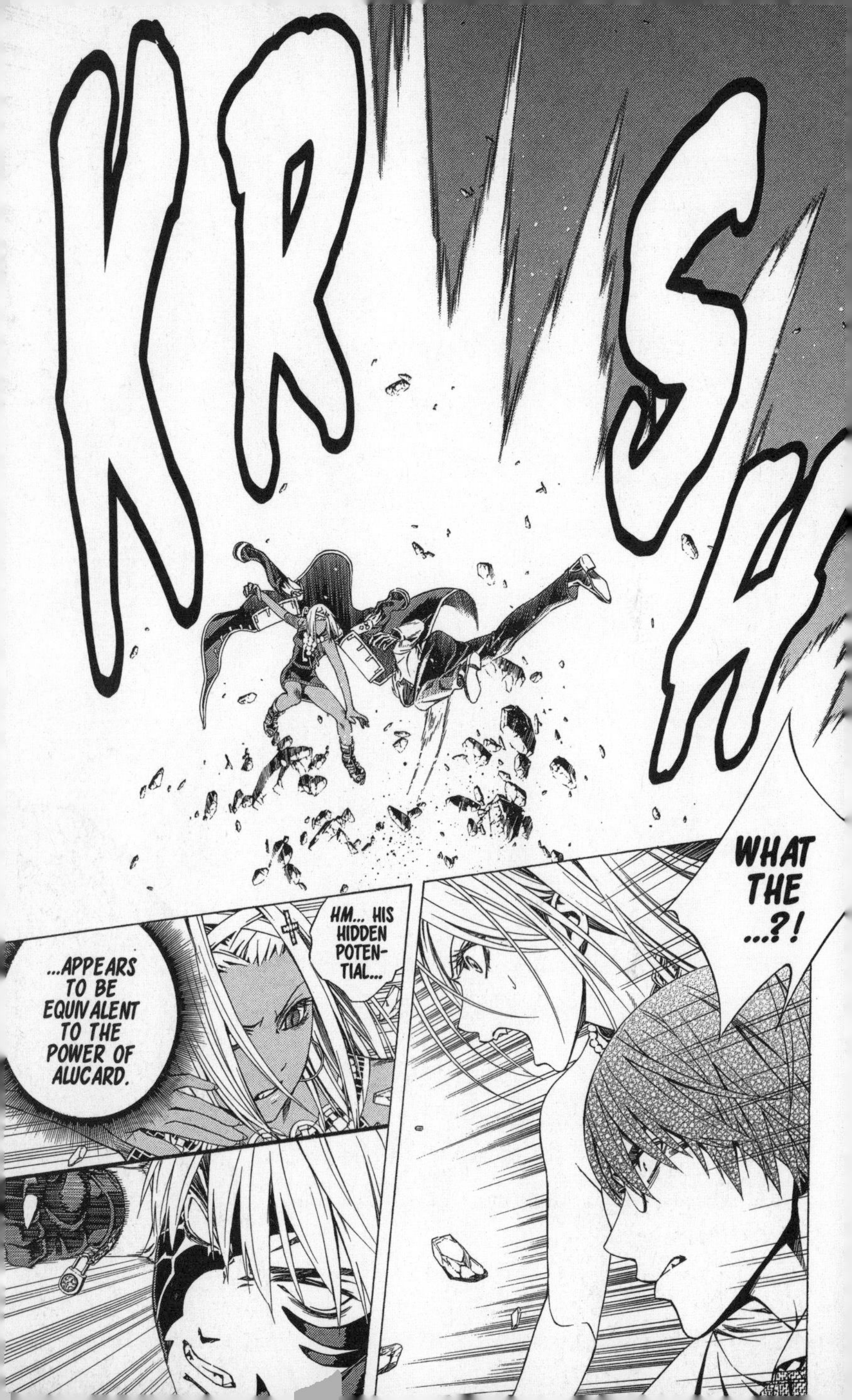
KRSSH
WHAT THE ...?!
HM... HIS HIDDEN POTEN-TIAL...
...APPEARS TO BE EQUIVALENT TO THE POWER OF ALUCARD.

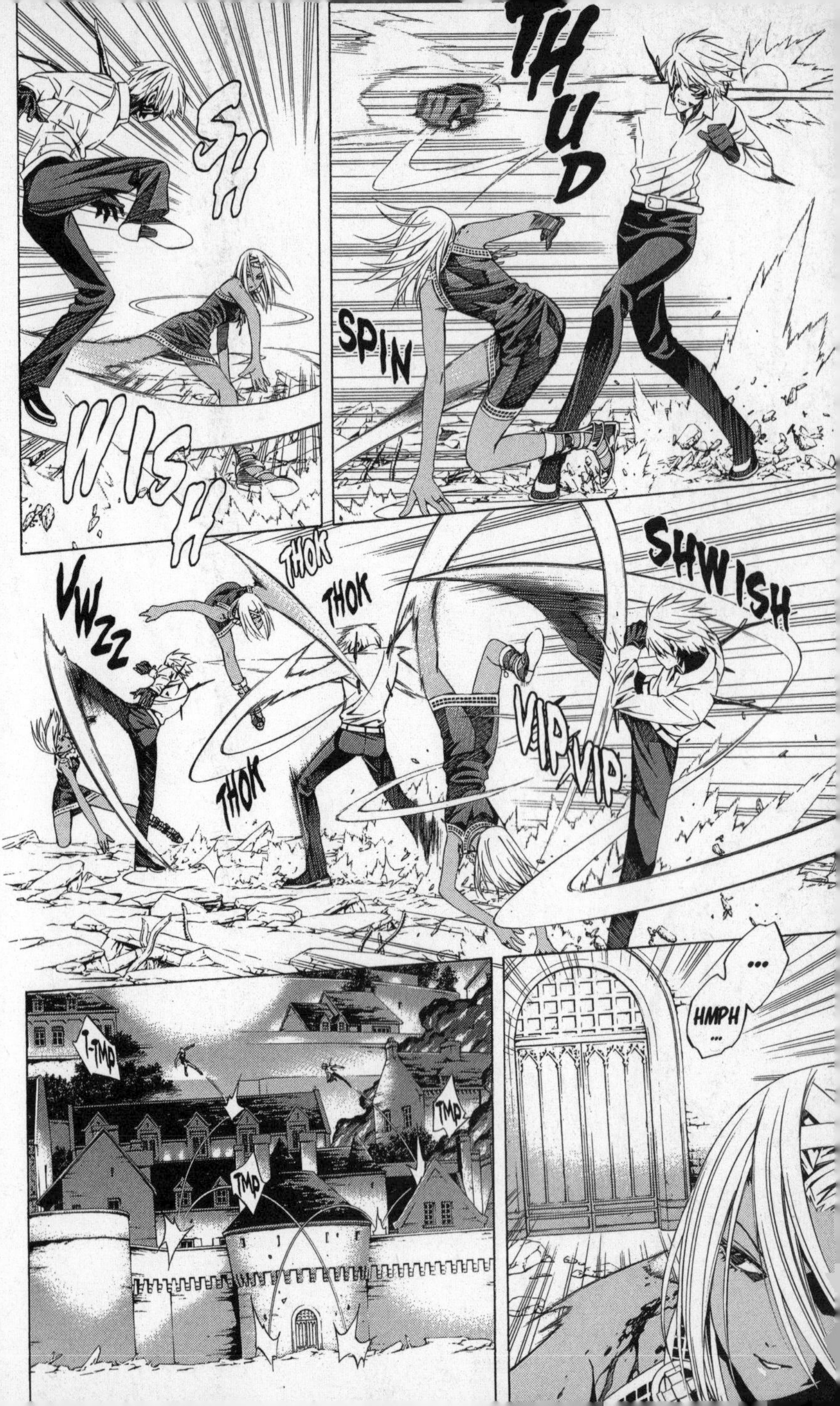
THUD
SPIN
SH
WISH
SHWISH
VIP VIP
THOK
THOK
THOK
VWZZZ
...
HMPH ...
T-TMP
TMP
TMP

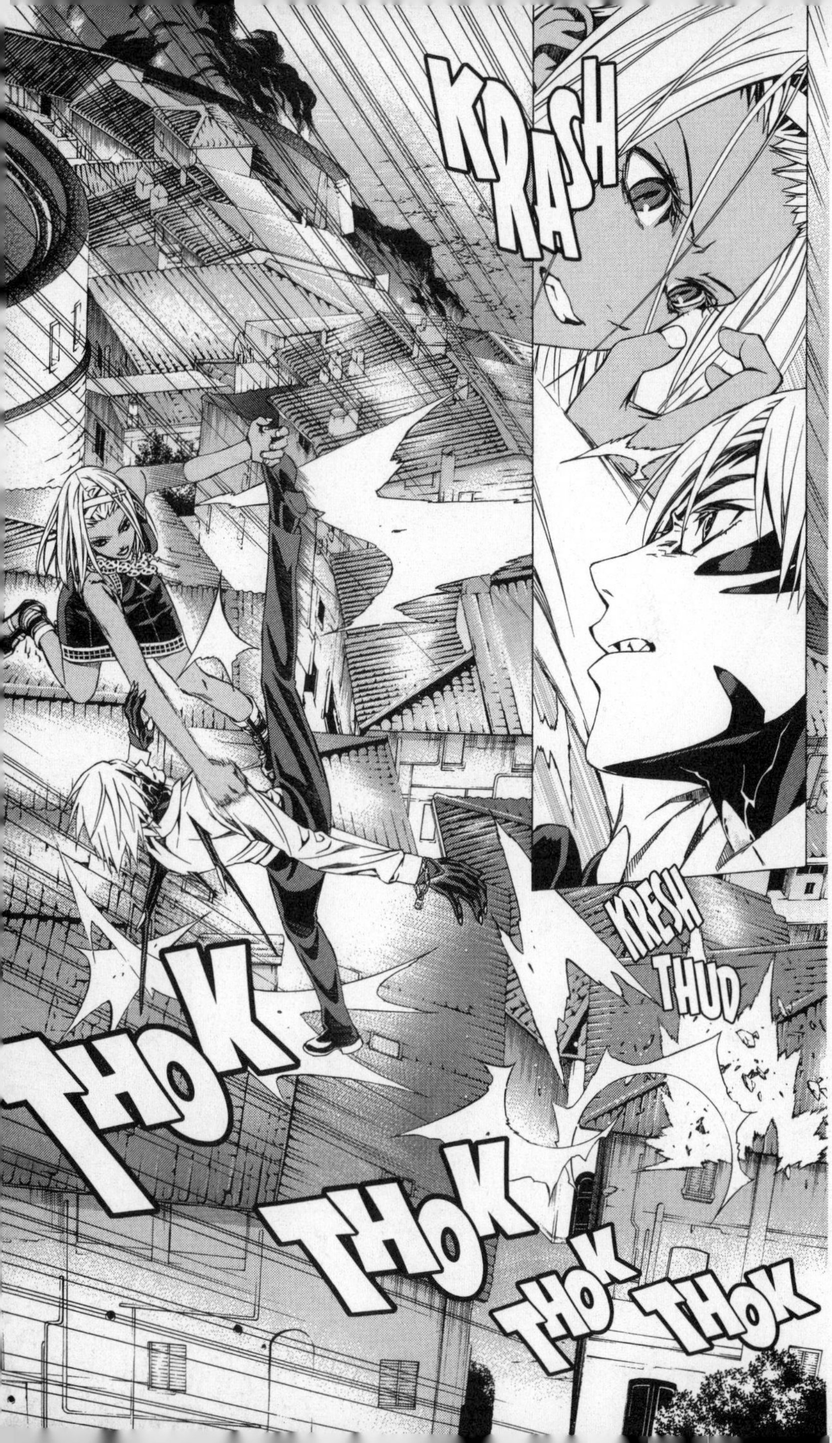
KRASH
KRESH
THUD
THOK
THOK
THOK
THOK

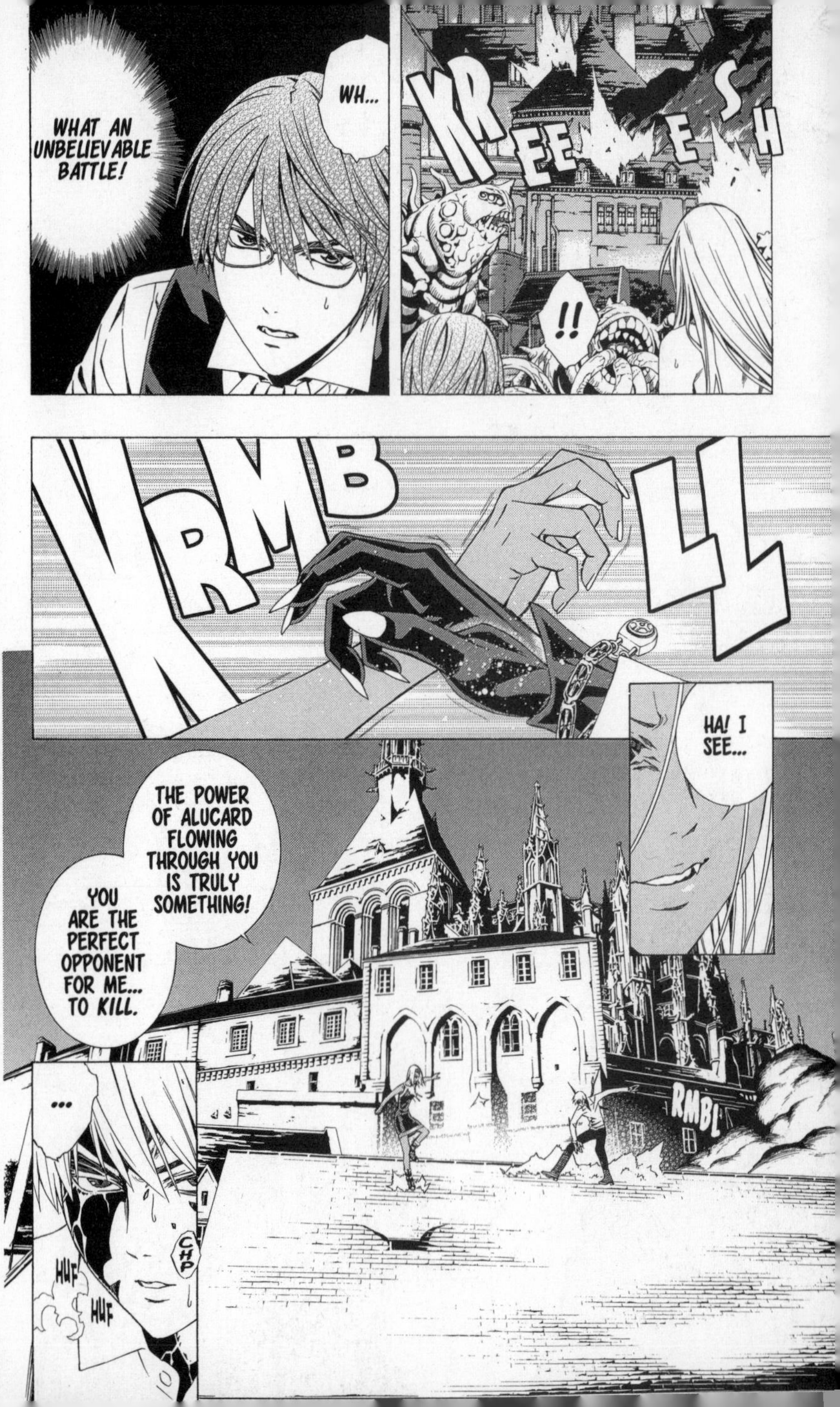
KREEESH
!!
WH...
WHAT AN UNBELIEVABLE BATTLE!
KRMBLL
HA! I SEE...
THE POWER OF ALUCARD FLOWING THROUGH YOU IS TRULY SOMETHING!
YOU ARE THE PERFECT OPPONENT FOR ME... TO KILL.
RMBL
...
CHP
HUF HUF

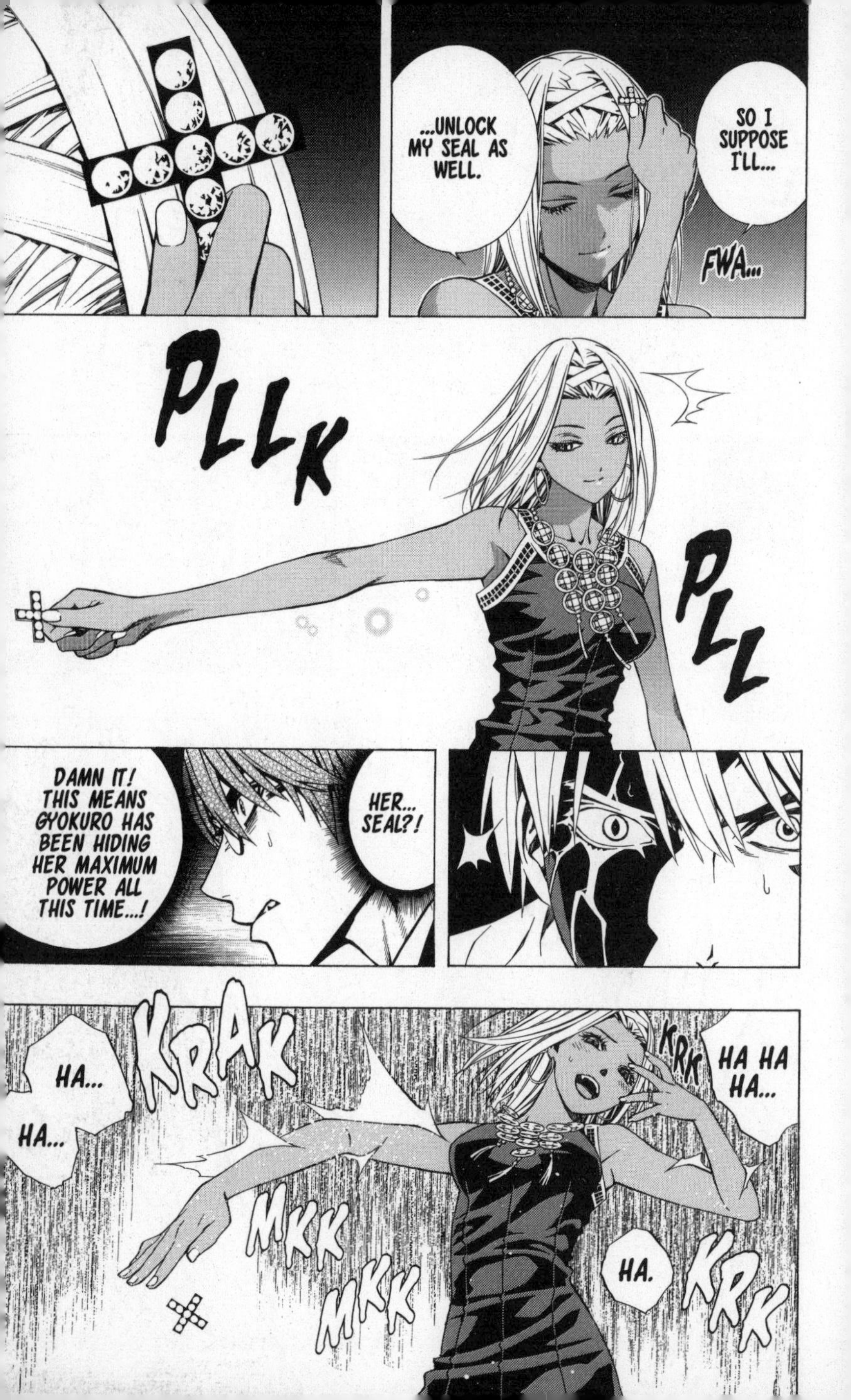
SO I SUPPOSE I'LL...
FWA...
...UNLOCK MY SEAL AS WELL.
PLLK
PLL
HER... SEAL?!
DAMN IT! THIS MEANS GYOKURO HAS BEEN HIDING HER MAXIMUM POWER ALL THIS TIME...!
HA HA HA...
KRK
KRAK
HA...
HA...
MKK
MKK
HA.
KRK

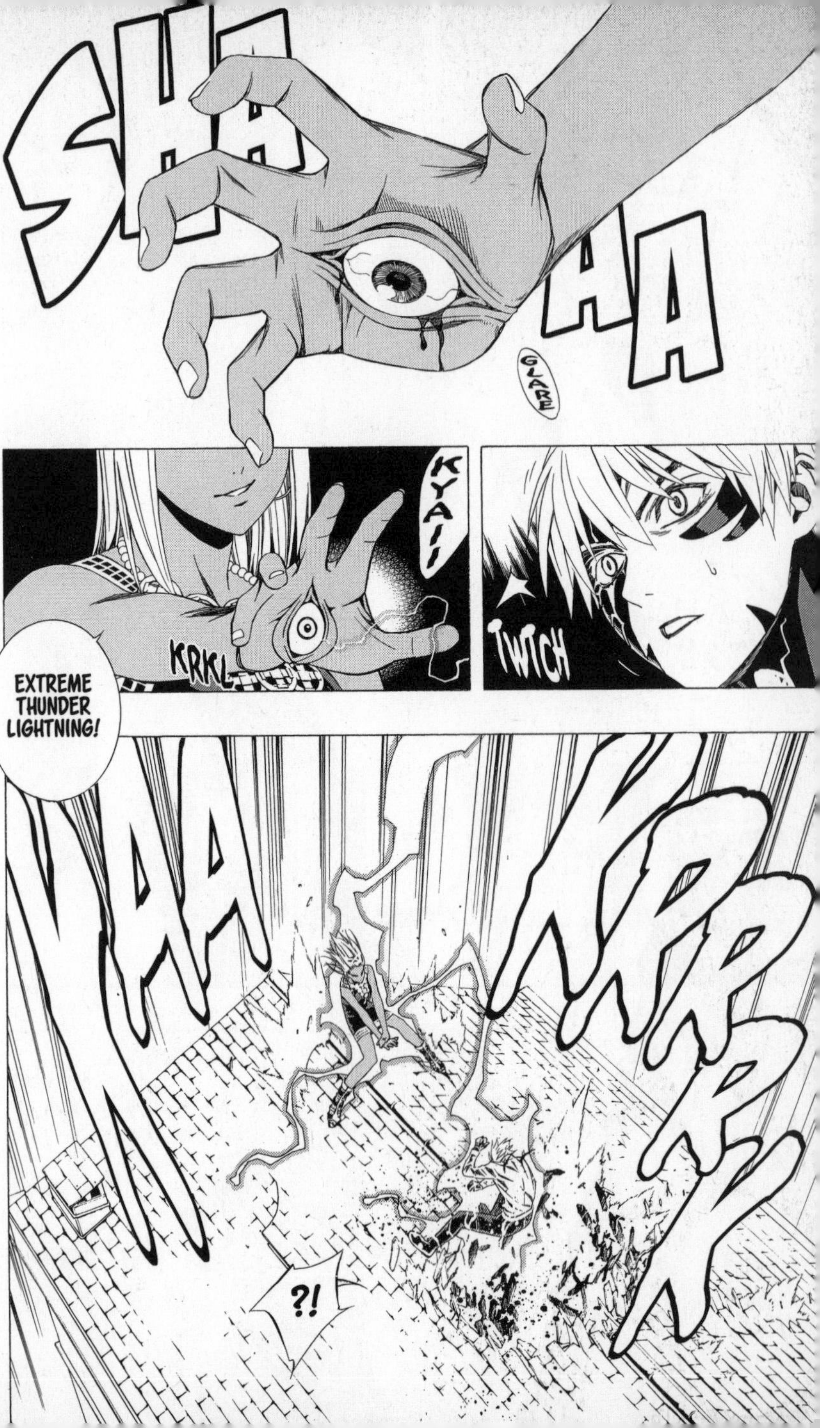
SHA
AA
GLARE
TWITCH
KYAII
KRKL
EXTREME THUNDER LIGHTNING!
?!

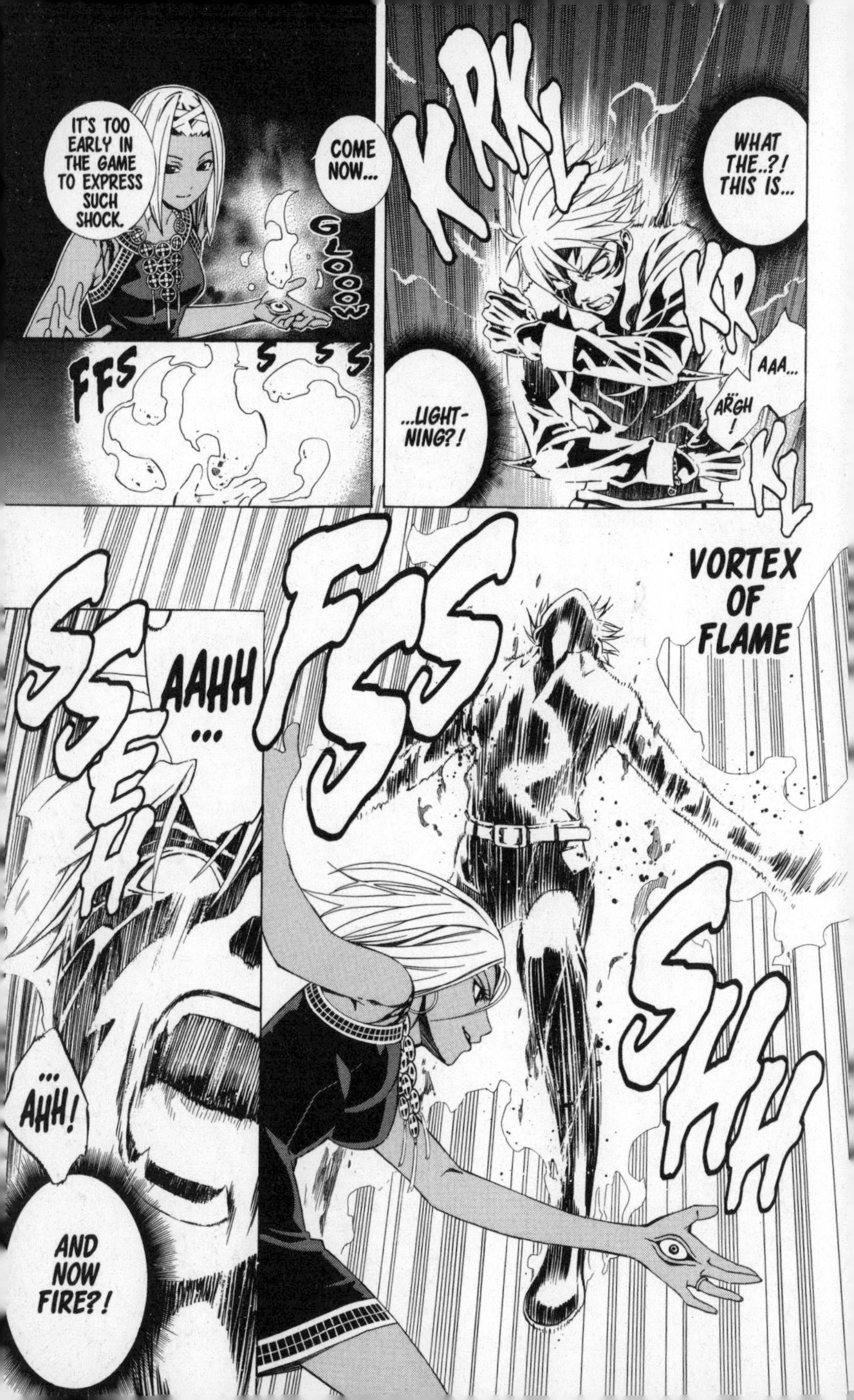
WHAT THE..?! THIS IS...
KRKL
KR
...LIGHTNING?!
AAA... ARGH!
KL
COME NOW...
IT'S TOO EARLY IN THE GAME TO EXPRESS SUCH SHOCK.
GLOOOOW
FFS
S S S
VORTEX OF FLAME
FSS
SHH
AAHH...
SSEH
...AHH!
AND NOW FIRE?!

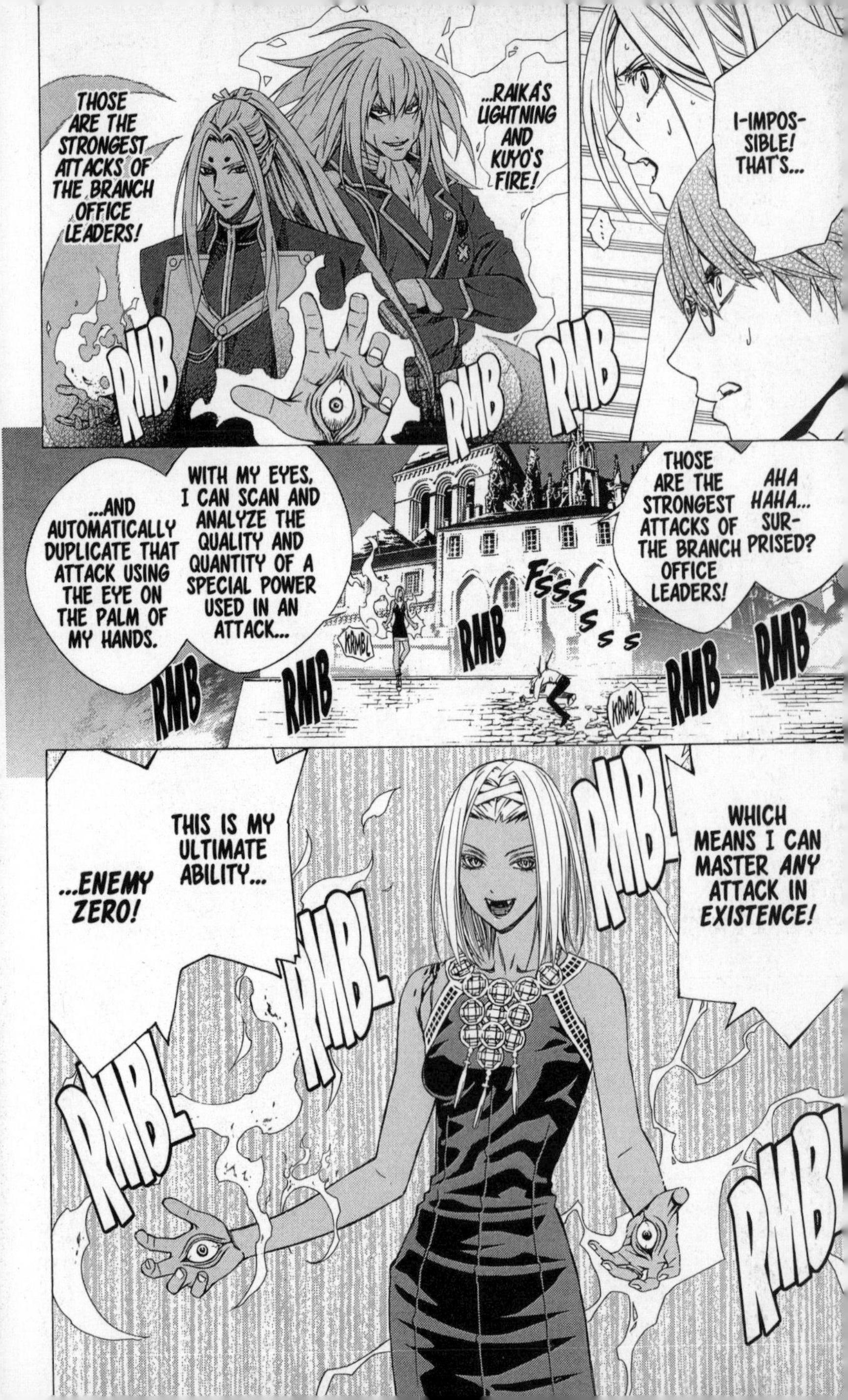
I-IMPOSSIBLE! THAT'S...
...
...RAIKA'S LIGHTNING AND KUYO'S FIRE!
THOSE ARE THE STRONGEST ATTACKS OF THE BRANCH OFFICE LEADERS!
RMB
RMB
RMB
AHA HAHA... SURPRISED?
THOSE ARE THE STRONGEST ATTACKS OF THE BRANCH OFFICE LEADERS!
RMB
RMB
KRMBL
FSSSSSSS
RMB
KRMBL
WITH MY EYES, I CAN SCAN AND ANALYZE THE QUALITY AND QUANTITY OF A SPECIAL POWER USED IN AN ATTACK...
...AND AUTOMATICALLY DUPLICATE THAT ATTACK USING THE EYE ON THE PALM OF MY HANDS.
RMB
RMB
WHICH MEANS I CAN MASTER ANY ATTACK IN EXISTENCE!
RMBL
THIS IS MY ULTIMATE ABILITY...
...ENEMY ZERO!
KMBL
RMBL
RMBL

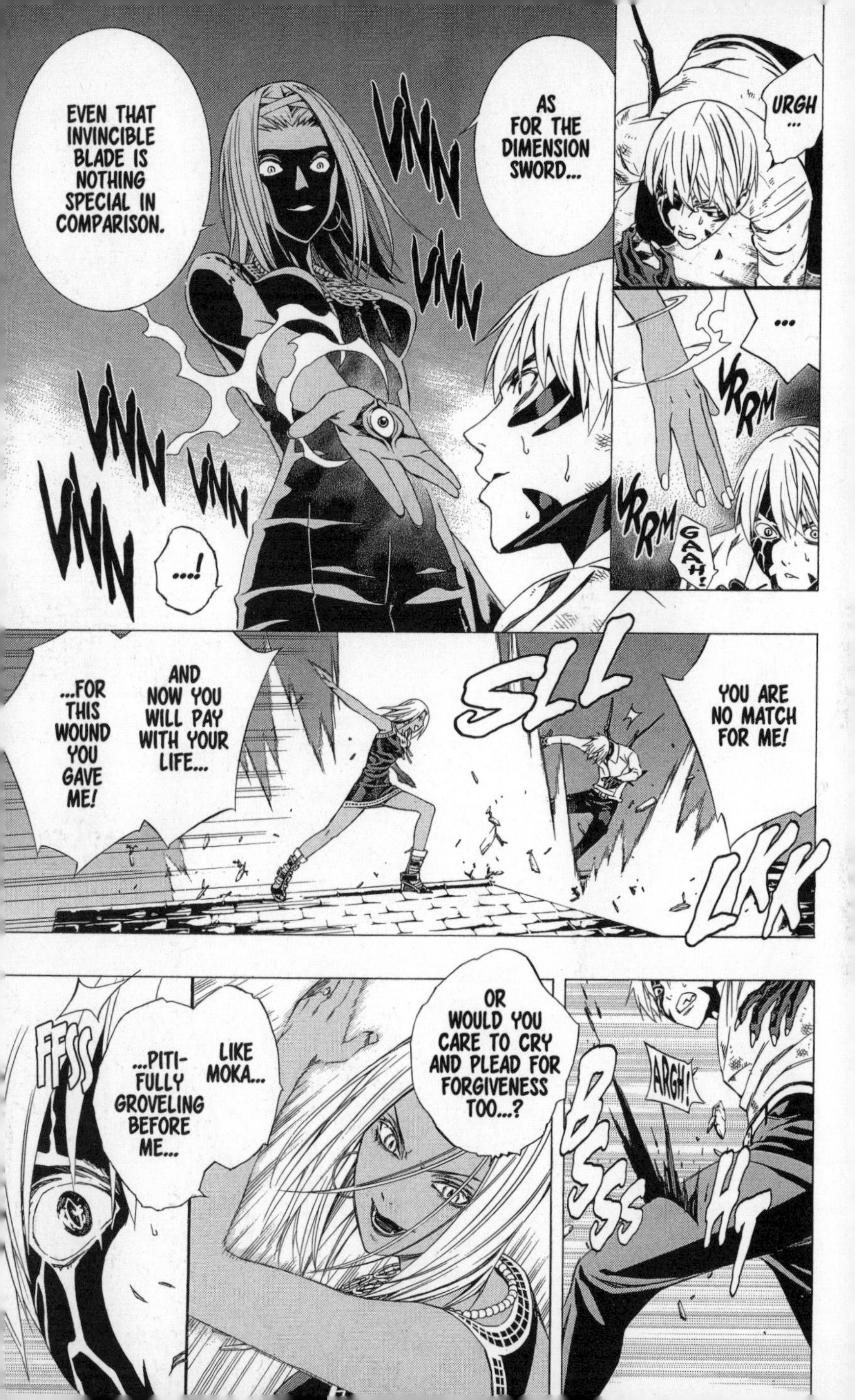
URGH...
...
VRRM
VRRM
GAAH!
AS FOR THE DIMENSION SWORD...
VNN
VNN
EVEN THAT INVINCIBLE BLADE IS NOTHING SPECIAL IN COMPARISON.
VNN
VNN
VNN
...!
YOU ARE NO MATCH FOR ME!
SLL
LKK
AND NOW YOU WILL PAY WITH YOUR LIFE...
...FOR THIS WOUND YOU GAVE ME!
ARGH!
BSSSHT
OR WOULD YOU CARE TO CRY AND PLEAD FOR FORGIVENESS TOO...?
LIKE MOKA...
...PITI-FULLY GROVELING BEFORE ME...
FFSS

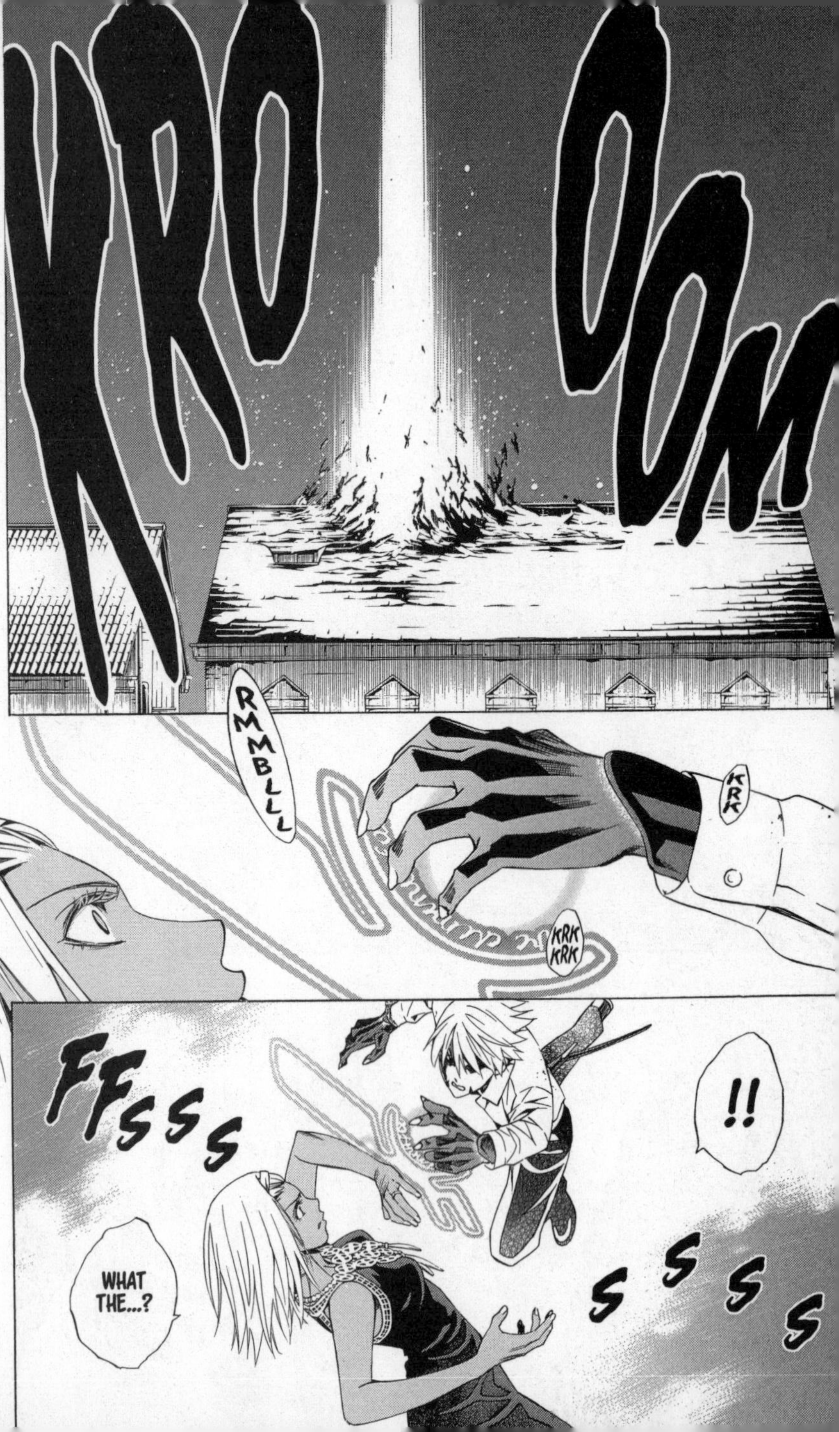
KROOOM
KRK
KRK KRK
RMMBLLL
!!
FFSSSS
SSSSS
WHAT THE...?

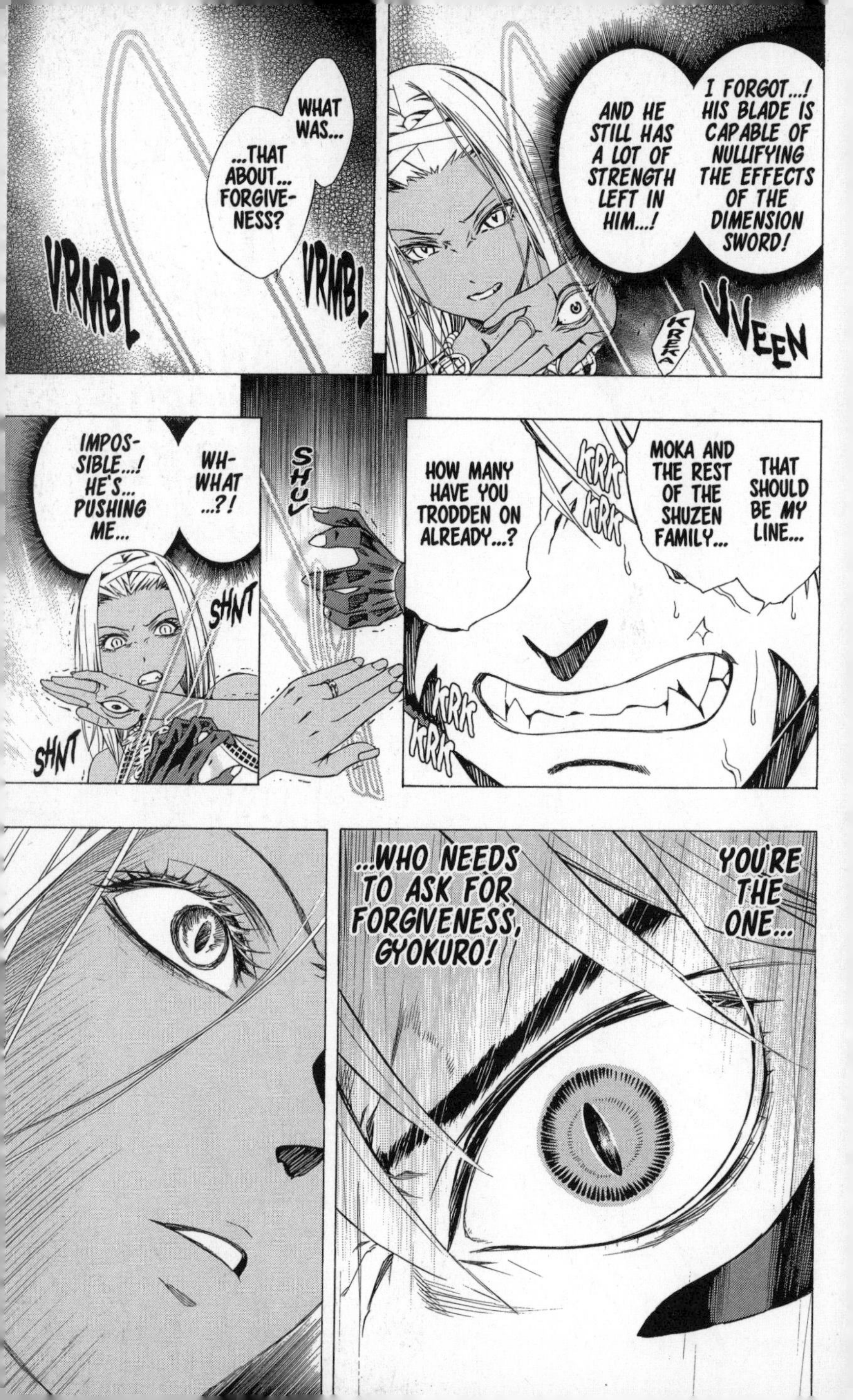
I FORGOT...! HIS BLADE IS CAPABLE OF NULLIFYING THE EFFECTS OF THE DIMENSION SWORD!
AND HE STILL HAS A LOT OF STRENGTH LEFT IN HIM...!
KREKA
VVEEN
WHAT WAS...
...THAT ABOUT... FORGIVENESS?
VRMBL
VRMBL
THAT SHOULD BE MY LINE...
MOKA AND THE REST OF THE SHUZEN FAMILY...
HOW MANY HAVE YOU TRODDEN ON ALREADY...?
KRK KRK
KRK KRK
SHU
WH-WHAT...?!
IMPOSSIBLE...! HE'S... PUSHING ME...
SHNT
SHNT
YOU'RE THE ONE...
...WHO NEEDS TO ASK FOR FORGIVENESS, GYOKURO!

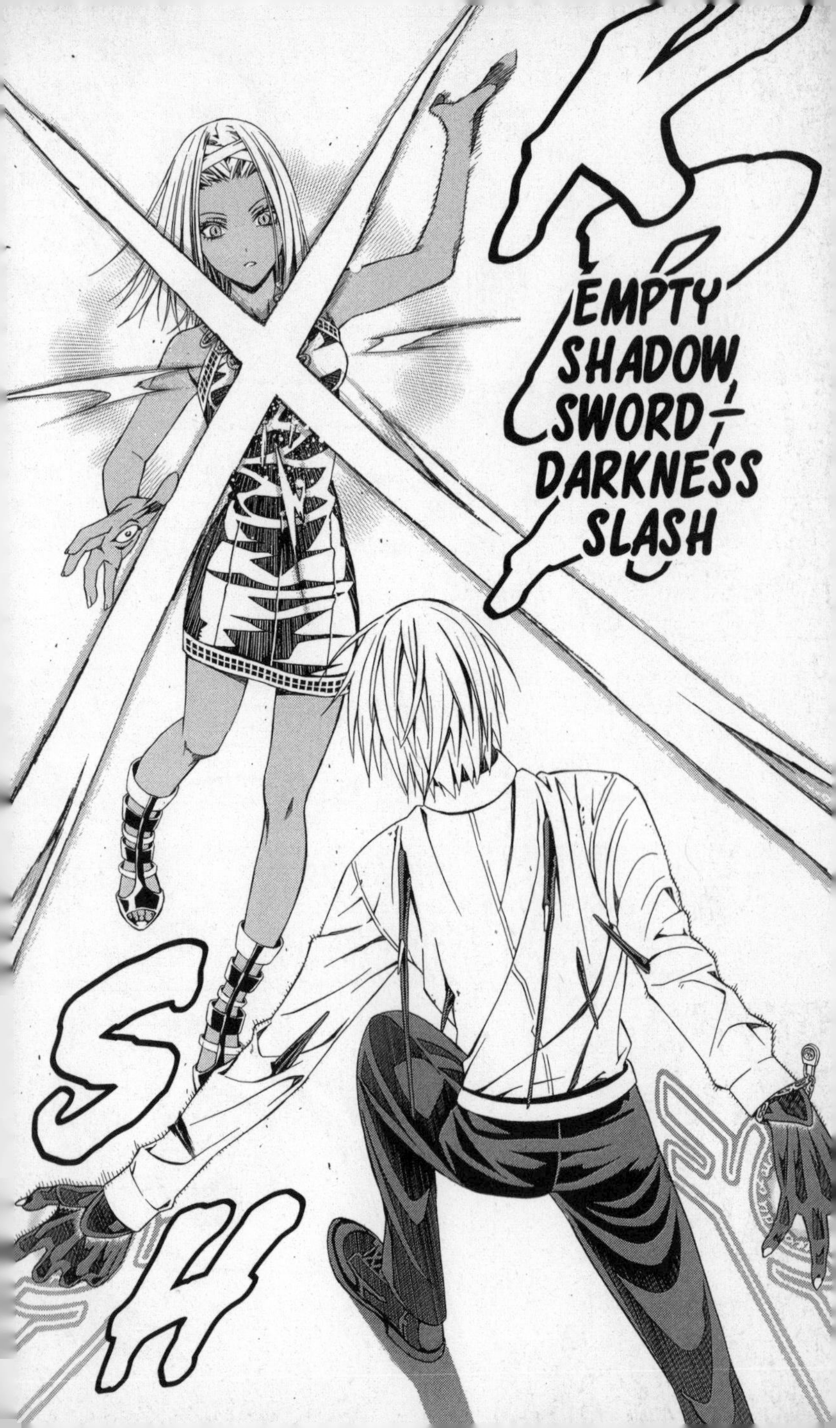
EMPTY SHADOW SWORD DARKNESS SLASH
SH

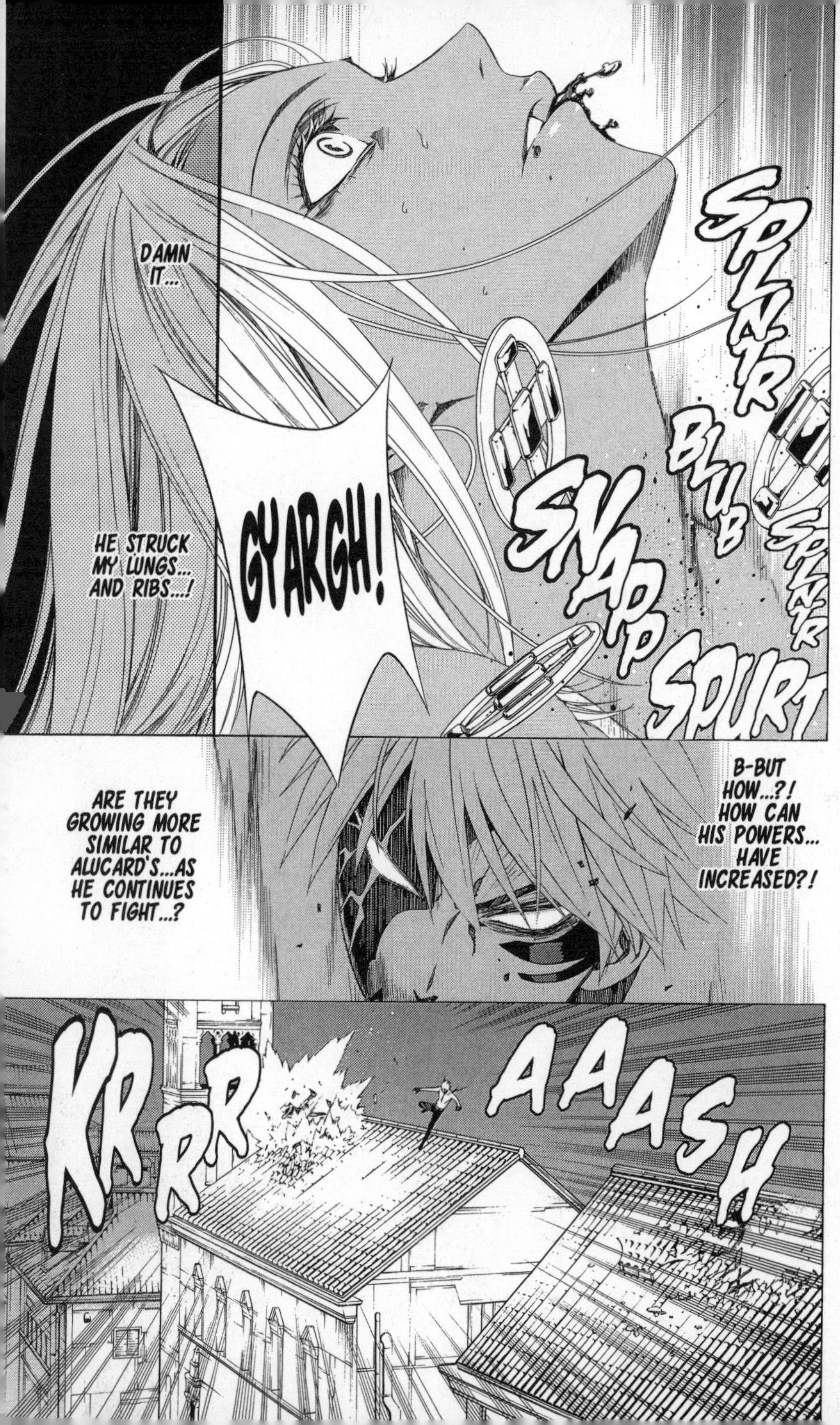
SPLNTR
BLUB
SNAP
SPLNTR
SPURT
GYARGH!
DAMN IT...
HE STRUCK MY LUNGS... AND RIBS...!
B-BUT HOW...?! HOW CAN HIS POWERS... HAVE INCREASED?!
ARE THEY GROWING MORE SIMILAR TO ALUCARD'S...AS HE CONTINUES TO FIGHT...?
KRRRAAAASH

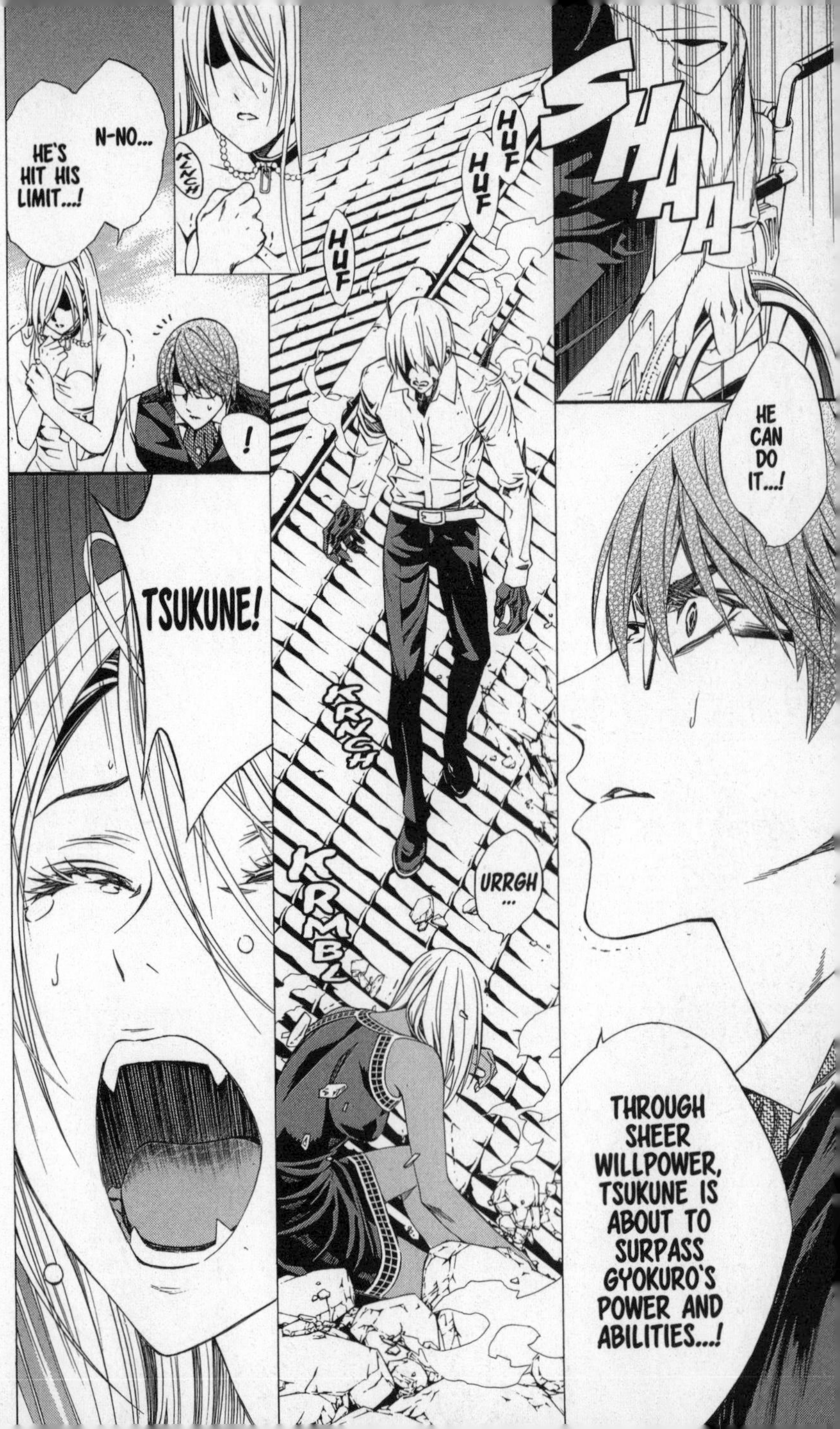
SHAAA
HE CAN DO IT...!
THROUGH SHEER WILLPOWER, TSUKUNE IS ABOUT TO SURPASS GYOKURO'S POWER AND ABILITIES...!
HUF
HUF
HUF
HUF
URRGH...
KRNCH
KRMBL
KLNCH
N-NO...
HE'S HIT HIS LIMIT...!
!
TSUKUNE!

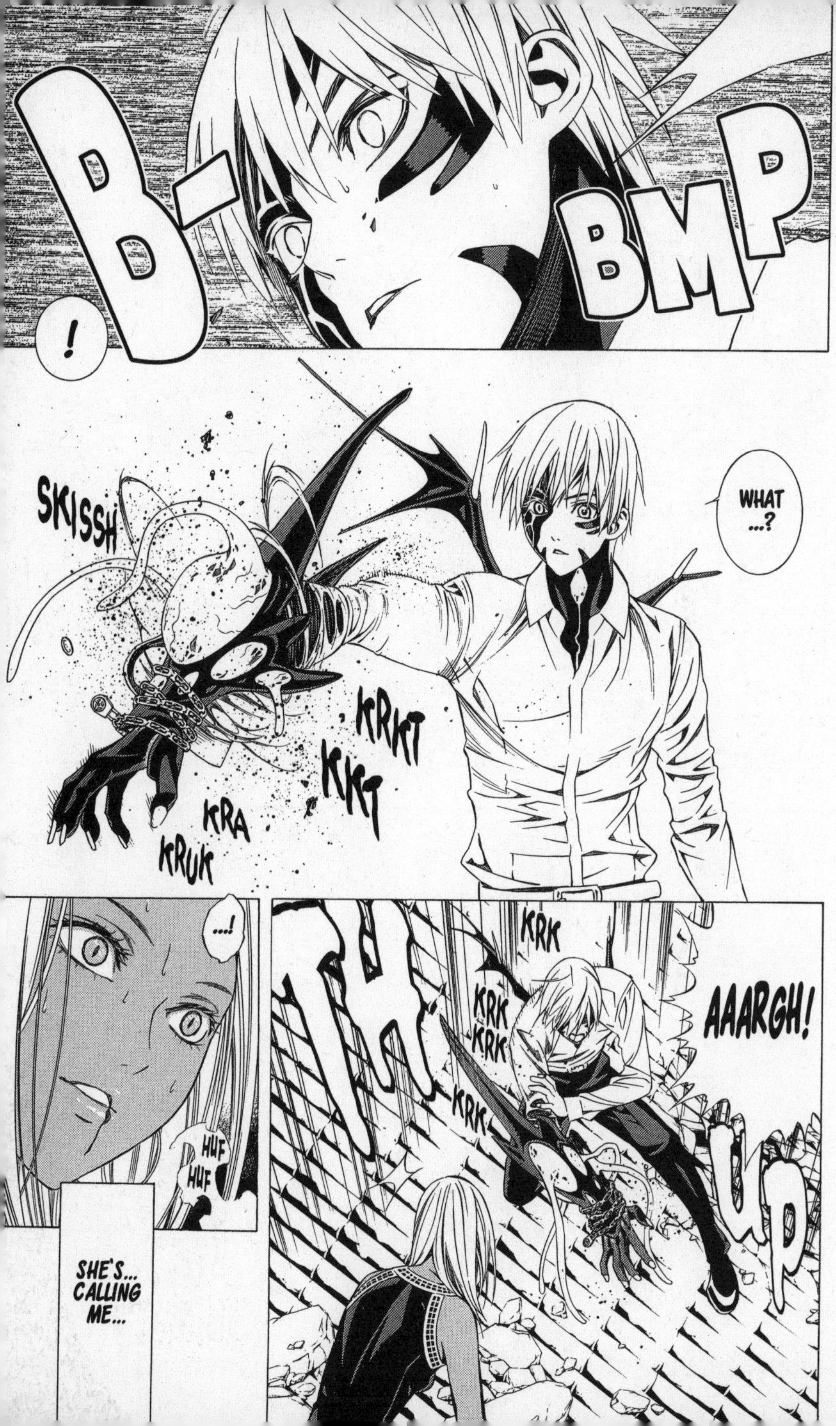
B-BMP
!
WHAT ...?
SKISSH
KRKT KKT
KRA KRUK
KRK
AAARGH!
KRK KRK
KRK
UP
...!
HUF HUF
SHE'S... CALLING ME...

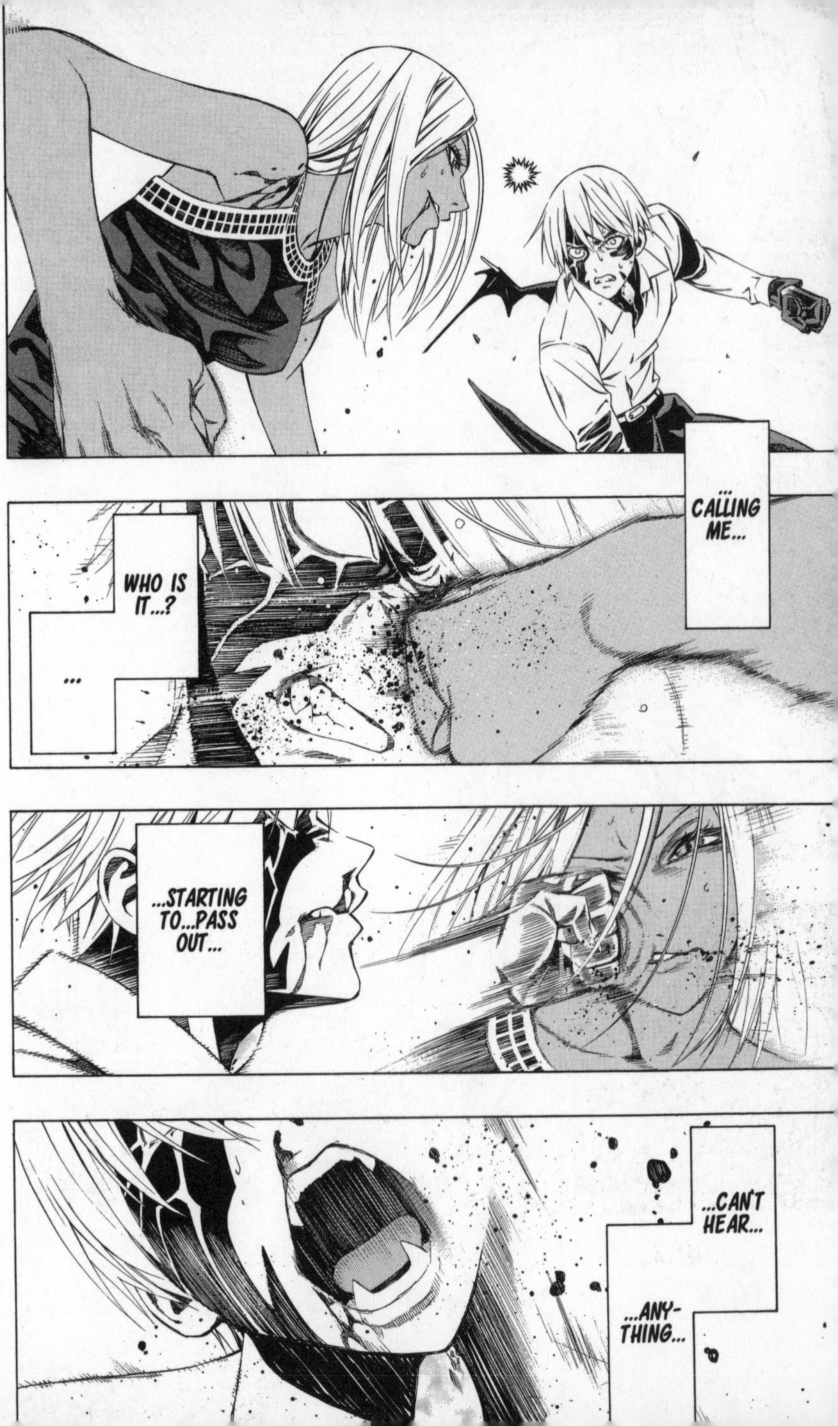
...CALLING ME...
WHO IS IT...?
...
...STARTING TO...PASS OUT...
...CAN'T HEAR...
...ANY-THING...

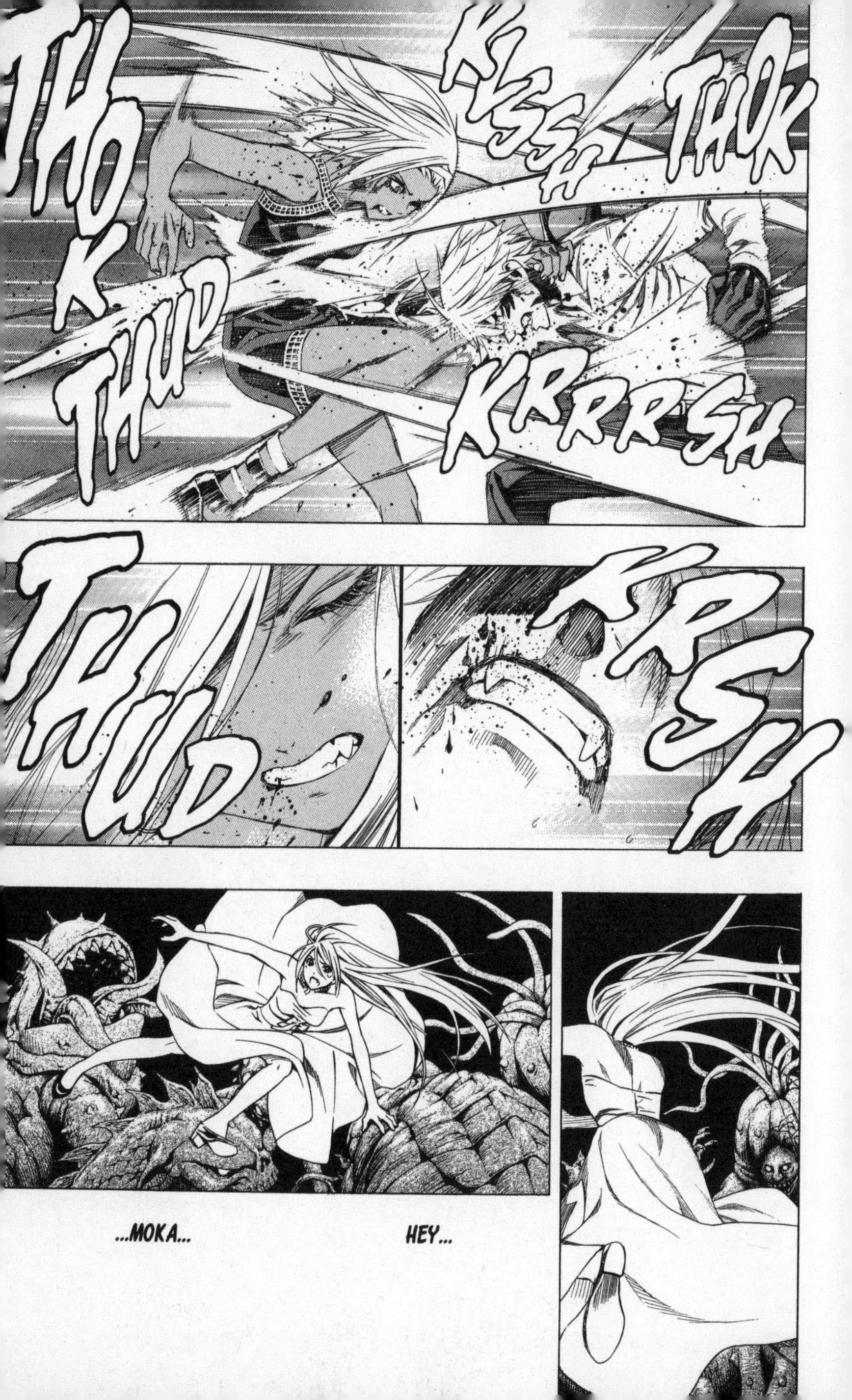
THOK
KISSH
THOK
KRRRSH
THUD
KRSH
THUD
HEY...
...MOKA...

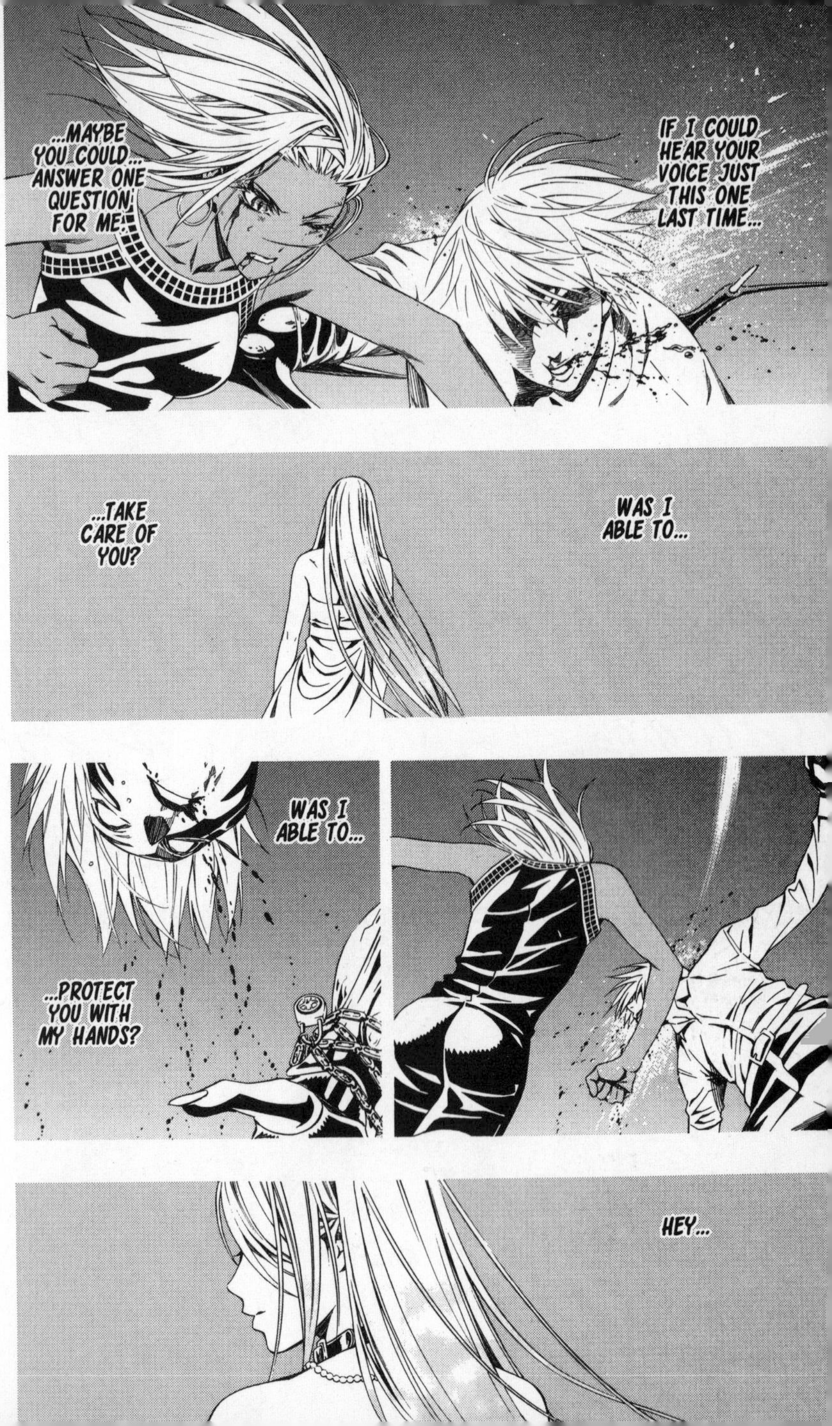
IF I COULD HEAR YOUR VOICE JUST THIS ONE LAST TIME...
...MAYBE YOU COULD... ANSWER ONE QUESTION FOR ME.
WAS I ABLE TO...
...TAKE CARE OF YOU?
WAS I ABLE TO...
...PROTECT YOU WITH MY HANDS?
HEY...

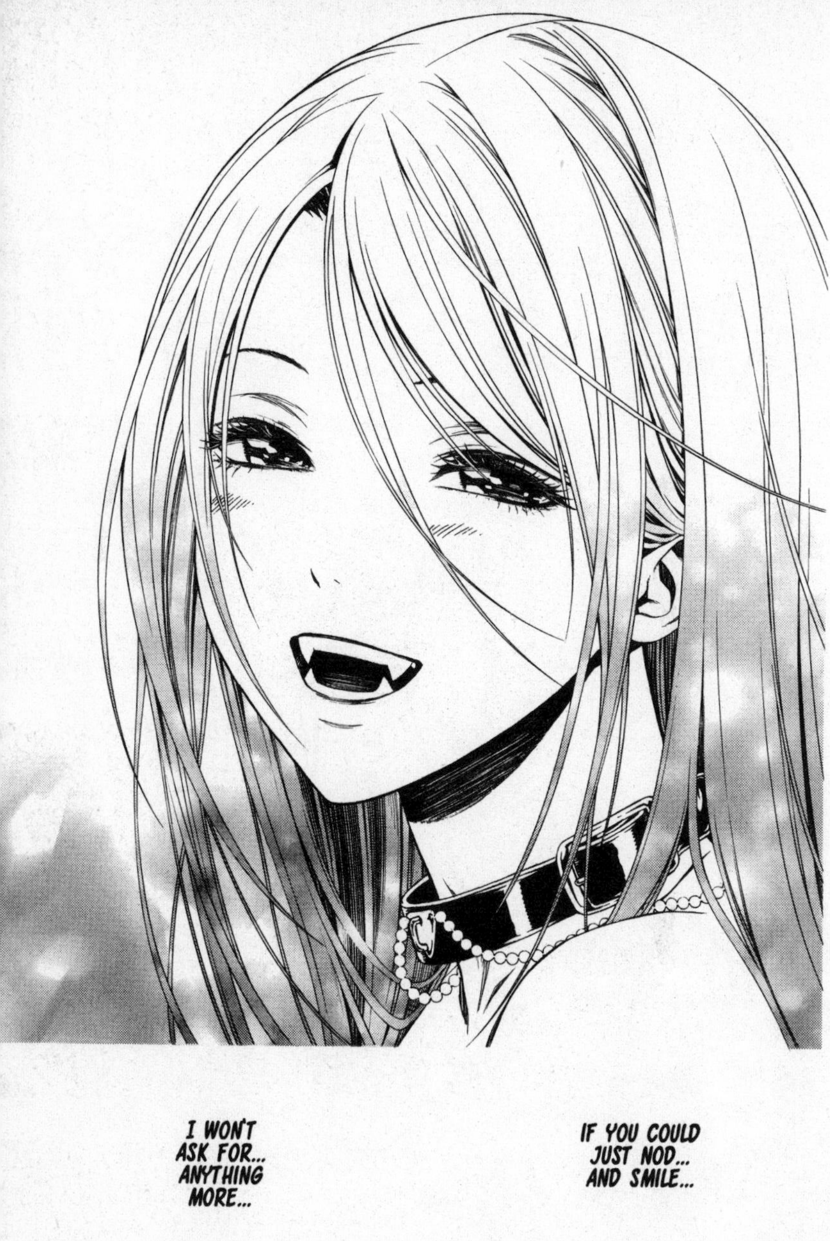
IF YOU COULD JUST NOD... AND SMILE...
I WON'T ASK FOR... ANYTHING MORE...

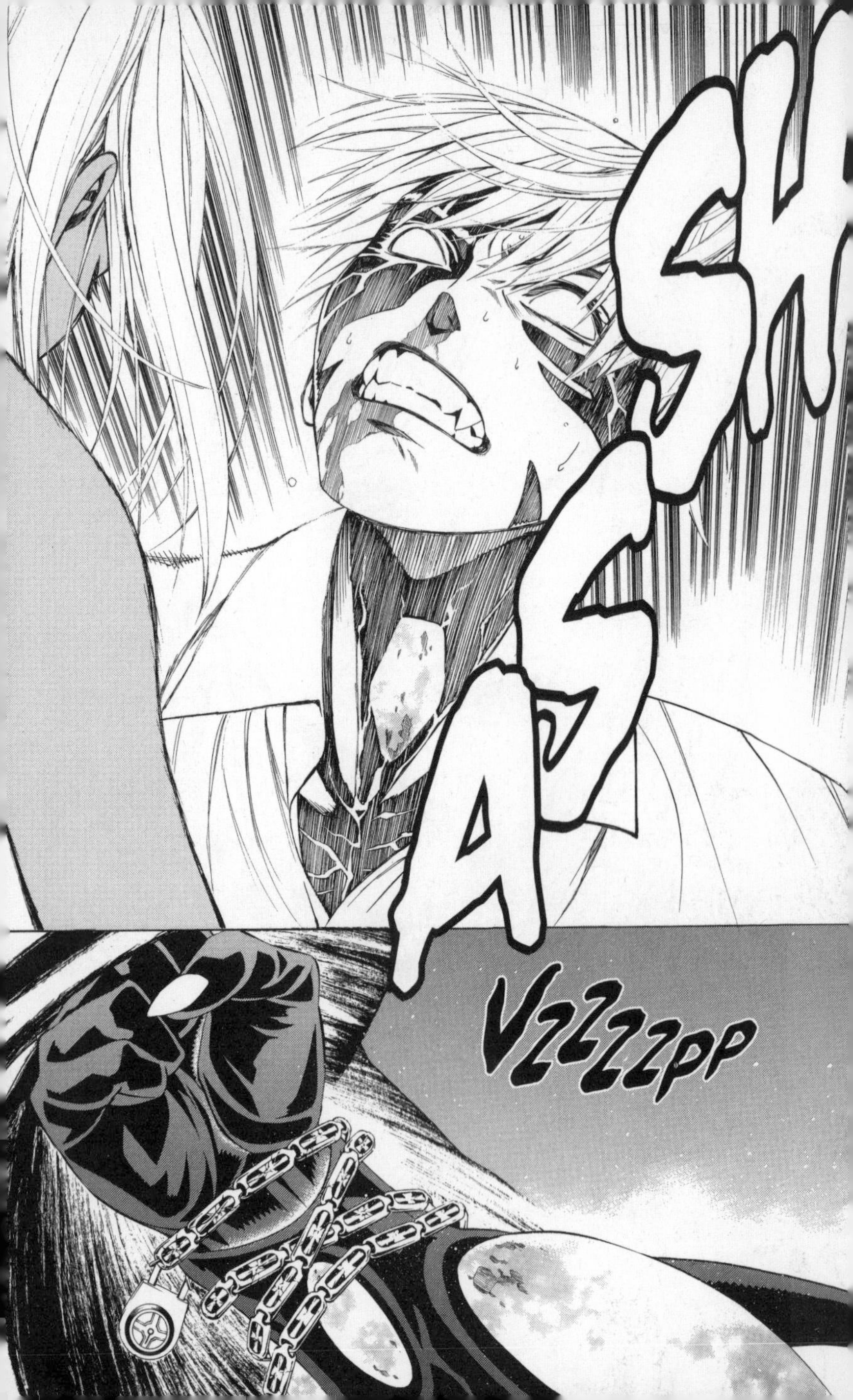
SHASH
VZZZZZPP

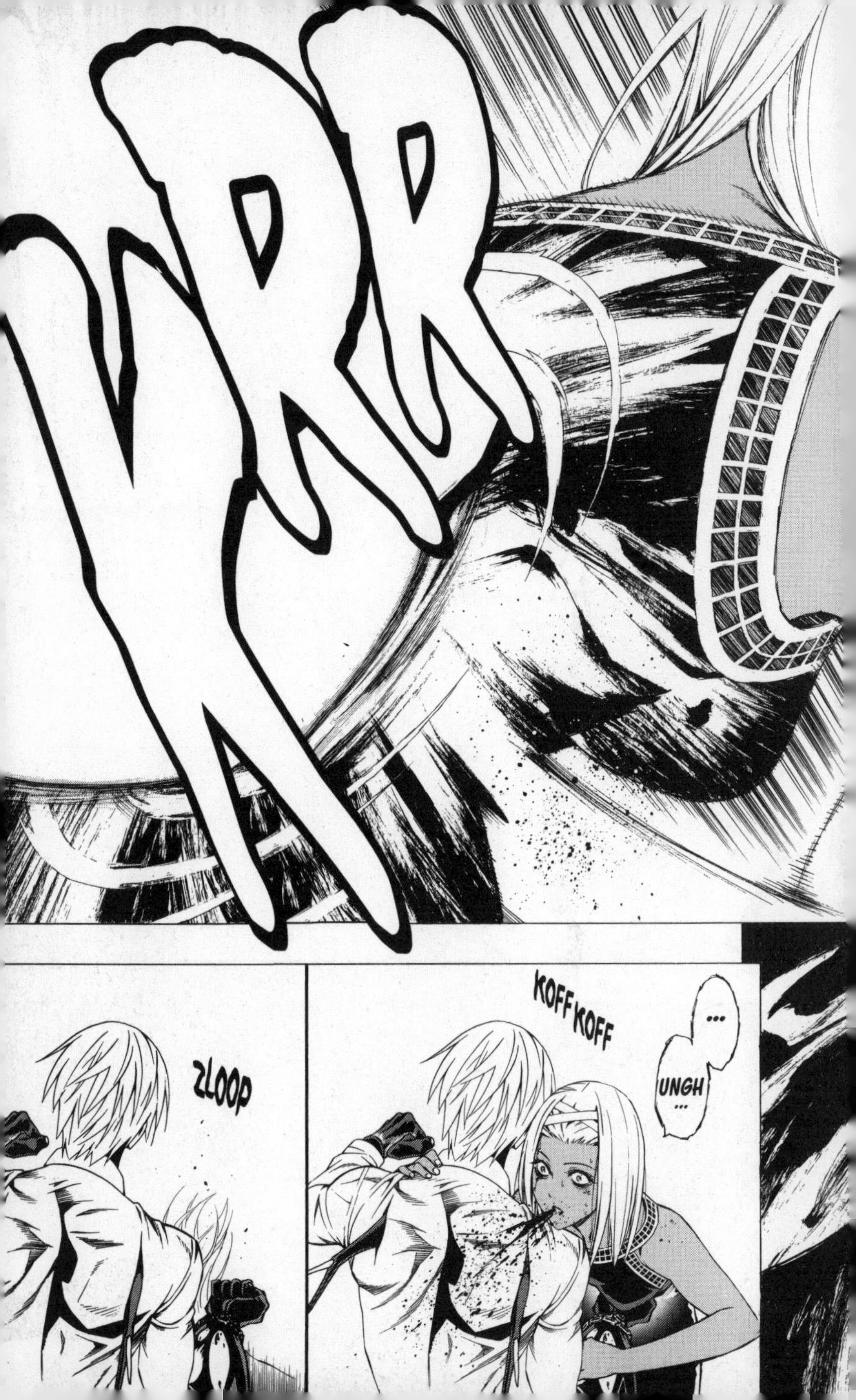
... UNGH ...
KOFF KOFF
ZLOOP

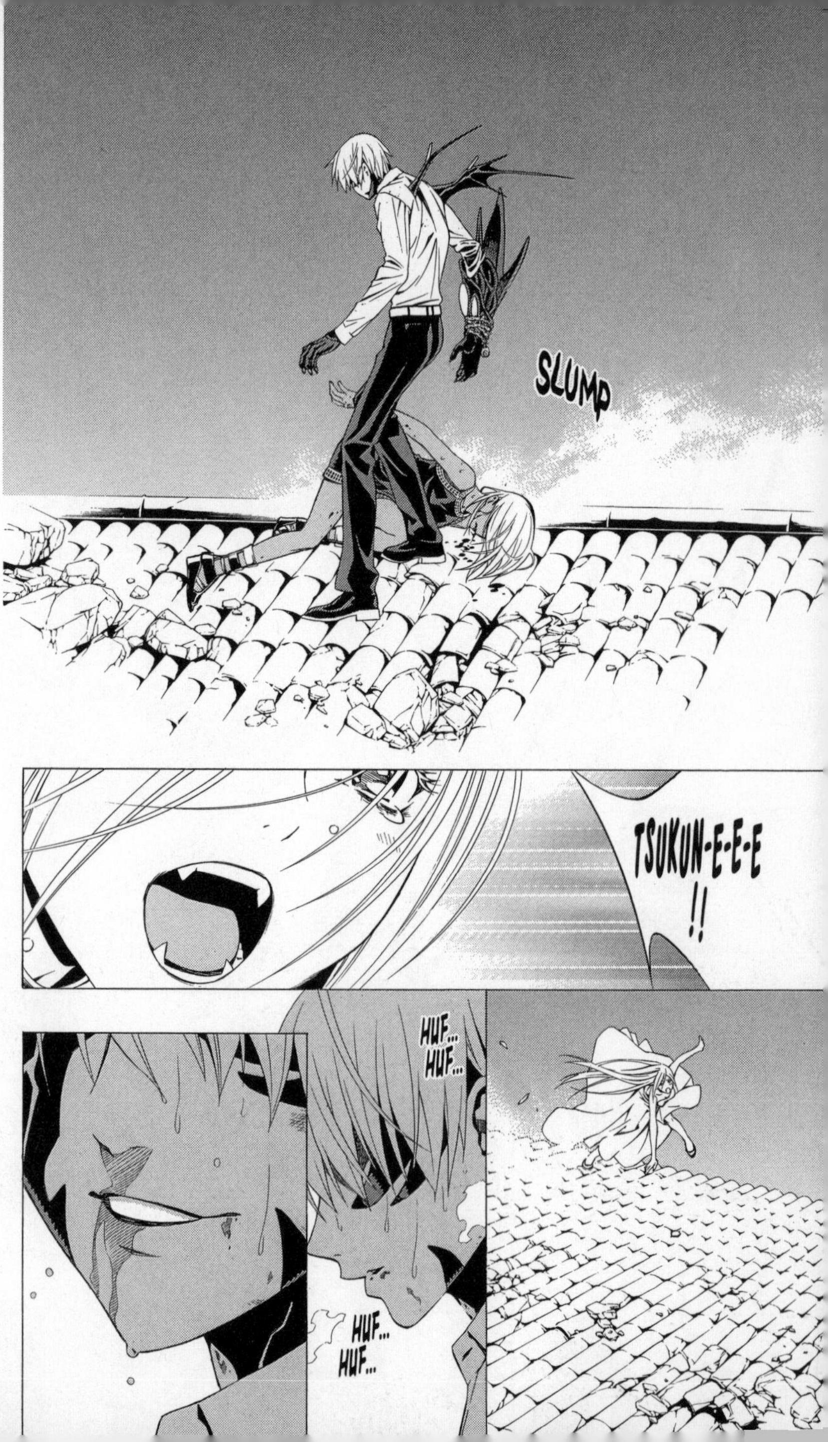
SLUMP
TSUKUN-E-E-E !!
HUF... HUF...
HUF... HUF...

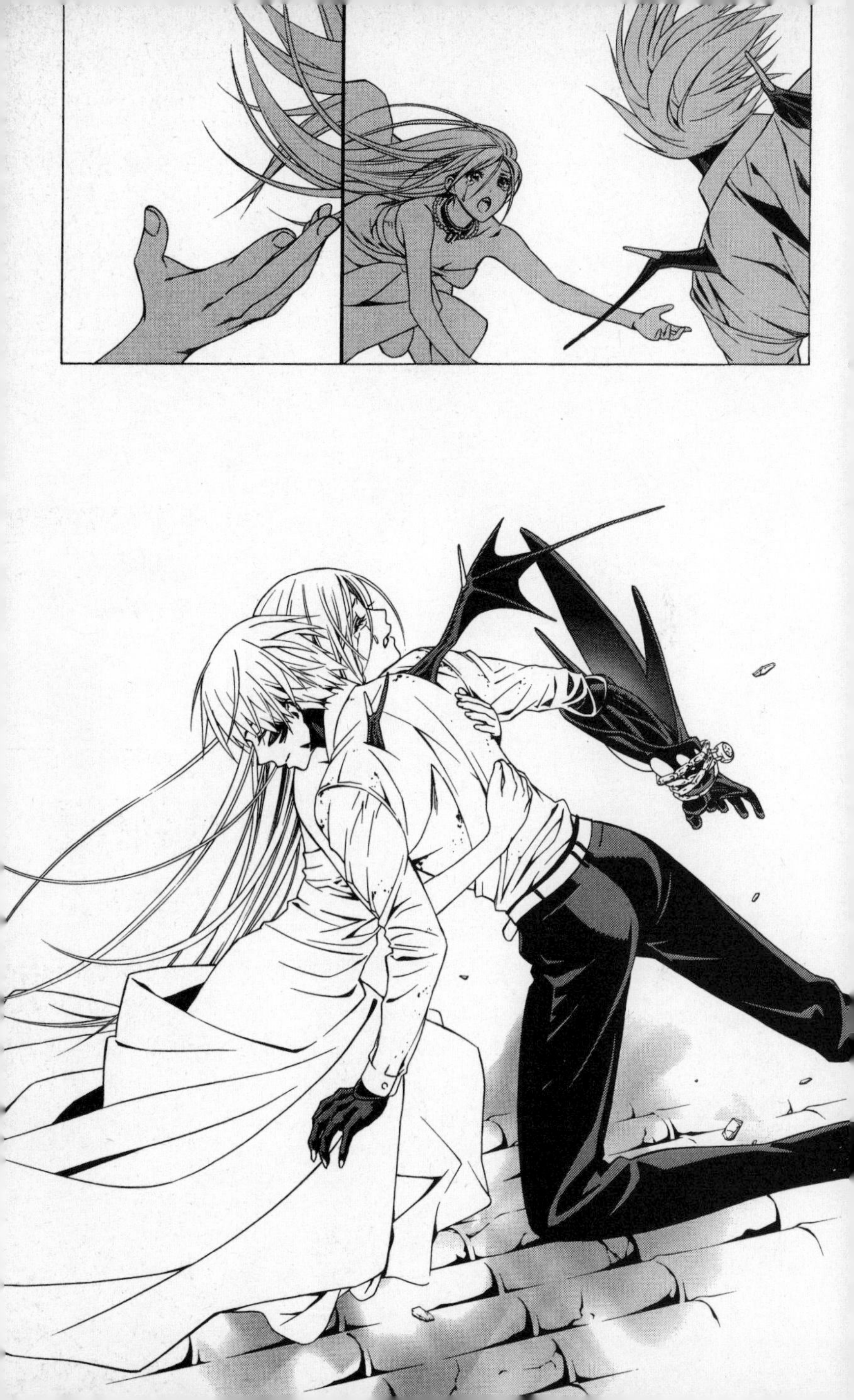

61: Countdown

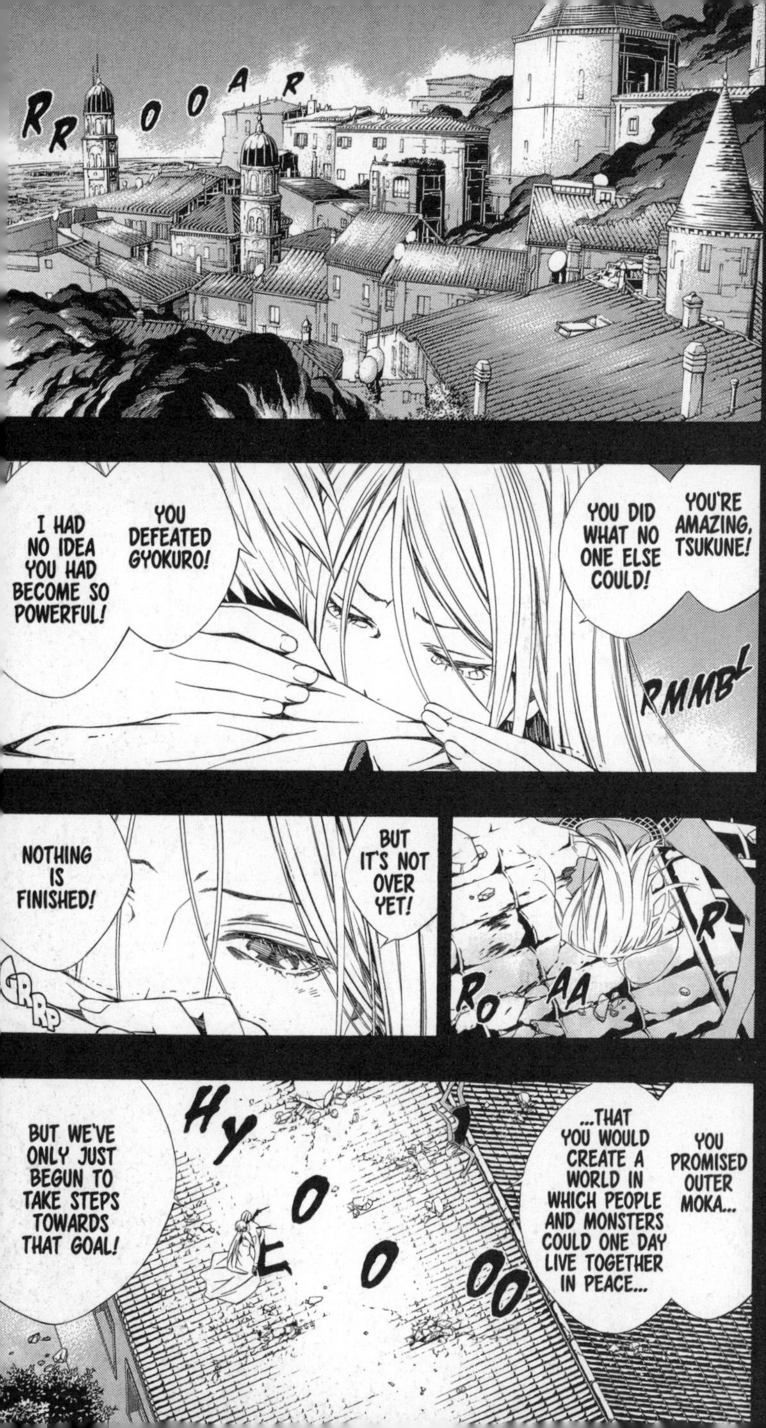
RROOAR
YOU'RE AMAZING, TSUKUNE!
YOU DID WHAT NO ONE ELSE COULD!
RMMBL
YOU DEFEATED GYOKURO!
I HAD NO IDEA YOU HAD BECOME SO POWERFUL!
ROAAR
BUT IT'S NOT OVER YET!
NOTHING IS FINISHED!
GRRRP
YOU PROMISED OUTER MOKA...
...THAT YOU WOULD CREATE A WORLD IN WHICH PEOPLE AND MONSTERS COULD ONE DAY LIVE TOGETHER IN PEACE...
HyOOOOO
BUT WE'VE ONLY JUST BEGUN TO TAKE STEPS TOWARDS THAT GOAL!

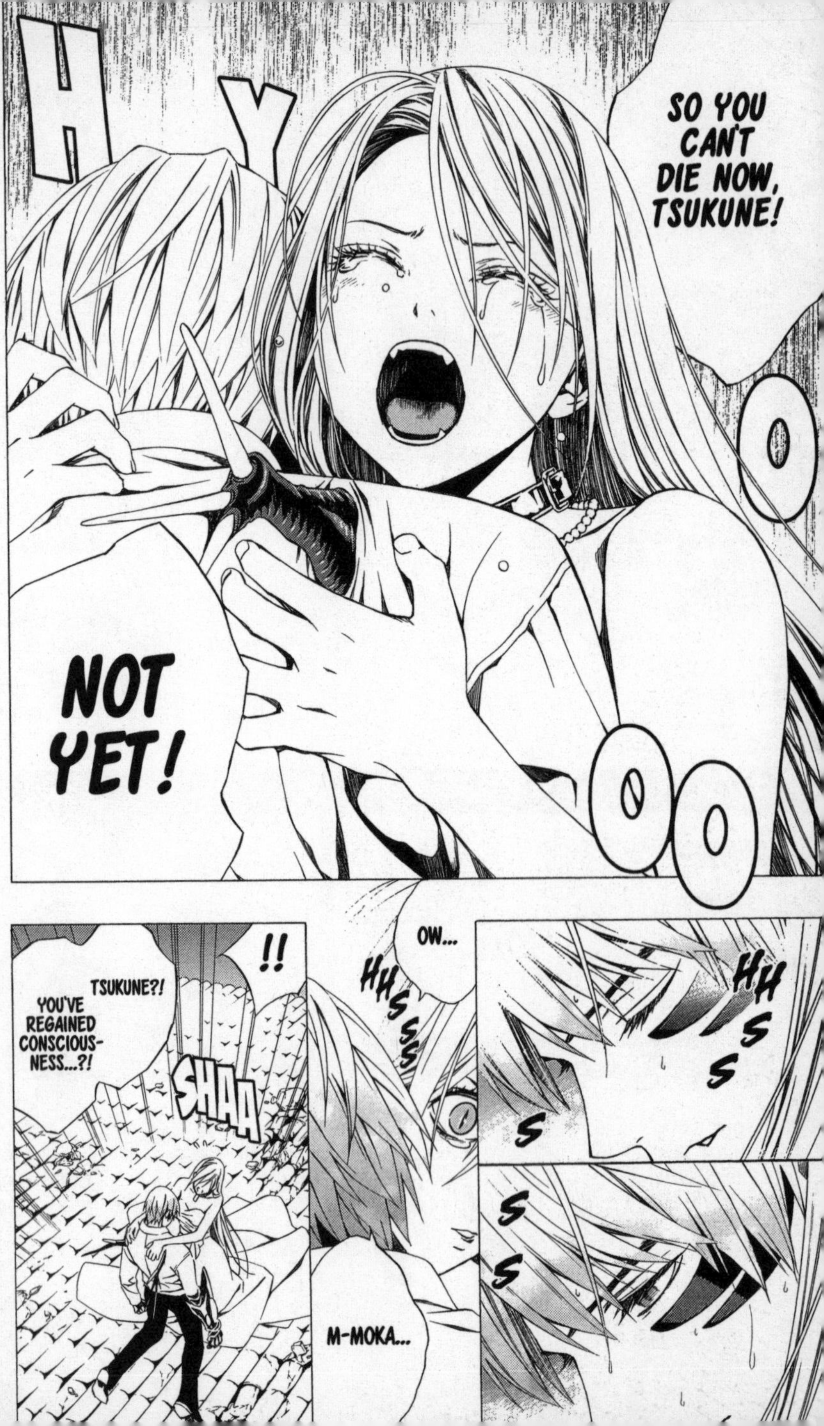
SO YOU CAN'T DIE NOW, TSUKUNE!
HYOOOO
NOT YET!
HHSSS
SSS
OW...
HHSSSS
M-MOKA...
!!
TSUKUNE?!
YOU'VE REGAINED CONSCIOUS-NESS...?!
SHAA

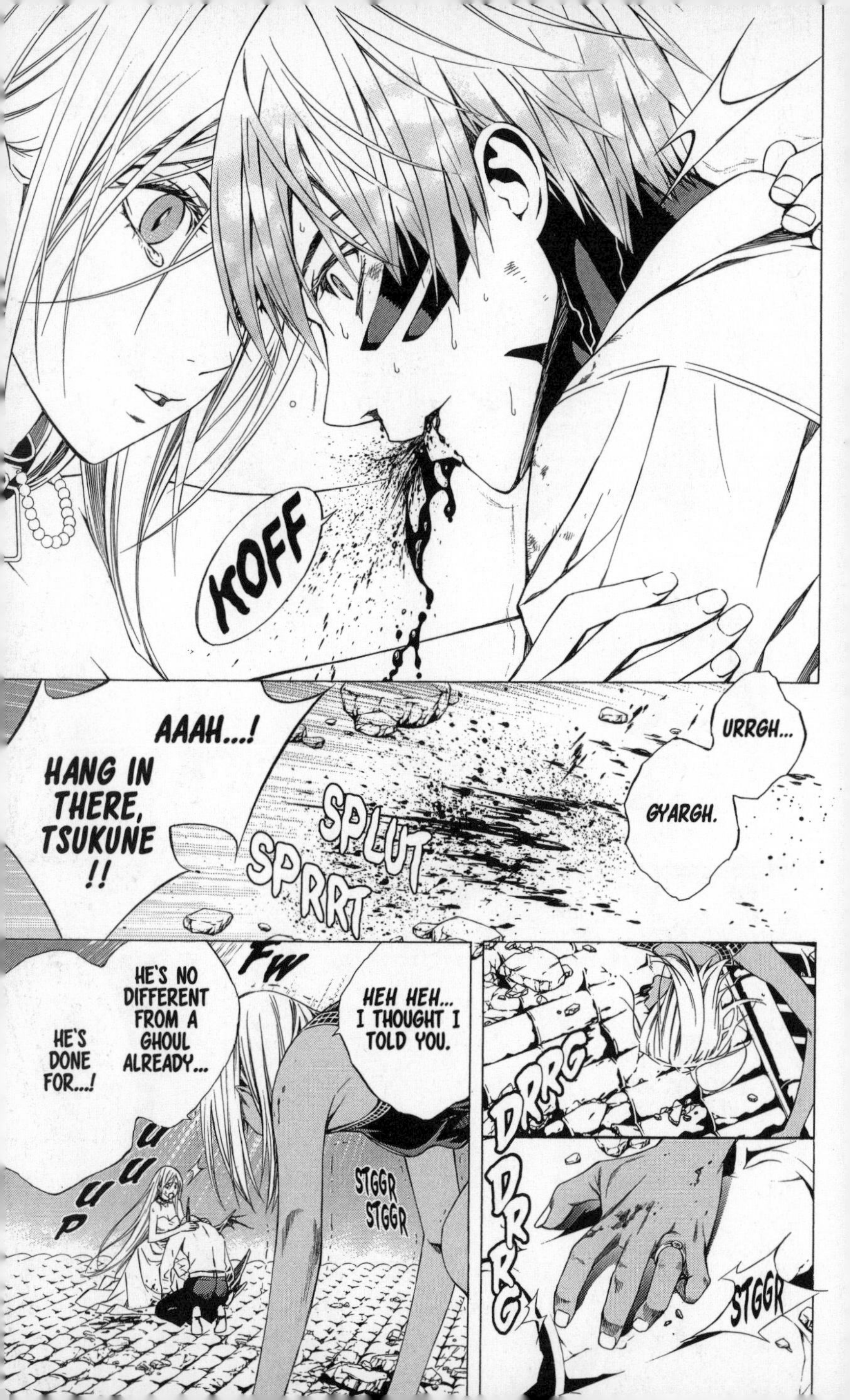
KOFF
URRGH...
GYARGH.
SPLUT
SPRRT
AAAH...!
HANG IN THERE, TSUKUNE!!
DRRG
DRRG
STGGR
FW
HEH HEH... I THOUGHT I TOLD YOU.
HE'S NO DIFFERENT FROM A GHOUL ALREADY...
HE'S DONE FOR...!
STGGR STGGR
UUUP

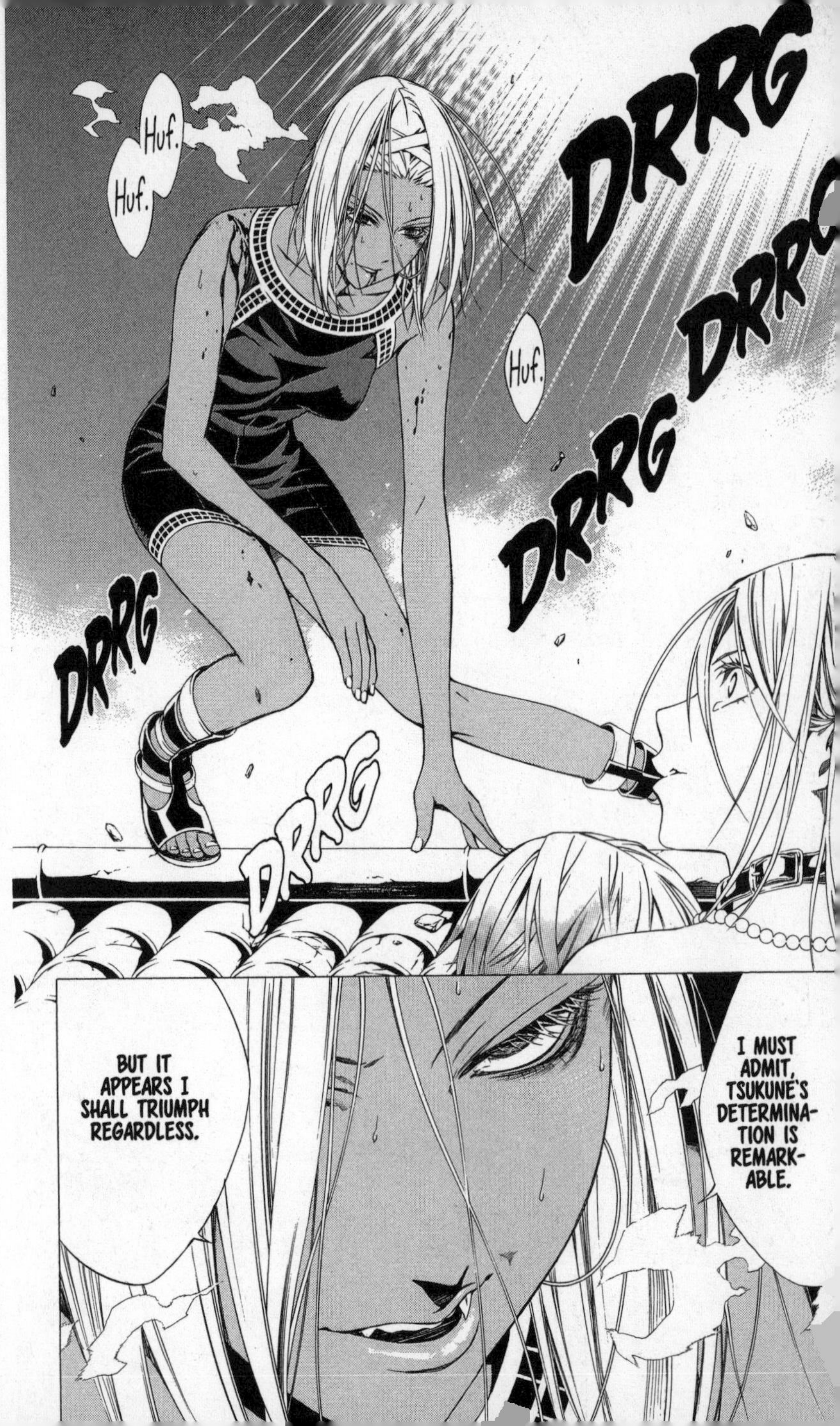
DRRG
DRRG DRRG DRRG
Huf.
Huf.
Huf.
DRRG
DRRG
I MUST ADMIT, TSUKUNE'S DETERMINATION IS REMARKABLE.
BUT IT APPEARS I SHALL TRIUMPH REGARDLESS.

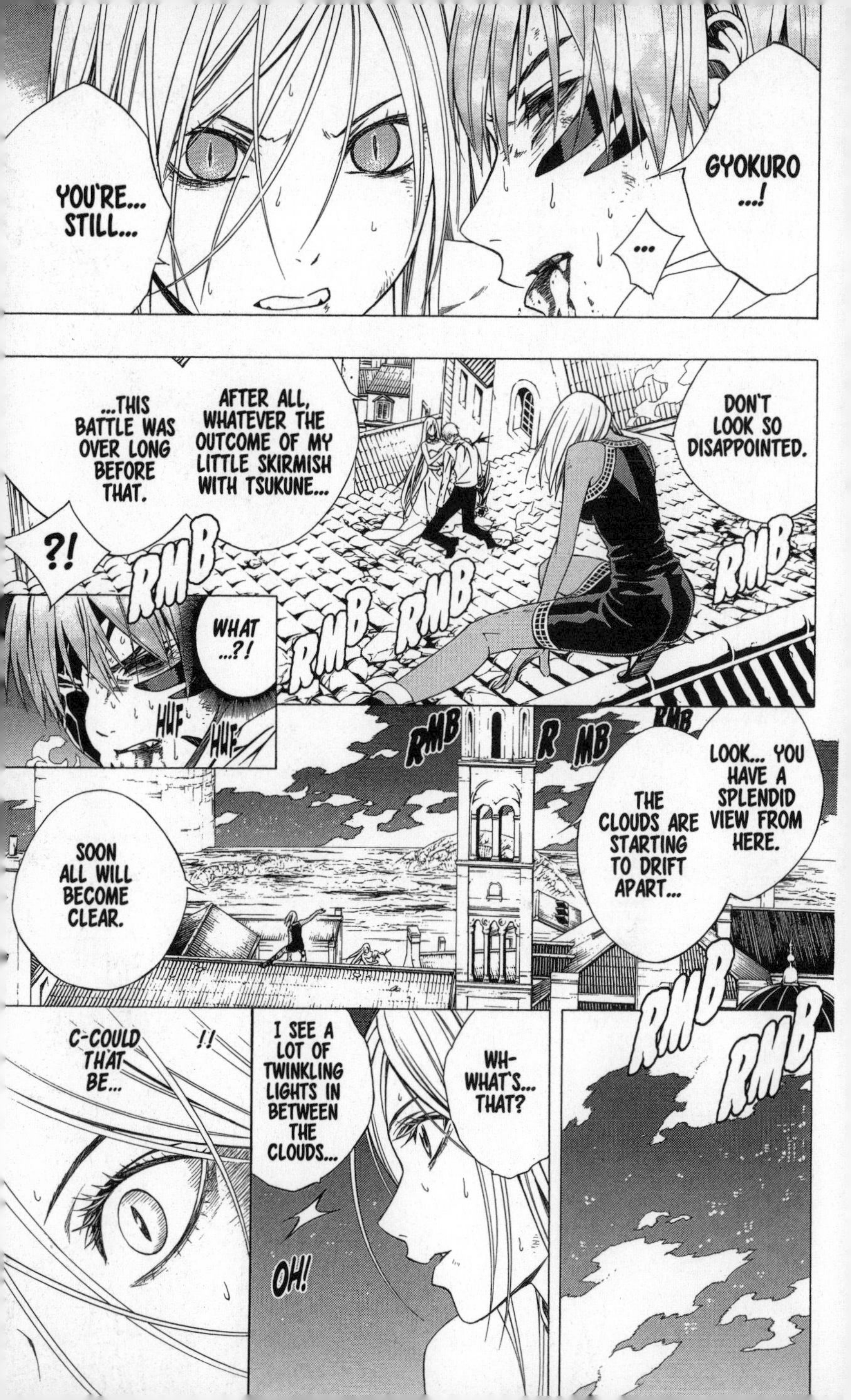
GYOKURO ...!
...
YOU'RE... STILL...
DON'T LOOK SO DISAPPOINTED.
AFTER ALL, WHATEVER THE OUTCOME OF MY LITTLE SKIRMISH WITH TSUKUNE...
...THIS BATTLE WAS OVER LONG BEFORE THAT.
RMB
RMB RMB
RMB
?!
WHAT ...?!
HUF HUF
RMB
R MB
RMB
LOOK... YOU HAVE A SPLENDID VIEW FROM HERE.
THE CLOUDS ARE STARTING TO DRIFT APART...
SOON ALL WILL BECOME CLEAR.
RMB
RMB
WH-WHAT'S... THAT?
I SEE A LOT OF TWINKLING LIGHTS IN BETWEEN THE CLOUDS...
OH!
!!
C-COULD THAT BE...

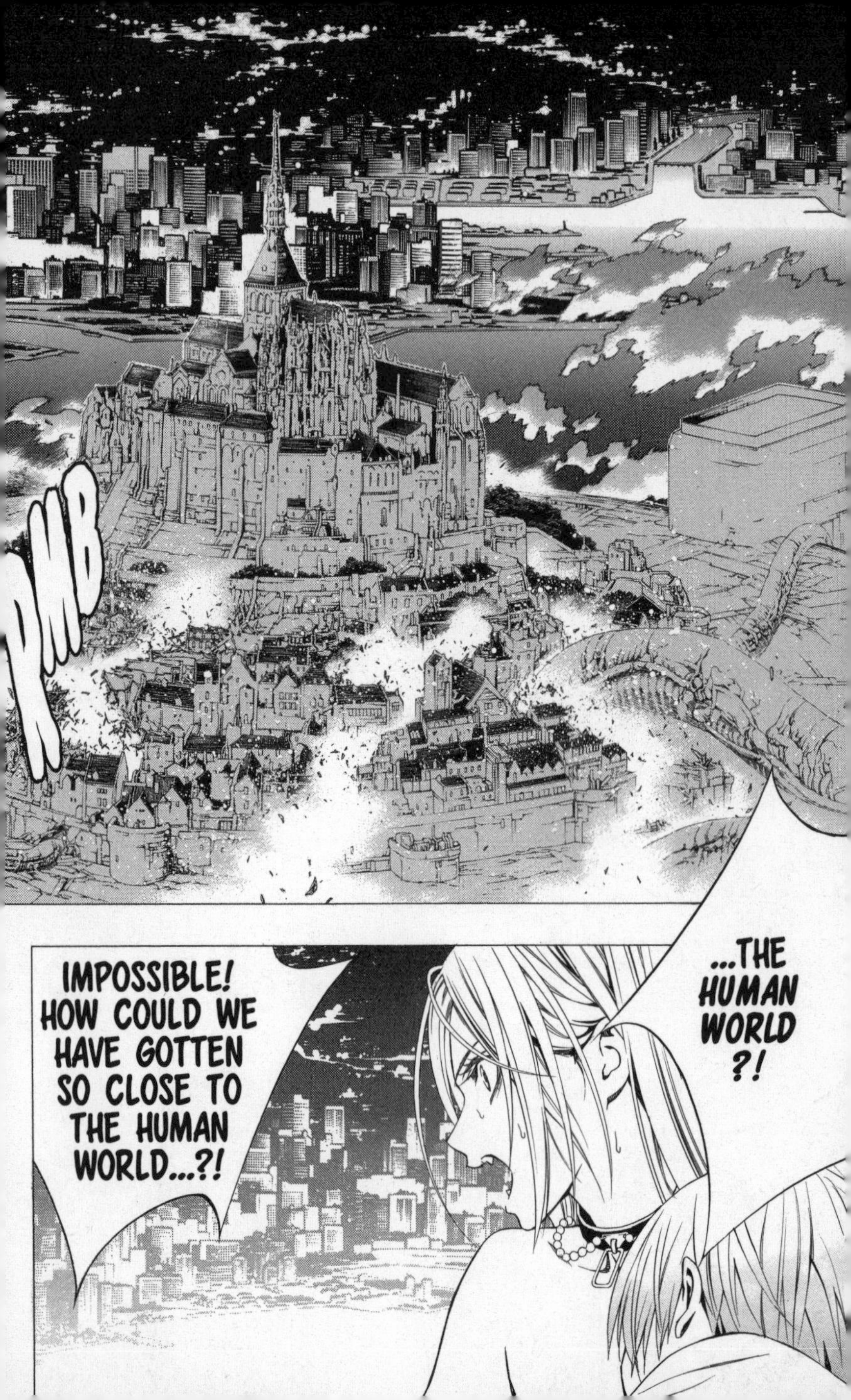
...THE HUMAN WORLD?!
IMPOSSIBLE! HOW COULD WE HAVE GOTTEN SO CLOSE TO THE HUMAN WORLD...?!

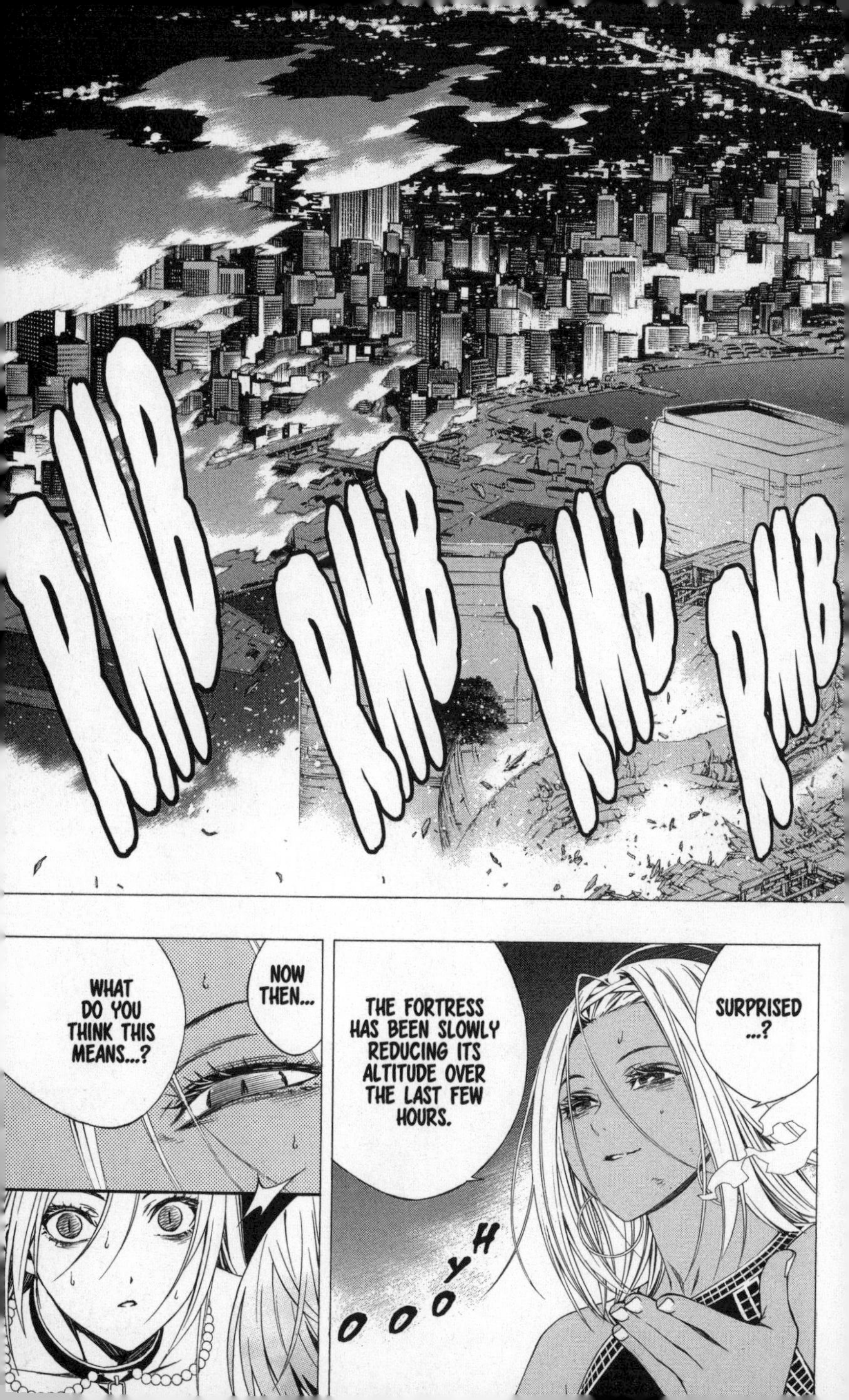
DMB DMB DMB DMB
SURPRISED ...?
THE FORTRESS HAS BEEN SLOWLY REDUCING ITS ALTITUDE OVER THE LAST FEW HOURS.
NOW THEN...
WHAT DO YOU THINK THIS MEANS...?

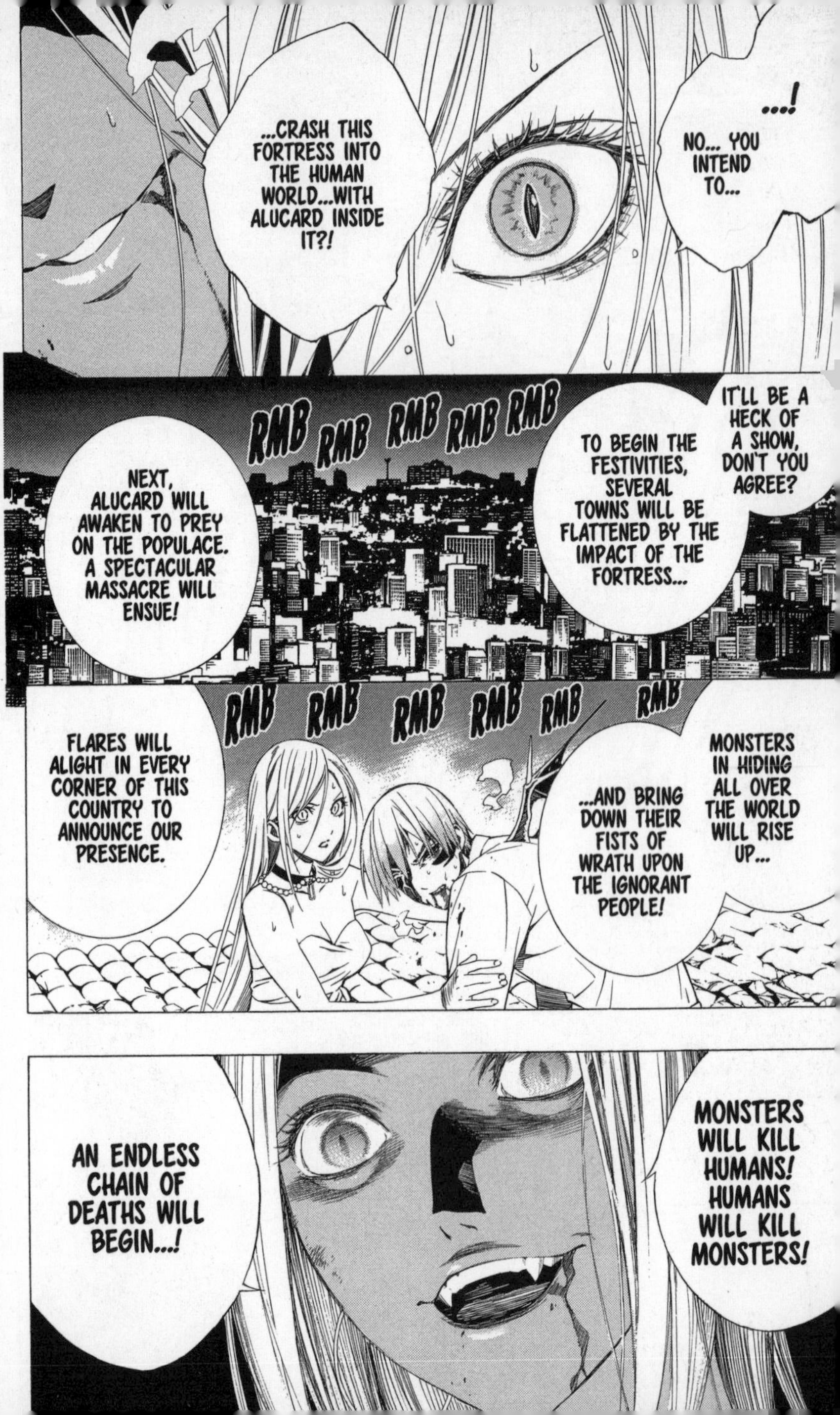
...!
NO... YOU INTEND TO...
...CRASH THIS FORTRESS INTO THE HUMAN WORLD...WITH ALUCARD INSIDE IT?!
IT'LL BE A HECK OF A SHOW, DON'T YOU AGREE?
TO BEGIN THE FESTIVITIES, SEVERAL TOWNS WILL BE FLATTENED BY THE IMPACT OF THE FORTRESS...
RMB RMB RMB RMB RMB
NEXT, ALUCARD WILL AWAKEN TO PREY ON THE POPULACE. A SPECTACULAR MASSACRE WILL ENSUE!
RMB RMB RMB RMB RMB RMB
MONSTERS IN HIDING ALL OVER THE WORLD WILL RISE UP...
...AND BRING DOWN THEIR FISTS OF WRATH UPON THE IGNORANT PEOPLE!
FLARES WILL ALIGHT IN EVERY CORNER OF THIS COUNTRY TO ANNOUNCE OUR PRESENCE.
MONSTERS WILL KILL HUMANS! HUMANS WILL KILL MONSTERS!
AN ENDLESS CHAIN OF DEATHS WILL BEGIN...!

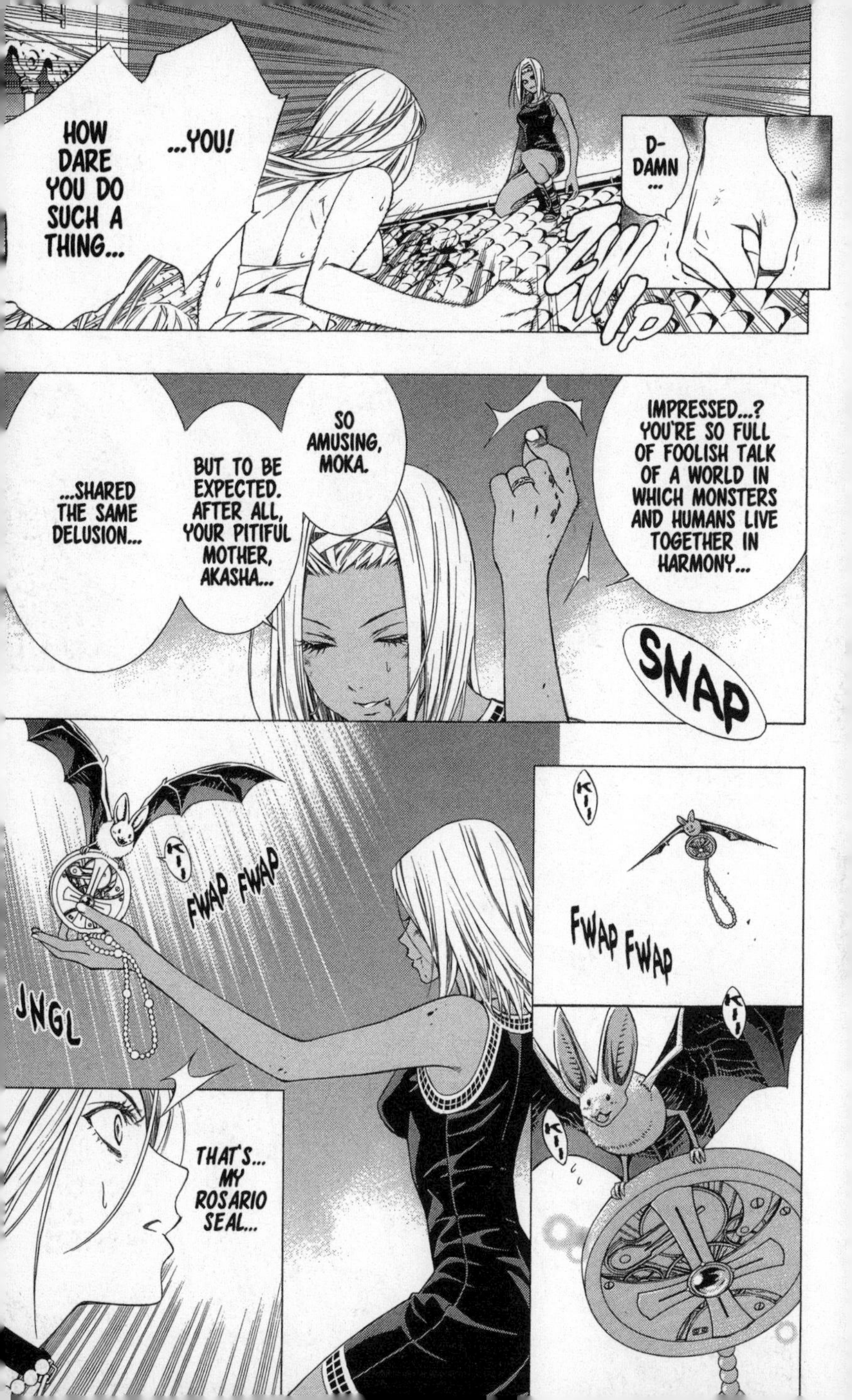
D-DAMN...
WHIP
...YOU!
HOW DARE YOU DO SUCH A THING...
IMPRESSED...? YOU'RE SO FULL OF FOOLISH TALK OF A WORLD IN WHICH MONSTERS AND HUMANS LIVE TOGETHER IN HARMONY...
SNAP
SO AMUSING, MOKA.
BUT TO BE EXPECTED. AFTER ALL, YOUR PITIFUL MOTHER, AKASHA...
...SHARED THE SAME DELUSION...
KII
FWAP FWAP
KII
KII
KII
FWAP FWAP
JNGL
THAT'S... MY ROSARIO SEAL...

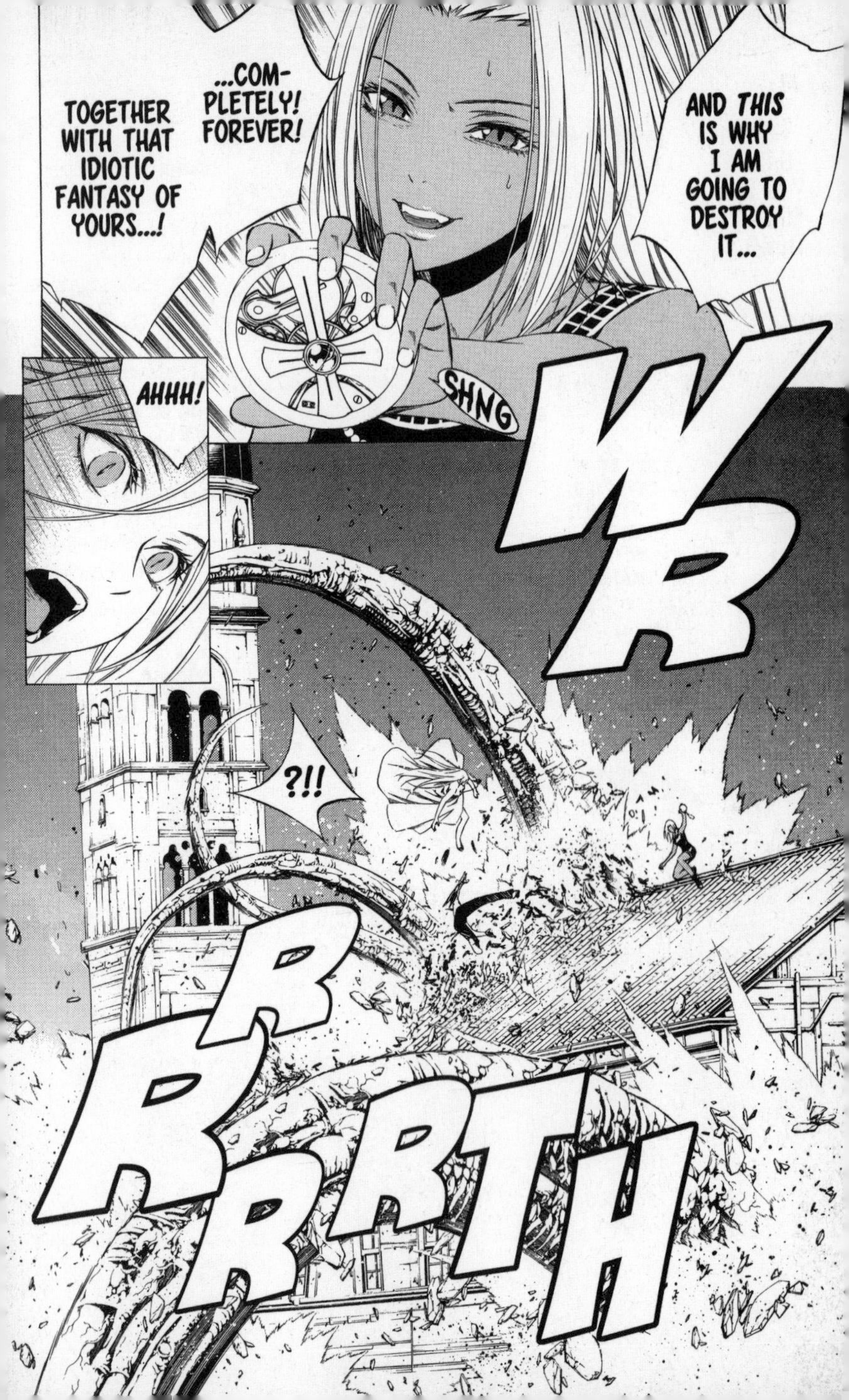
AND THIS IS WHY I AM GOING TO DESTROY IT...
...COMPLETELY! FOREVER!
TOGETHER WITH THAT IDIOTIC FANTASY OF YOURS...!
SHNG
AHHH!
WRB
?!!
RRRTH

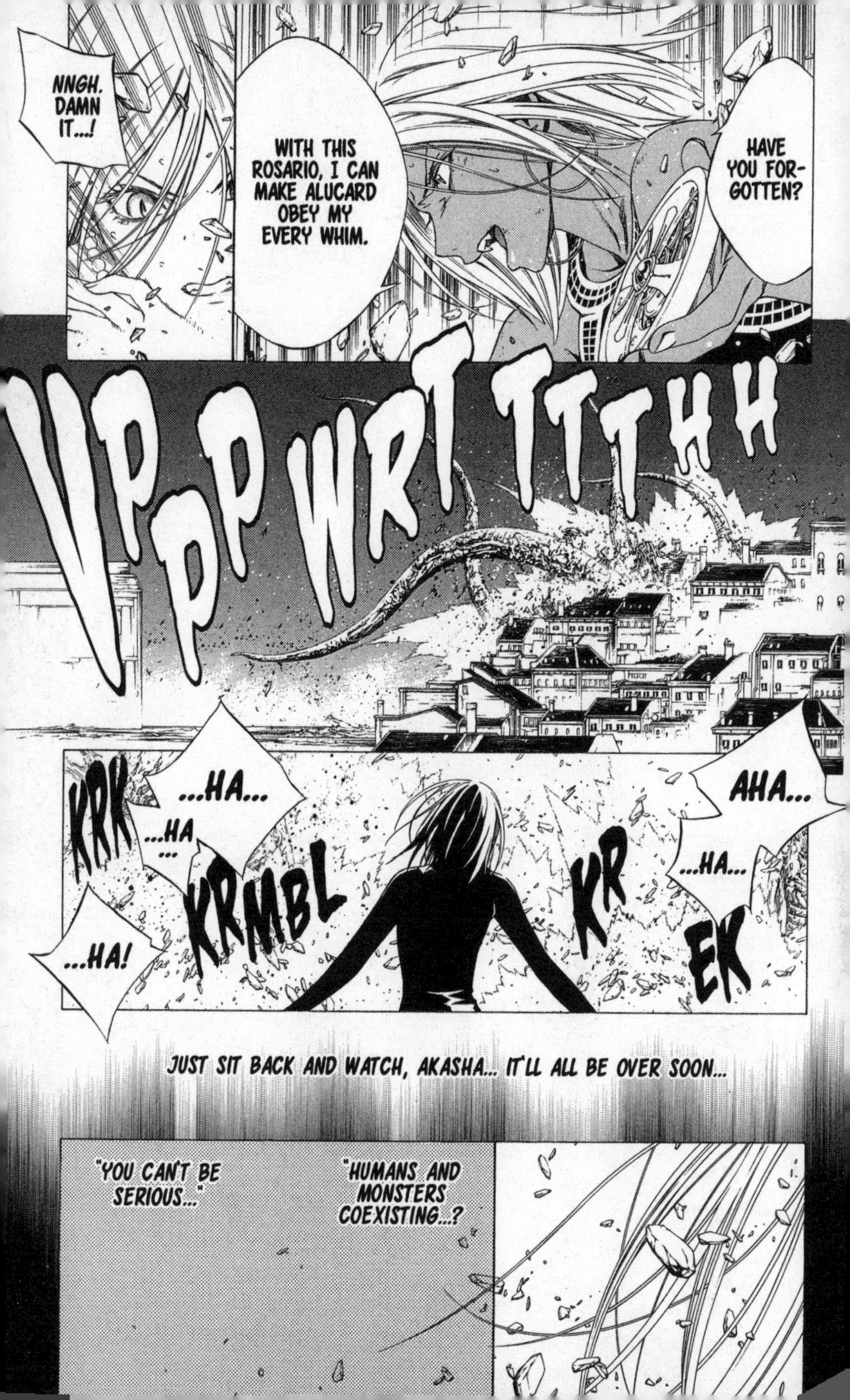
HAVE YOU FOR-GOTTEN?
WITH THIS ROSARIO, I CAN MAKE ALUCARD OBEY MY EVERY WHIM.
NNGH. DAMN IT...!
VP PP WRT TTT H H
AHA...
...HA...
KR EK
KRMBL
...HA...
...HA ...
...HA!
KRK
JUST SIT BACK AND WATCH, AKASHA... IT'LL ALL BE OVER SOON...
"HUMANS AND MONSTERS COEXISTING...?
"YOU CAN'T BE SERIOUS..."

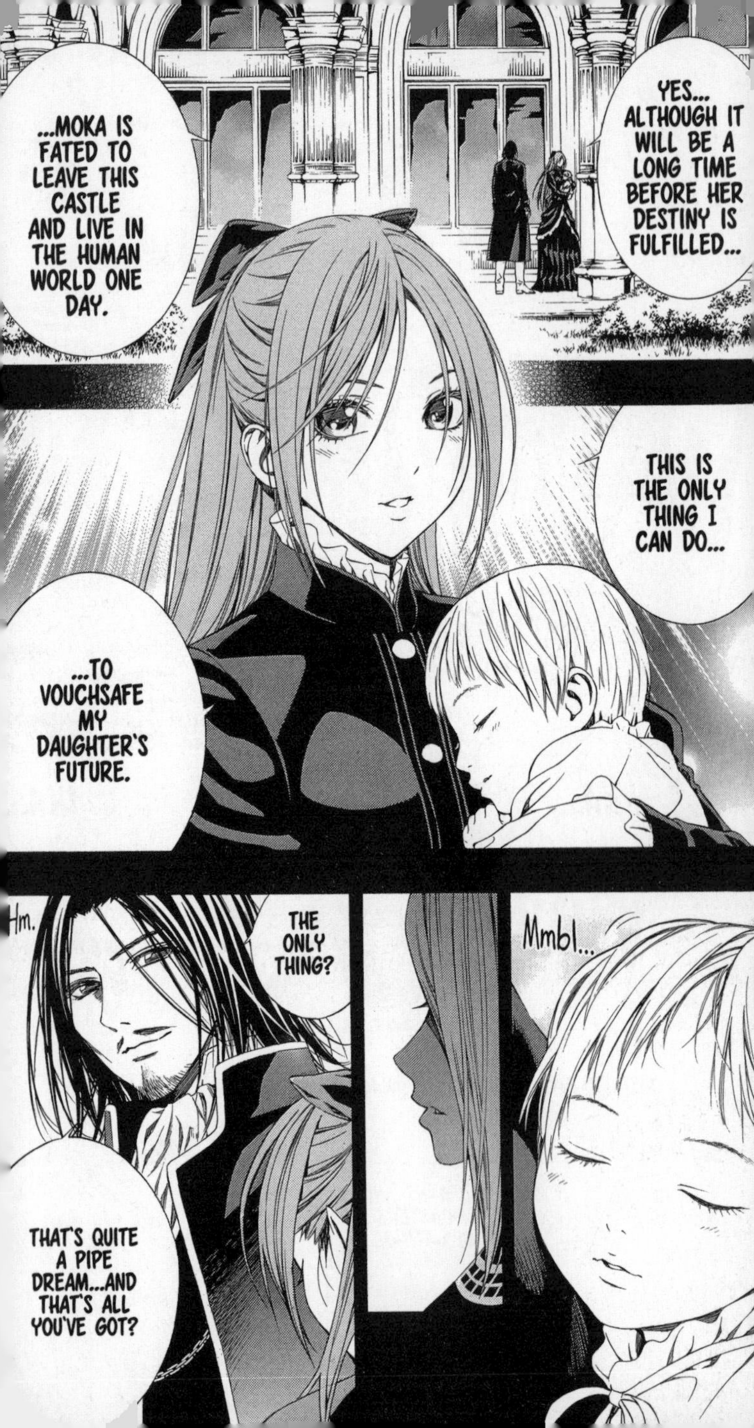
YES... ALTHOUGH IT WILL BE A LONG TIME BEFORE HER DESTINY IS FULFILLED...
...MOKA IS FATED TO LEAVE THIS CASTLE AND LIVE IN THE HUMAN WORLD ONE DAY.
THIS IS THE ONLY THING I CAN DO...
...TO VOUCHSAFE MY DAUGHTER'S FUTURE.
Mmbl...
THE ONLY THING?
Hm.
THAT'S QUITE A PIPE DREAM...AND THAT'S ALL YOU'VE GOT?

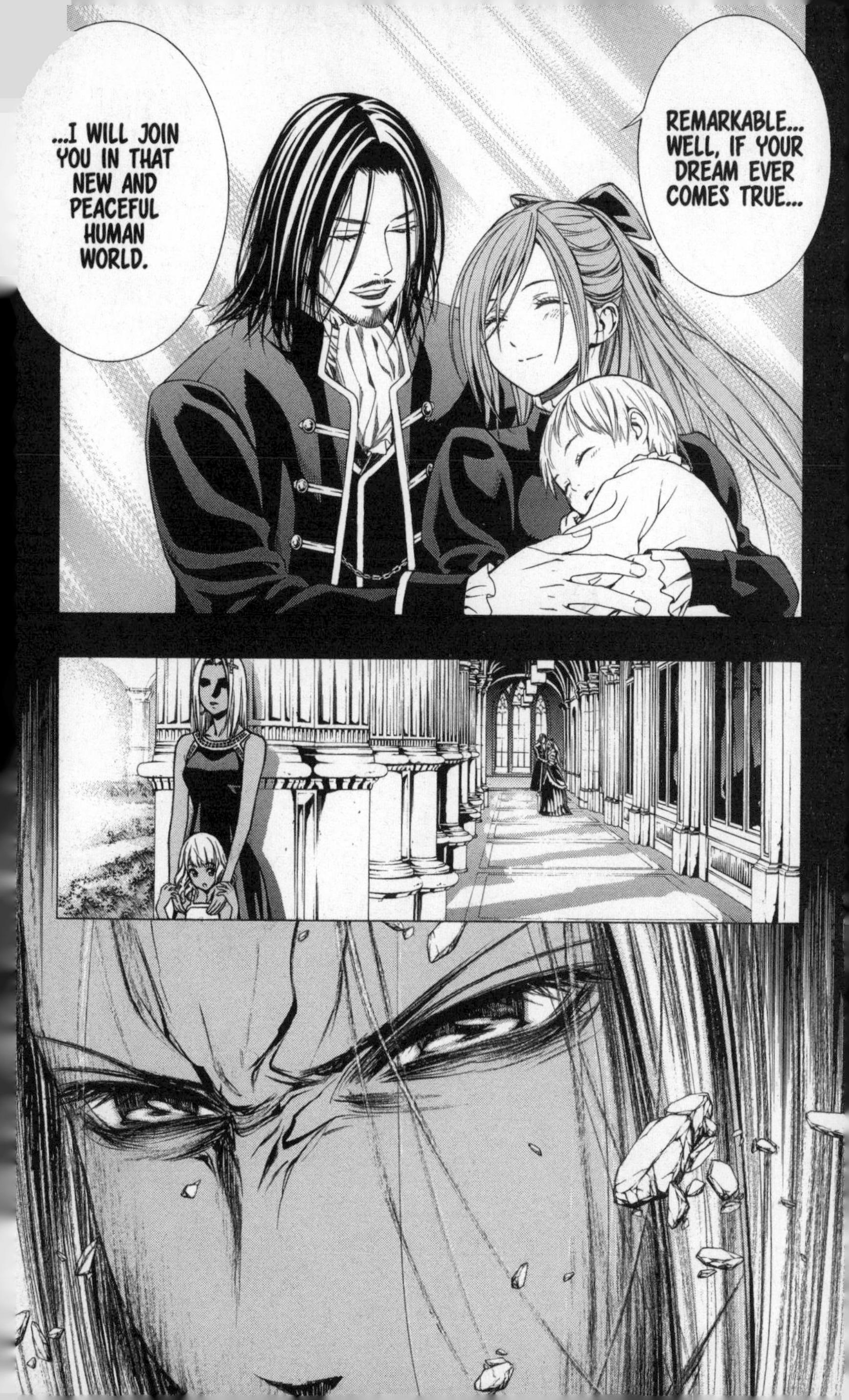
REMARKABLE... WELL, IF YOUR DREAM EVER COMES TRUE...
...I WILL JOIN YOU IN THAT NEW AND PEACEFUL HUMAN WORLD.

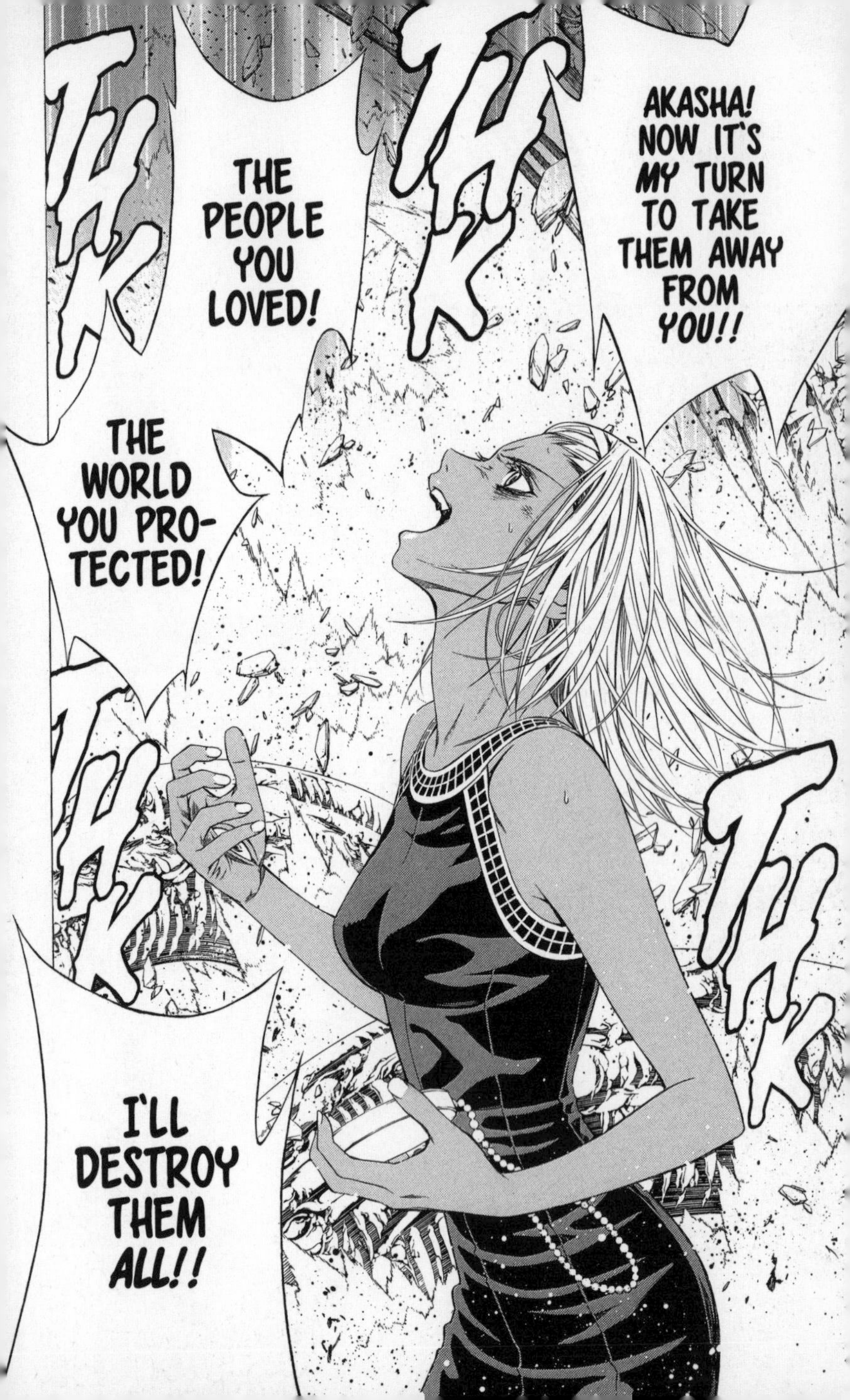
THK
AKASHA! NOW IT'S MY TURN TO TAKE THEM AWAY FROM YOU!!
THK
THE PEOPLE YOU LOVED!
THE WORLD YOU PRO-TECTED!
THK
THK
I'LL DESTROY THEM ALL!!

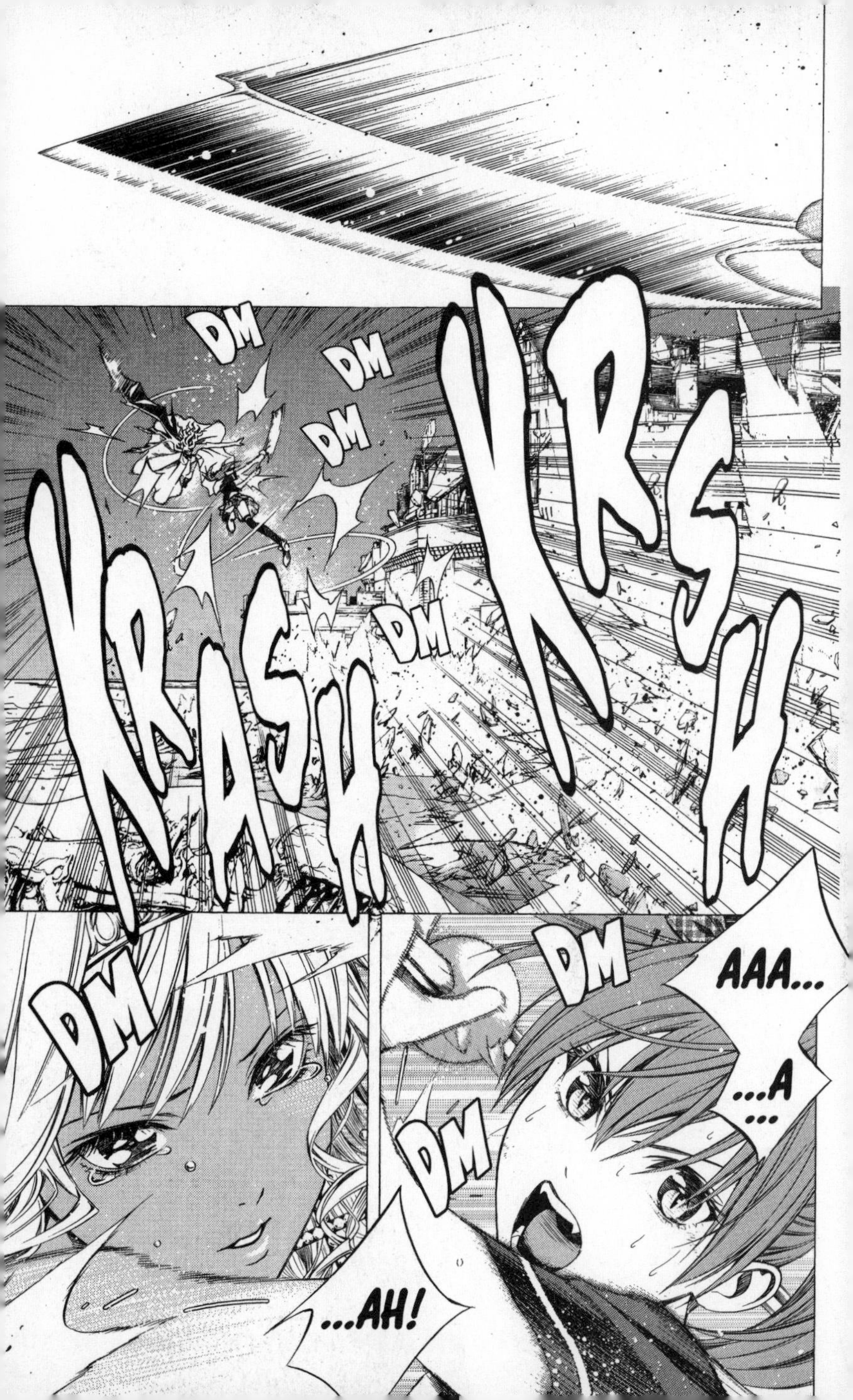
KRSH
KRASH
DM
DM
DM
DM
DM
AAA...
...A...
DM
DM
...AH!

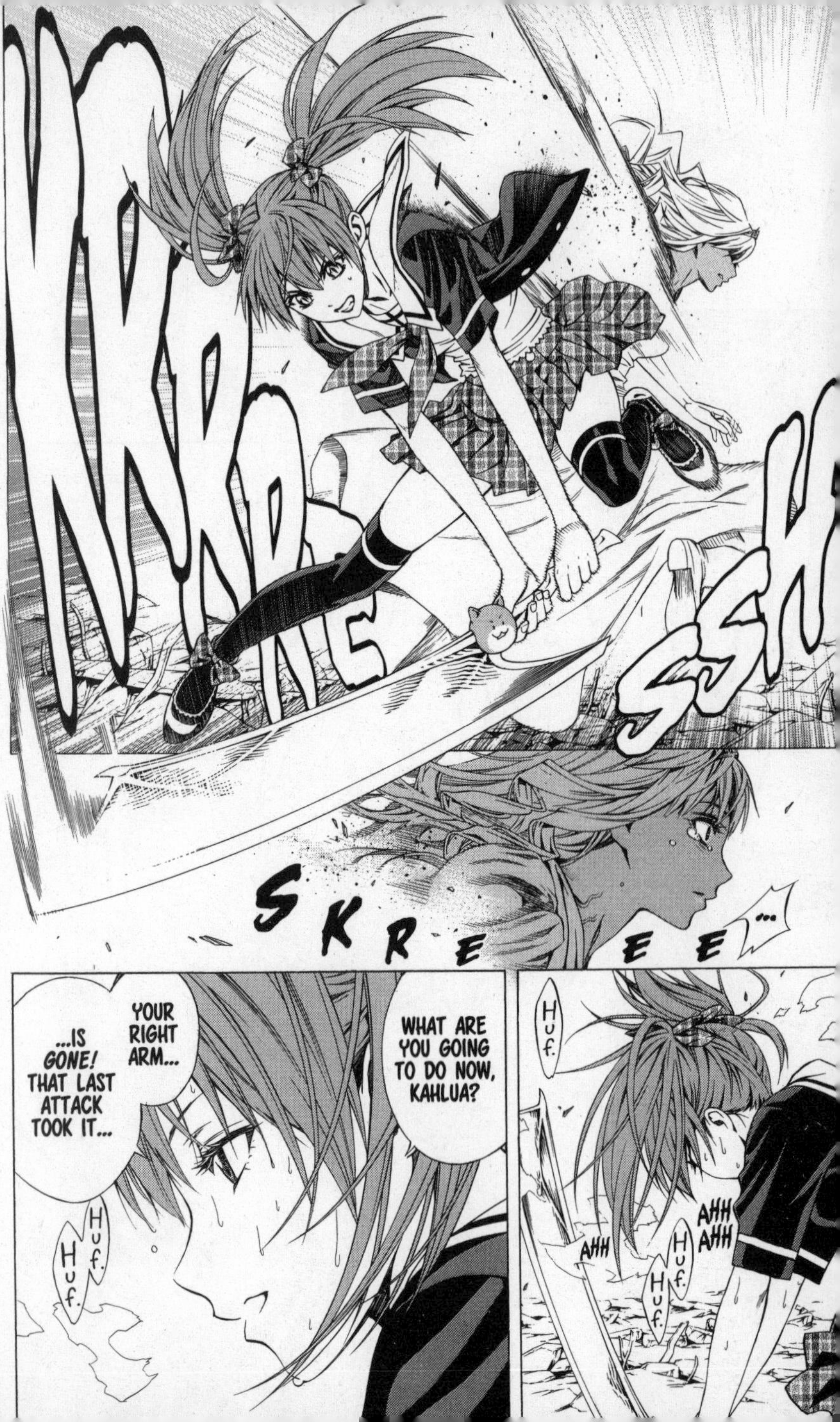
SKREEEE...
Huf.
AHH AHH
Huf. Huf.
AHH
WHAT ARE YOU GOING TO DO NOW, KAHLUA?
YOUR RIGHT ARM...
...IS GONE! THAT LAST ATTACK TOOK IT...
Huf. Huf.

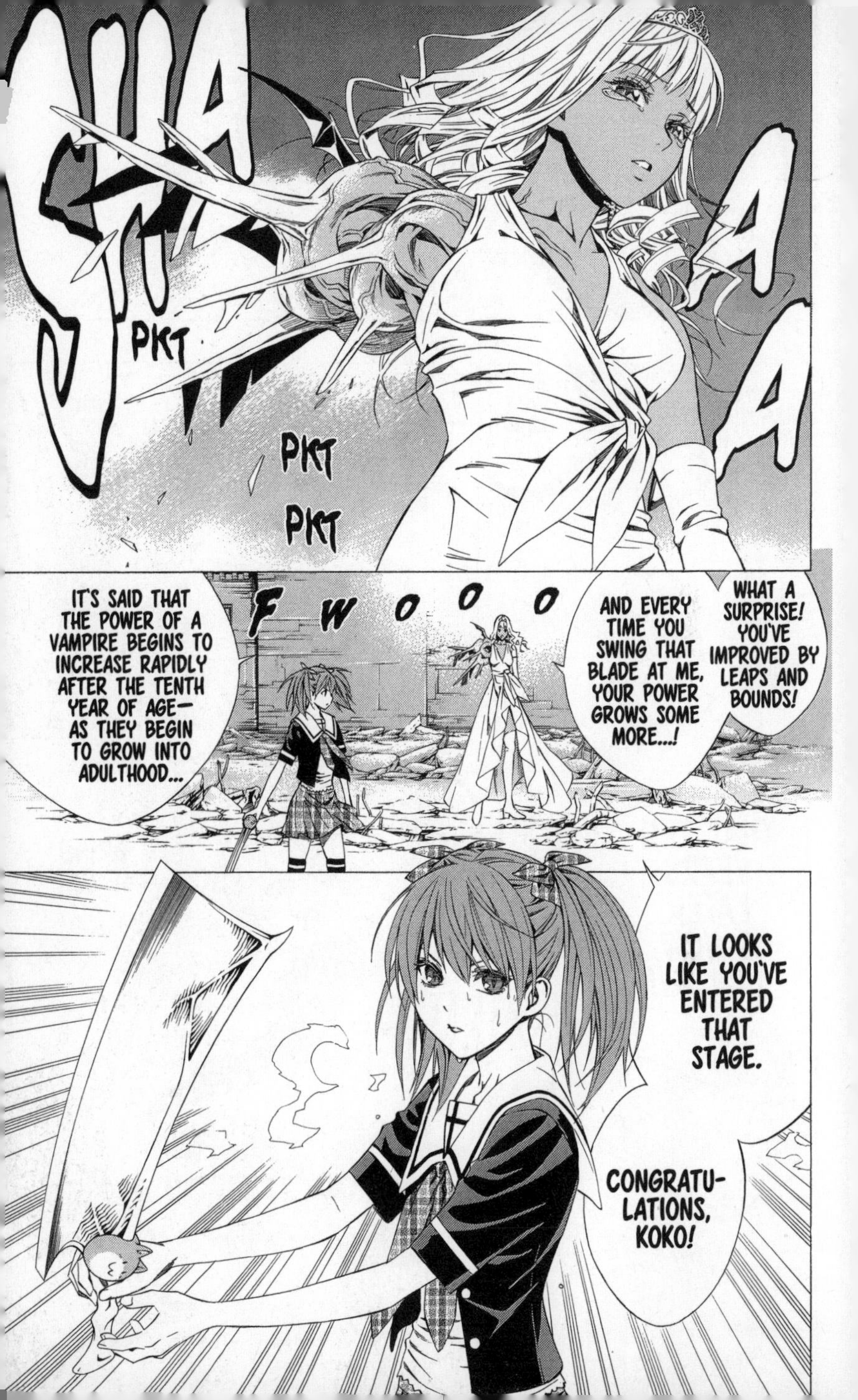
SHAAAA
PKT
PKT
PKT
WHAT A SURPRISE! YOU'VE IMPROVED BY LEAPS AND BOUNDS!
AND EVERY TIME YOU SWING THAT BLADE AT ME, YOUR POWER GROWS SOME MORE...!
FWOOO
IT'S SAID THAT THE POWER OF A VAMPIRE BEGINS TO INCREASE RAPIDLY AFTER THE TENTH YEAR OF AGE—AS THEY BEGIN TO GROW INTO ADULTHOOD...
IT LOOKS LIKE YOU'VE ENTERED THAT STAGE.
CONGRATULATIONS, KOKO!

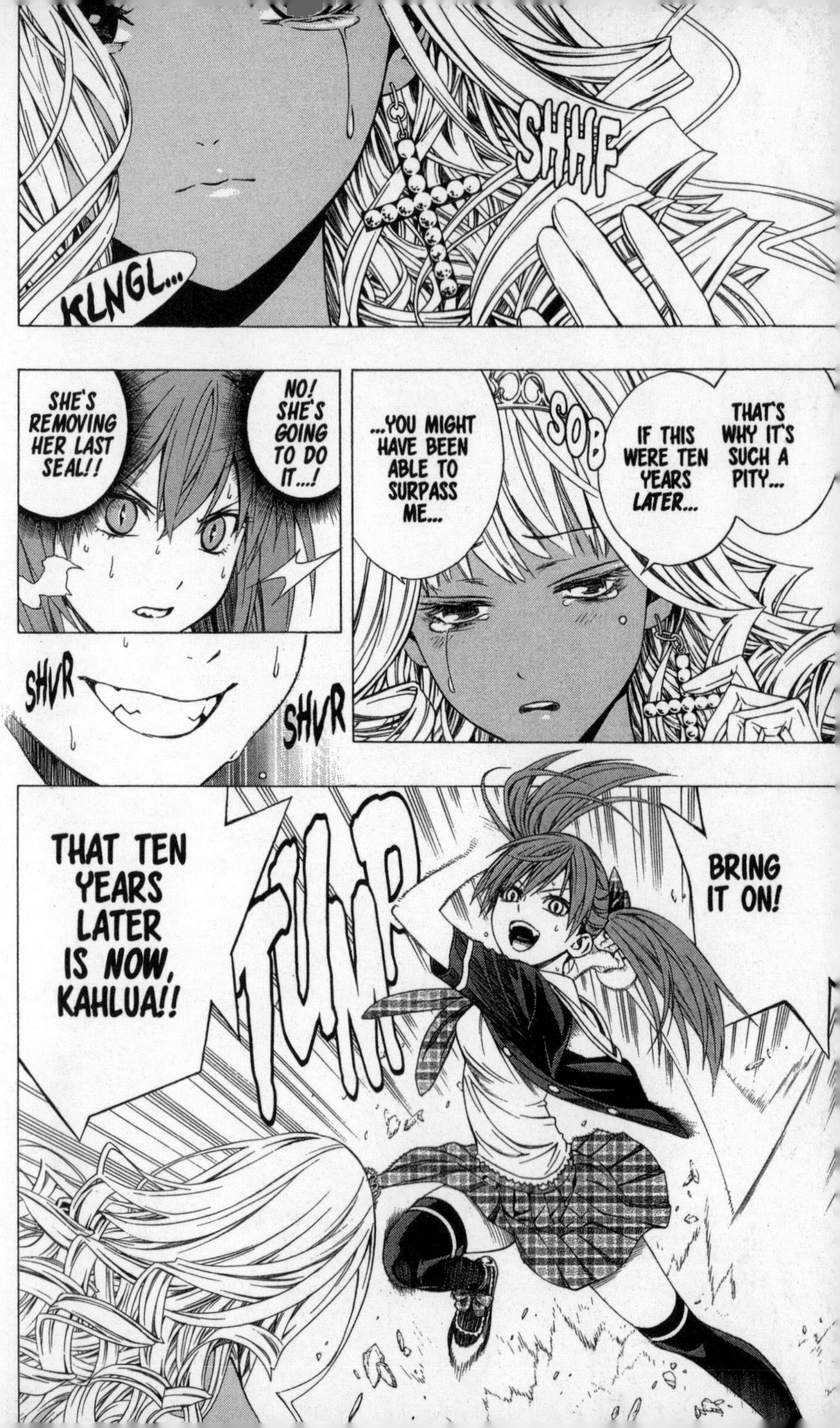
SHHF
KLNGL...
THAT'S WHY IT'S SUCH A PITY...
IF THIS WERE TEN YEARS LATER...
SOB
...YOU MIGHT HAVE BEEN ABLE TO SURPASS ME...
NO! SHE'S GOING TO DO IT...!
SHE'S REMOVING HER LAST SEAL!!
SHVR
SHVR
BRING IT ON!
TUMP
THAT TEN YEARS LATER IS NOW, KAHLUA!!

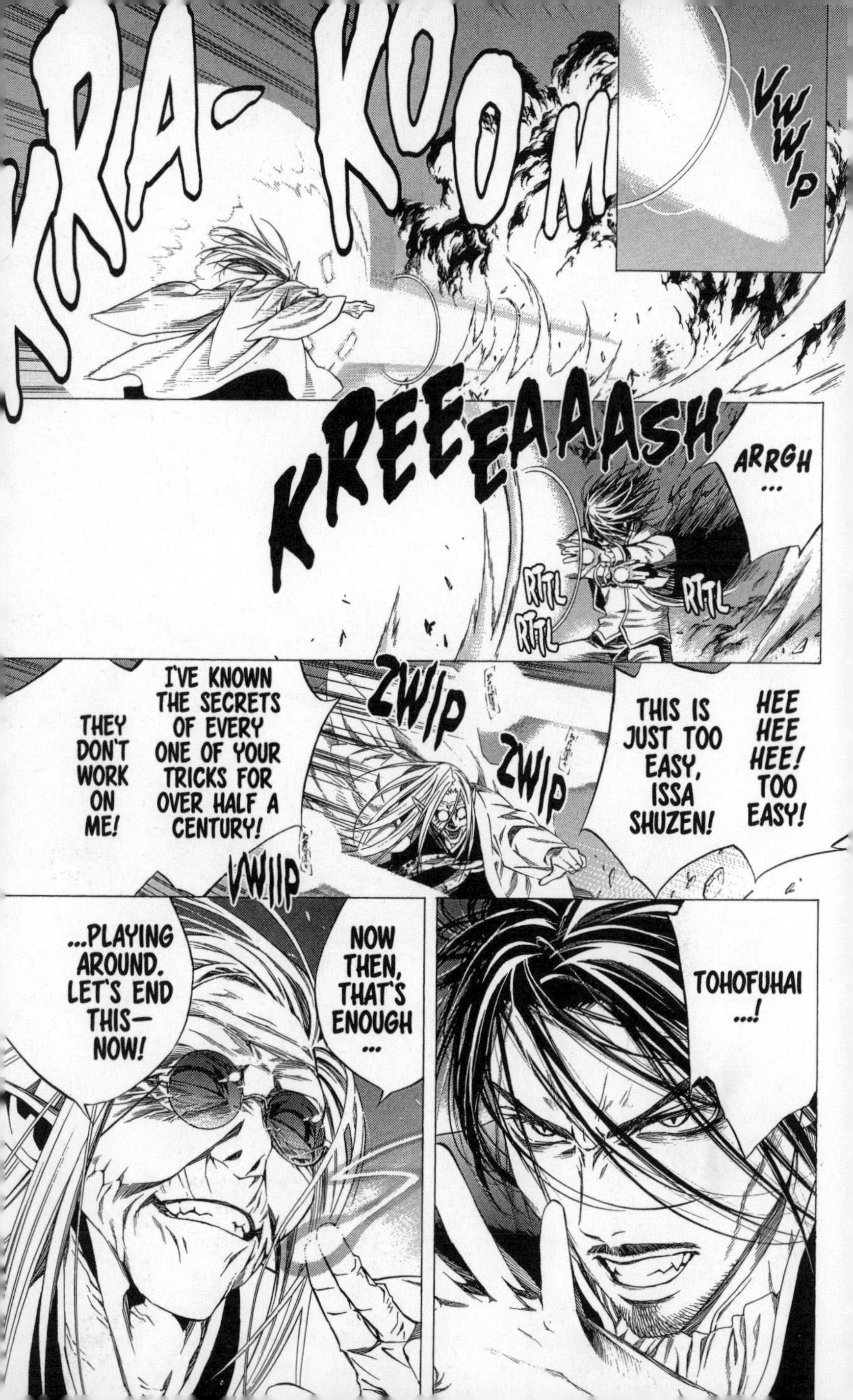
VWWIP
RA-KOOM
KREEAAASH
ARRGH...
RTTL
RTTL
RTTL
HEE HEE HEE! TOO EASY!
THIS IS JUST TOO EASY, ISSA SHUZEN!
ZWIP
ZWIP
I'VE KNOWN THE SECRETS OF EVERY ONE OF YOUR TRICKS FOR OVER HALF A CENTURY!
THEY DON'T WORK ON ME!
VWIIP
TOHOFUHAI ...!
NOW THEN, THAT'S ENOUGH ...
...PLAYING AROUND. LET'S END THIS—NOW!

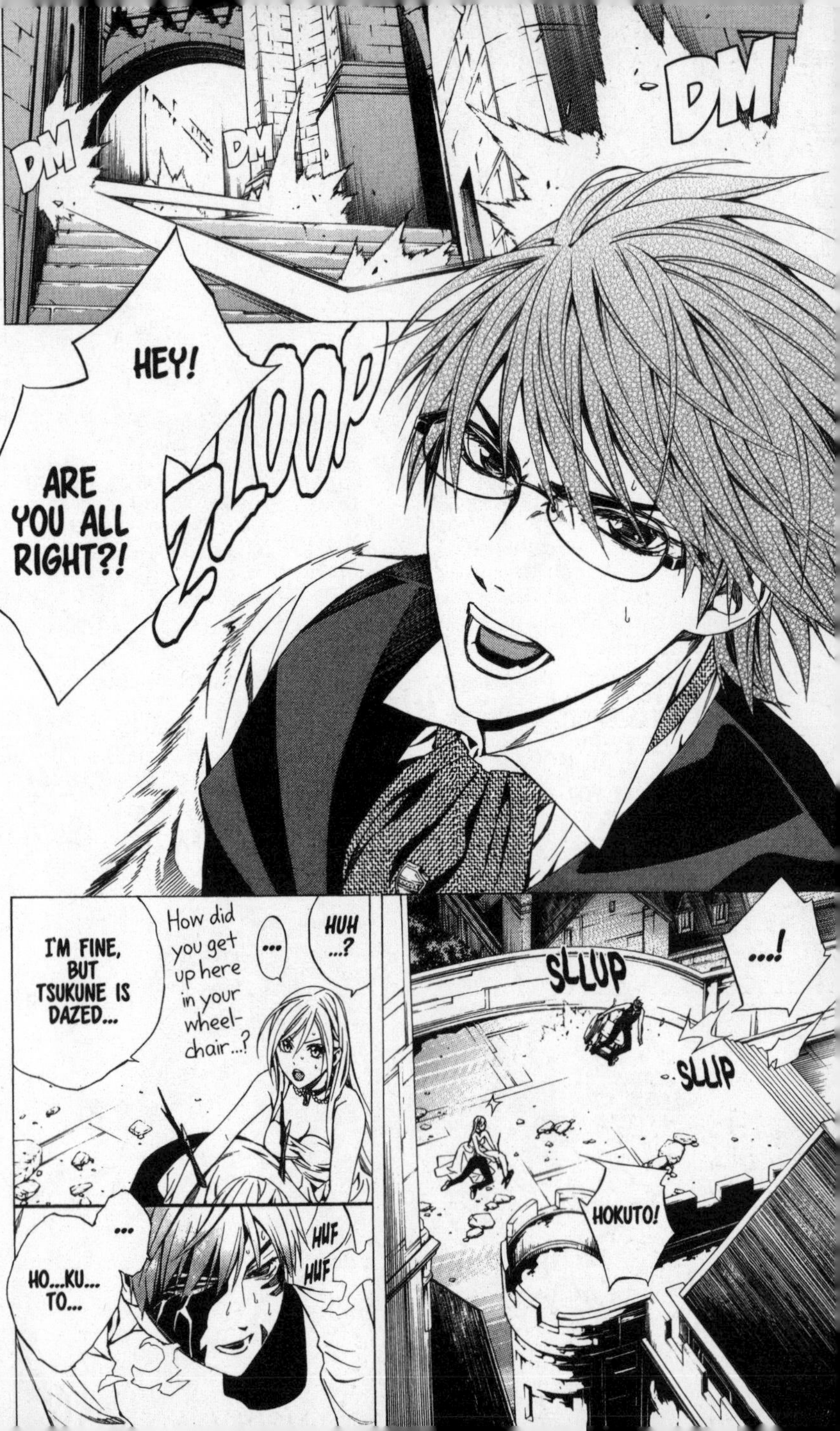
DM
DM
DM
ZLOOP
HEY!
ARE YOU ALL RIGHT?!
...!
SLLUP
SLLUP
HOKUTO!
HUH ...?
...
How did you get up here in your wheel-chair...?
I'M FINE, BUT TSUKUNE IS DAZED...
HUF
HUF
...
HO...KU... TO...

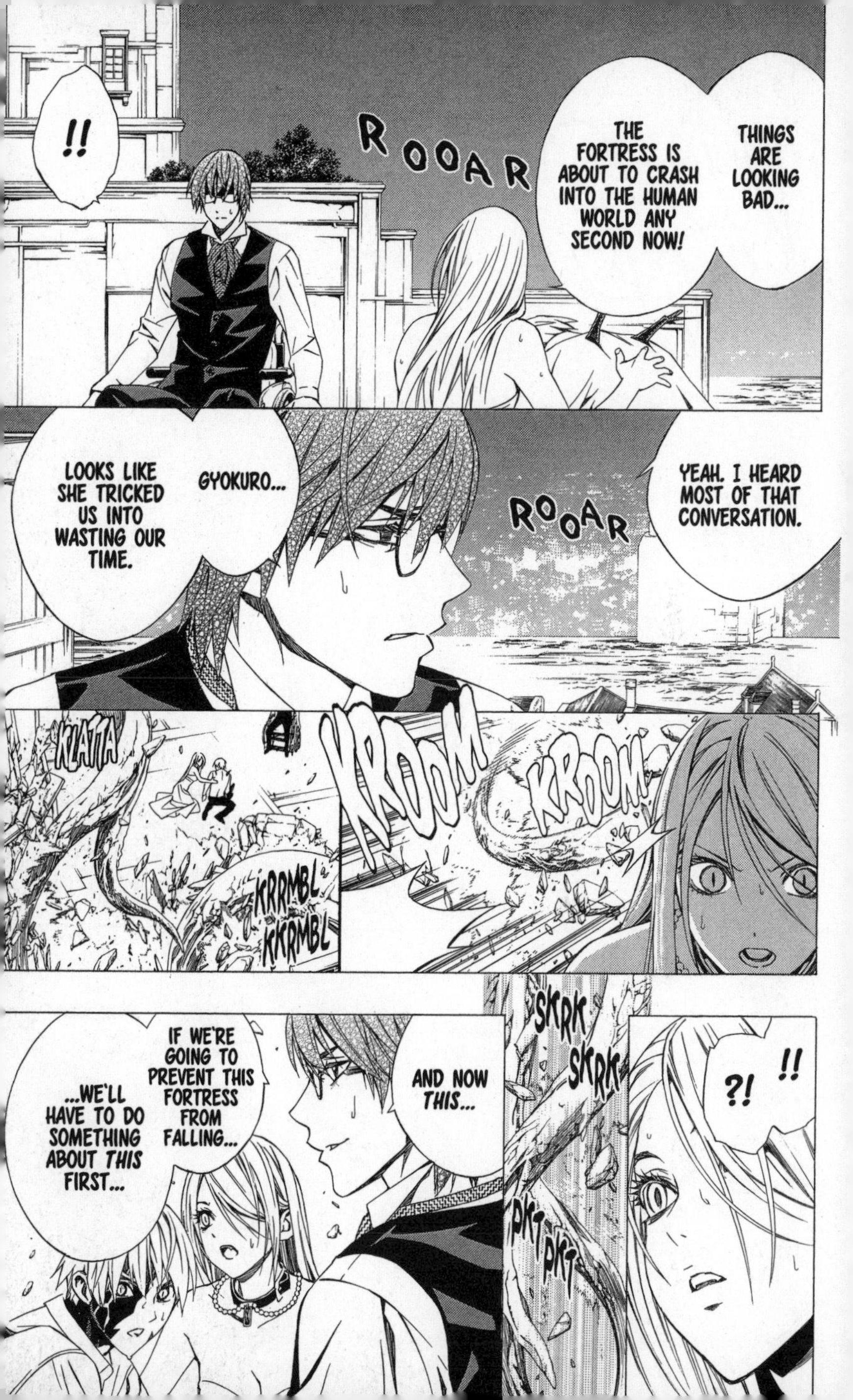
THINGS ARE LOOKING BAD...
THE FORTRESS IS ABOUT TO CRASH INTO THE HUMAN WORLD ANY SECOND NOW!
ROOAR
!!
YEAH. I HEARD MOST OF THAT CONVERSATION.
ROOAR
GYOKURO...
LOOKS LIKE SHE TRICKED US INTO WASTING OUR TIME.
KROOM
KROOM
KLATTA
KRRMBL KRRMBL
!!
?!
SKRK SKRK
PKT PKT
AND NOW THIS...
IF WE'RE GOING TO PREVENT THIS FORTRESS FROM FALLING...
...WE'LL HAVE TO DO SOMETHING ABOUT THIS FIRST...

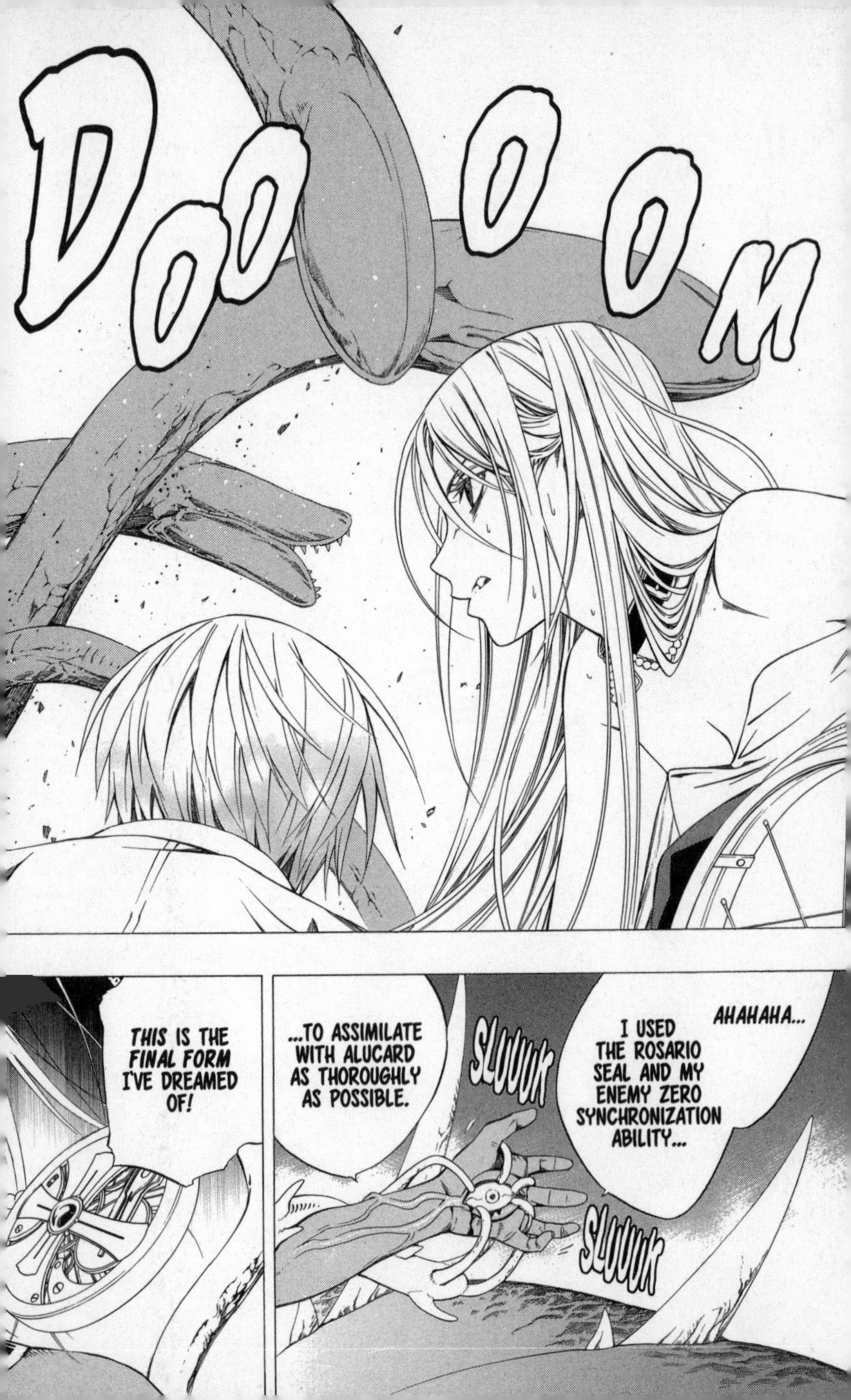
DOOOOOM
AHAHAHA...
I USED THE ROSARIO SEAL AND MY ENEMY ZERO SYNCHRONIZATION ABILITY...
SLUUUK
...TO ASSIMILATE WITH ALUCARD AS THOROUGHLY AS POSSIBLE.
SLUUUK
THIS IS THE FINAL FORM I'VE DREAMED OF!

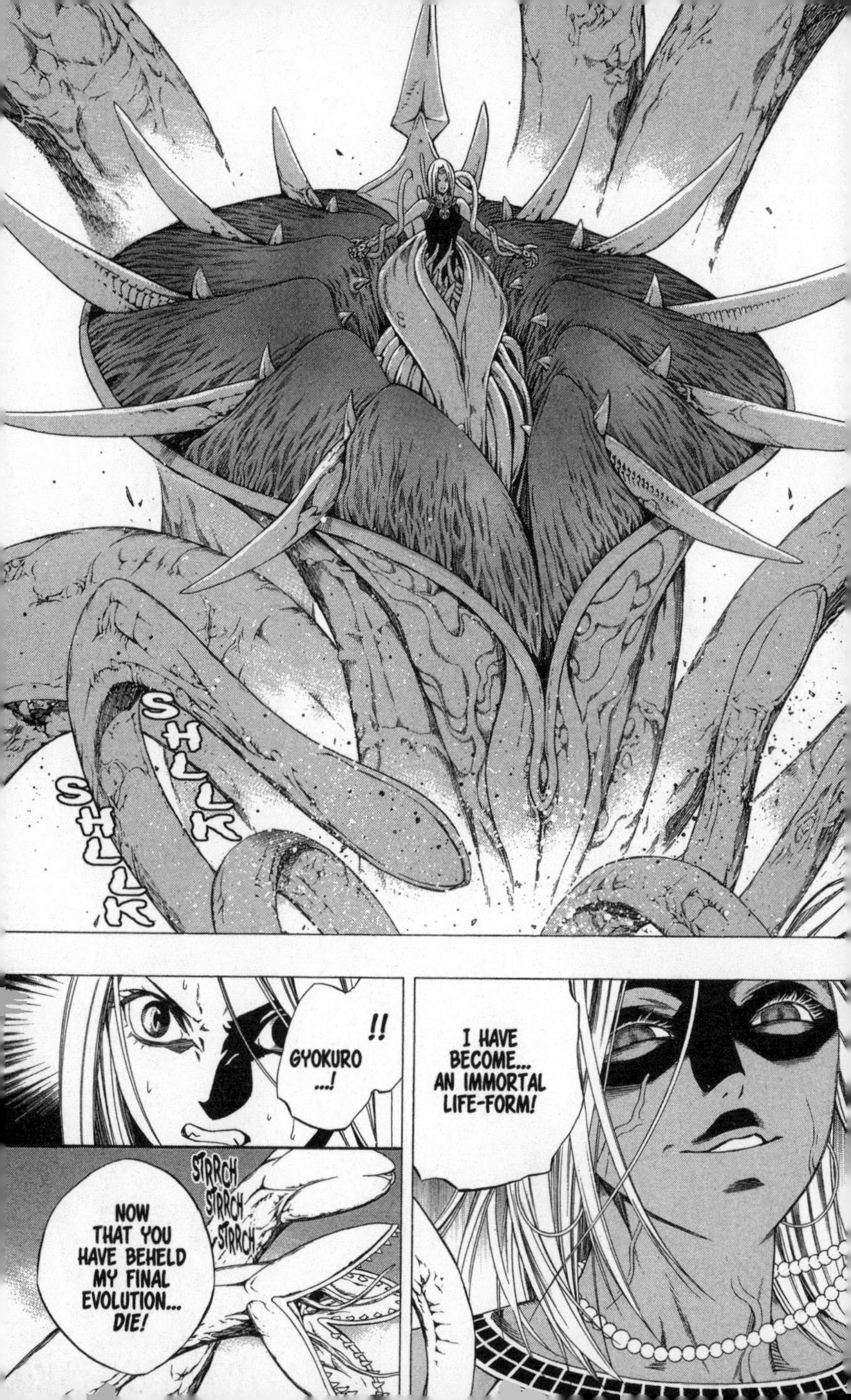
SHLLK
SHLLK
I HAVE BECOME... AN IMMORTAL LIFE-FORM!
!!
GYOKURO ...!
STRRCH STRRCH STRRCH
NOW THAT YOU HAVE BEHELD MY FINAL EVOLUTION... DIE!

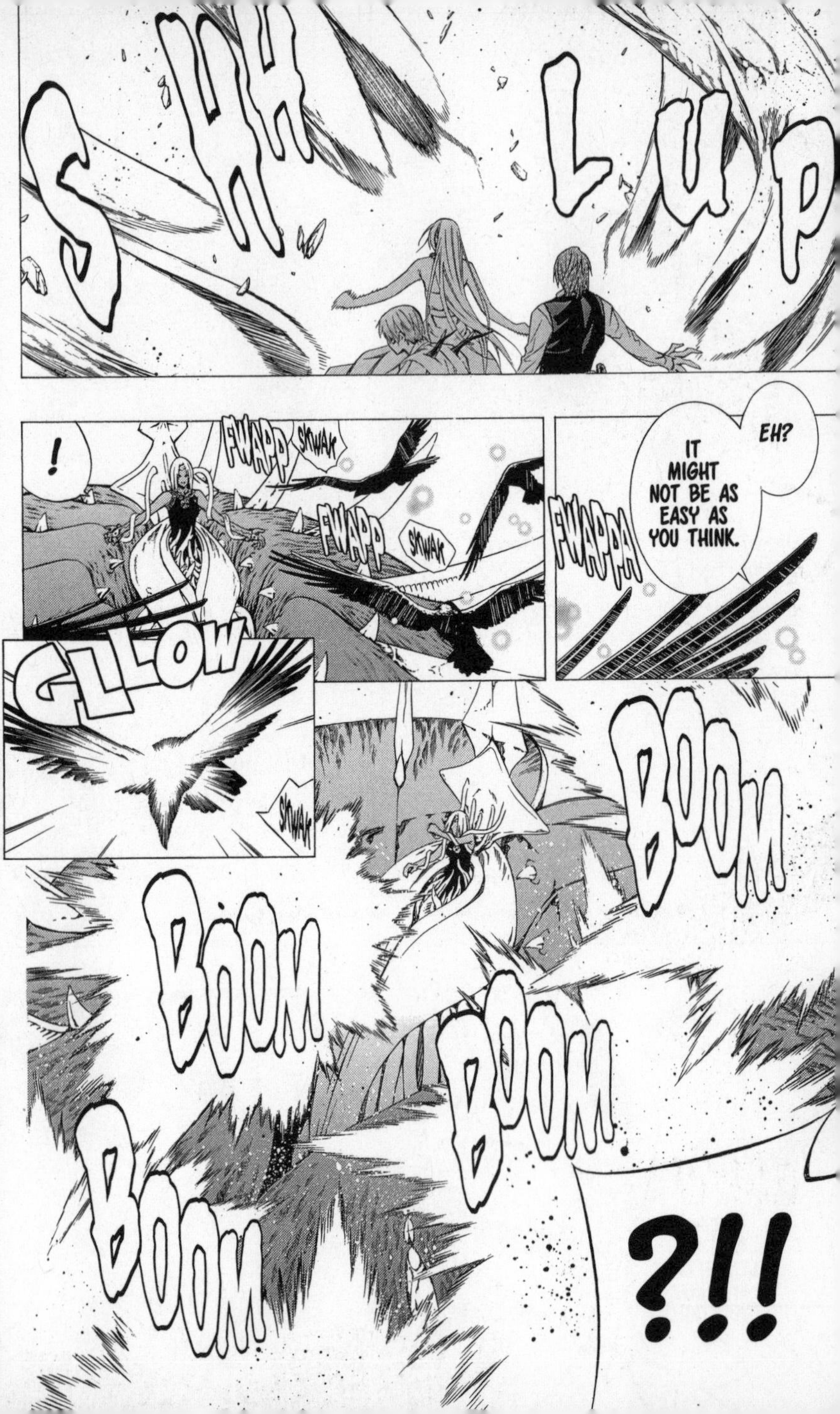
SHH
LUP
EH?
IT MIGHT NOT BE AS EASY AS YOU THINK.
FWAPPA
!
FWAPP
SKWAK
FWAPP
SKWAK
GLLOW
SKWAK
BOOM
BOOM
BOOM
BOOM
?!!

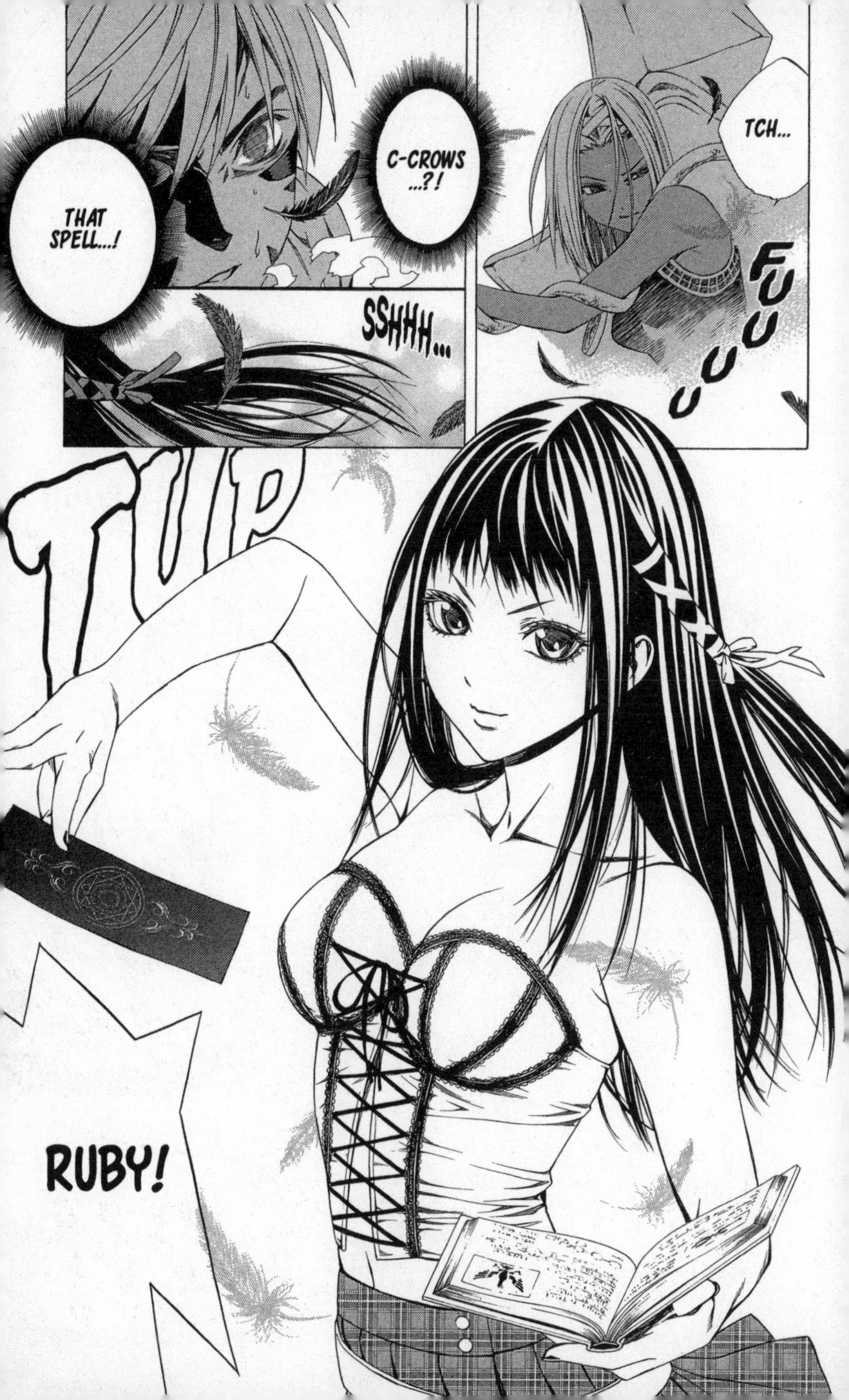
TCH...
FUUUUUU
C-CROWS ...?!
THAT SPELL...!
SSHHH...
TUP
RUBY!

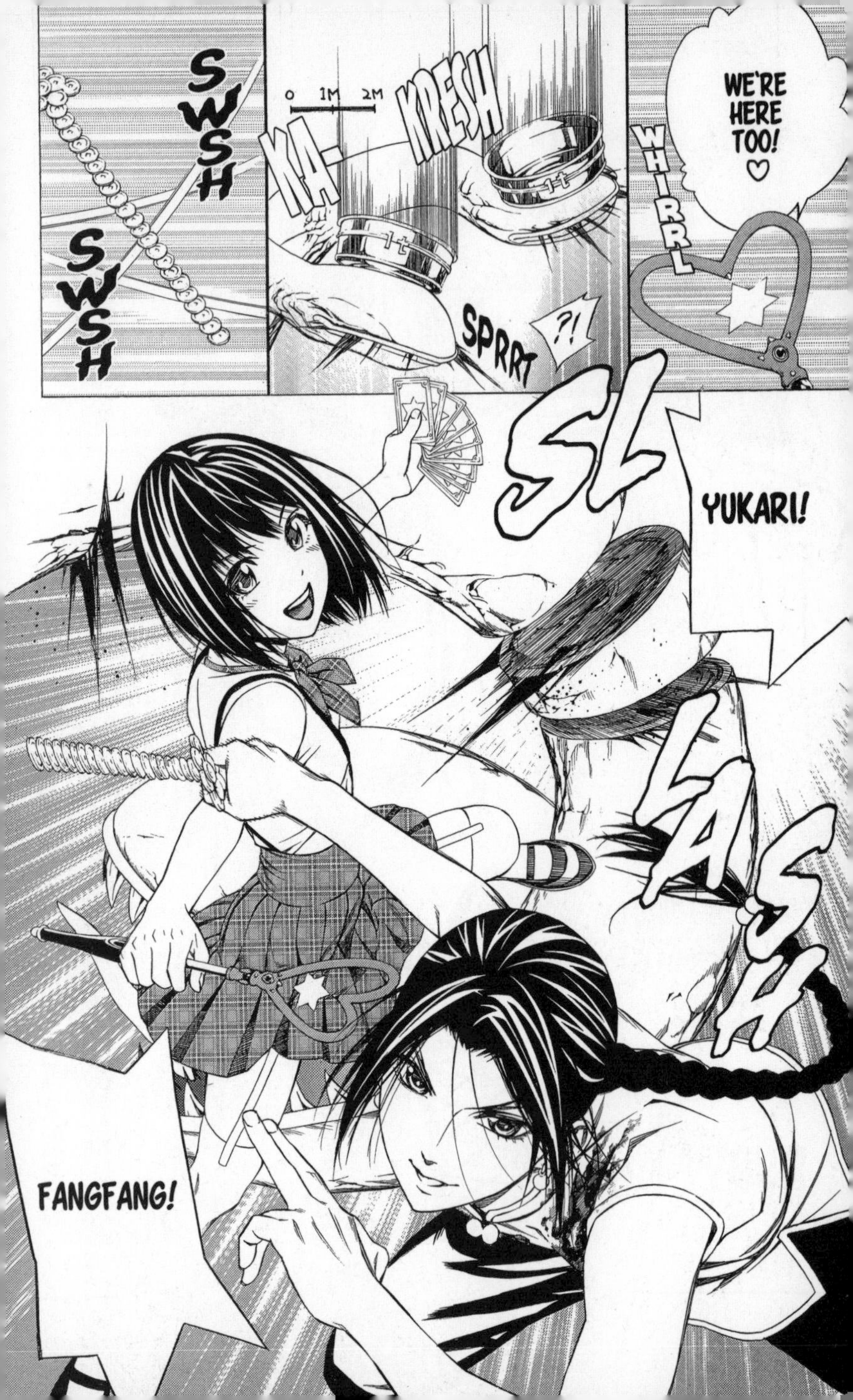

WE'RE HERE TOO! ♡
WHIRRL
0 1M 2M
KA-KRESH
SPRRT
?!
SWSH
SWSH
SLASH
YUKARI!
FANGFANG!

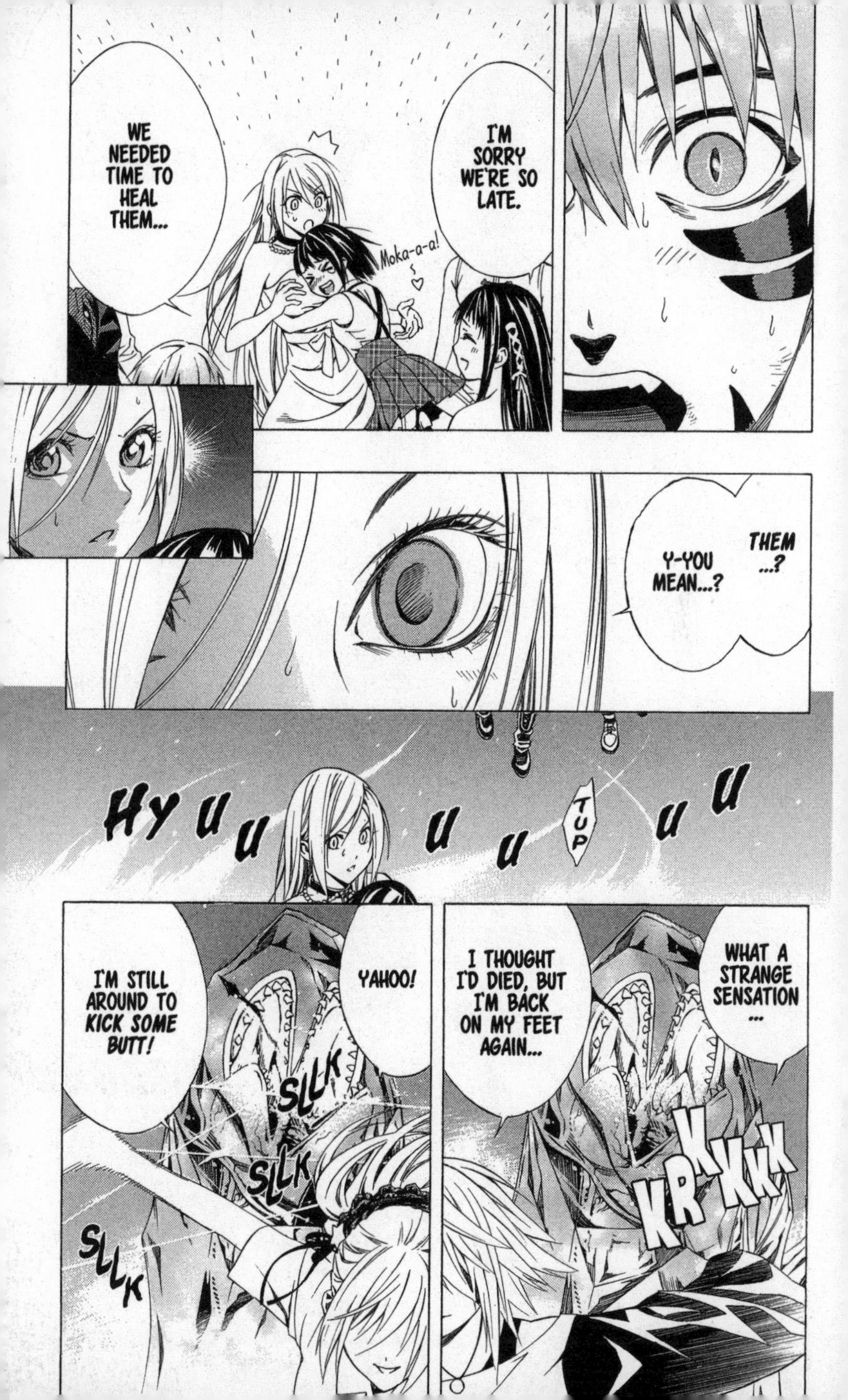
I'M SORRY WE'RE SO LATE.
WE NEEDED TIME TO HEAL THEM...
Moka-a-a!
THEM ...?
Y-YOU MEAN...?
HYUUUUUUU
TUP
WHAT A STRANGE SENSATION ...
I THOUGHT I'D DIED, BUT I'M BACK ON MY FEET AGAIN...
KRKKKKK
YAHOO!
I'M STILL AROUND TO KICK SOME BUTT!
SLLK
SLLK
SLLK

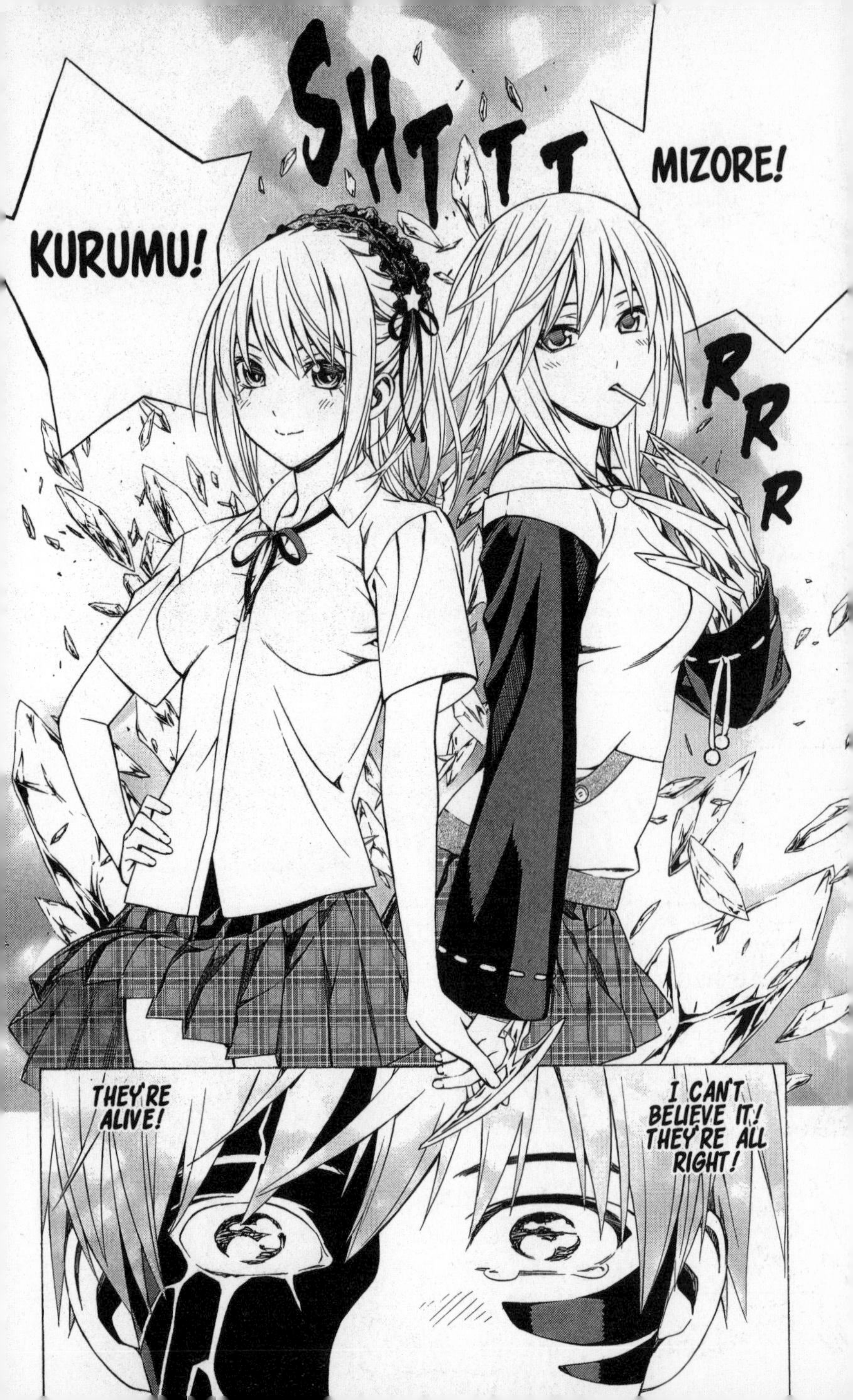
SHTTT
RRR
MIZORE!
KURUMU!
I CAN'T BELIEVE IT! THEY'RE ALL RIGHT!
THEY'RE ALIVE!

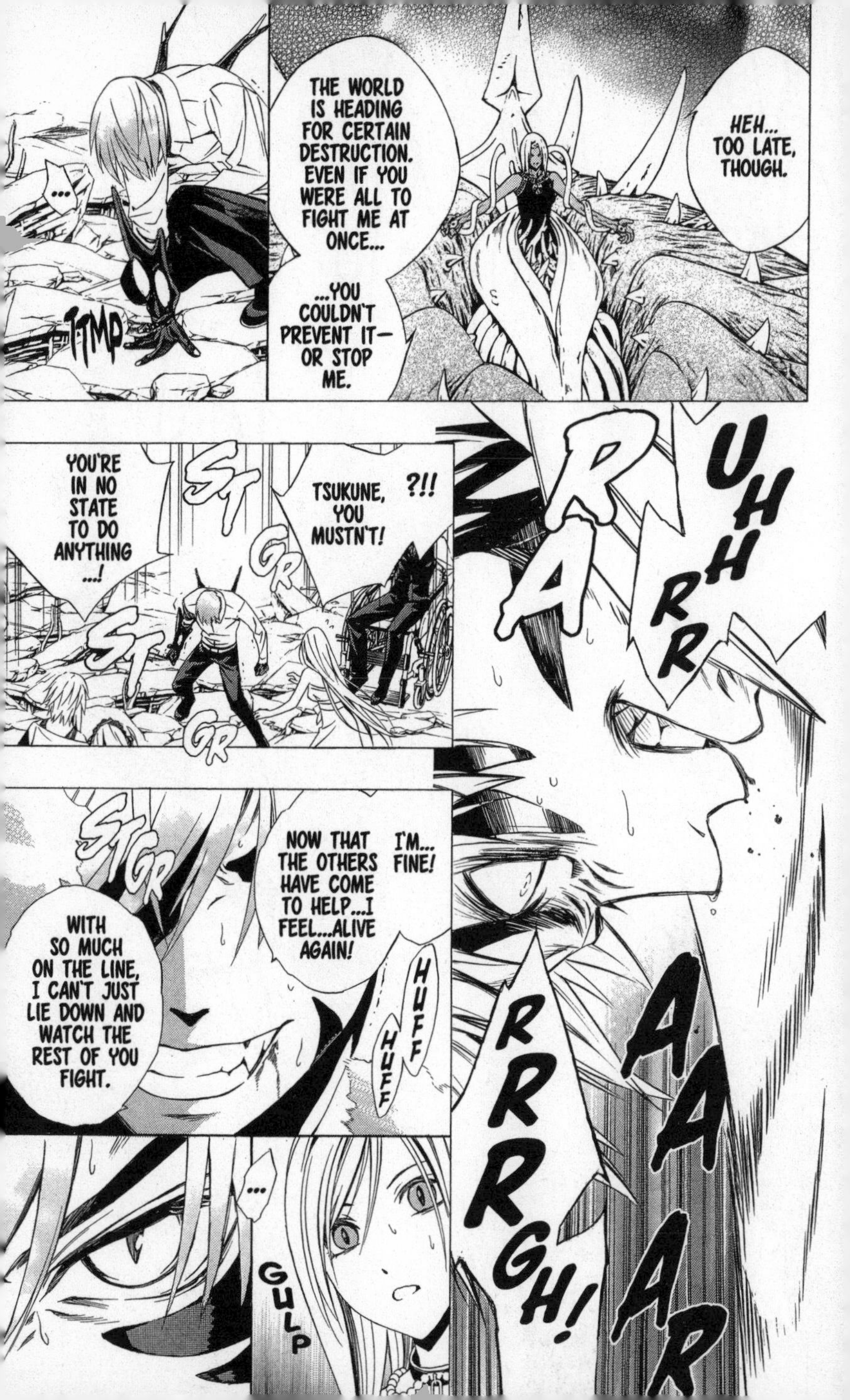
HEH... TOO LATE, THOUGH.
THE WORLD IS HEADING FOR CERTAIN DESTRUCTION. EVEN IF YOU WERE ALL TO FIGHT ME AT ONCE...
...YOU COULDN'T PREVENT IT—OR STOP ME.
...
TMP
RAUHHRRR
AAAR
RRRRGH!
?!!
TSUKUNE, YOU MUSTN'T!
YOU'RE IN NO STATE TO DO ANYTHING...!
ST
GR
ST
GR
I'M... FINE!
NOW THAT THE OTHERS HAVE COME TO HELP...I FEEL...ALIVE AGAIN!
WITH SO MUCH ON THE LINE, I CAN'T JUST LIE DOWN AND WATCH THE REST OF YOU FIGHT.
STGR
HUFF
HUFF
GULP
...

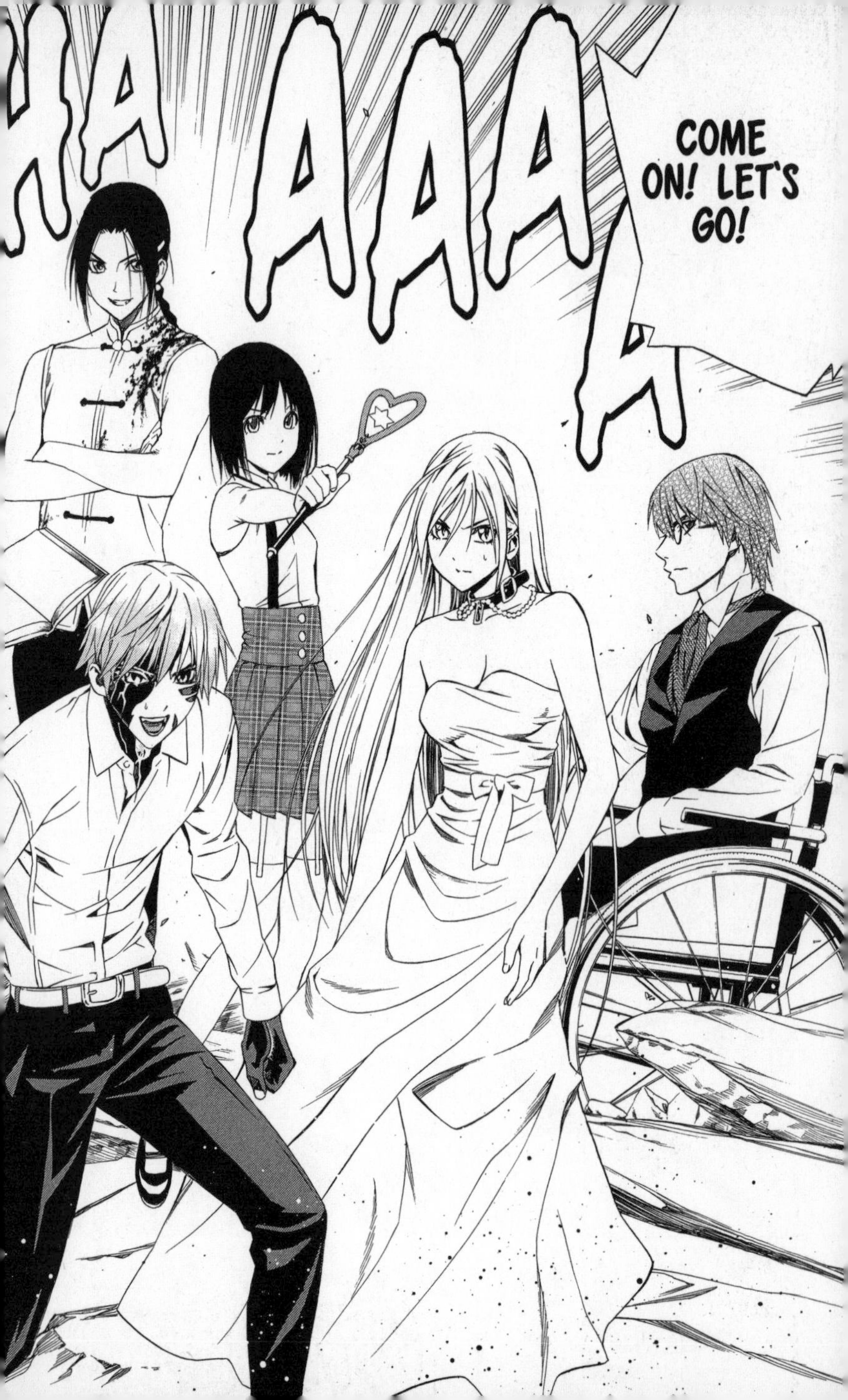
COME ON! LET'S GO!
HAAAA

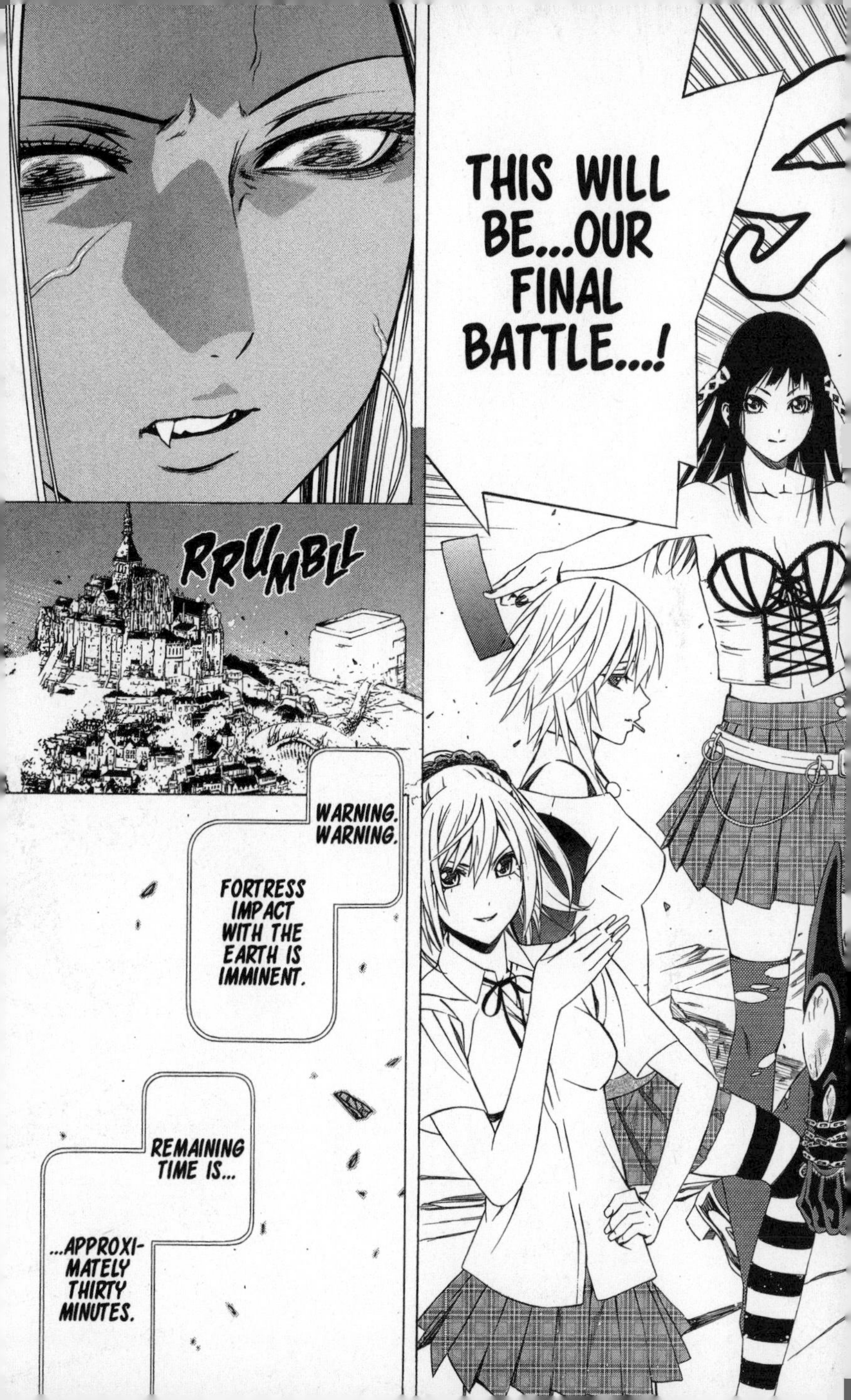
THIS WILL BE...OUR FINAL BATTLE...!
RRUMBLL
WARNING. WARNING.
FORTRESS IMPACT WITH THE EARTH IS IMMINENT.
REMAINING TIME IS...
...APPROXI-MATELY THIRTY MINUTES.

62: We're Not Alone

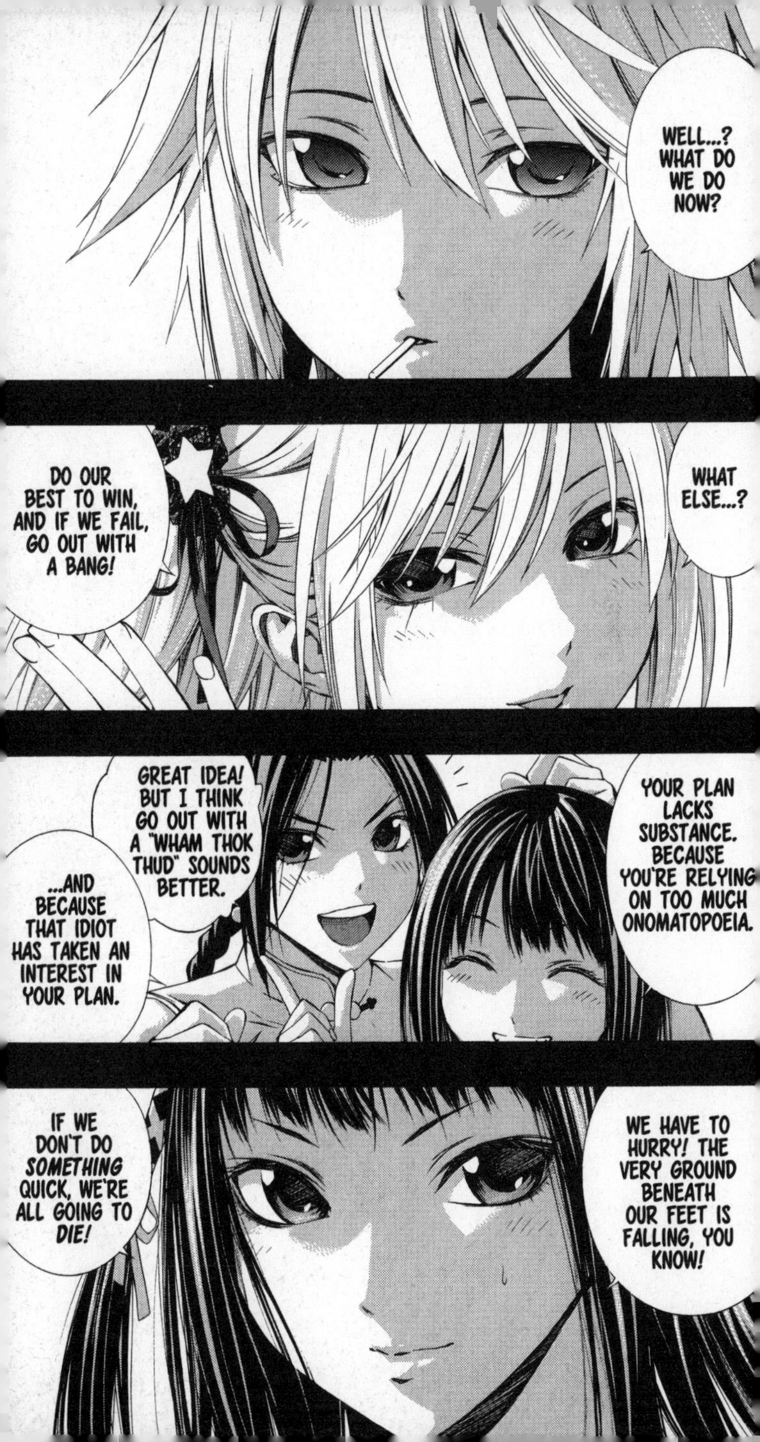
WELL...? WHAT DO WE DO NOW?
WHAT ELSE...?
DO OUR BEST TO WIN, AND IF WE FAIL, GO OUT WITH A BANG!
YOUR PLAN LACKS SUBSTANCE. BECAUSE YOU'RE RELYING ON TOO MUCH ONOMATOPOEIA.
GREAT IDEA! BUT I THINK GO OUT WITH A "WHAM THOK THUD" SOUNDS BETTER.
...AND BECAUSE THAT IDIOT HAS TAKEN AN INTEREST IN YOUR PLAN.
WE HAVE TO HURRY! THE VERY GROUND BENEATH OUR FEET IS FALLING, YOU KNOW!
IF WE DON'T DO *SOMETHING* QUICK, WE'RE ALL GOING TO *DIE!*

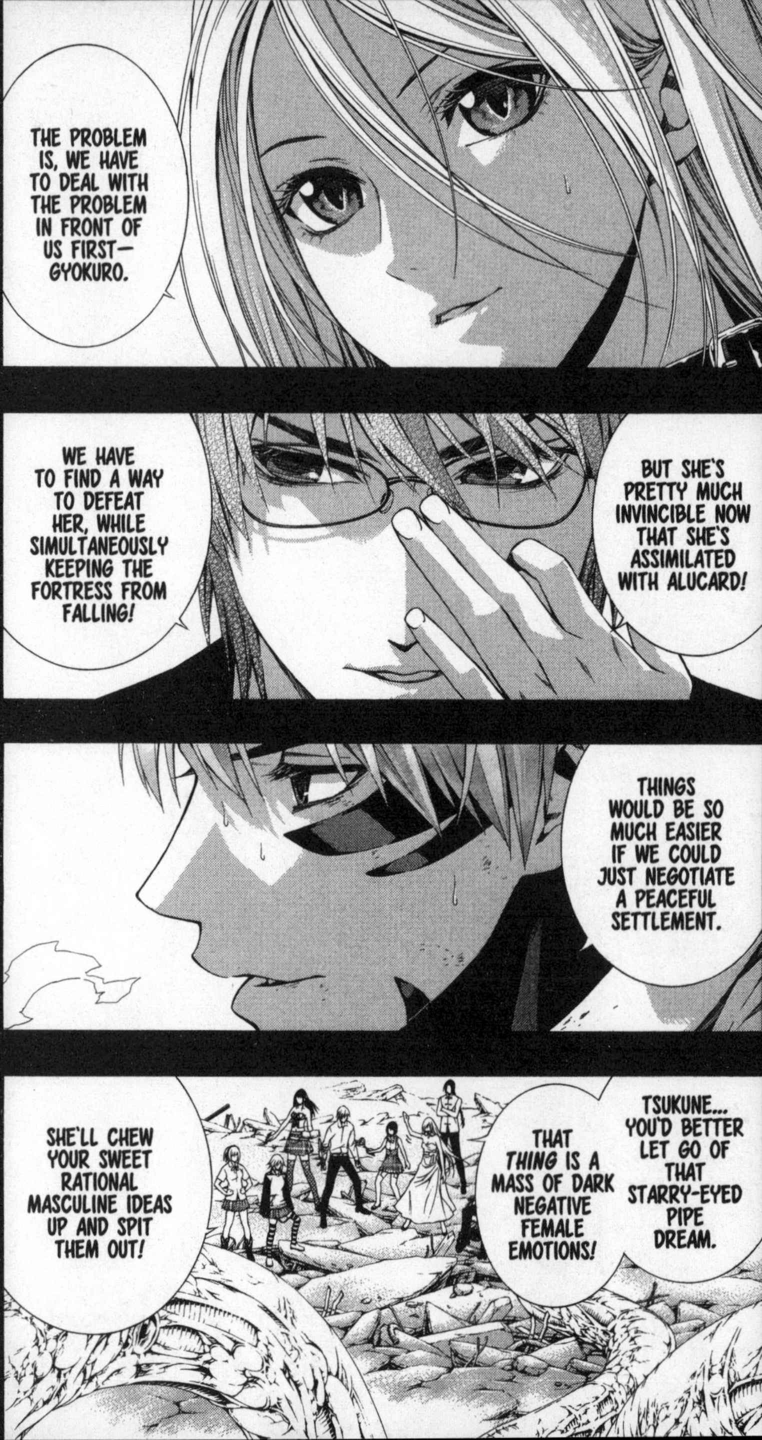
THE PROBLEM IS, WE HAVE TO DEAL WITH THE PROBLEM IN FRONT OF US FIRST— GYOKURO.
BUT SHE'S PRETTY MUCH INVINCIBLE NOW THAT SHE'S ASSIMILATED WITH ALUCARD!
WE HAVE TO FIND A WAY TO DEFEAT HER, WHILE SIMULTANEOUSLY KEEPING THE FORTRESS FROM FALLING!
THINGS WOULD BE SO MUCH EASIER IF WE COULD JUST NEGOTIATE A PEACEFUL SETTLEMENT.
TSUKUNE... YOU'D BETTER LET GO OF THAT STARRY-EYED PIPE DREAM.
THAT *THING* IS A MASS OF DARK NEGATIVE FEMALE EMOTIONS!
SHE'LL CHEW YOUR SWEET RATIONAL MASCULINE IDEAS UP AND SPIT THEM OUT!

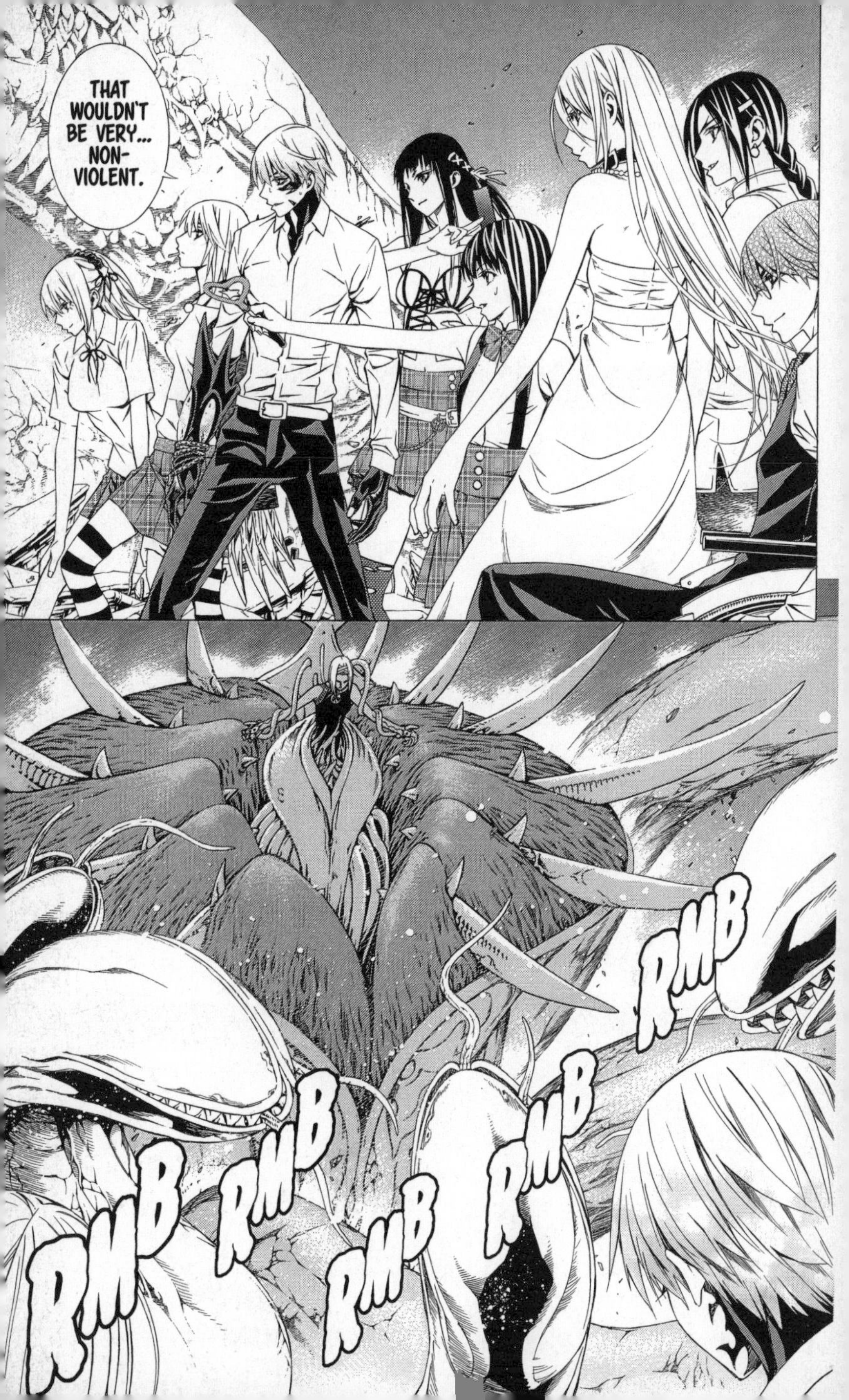

THAT WOULDN'T BE VERY... NON-VIOLENT.
RMB
RMB
RMB
RMB
RMB

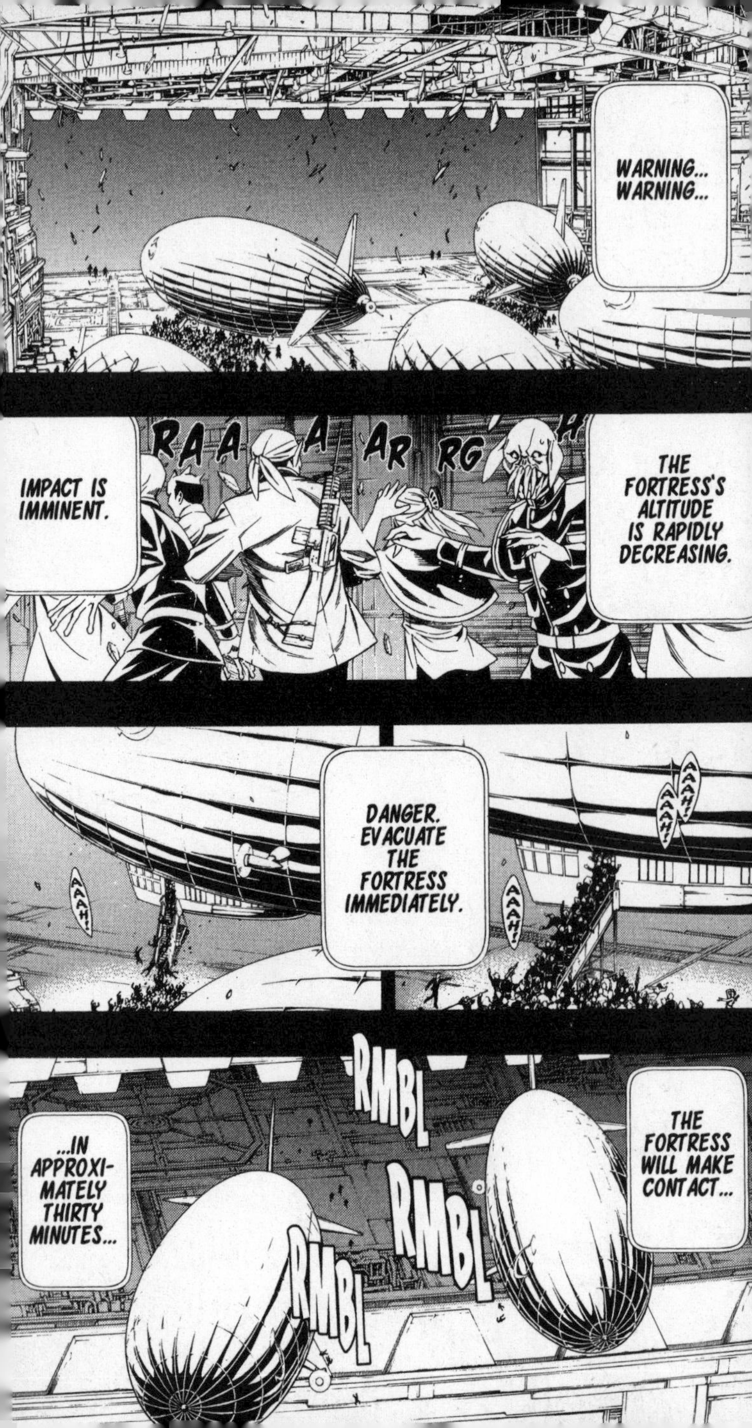
WARNING... WARNING...
THE FORTRESS'S ALTITUDE IS RAPIDLY DECREASING.
RAAAARRG
IMPACT IS IMMINENT.
AAAH!
AAAH!
DANGER. EVACUATE THE FORTRESS IMMEDIATELY.
AAAH!
AAAH!
THE FORTRESS WILL MAKE CONTACT...
RMBL
RMBL
RMBL
...IN APPROXIMATELY THIRTY MINUTES...

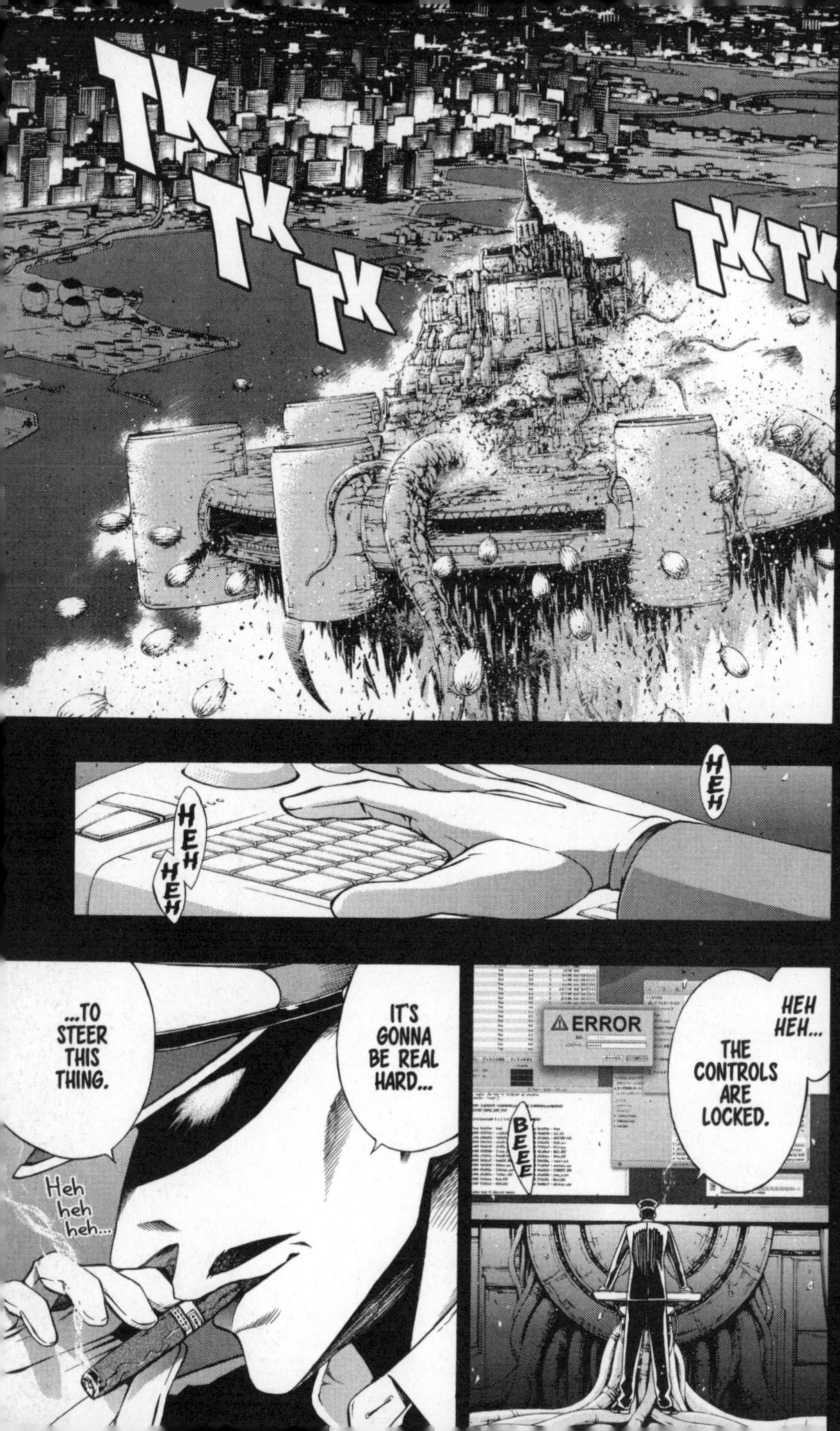
TKTK
TK TK TK
HEH
HEH HEH
HEH HEH... THE CONTROLS ARE LOCKED.
ERROR
BEEE
IT'S GONNA BE REAL HARD...
...TO STEER THIS THING.
Heh heh heh...

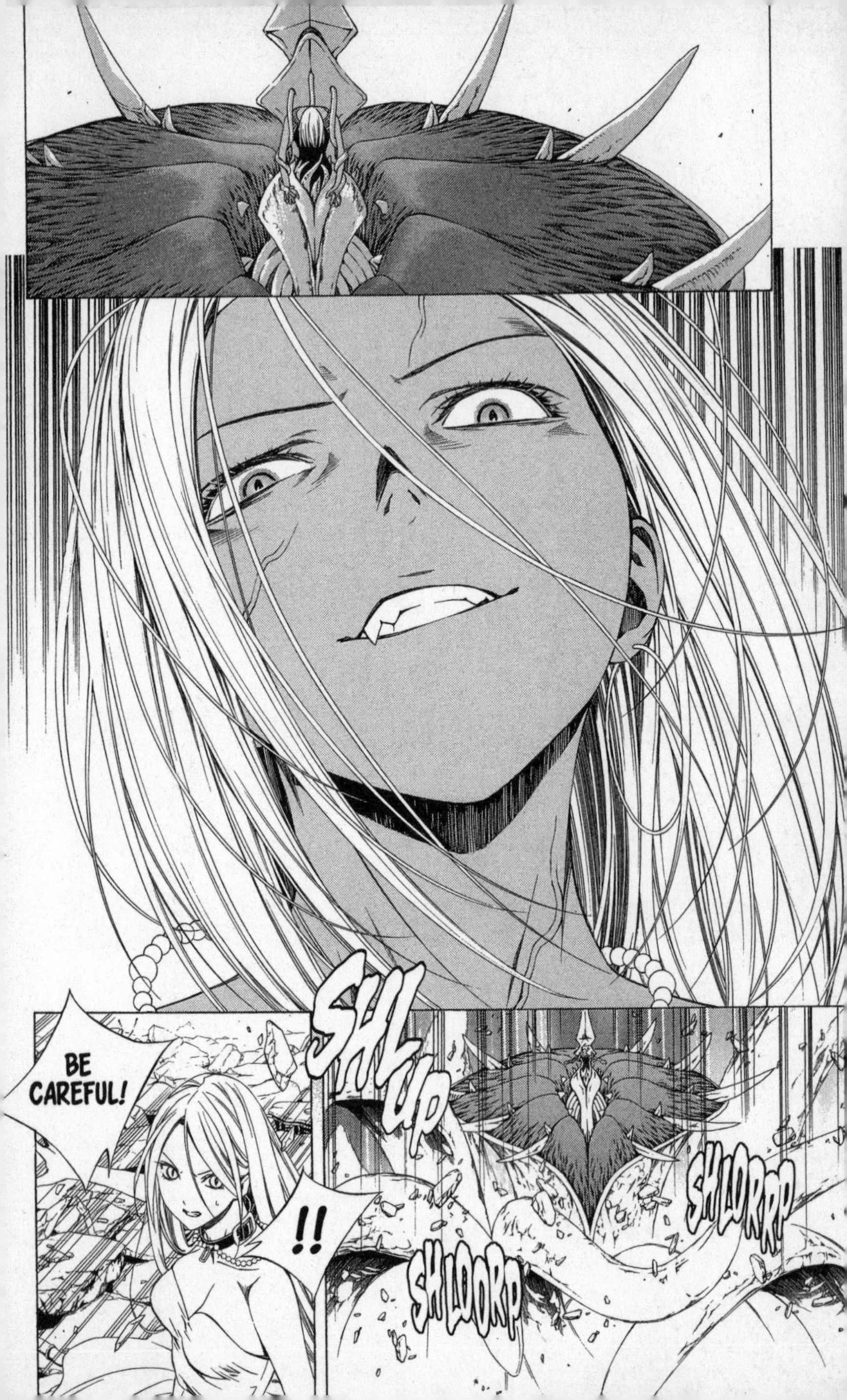
SHLORRP
SHLOORP
SHLUP
!!
BE CAREFUL!

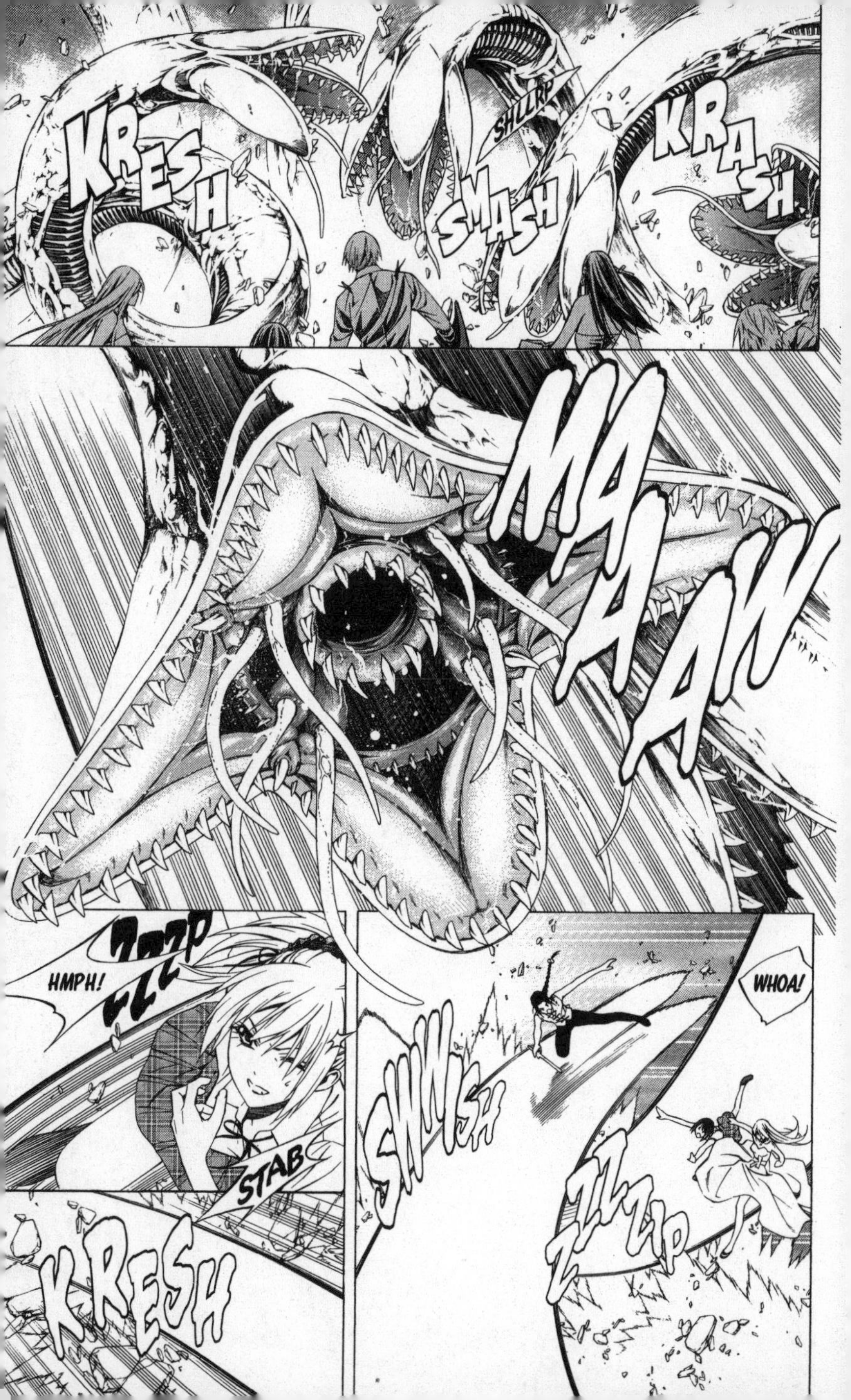
KRASH
SHLLRP
SMASH
KRESH
MAAAN
WHOA!
ZZZZIP
SWWISH
HMPH!
ZZZP
STAB
KRESH

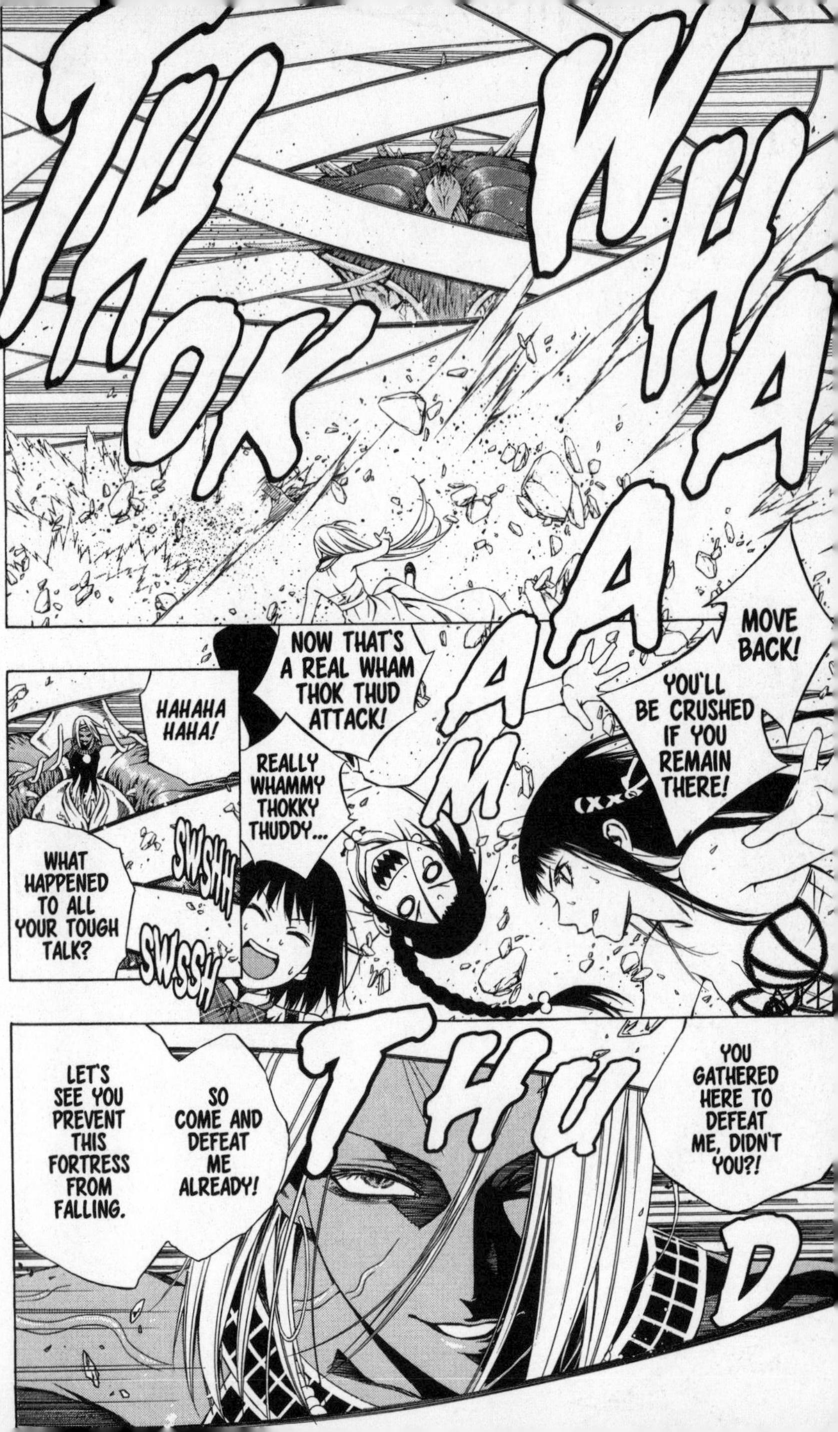

WHAAAAM
THOK
MOVE BACK!
YOU'LL BE CRUSHED IF YOU REMAIN THERE!
NOW THAT'S A REAL WHAM THOK THUD ATTACK!
REALLY WHAMMY THOKKY THUDDY...
SWSHH
SWSSH
HAHAHA HAHA!
WHAT HAPPENED TO ALL YOUR TOUGH TALK?
YOU GATHERED HERE TO DEFEAT ME, DIDN'T YOU?!
THUD
SO COME AND DEFEAT ME ALREADY!
LET'S SEE YOU PREVENT THIS FORTRESS FROM FALLING.

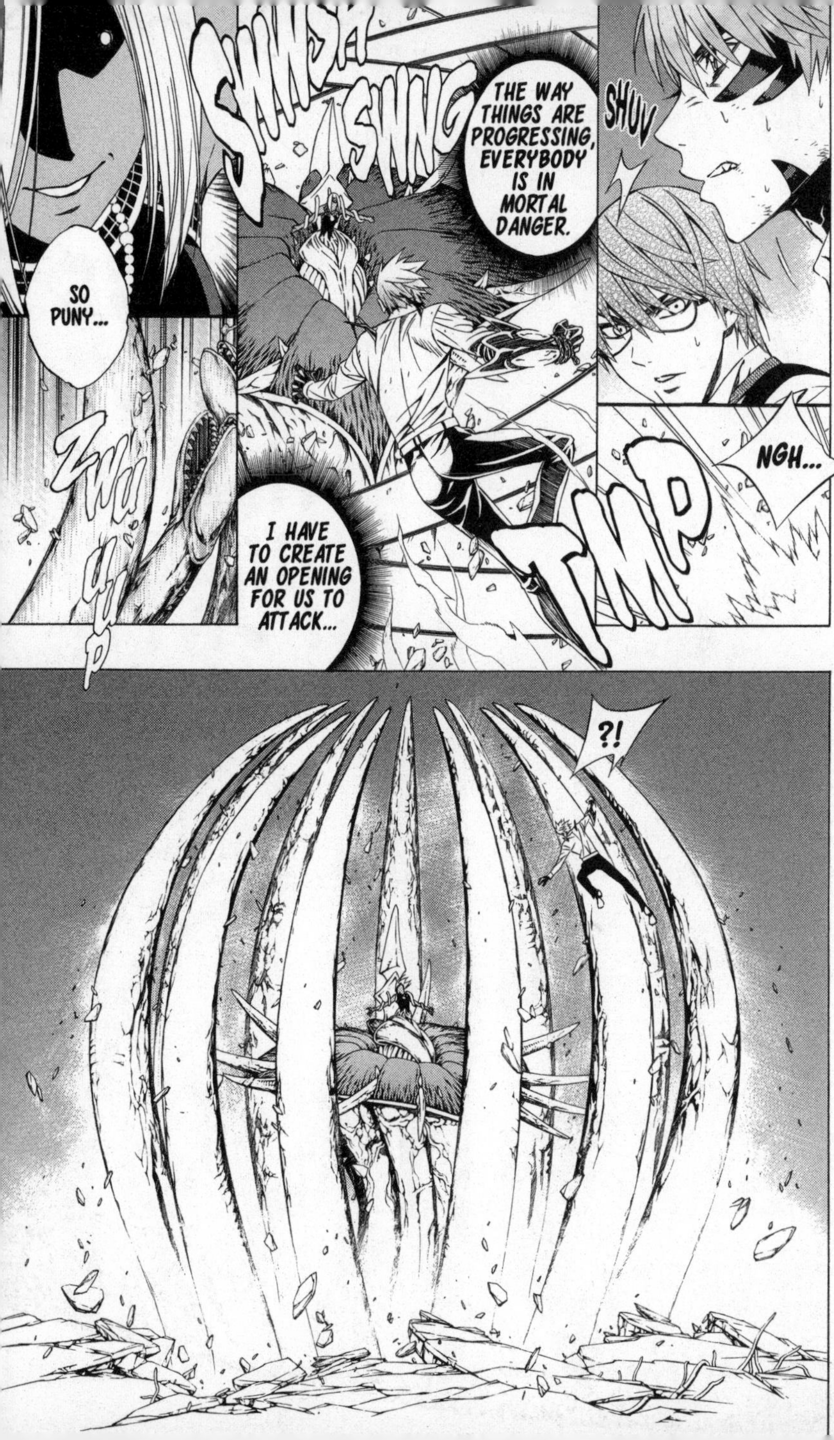
SHUV
NGH...
TMP
SWNG
THE WAY THINGS ARE PROGRESSING, EVERYBODY IS IN MORTAL DANGER.
I HAVE TO CREATE AN OPENING FOR US TO ATTACK...
SO PUNY...
?!

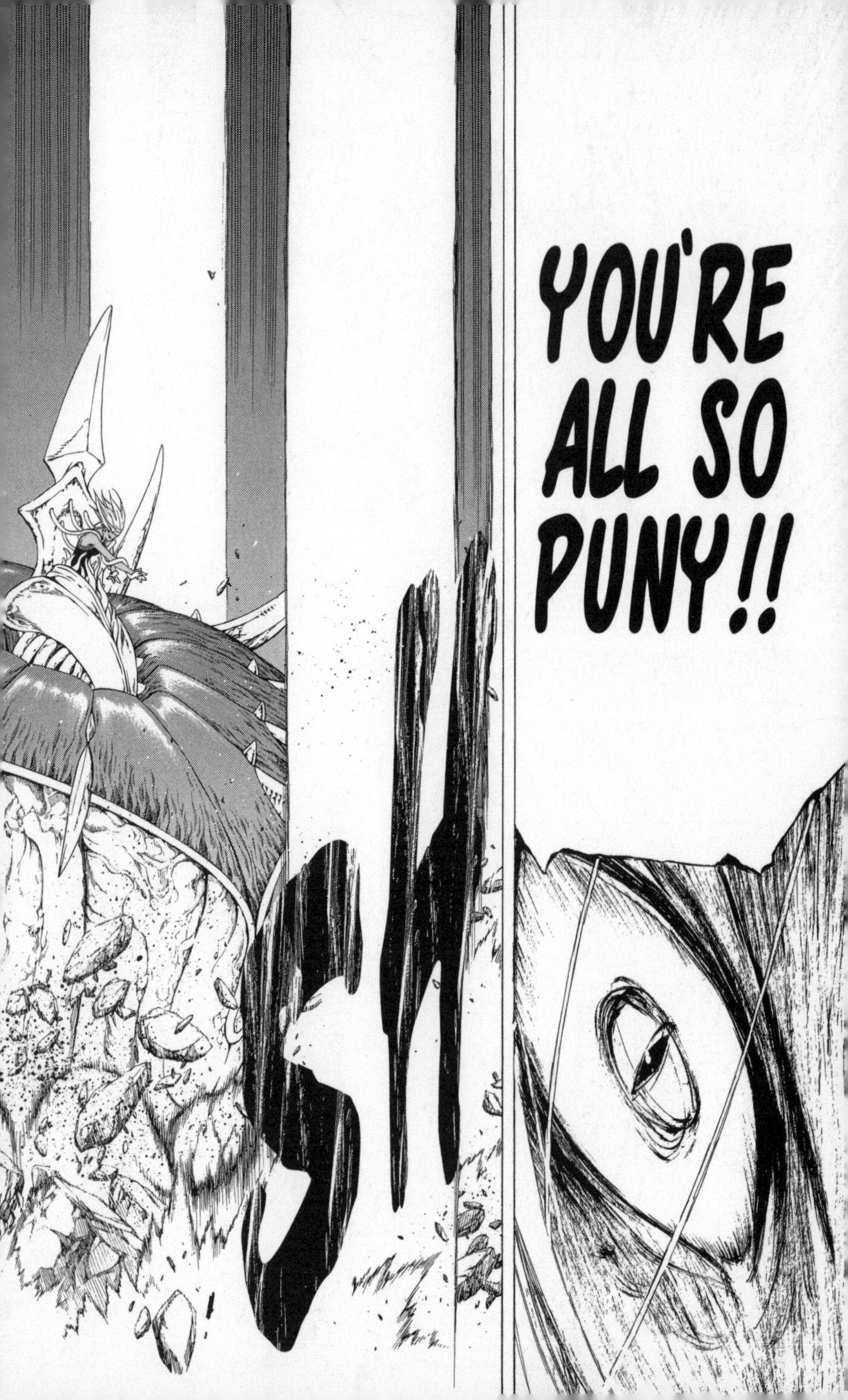
YOU'RE ALL SO PUNY!!
SHH

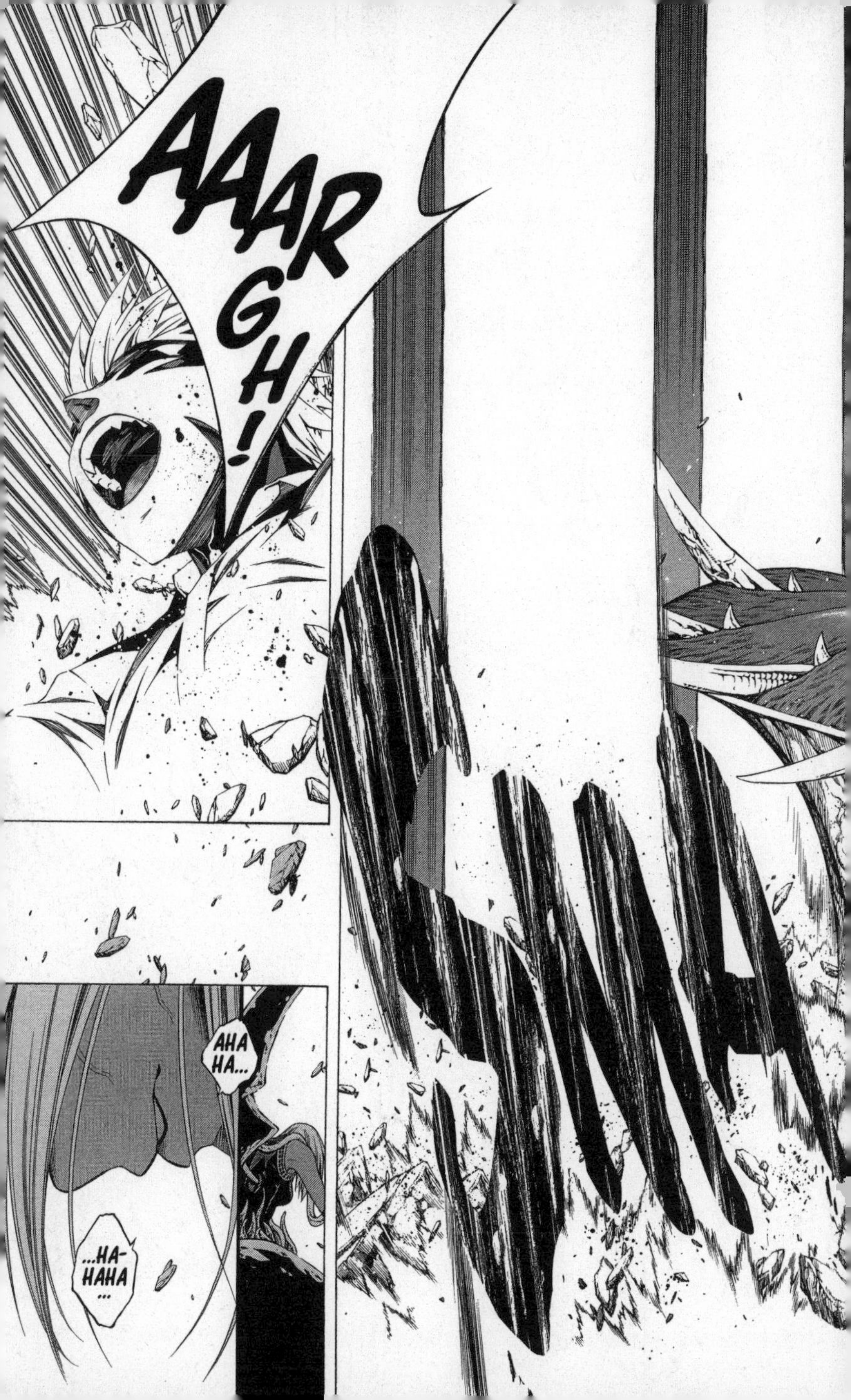
AAARGH!
AHAHA...
...HA-HAHA...

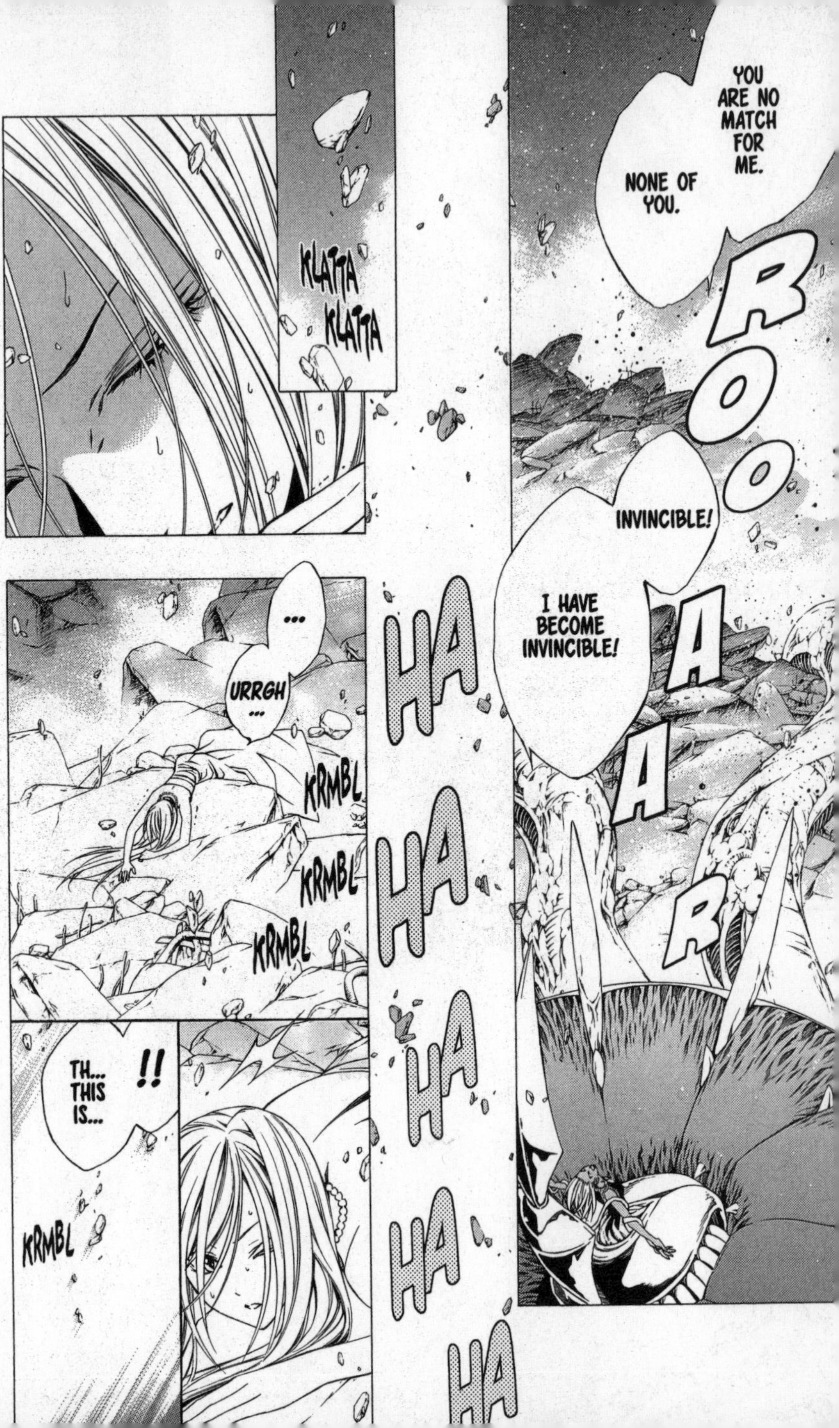
YOU ARE NO MATCH FOR ME.
NONE OF YOU.
ROOAAR
INVINCIBLE!
I HAVE BECOME INVINCIBLE!
HA HA HA HA HA
KLATTA KLATTA
...
URRGH...
KRMBL
KRMBL
KRMBL
!!
TH... THIS IS...
KRMBL

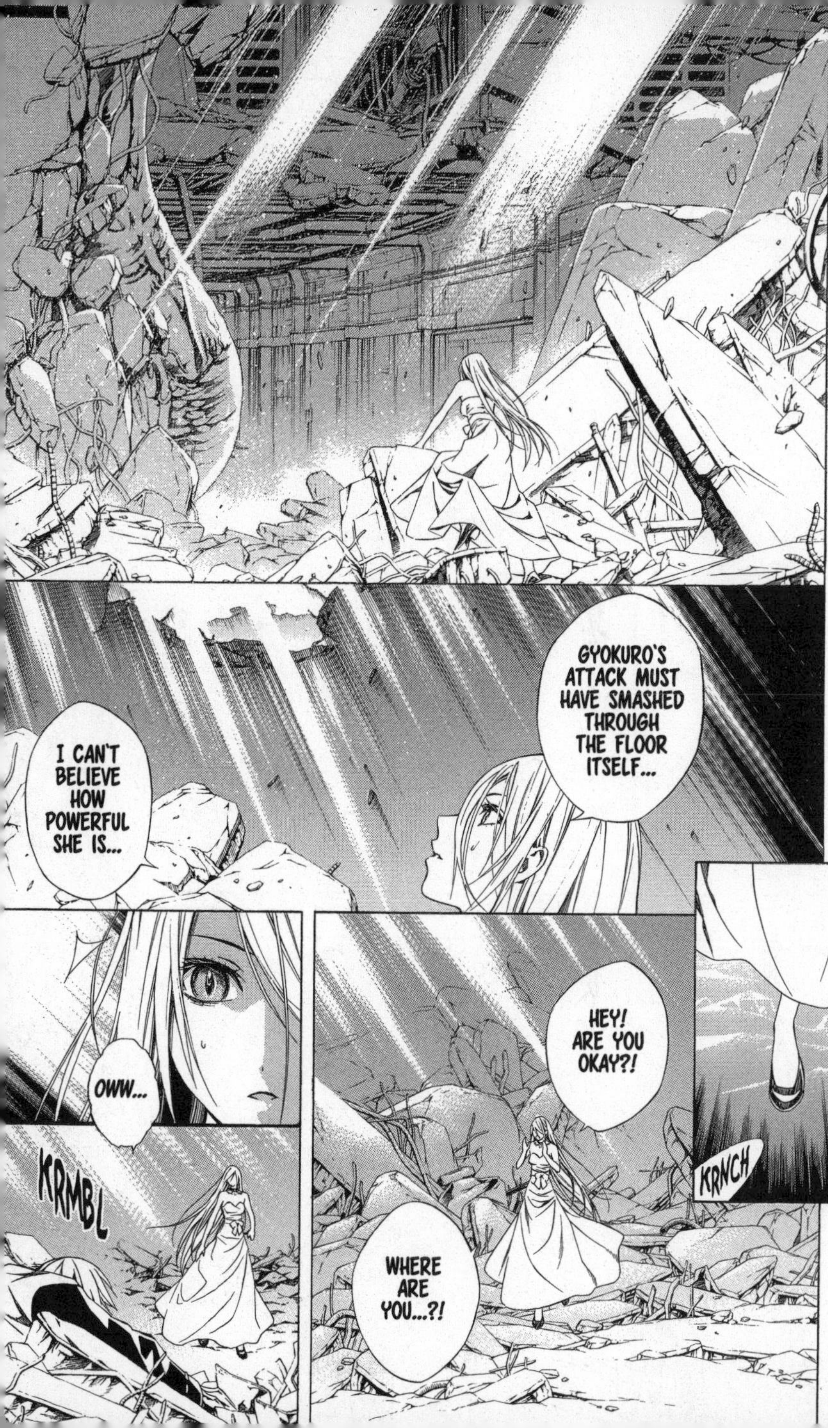
GYOKURO'S ATTACK MUST HAVE SMASHED THROUGH THE FLOOR ITSELF...
I CAN'T BELIEVE HOW POWERFUL SHE IS...
KRNCH
HEY! ARE YOU OKAY?!
WHERE ARE YOU...?!
OWW...
KRMBL

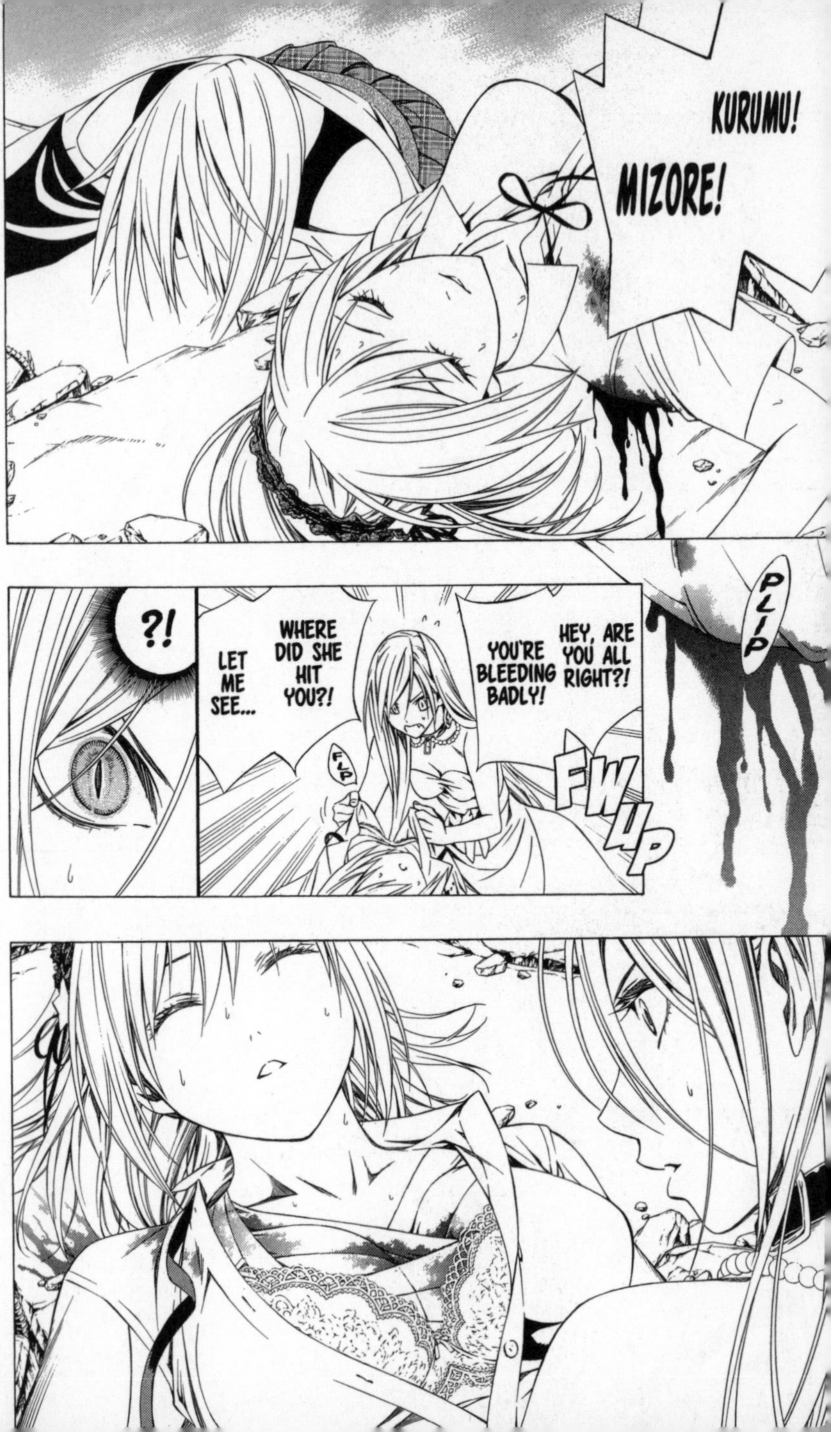
KURUMU!
MIZORE!
PLIP
HEY, ARE YOU ALL RIGHT?!
YOU'RE BLEEDING BADLY!
FWUP
WHERE DID SHE HIT YOU?!
LET ME SEE...
FLIP
?!

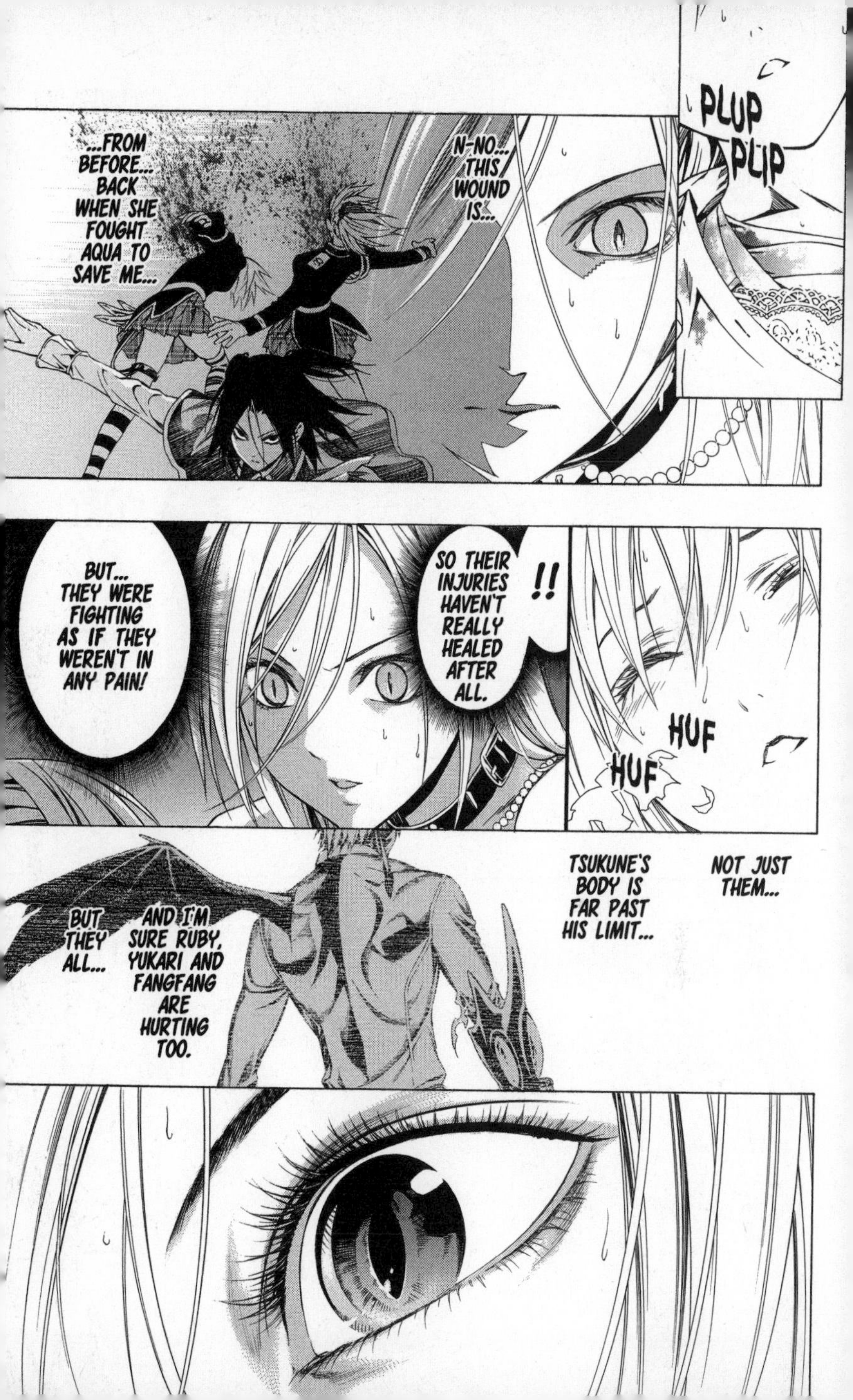
PLUP PLIP
N-NO... THIS WOUND IS...
...FROM BEFORE... BACK WHEN SHE FOUGHT AQUA TO SAVE ME...
HUF HUF
!!
SO THEIR INJURIES HAVEN'T REALLY HEALED AFTER ALL.
BUT... THEY WERE FIGHTING AS IF THEY WEREN'T IN ANY PAIN!
NOT JUST THEM...
TSUKUNE'S BODY IS FAR PAST HIS LIMIT...
AND I'M SURE RUBY, YUKARI AND FANGFANG ARE HURTING TOO.
BUT THEY ALL...

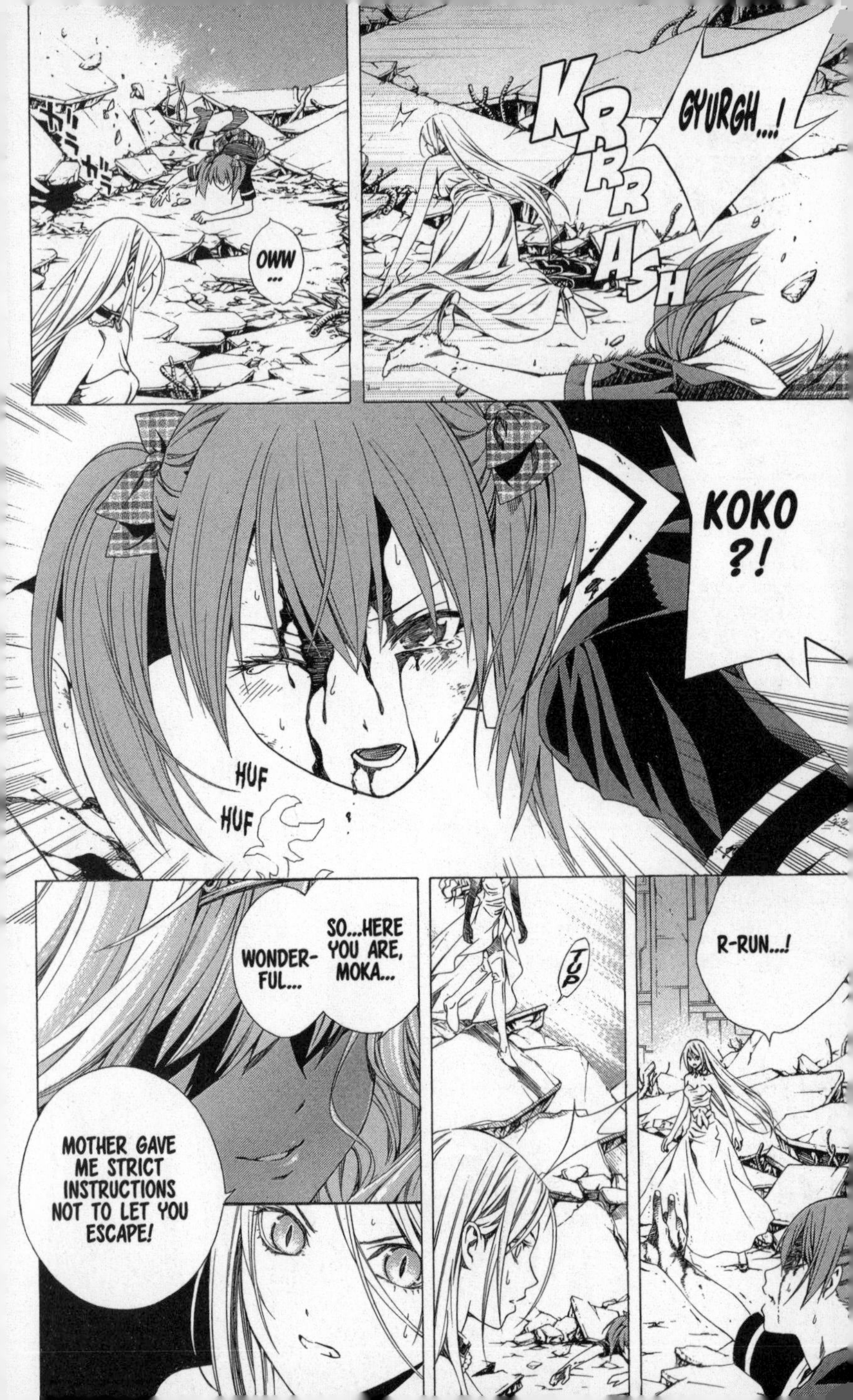
GYURGH...!
KRRRASH
OWW...
KOKO?!
HUF
HUF
R-RUN...!
TUP
SO...HERE YOU ARE, MOKA...
WONDERFUL...
MOTHER GAVE ME STRICT INSTRUCTIONS NOT TO LET YOU ESCAPE!

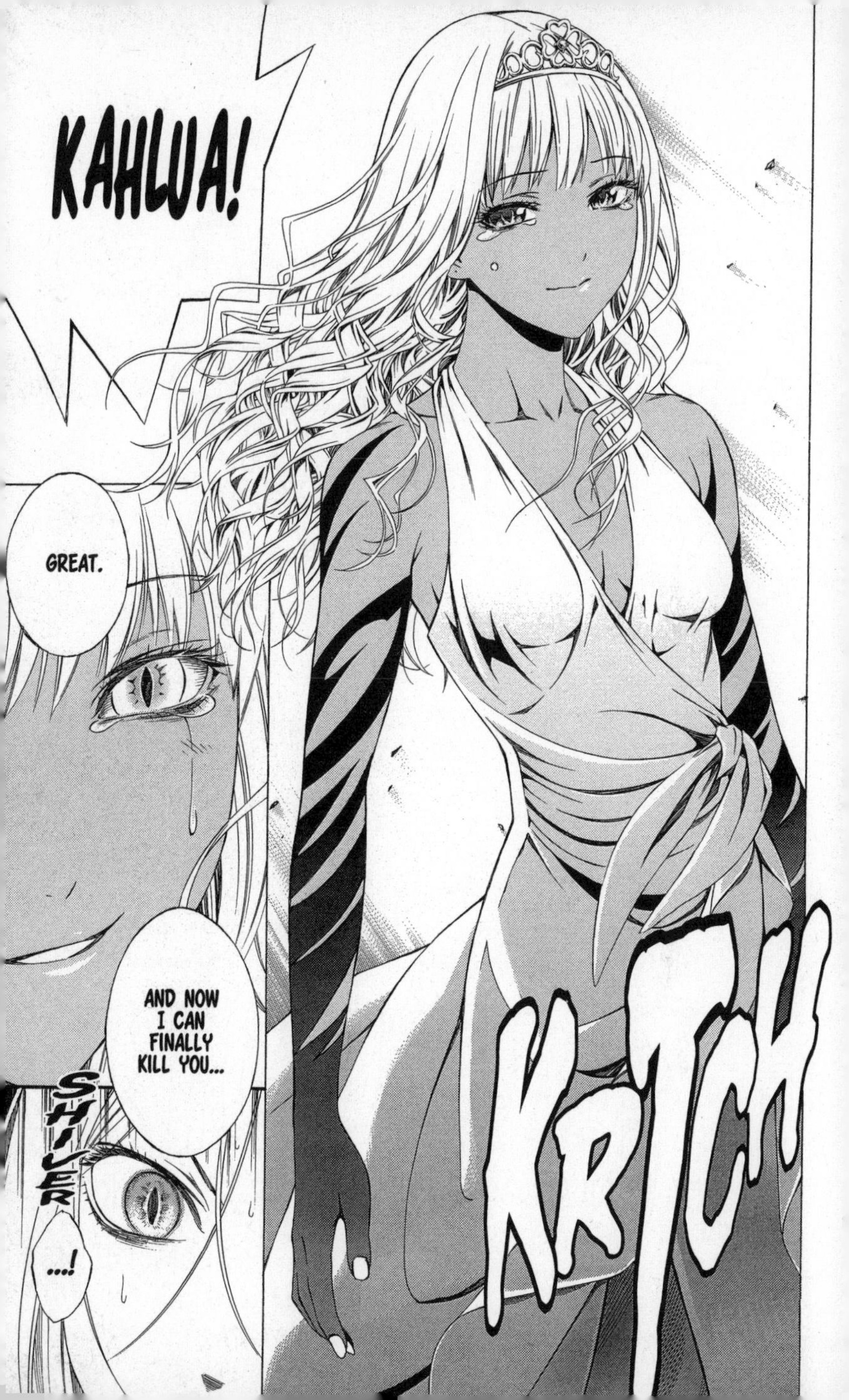
KAHLUA!
KRTCH
GREAT.
AND NOW I CAN FINALLY KILL YOU...
SHIVER
...!

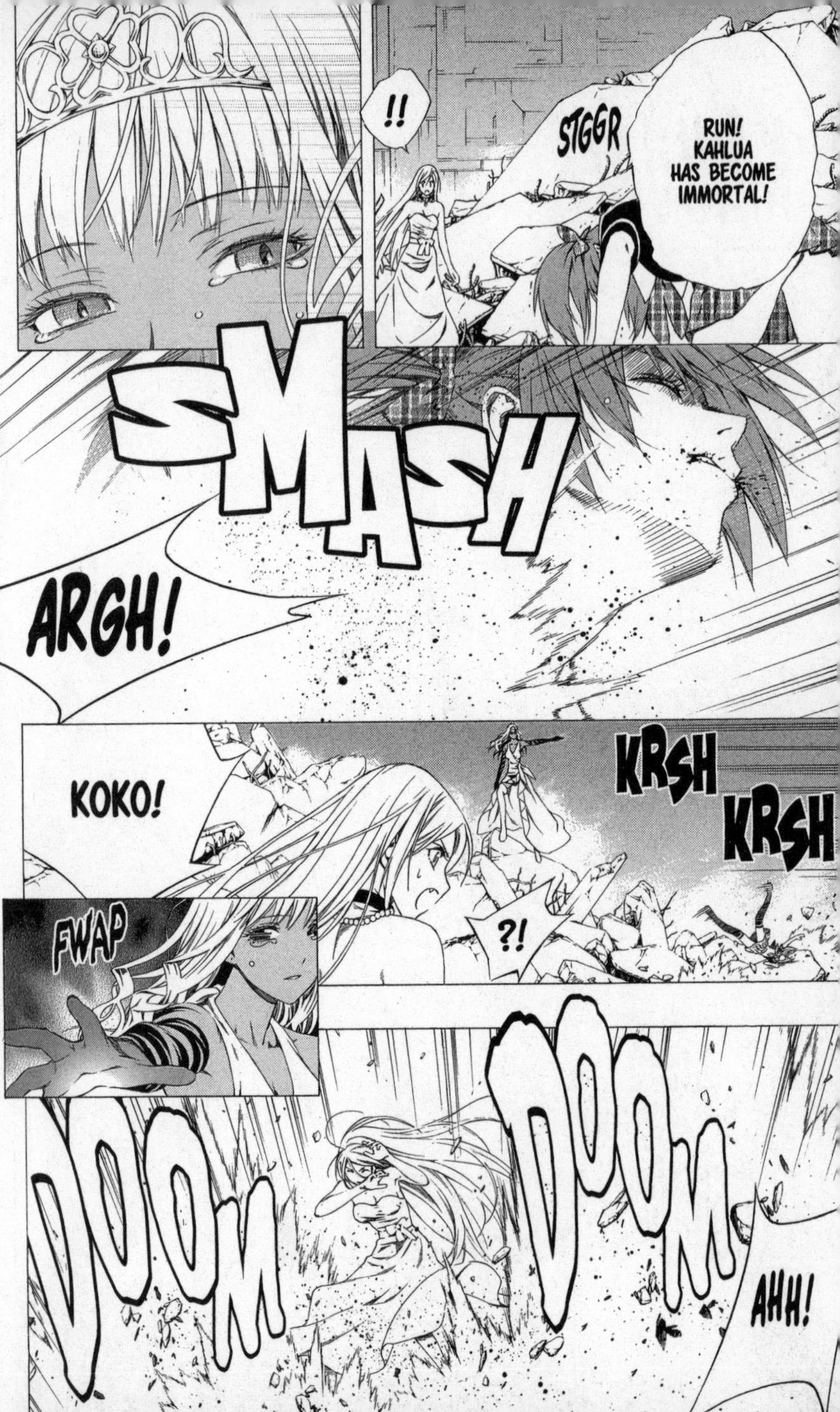
STGGR
RUN! KAHLUA HAS BECOME IMMORTAL!
!!
SMASH
ARGH!
KRSH
KRSH
?!
KOKO!
FWAP
DOOM
DOOM
AHH!

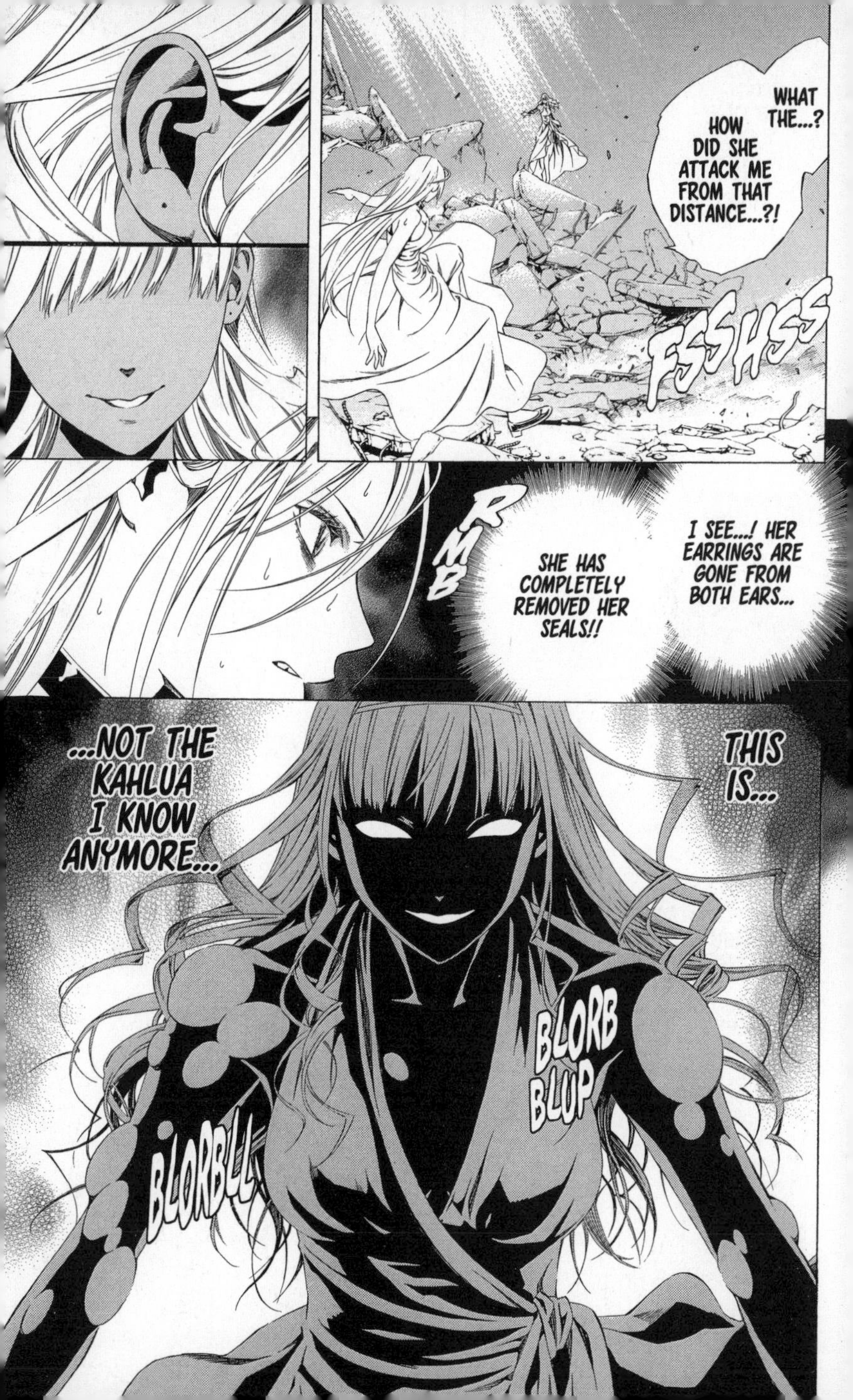
WHAT THE...?
HOW DID SHE ATTACK ME FROM THAT DISTANCE...?!
FSSHSS
I SEE...! HER EARRINGS ARE GONE FROM BOTH EARS...
SHE HAS COMPLETELY REMOVED HER SEALS!!
RMB
THIS IS...
...NOT THE KAHLUA I KNOW ANYMORE...
BLORB BLUP
BLORBLL

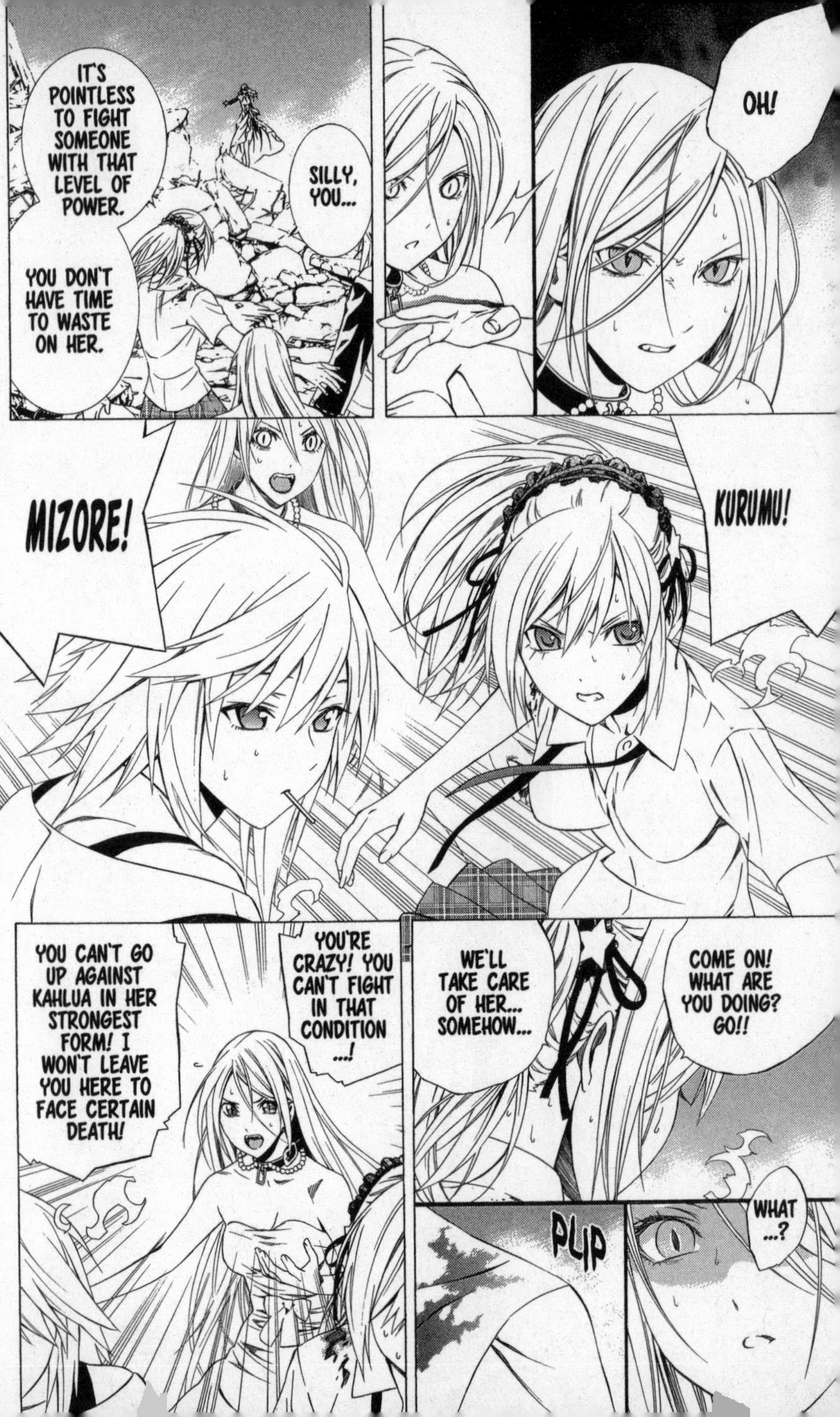
OH!
SILLY, YOU...
IT'S POINTLESS TO FIGHT SOMEONE WITH THAT LEVEL OF POWER.
YOU DON'T HAVE TIME TO WASTE ON HER.
KURUMU!
MIZORE!
COME ON! WHAT ARE YOU DOING? GO!!
WE'LL TAKE CARE OF HER... SOMEHOW...
WHAT ...?
PLIP
YOU'RE CRAZY! YOU CAN'T FIGHT IN THAT CONDITION ...!
YOU CAN'T GO UP AGAINST KAHLUA IN HER STRONGEST FORM! I WON'T LEAVE YOU HERE TO FACE CERTAIN DEATH!

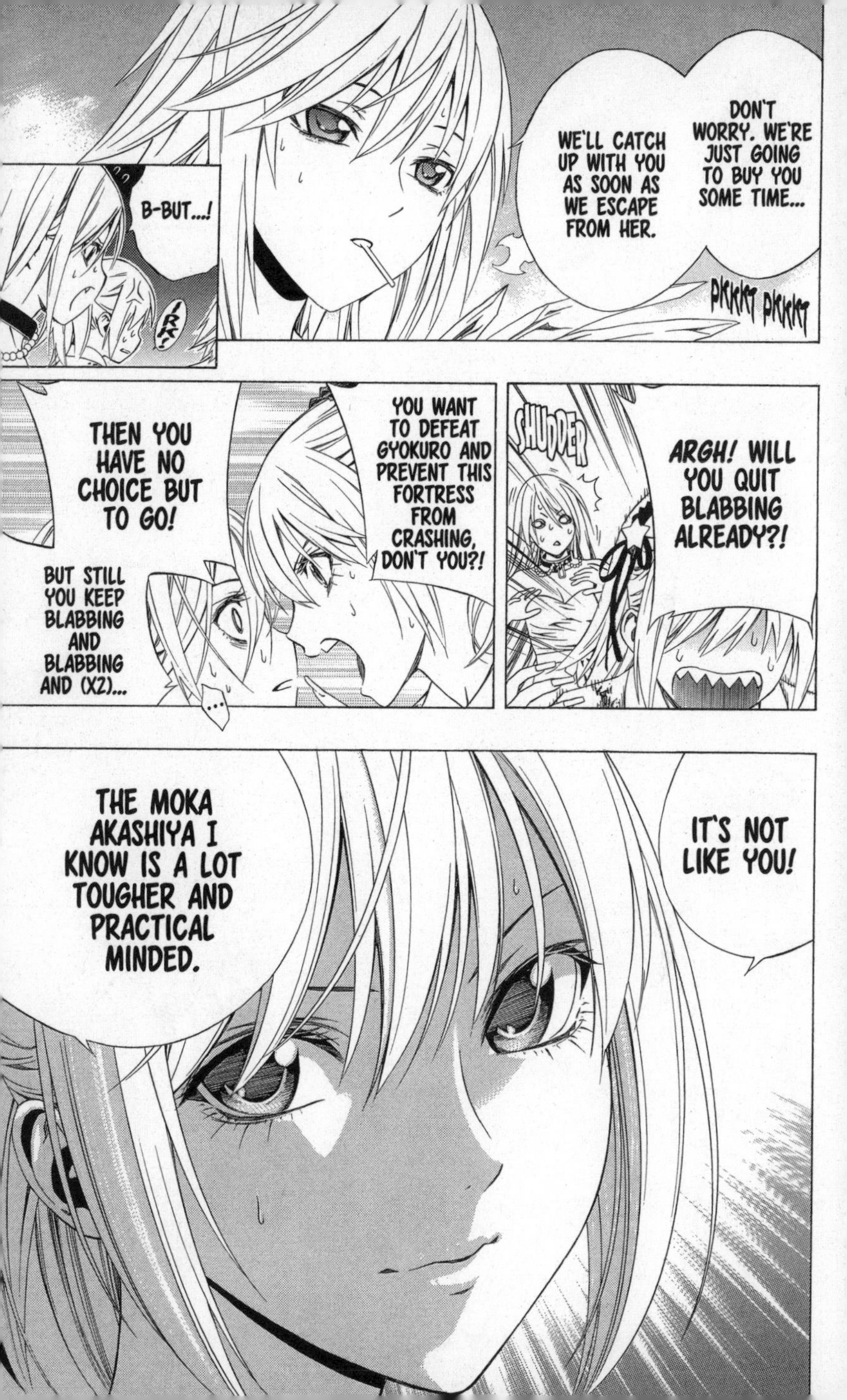
DON'T WORRY. WE'RE JUST GOING TO BUY YOU SOME TIME...
WE'LL CATCH UP WITH YOU AS SOON AS WE ESCAPE FROM HER.
B-BUT...!
IRK!
SHUDDER
ARGH! WILL YOU QUIT BLABBING ALREADY?!
YOU WANT TO DEFEAT GYOKURO AND PREVENT THIS FORTRESS FROM CRASHING, DON'T YOU?!
THEN YOU HAVE NO CHOICE BUT TO GO!
BUT STILL YOU KEEP BLABBING AND BLABBING AND (X2)...
...
IT'S NOT LIKE YOU!
THE MOKA AKASHIYA I KNOW IS A LOT TOUGHER AND PRACTICAL MINDED.

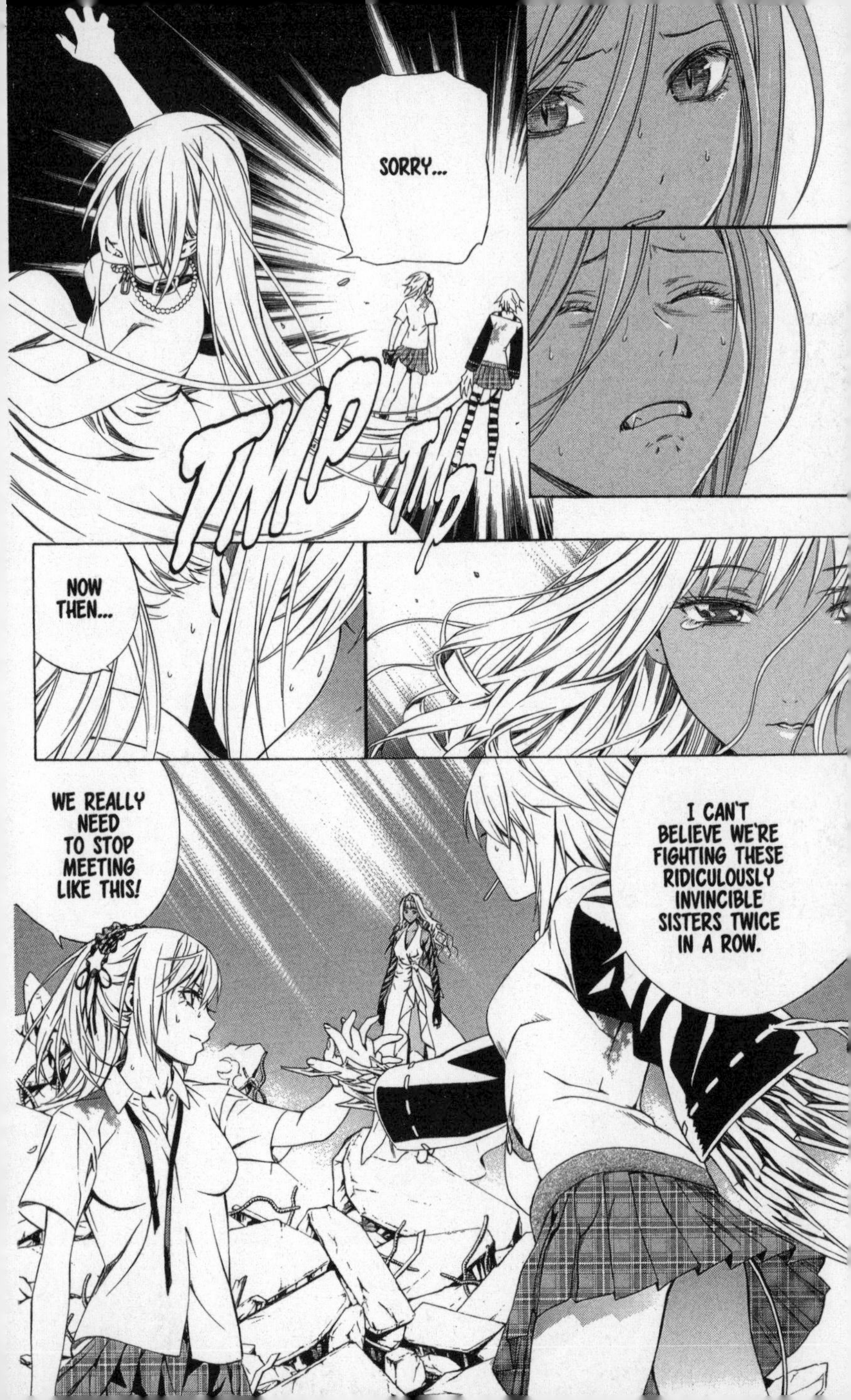
SORRY...
TMP TMP
NOW THEN...
I CAN'T BELIEVE WE'RE FIGHTING THESE RIDICULOUSLY INVINCIBLE SISTERS TWICE IN A ROW.
WE REALLY NEED TO STOP MEETING LIKE THIS!

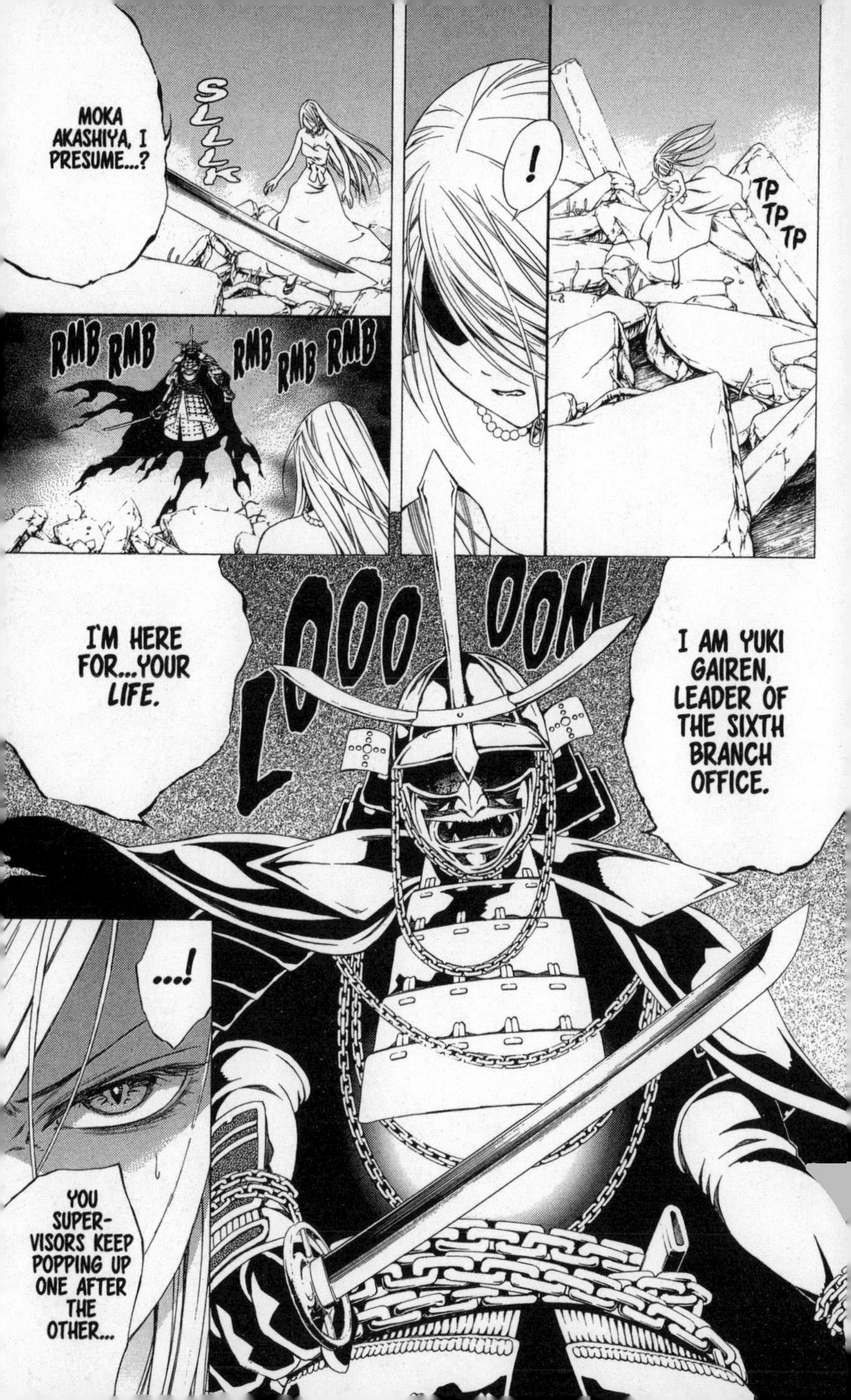
TP TP TP
!
SLLK
MOKA AKASHIYA, I PRESUME...?
RMB RMB RMB RMB RMB
I AM YUKI GAIREN, LEADER OF THE SIXTH BRANCH OFFICE.
LOOOOOOM
I'M HERE FOR...YOUR *LIFE.*
...!
YOU SUPER-VISORS KEEP POPPING UP ONE AFTER THE OTHER...

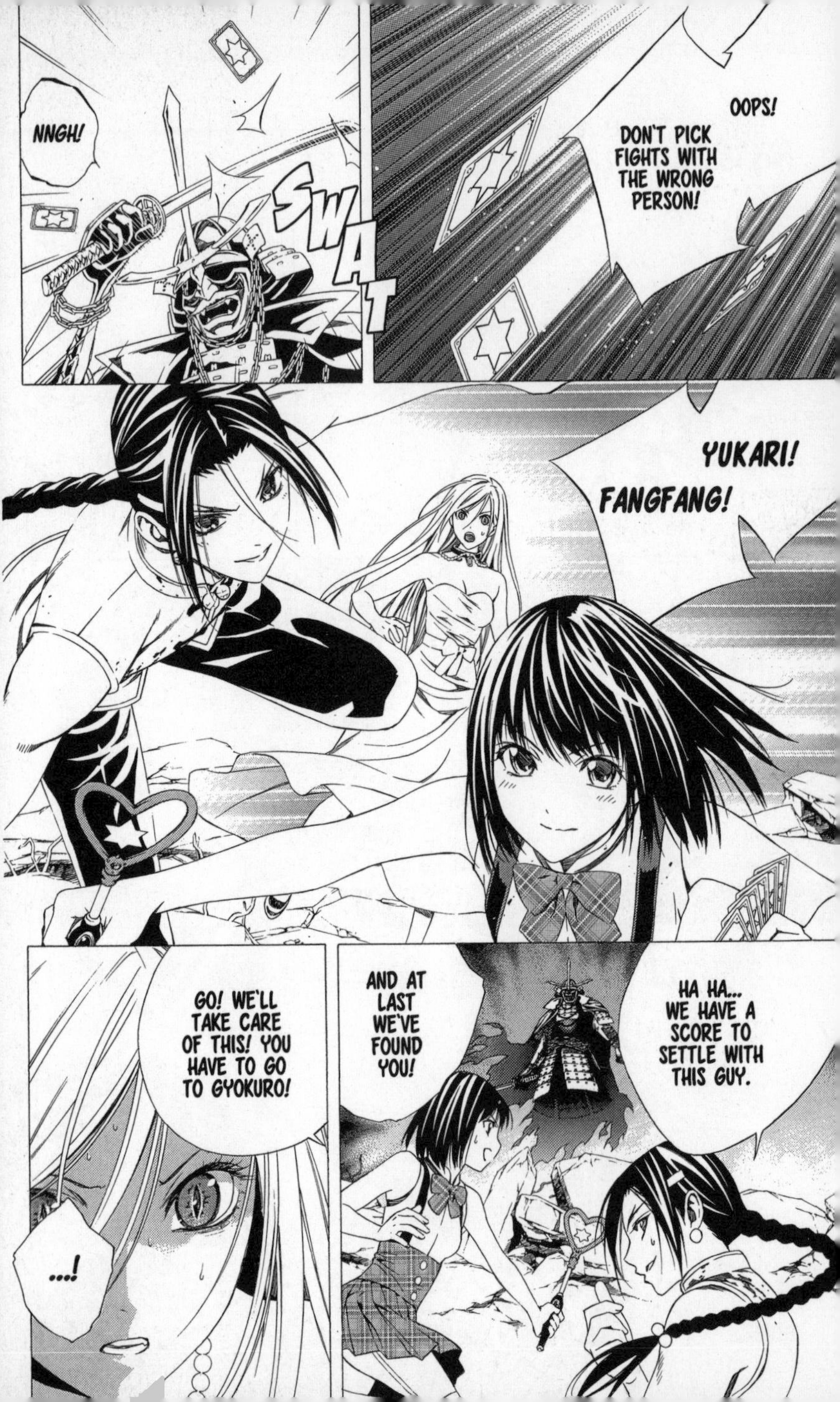
OOPS!
DON'T PICK FIGHTS WITH THE WRONG PERSON!
SWAT
NNGH!
YUKARI!
FANGFANG!
HA HA... WE HAVE A SCORE TO SETTLE WITH THIS GUY.
AND AT LAST WE'VE FOUND YOU!
GO! WE'LL TAKE CARE OF THIS! YOU HAVE TO GO TO GYOKURO!
...!

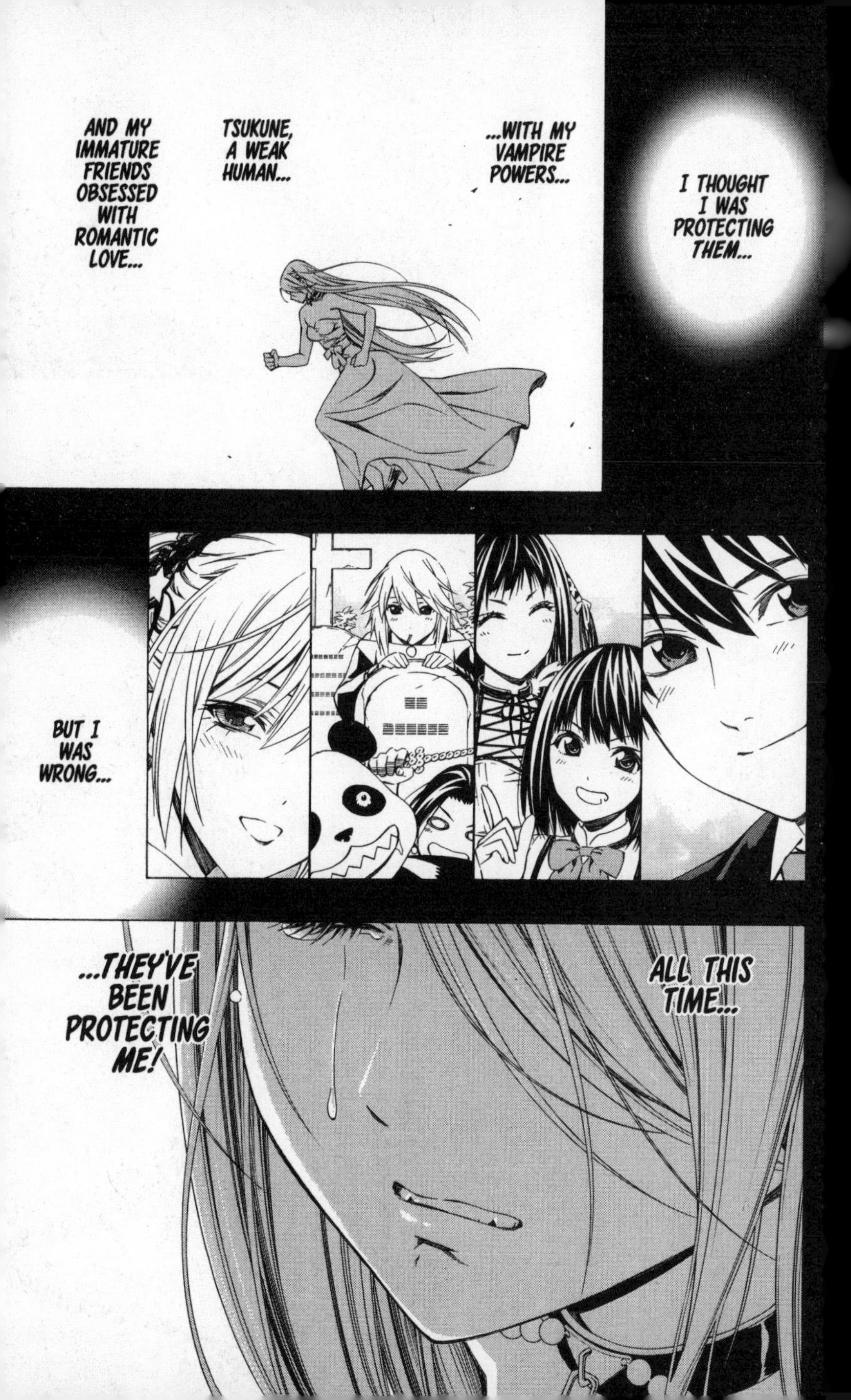
I THOUGHT I WAS PROTECTING THEM...
...WITH MY VAMPIRE POWERS...
TSUKUNE, A WEAK HUMAN...
AND MY IMMATURE FRIENDS OBSESSED WITH ROMANTIC LOVE...
BUT I WAS WRONG...
ALL THIS TIME...
...THEY'VE BEEN PROTECTING ME!

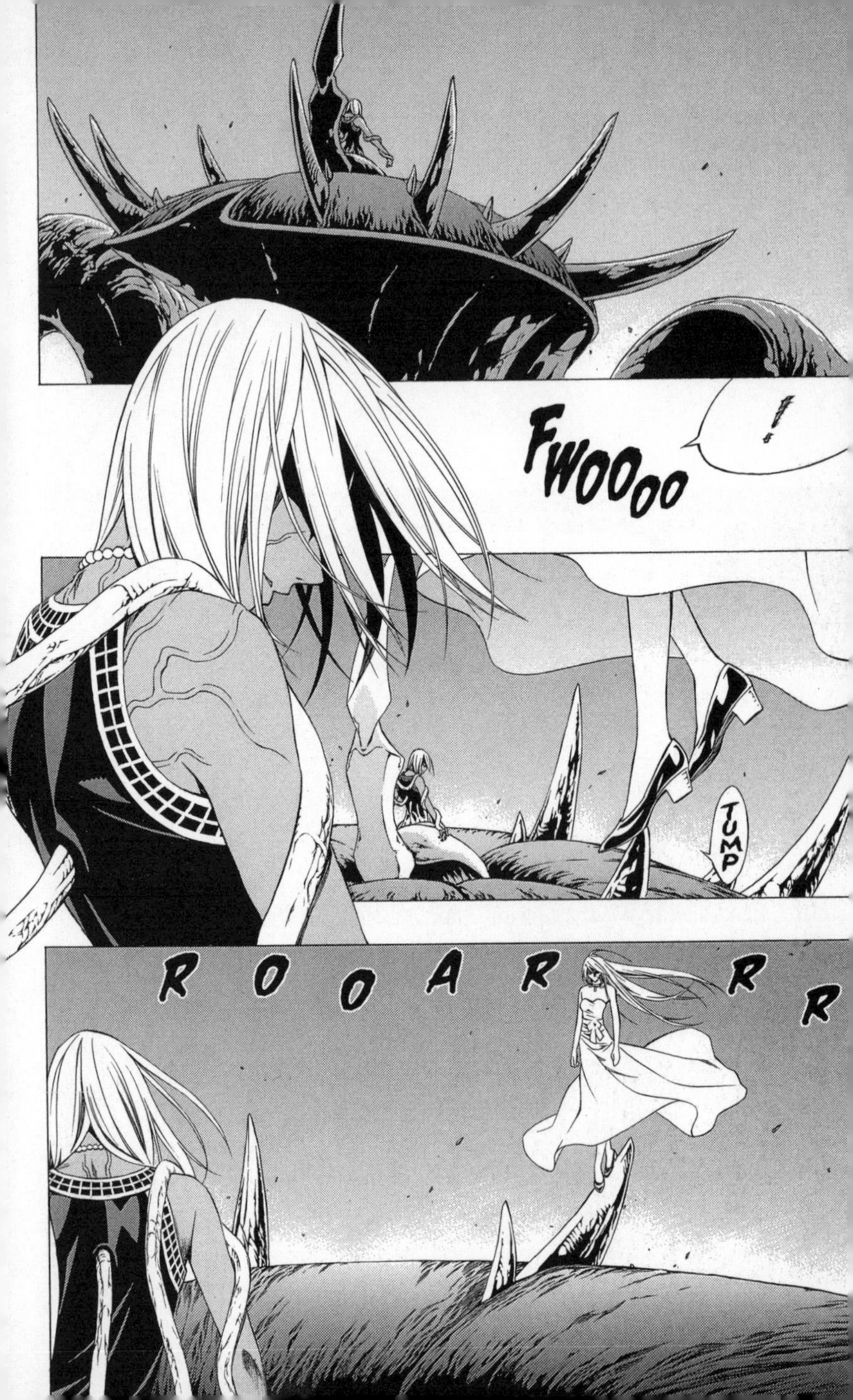
FWOOOO
!
TUMP
ROOARRR

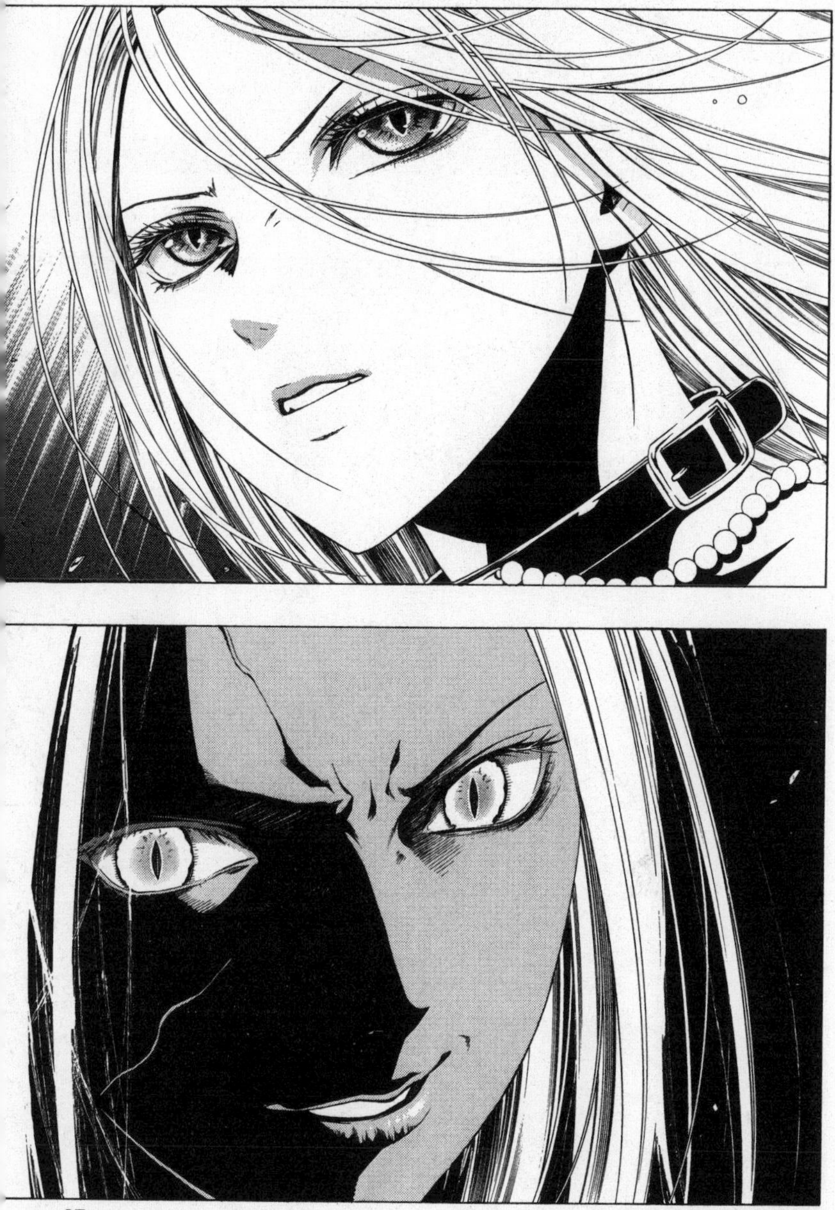

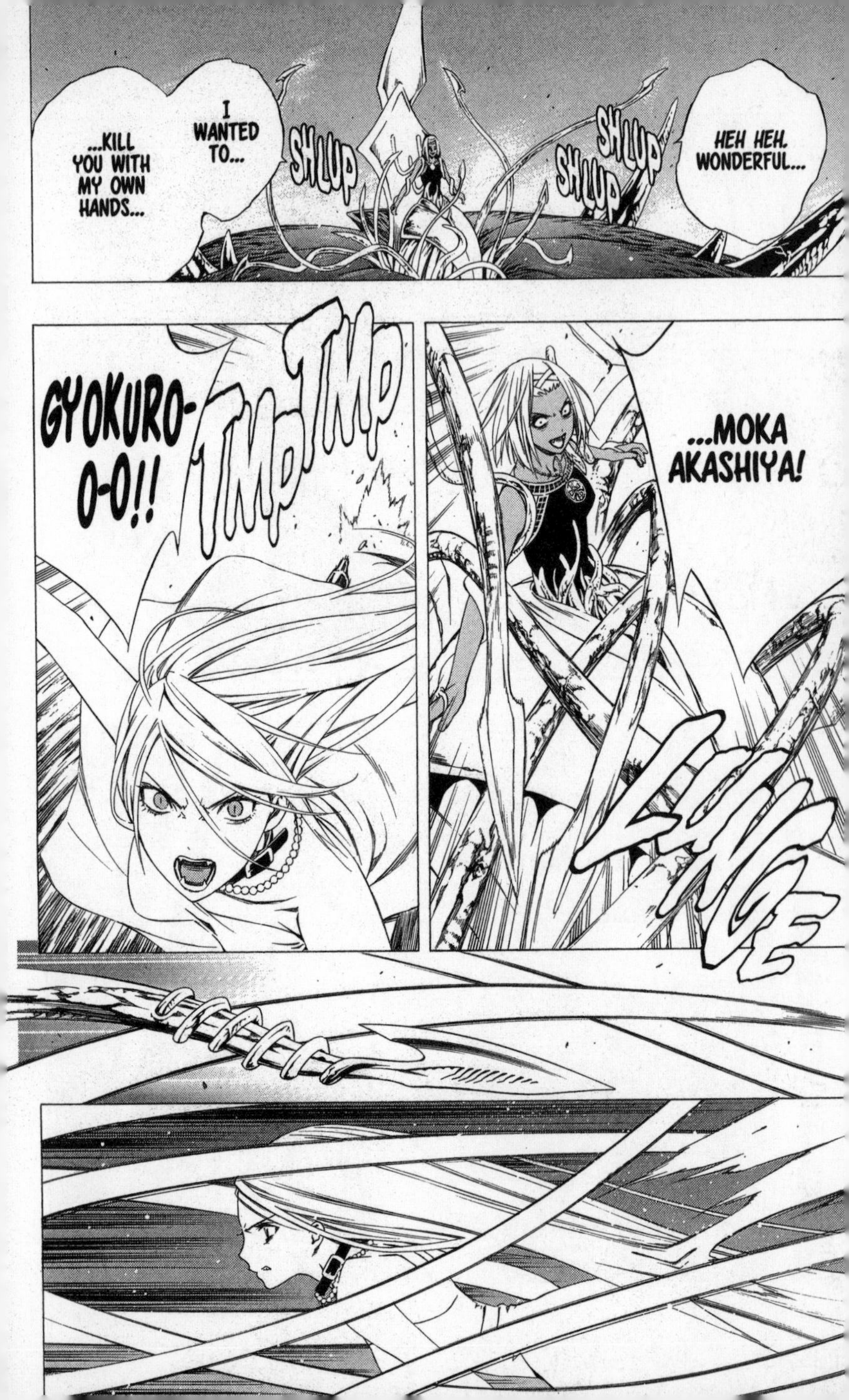
HEH HEH. WONDERFUL...
SHLUP
SHLUP
SHLUP
I WANTED TO...
...KILL YOU WITH MY OWN HANDS...
...MOKA AKASHIYA!
LUNGE
TMP TMP
GYOKURO-O-O!!

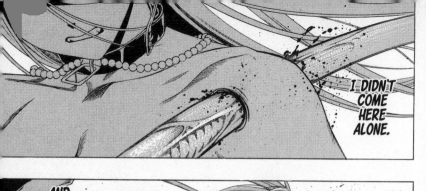

I DIDN'T COME HERE ALONE.

AND I'M NOT FIGHTING ALONE.

SO...

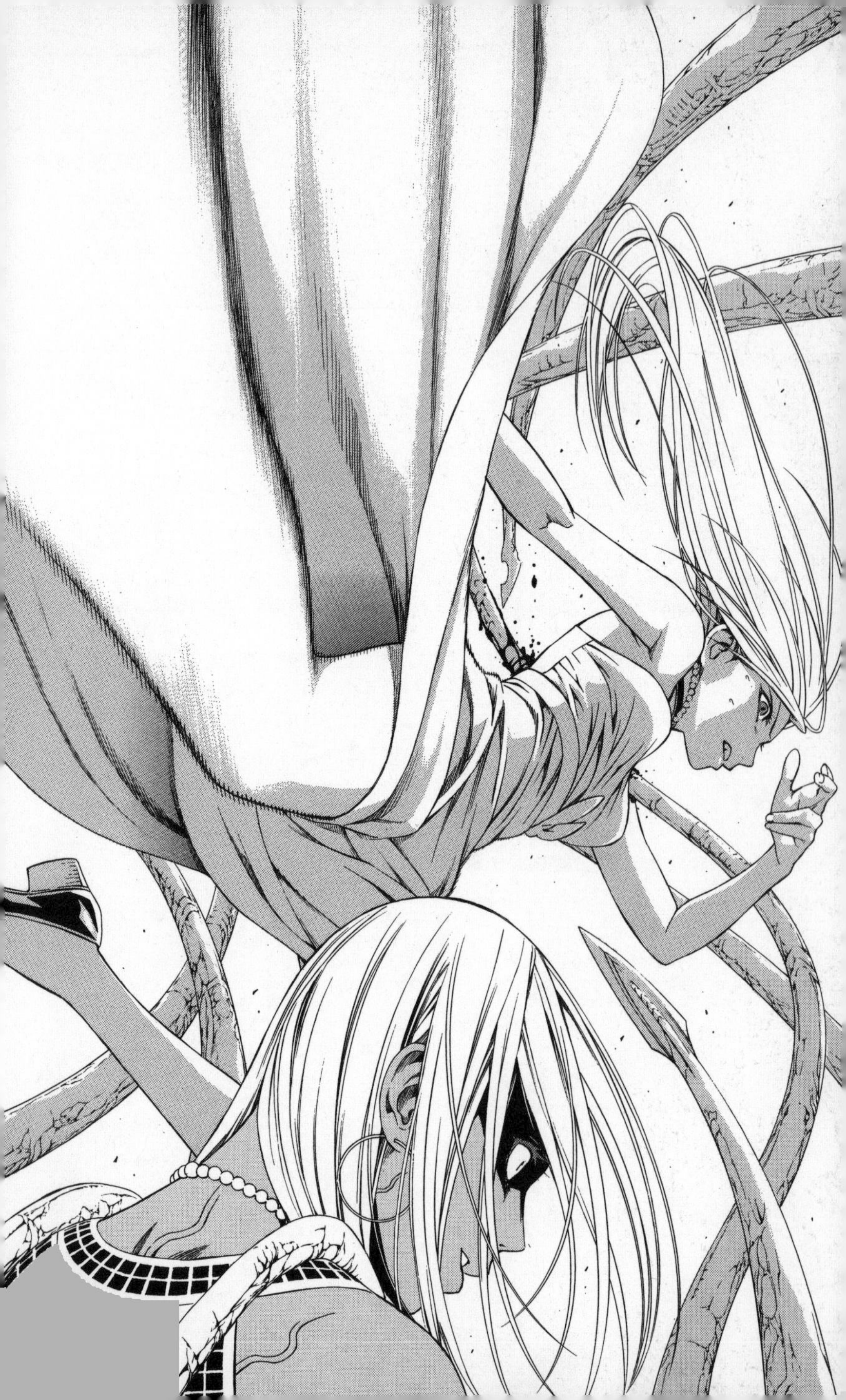

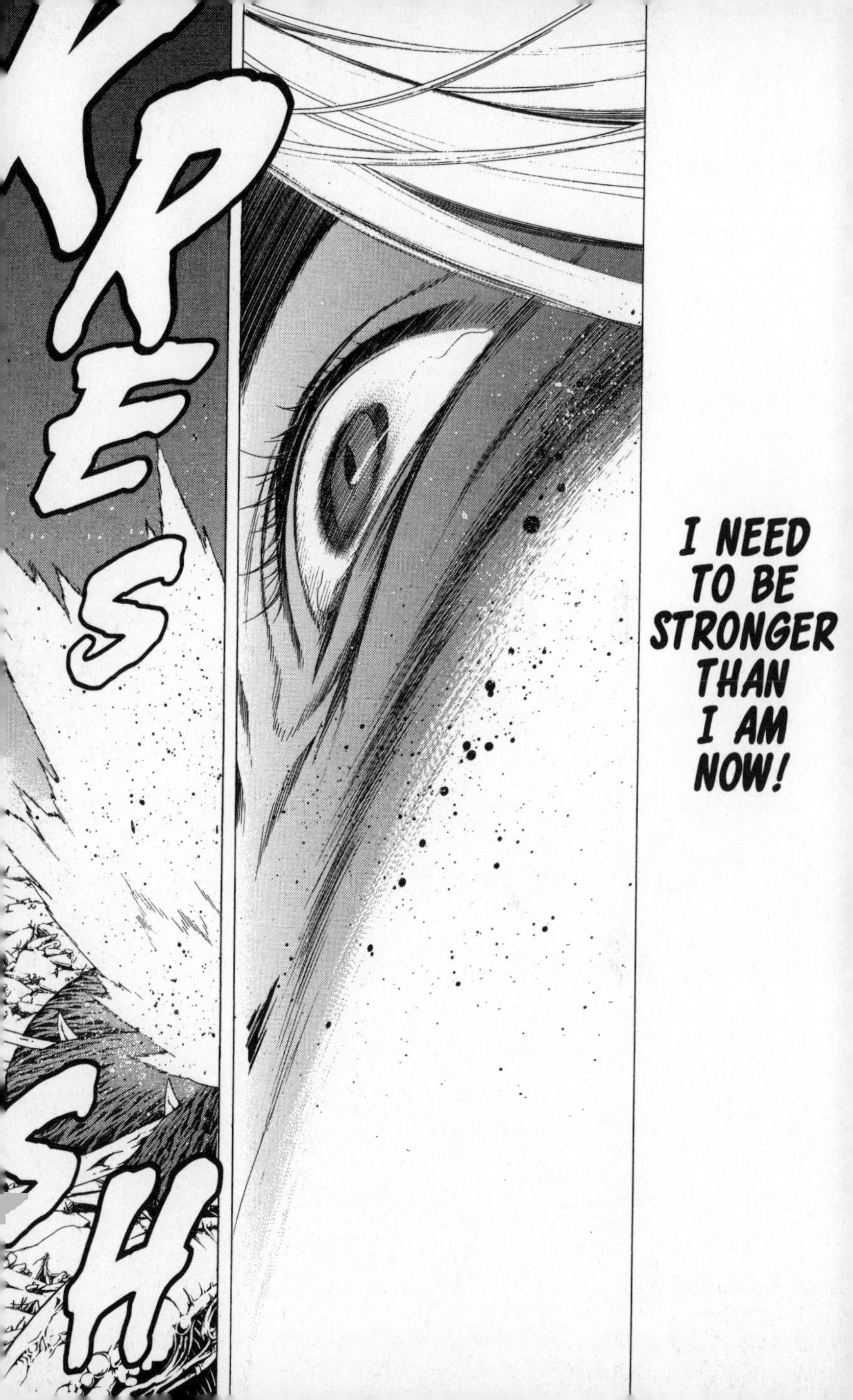
I NEED TO BE STRONGER THAN I AM NOW!

63: Last Waltz

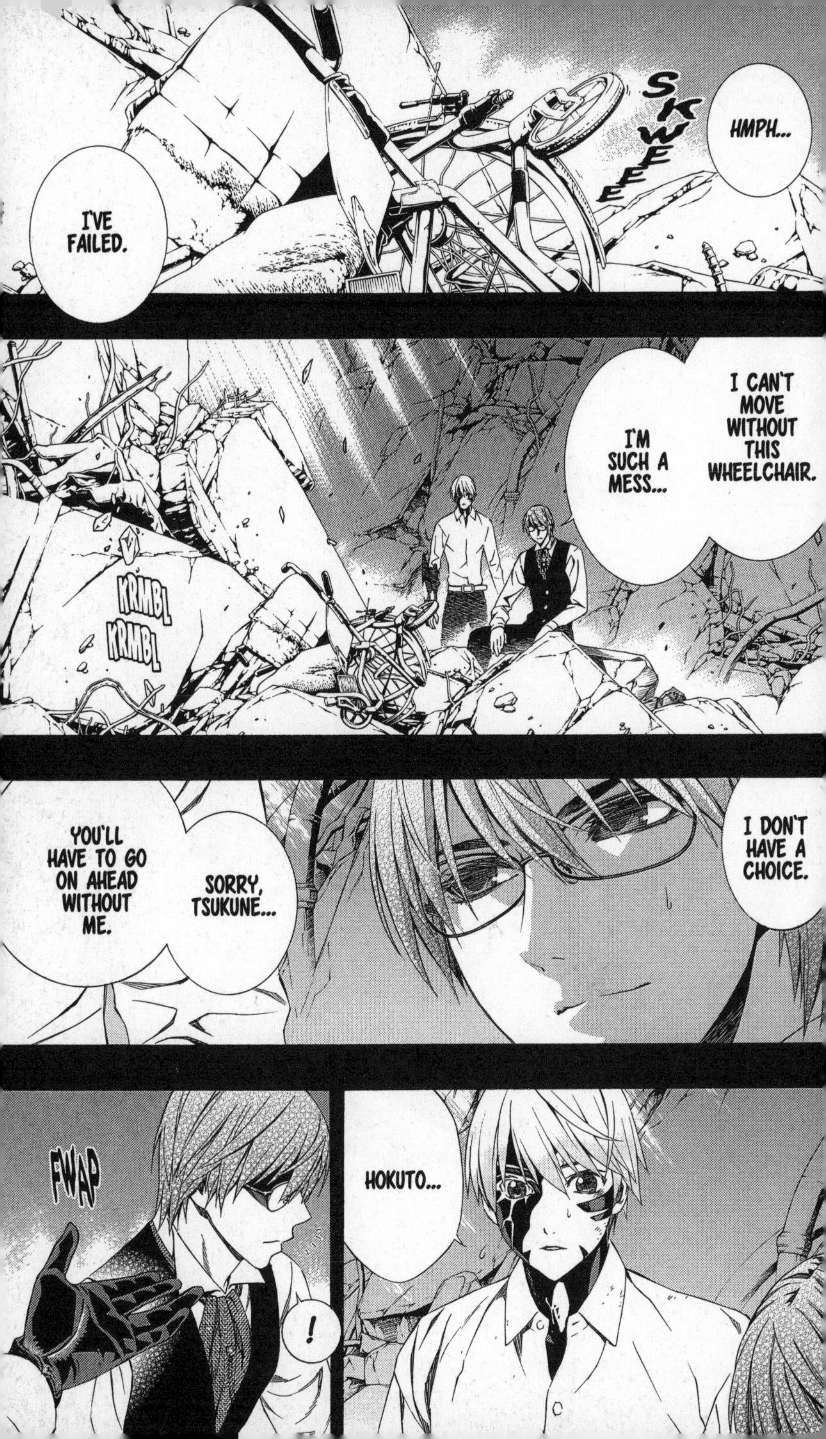
HMPH...
SKWEEE
I'VE FAILED.
I CAN'T MOVE WITHOUT THIS WHEELCHAIR.
I'M SUCH A MESS...
KRMBL KRMBL
I DON'T HAVE A CHOICE.
SORRY, TSUKUNE...
YOU'LL HAVE TO GO ON AHEAD WITHOUT ME.
HOKUTO...
FWAP
!

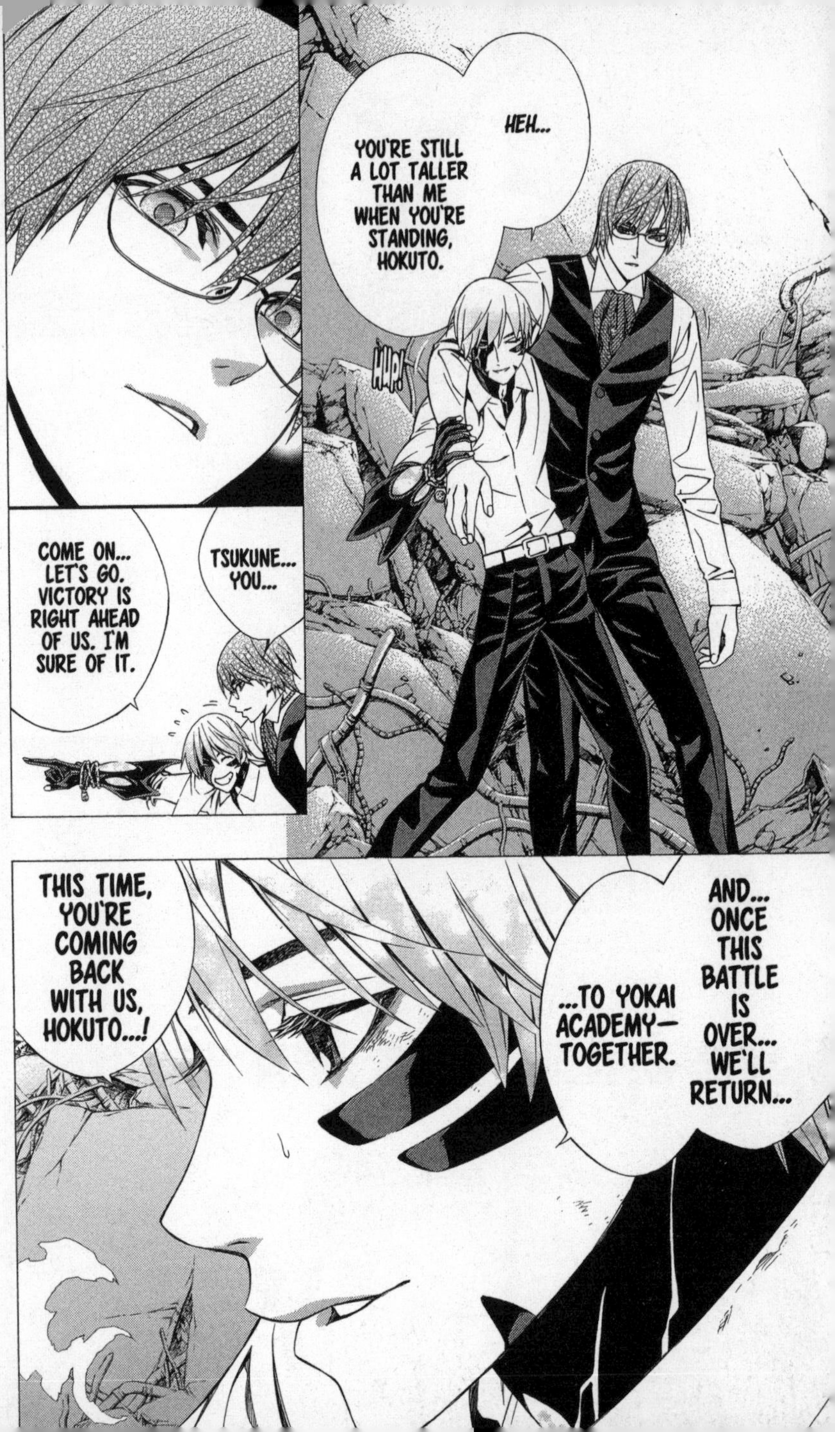
HEH...
YOU'RE STILL A LOT TALLER THAN ME WHEN YOU'RE STANDING, HOKUTO.
HUP!
TSUKUNE... YOU...
COME ON... LET'S GO. VICTORY IS RIGHT AHEAD OF US. I'M SURE OF IT.
AND... ONCE THIS BATTLE IS OVER... WE'LL RETURN...
...TO YOKAI ACADEMY—TOGETHER.
THIS TIME, YOU'RE COMING BACK WITH US, HOKUTO...!

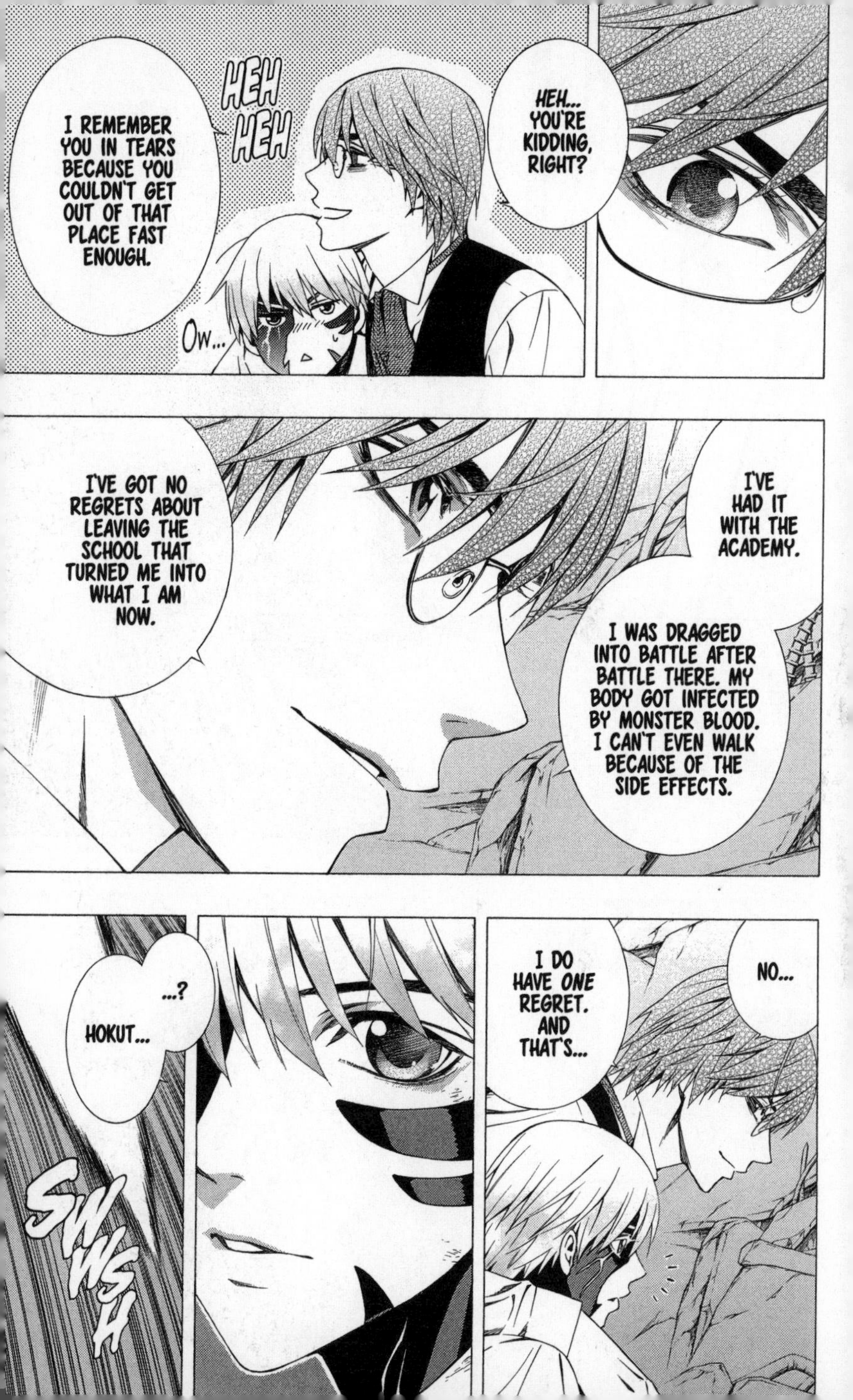
HEH... YOU'RE KIDDING, RIGHT?
HEH HEH
I REMEMBER YOU IN TEARS BECAUSE YOU COULDN'T GET OUT OF THAT PLACE FAST ENOUGH.
OW...
I'VE HAD IT WITH THE ACADEMY.
I WAS DRAGGED INTO BATTLE AFTER BATTLE THERE. MY BODY GOT INFECTED BY MONSTER BLOOD. I CAN'T EVEN WALK BECAUSE OF THE SIDE EFFECTS.
I'VE GOT NO REGRETS ABOUT LEAVING THE SCHOOL THAT TURNED ME INTO WHAT I AM NOW.
NO...
I DO HAVE ONE REGRET. AND THAT'S...
...?
HOKUT...
SWISH

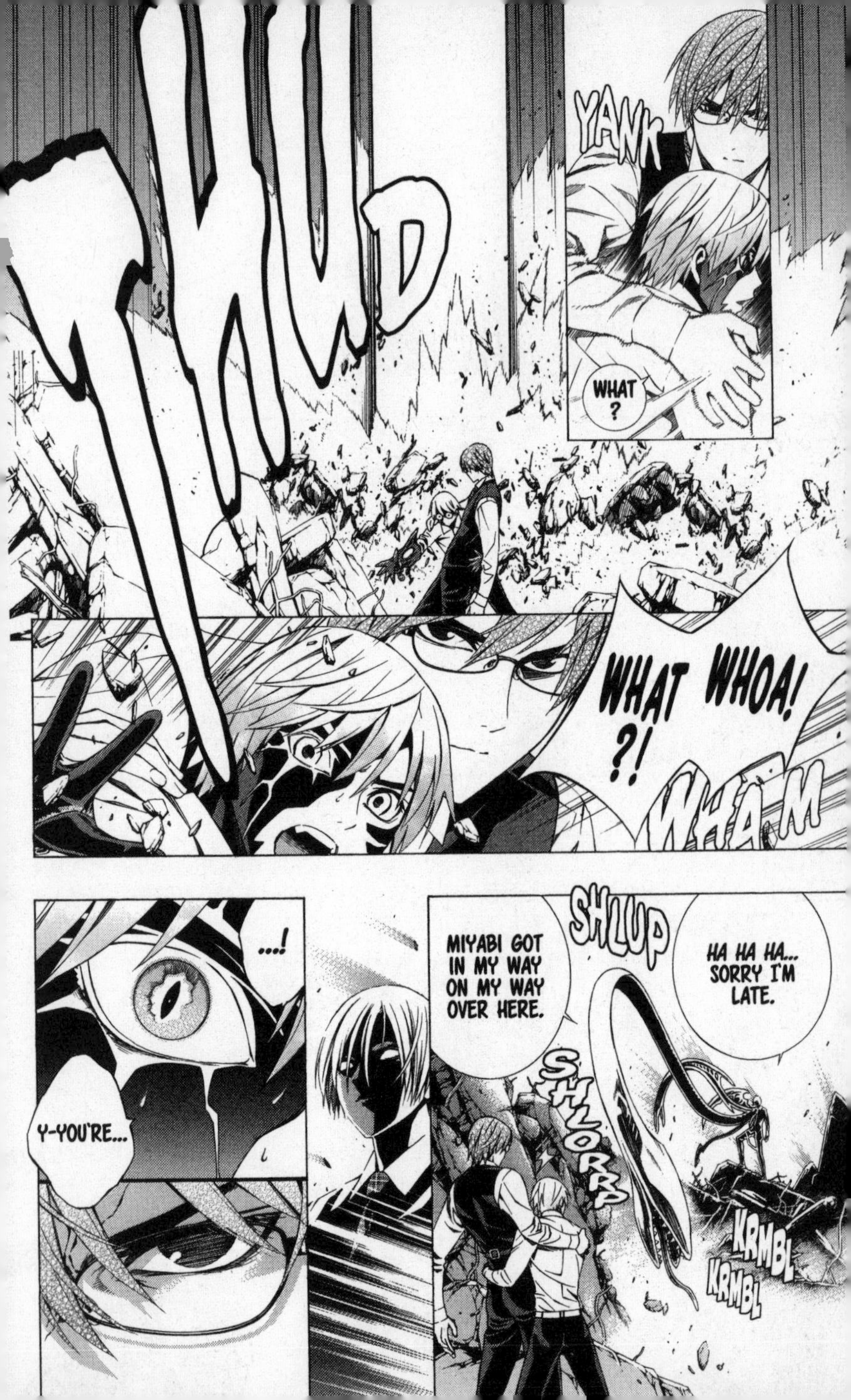
YANK
WHAT ?
THUD
WHOA!
WHAT ?!
WHAM
HA HA HA... SORRY I'M LATE.
SHLUP
MIYABI GOT IN MY WAY ON MY WAY OVER HERE.
SHLORRP
KRMBL
KRMBL
...!
Y-YOU'RE...

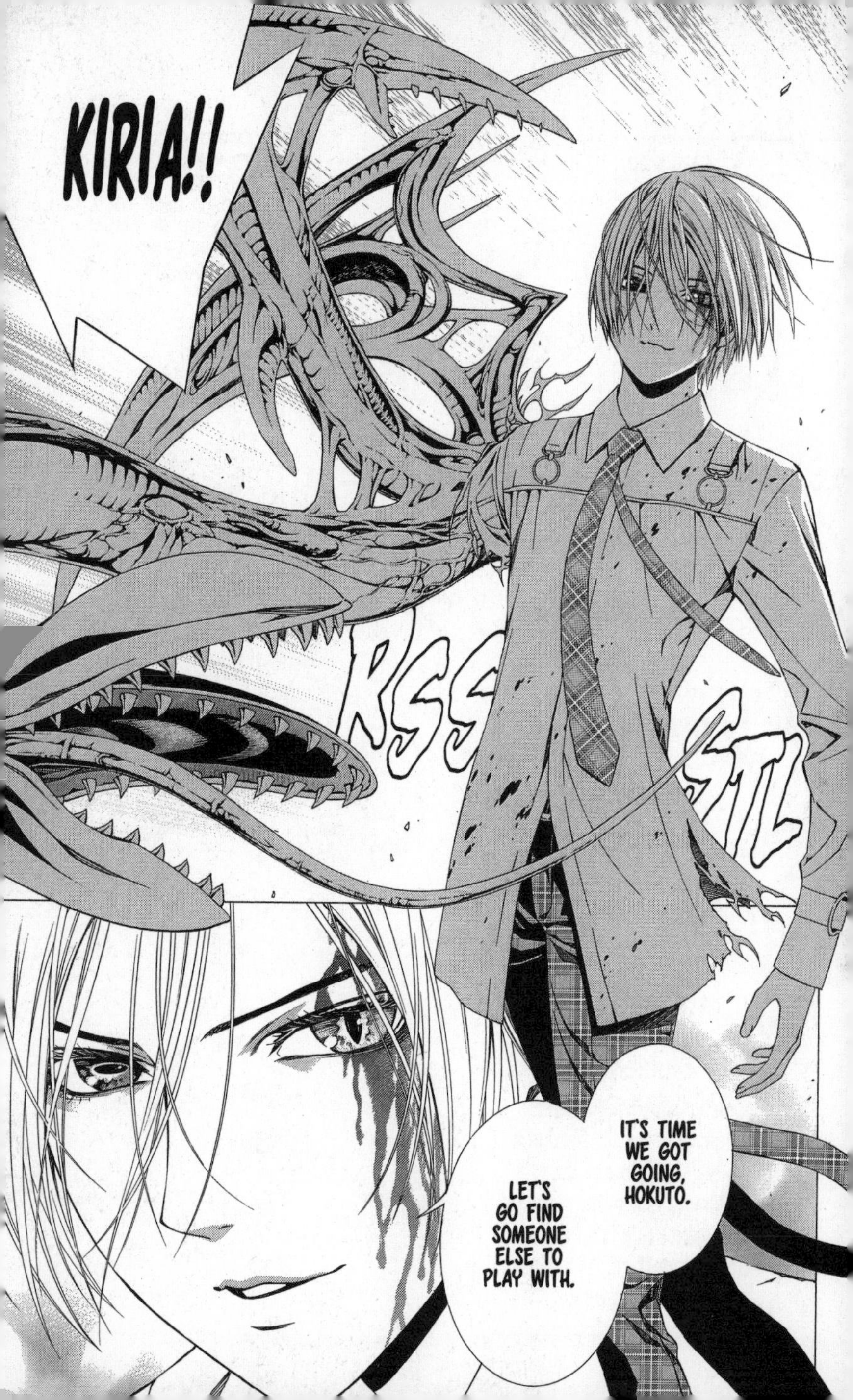
KIRIA!!
RSSSSTL
IT'S TIME WE GOT GOING, HOKUTO.
LET'S GO FIND SOMEONE ELSE TO PLAY WITH.

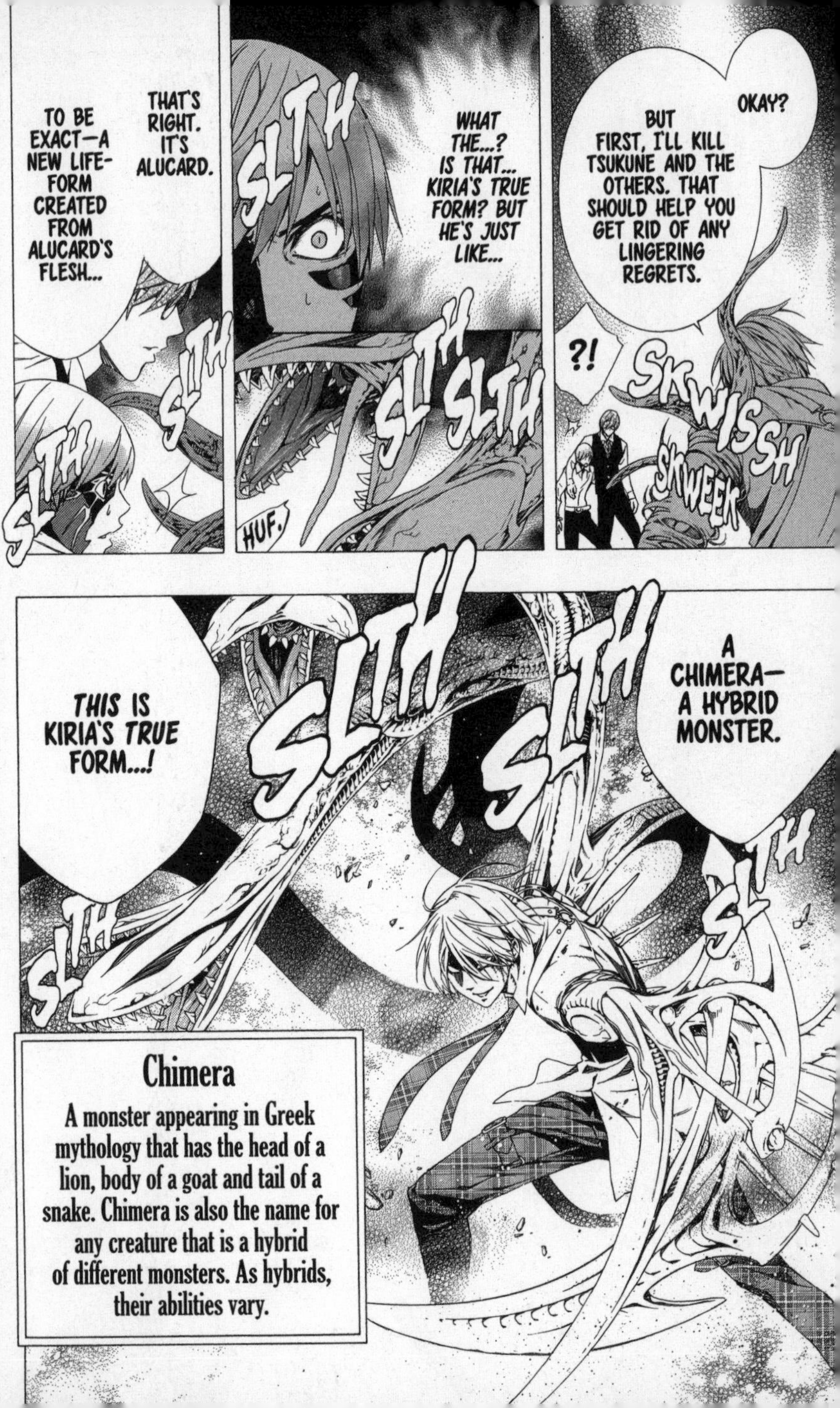
BUT FIRST, I'LL KILL TSUKUNE AND THE OTHERS. THAT SHOULD HELP YOU GET RID OF ANY LINGERING REGRETS.
OKAY?
?!
SKWISSH
SKWEEK
WHAT THE...? IS THAT... KIRIA'S TRUE FORM? BUT HE'S JUST LIKE...
SLTH
SLTH SLTH
HUF.
THAT'S RIGHT. IT'S ALUCARD.
TO BE EXACT—A NEW LIFE-FORM CREATED FROM ALUCARD'S FLESH...
SLTH
SLTH
A CHIMERA—A HYBRID MONSTER.
SLTH
SLTH
SLTH
SLTH
THIS IS KIRIA'S TRUE FORM...!
SLTH
Chimera
A monster appearing in Greek mythology that has the head of a lion, body of a goat and tail of a snake. Chimera is also the name for any creature that is a hybrid of different monsters. As hybrids, their abilities vary.

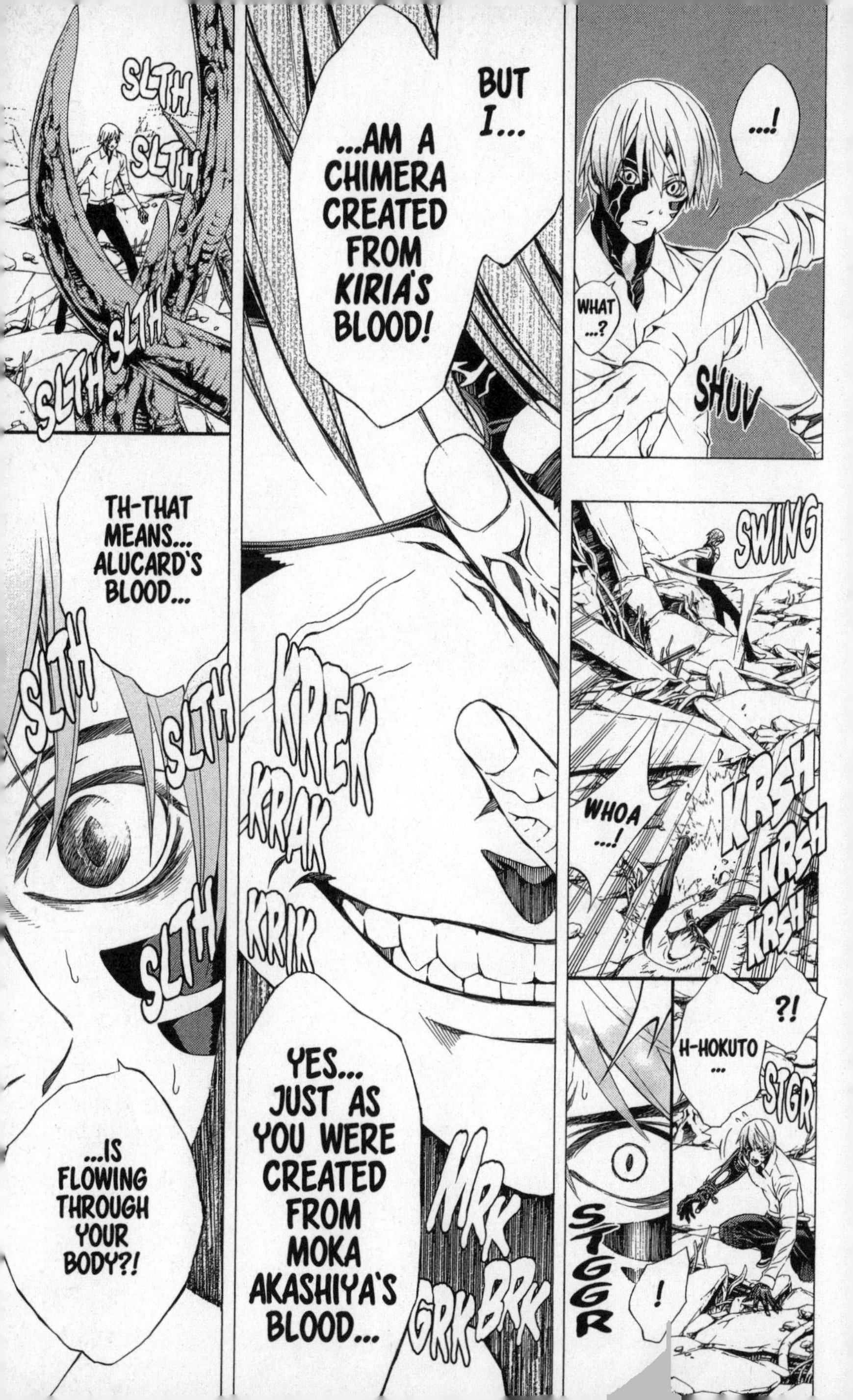
...!
WHAT ...?
SHUV
SWING
WHOA ...!
KRSH KRSH KRSH
?!
H-HOKUTO ...
STGR
STGGR
!
BUT I...
...AM A CHIMERA CREATED FROM KIRIA'S BLOOD!
KREK KRAK KRIK
YES... JUST AS YOU WERE CREATED FROM MOKA AKASHIYA'S BLOOD...
MRK BRK GRK
SLTH SLTH SLTH SLTH
TH-THAT MEANS... ALUCARD'S BLOOD...
SLTH SLTH SLTH
...IS FLOWING THROUGH YOUR BODY?!

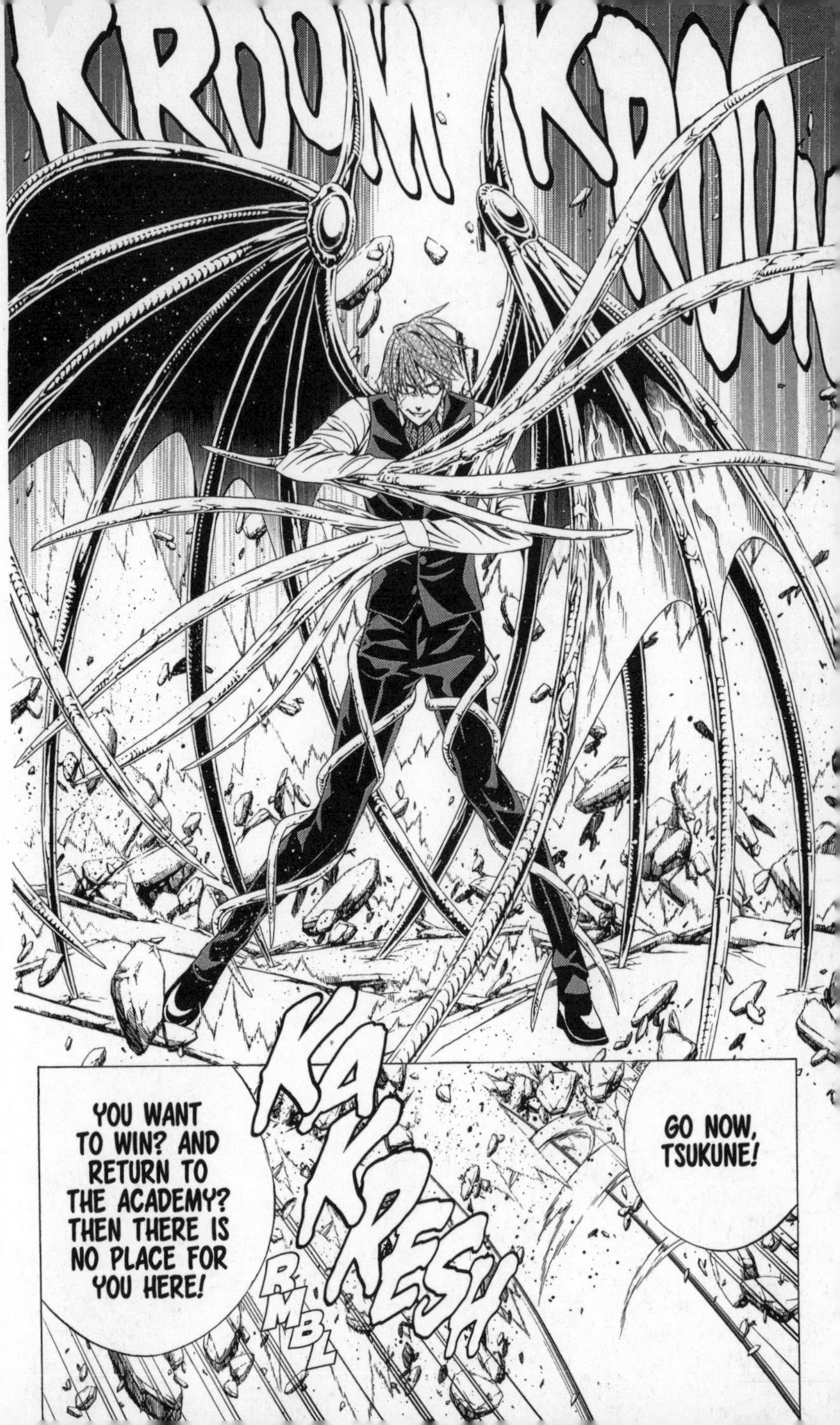
KROOM KROOM
GO NOW, TSUKUNE!
KA-KRESH
RMBL
YOU WANT TO WIN? AND RETURN TO THE ACADEMY? THEN THERE IS NO PLACE FOR YOU HERE!

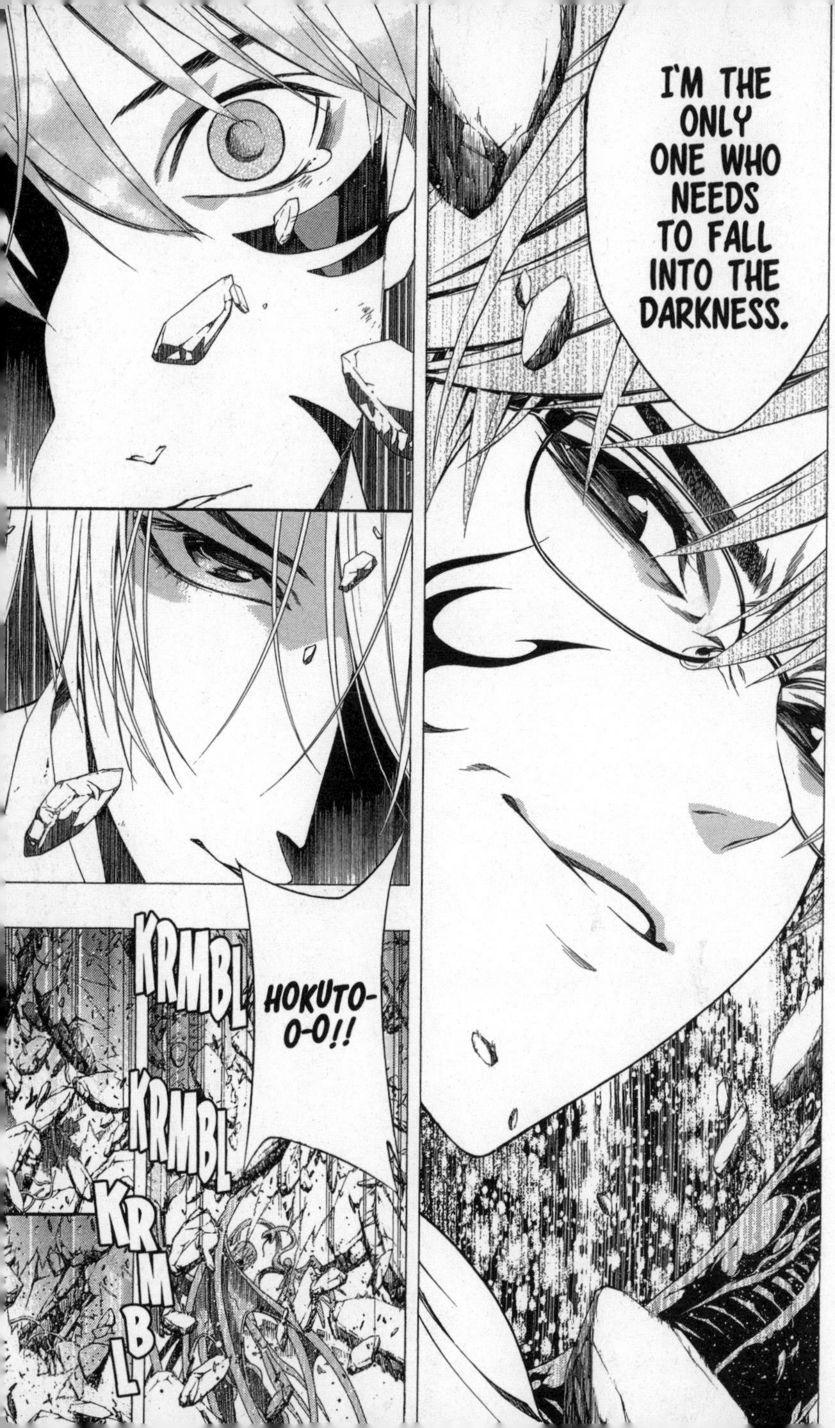
I'M THE ONLY ONE WHO NEEDS TO FALL INTO THE DARKNESS.
HOKUTO-O-O!!
KRMBL
KRMBL
KRMBL

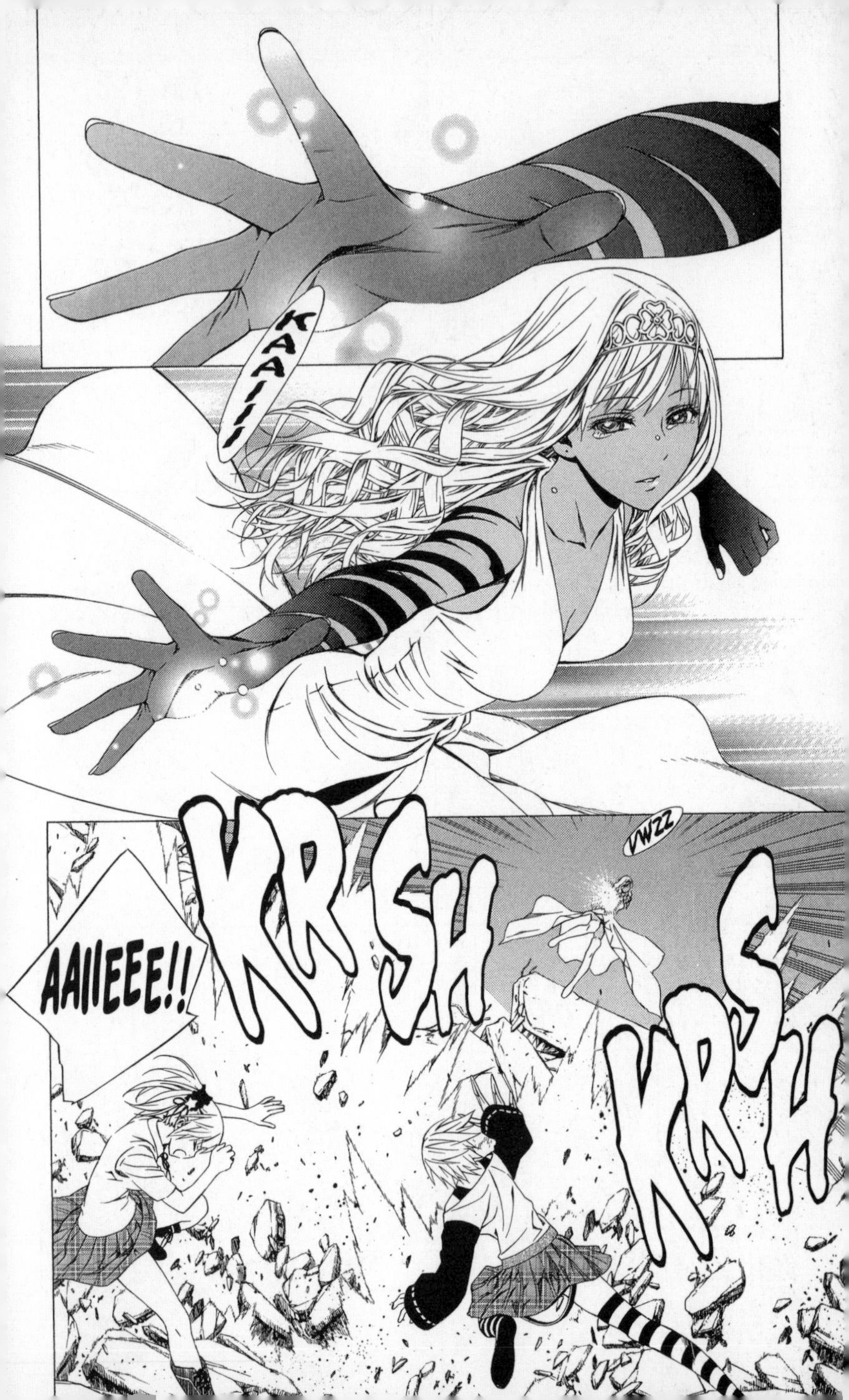
KAAIII
VWZZ
KRSH
KRSH
AAIIEEE!!

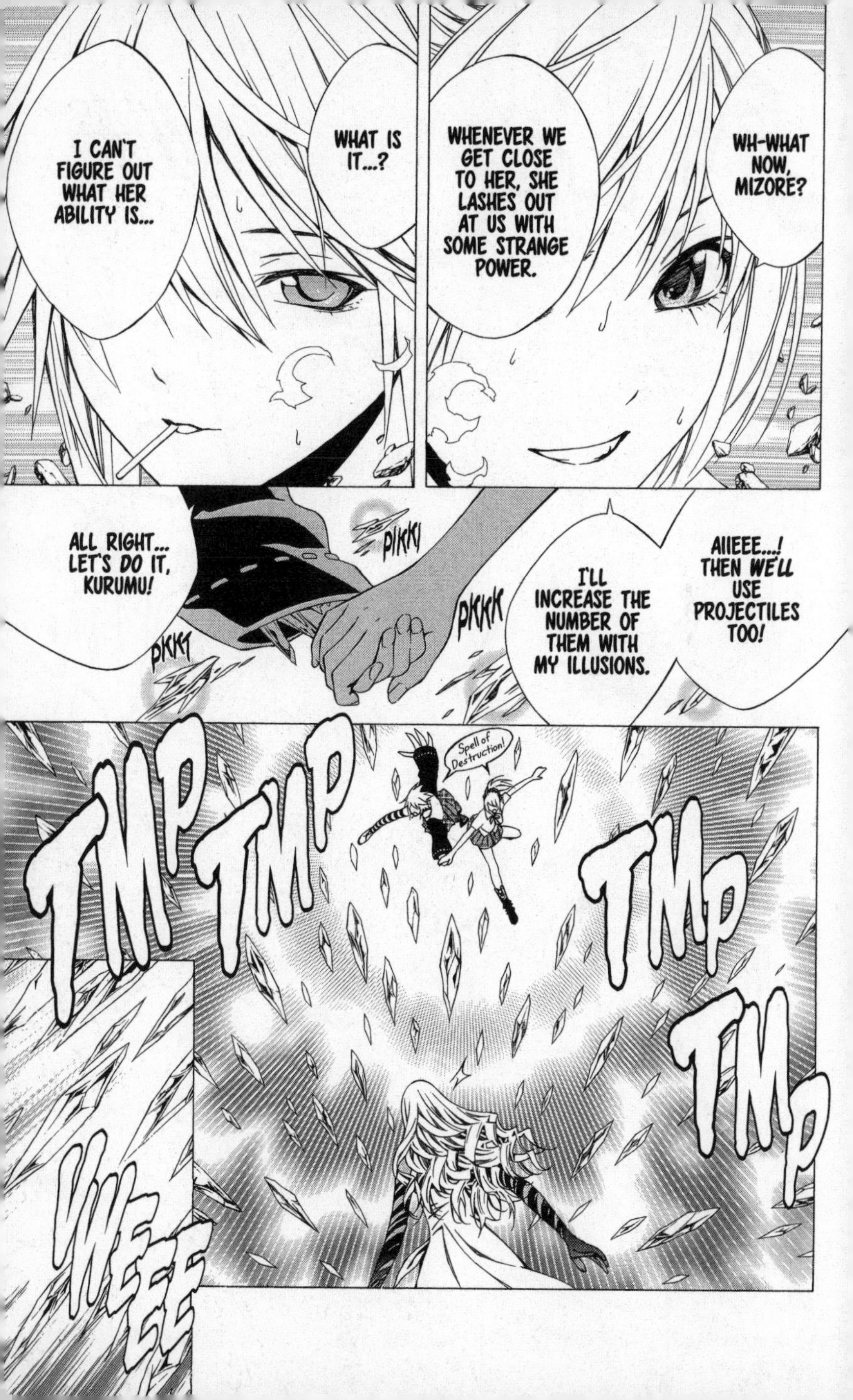
WH-WHAT NOW, MIZORE?
WHENEVER WE GET CLOSE TO HER, SHE LASHES OUT AT US WITH SOME STRANGE POWER.
WHAT IS IT...?
I CAN'T FIGURE OUT WHAT HER ABILITY IS...
AIIEEE...! THEN WE'LL USE PROJECTILES TOO!
I'LL INCREASE THE NUMBER OF THEM WITH MY ILLUSIONS.
PIKKK
PIKKI
ALL RIGHT... LET'S DO IT, KURUMU!
PIKKI
Spell of Destruction!
TMP TMP
TMP TMP
TMP
TMP
WHEEE

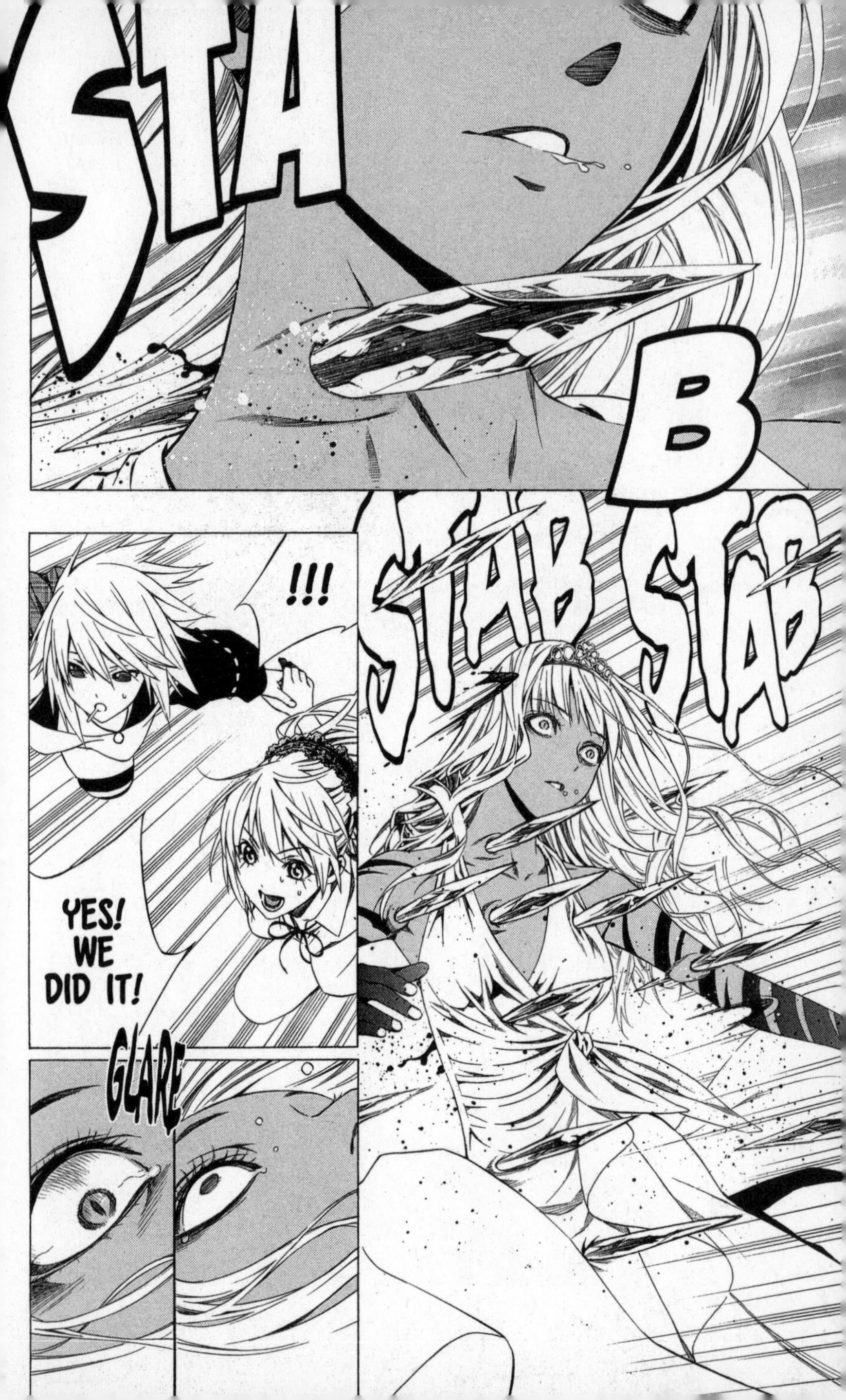
STAB
STAB STAB
!!!
YES! WE DID IT!
GLARE

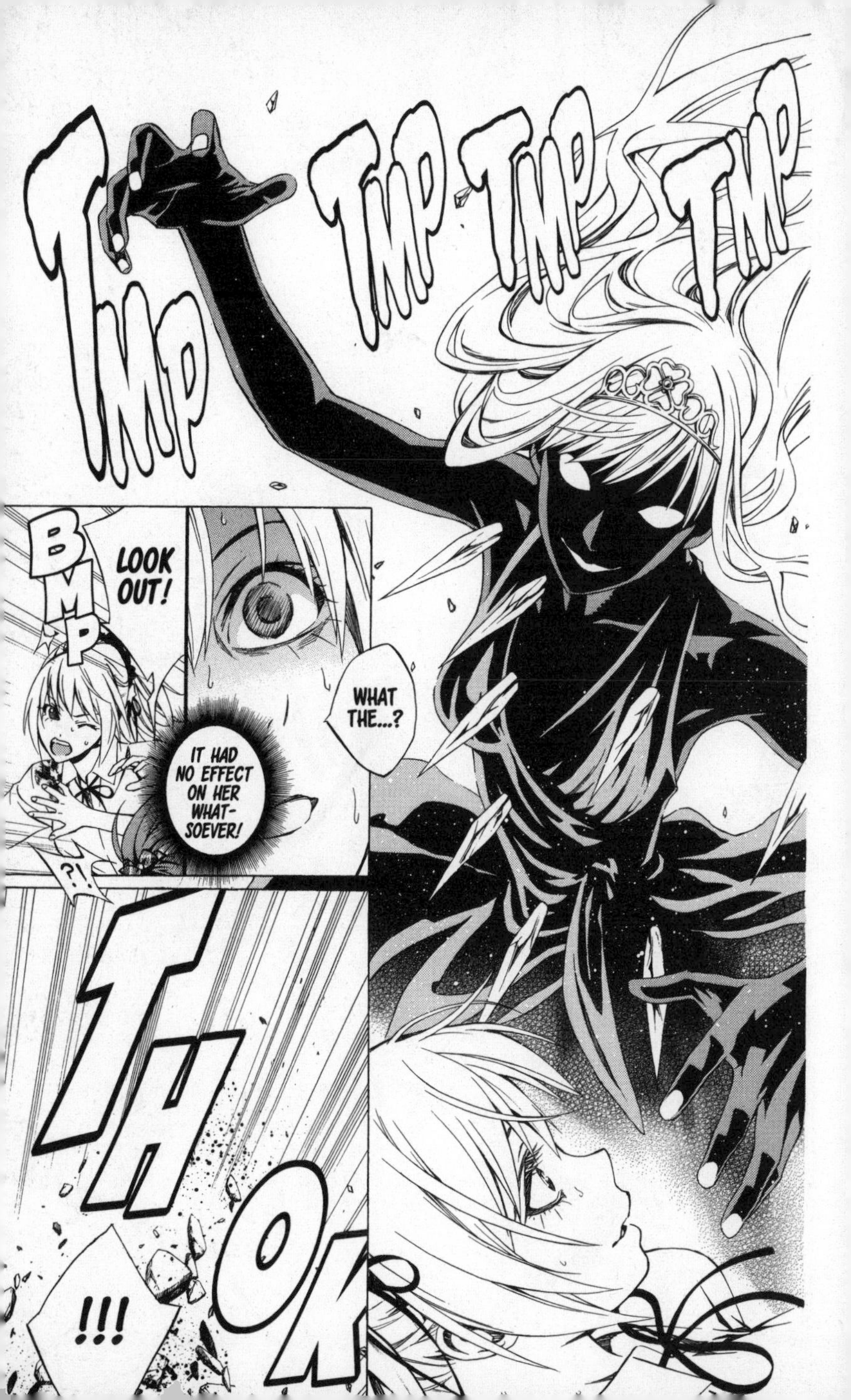
TMP
TMP
TMP
TMP
WHAT THE...?
IT HAD NO EFFECT ON HER WHAT-SOEVER!
BMP
LOOK OUT!
?!
THOK
!!!

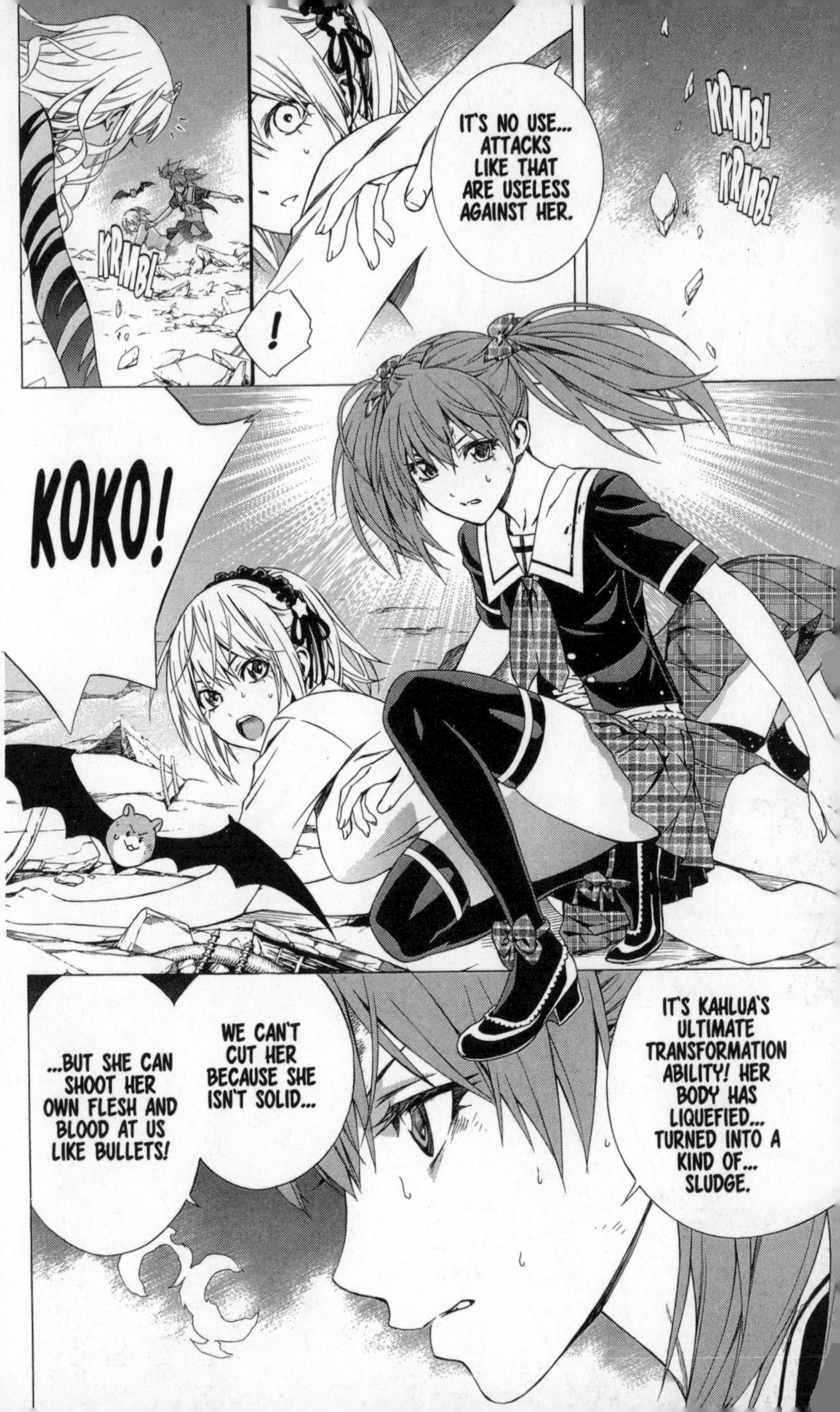
KRMBL KRMBL
IT'S NO USE... ATTACKS LIKE THAT ARE USELESS AGAINST HER.
!
KRMBL
KOKO!
IT'S KAHLUA'S ULTIMATE TRANSFORMATION ABILITY! HER BODY HAS LIQUEFIED... TURNED INTO A KIND OF... SLUDGE.
WE CAN'T CUT HER BECAUSE SHE ISN'T SOLID...
...BUT SHE CAN SHOOT HER OWN FLESH AND BLOOD AT US LIKE BULLETS!

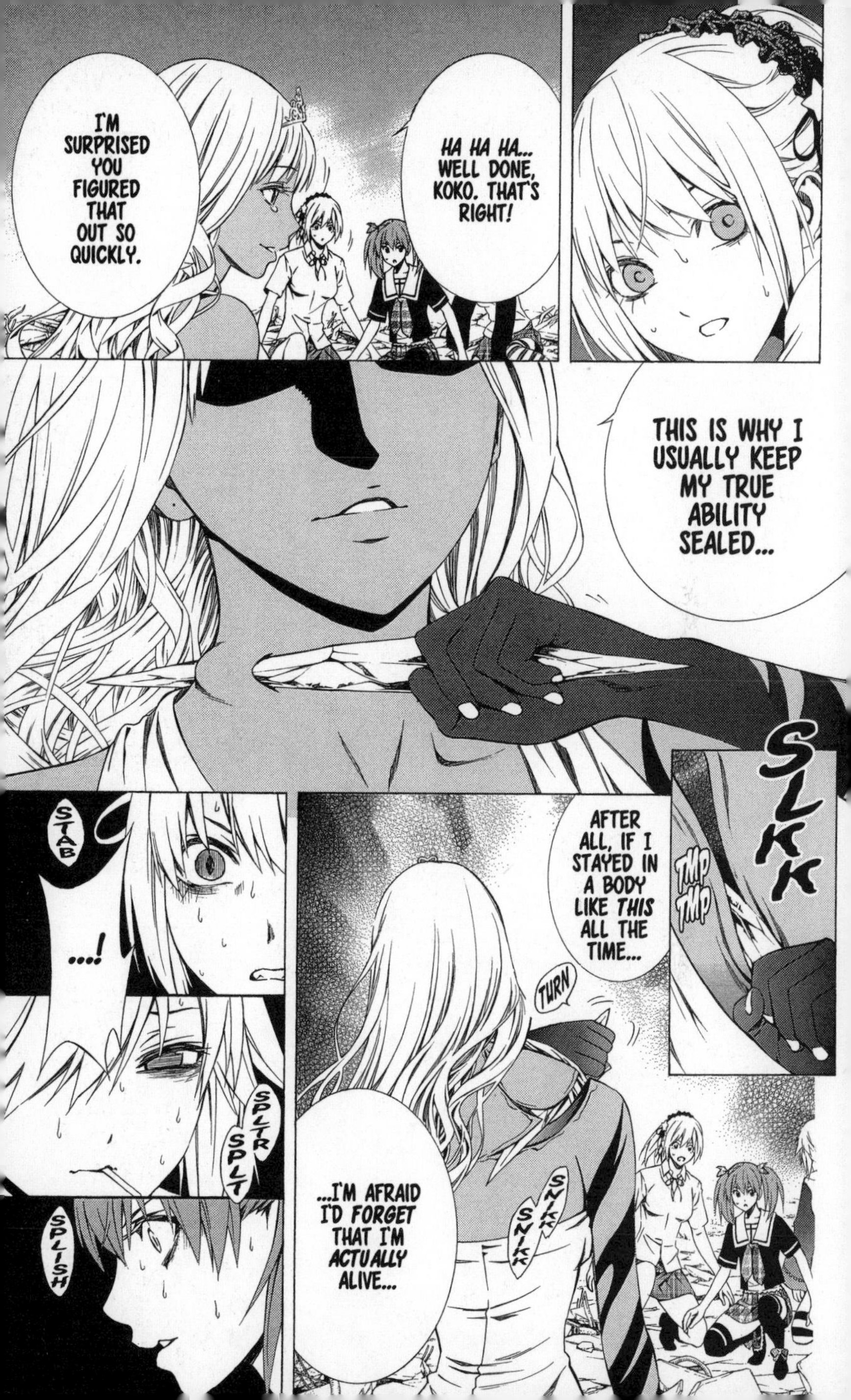
HA HA HA... WELL DONE, KOKO. THAT'S RIGHT!
I'M SURPRISED YOU FIGURED THAT OUT SO QUICKLY.
THIS IS WHY I USUALLY KEEP MY TRUE ABILITY SEALED...
SLKK
TMP TMP
AFTER ALL, IF I STAYED IN A BODY LIKE *THIS* ALL THE TIME...
TURN
SNIKK SNIKK
...I'M AFRAID I'D FORGET THAT I'M *ACTUALLY* ALIVE...
STAB
...!
SPLTR SPLT
SPLISH

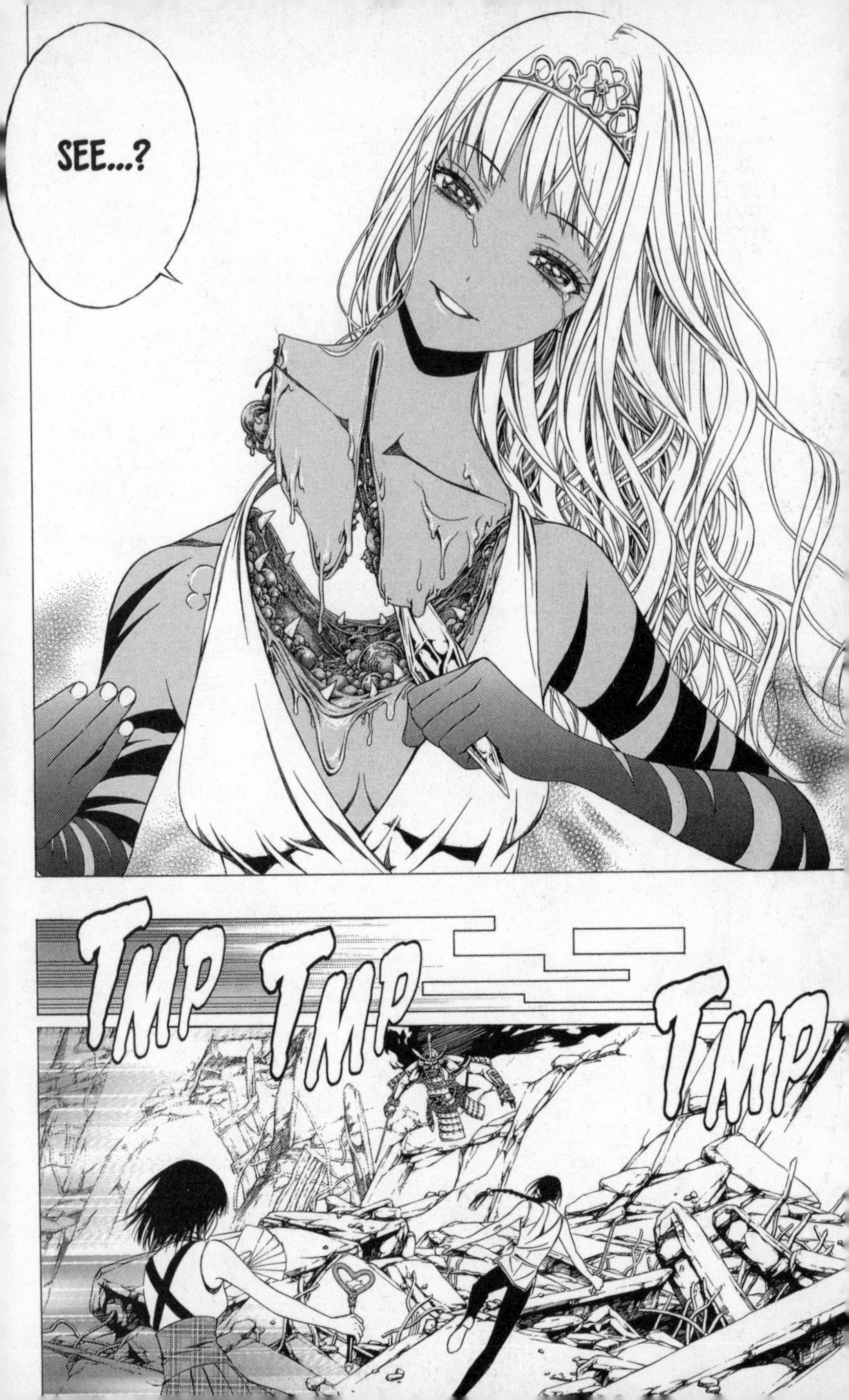
SEE...?
TMP TMP
TMP

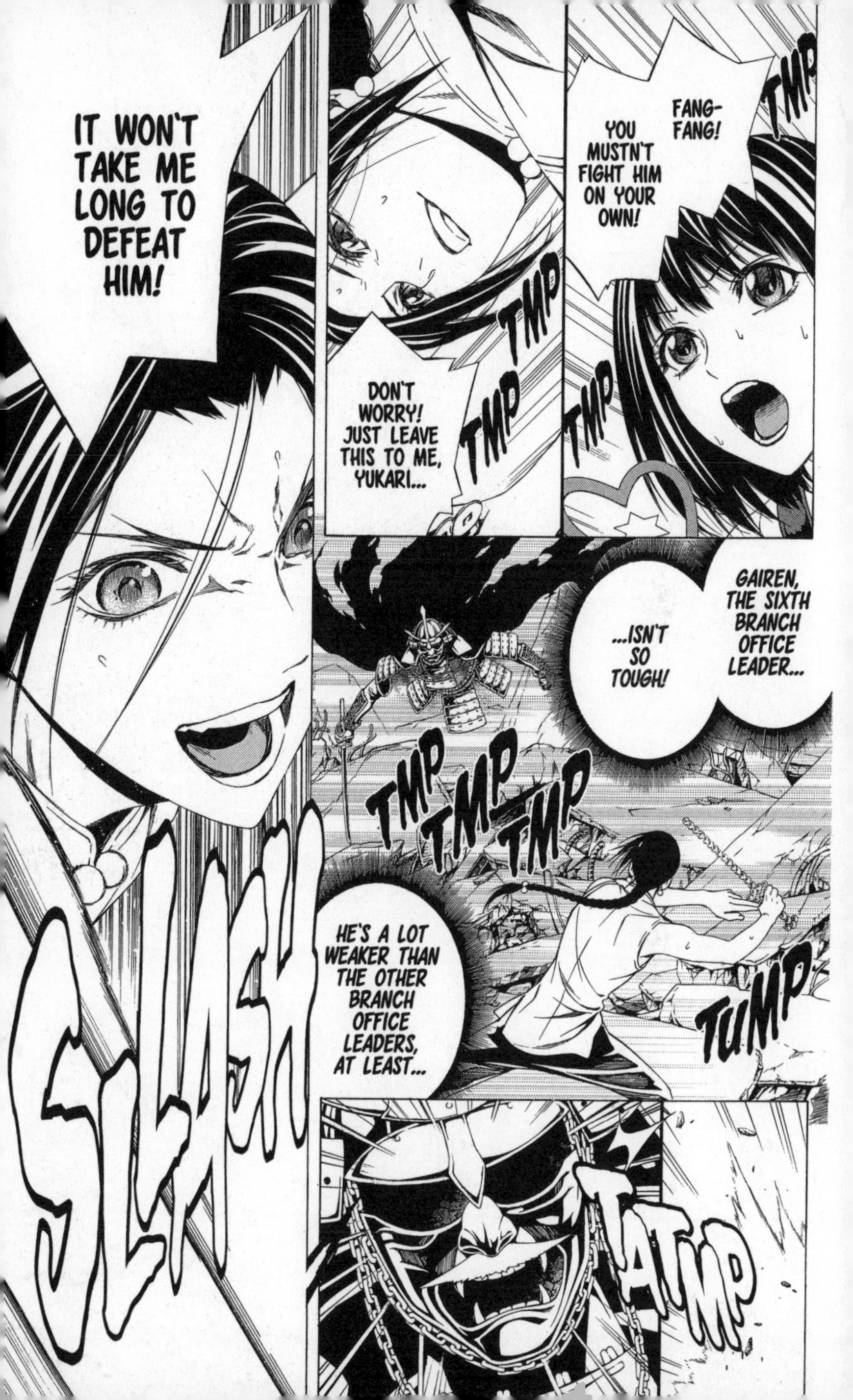
TMP
FANG-FANG!
YOU MUSTN'T FIGHT HIM ON YOUR OWN!
TMP
TMP
TMP
DON'T WORRY! JUST LEAVE THIS TO ME, YUKARI...
GAIREN, THE SIXTH BRANCH OFFICE LEADER...
...ISN'T SO TOUGH!
TMP TMP TMP
TUMP
HE'S A LOT WEAKER THAN THE OTHER BRANCH OFFICE LEADERS, AT LEAST...
TATMP
IT WON'T TAKE ME LONG TO DEFEAT HIM!
SLASH

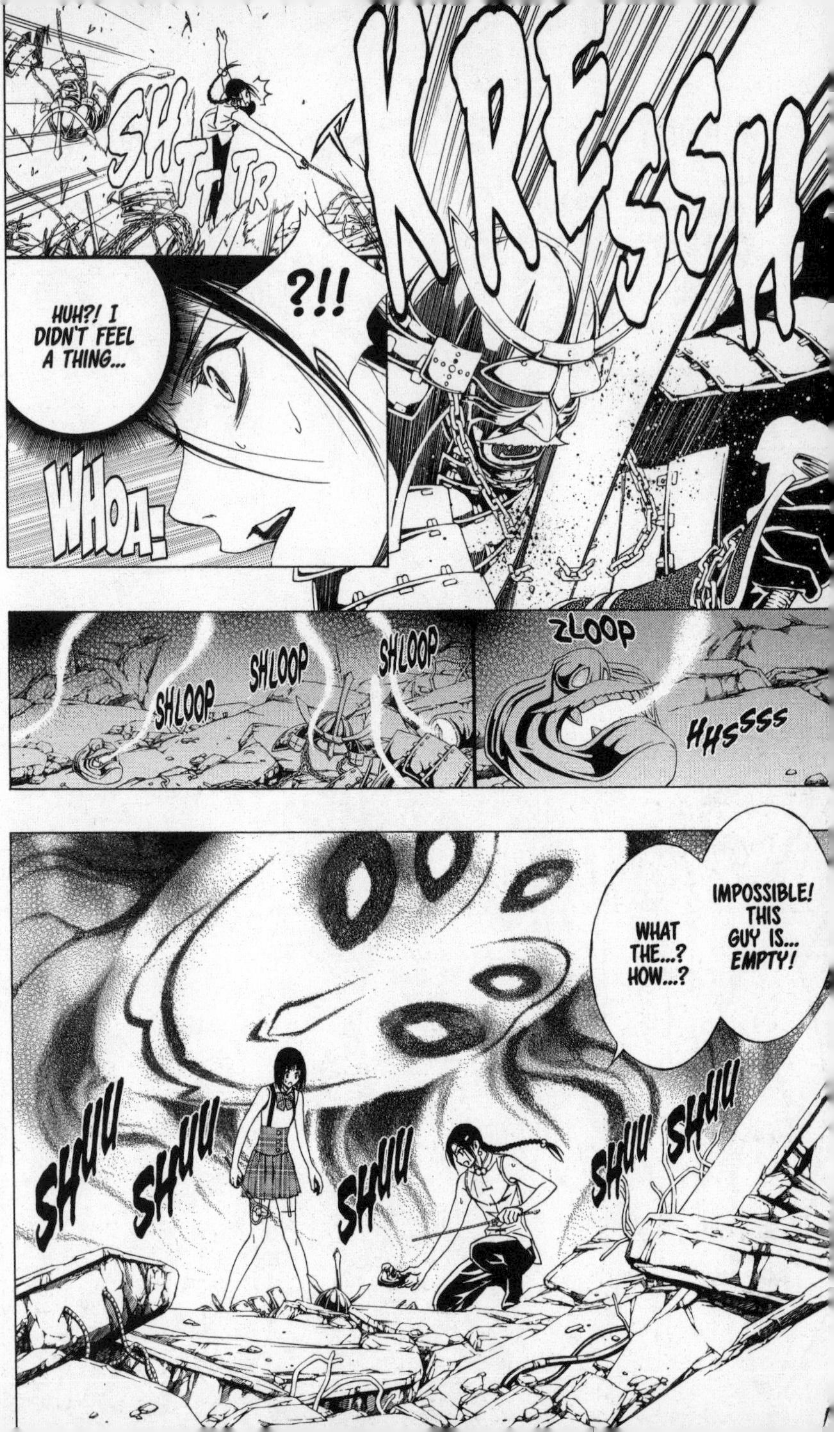
KRESSH
SH TT TR
?!!
HUH?! I DIDN'T FEEL A THING...
WHOA!
ZLOOP
HHSSSS
SHLOOP
SHLOOP
SHLOOP
IMPOSSIBLE! THIS GUY IS... EMPTY!
WHAT THE...? HOW...?
SHUU SHUU
SHUU
SHUU SHUU

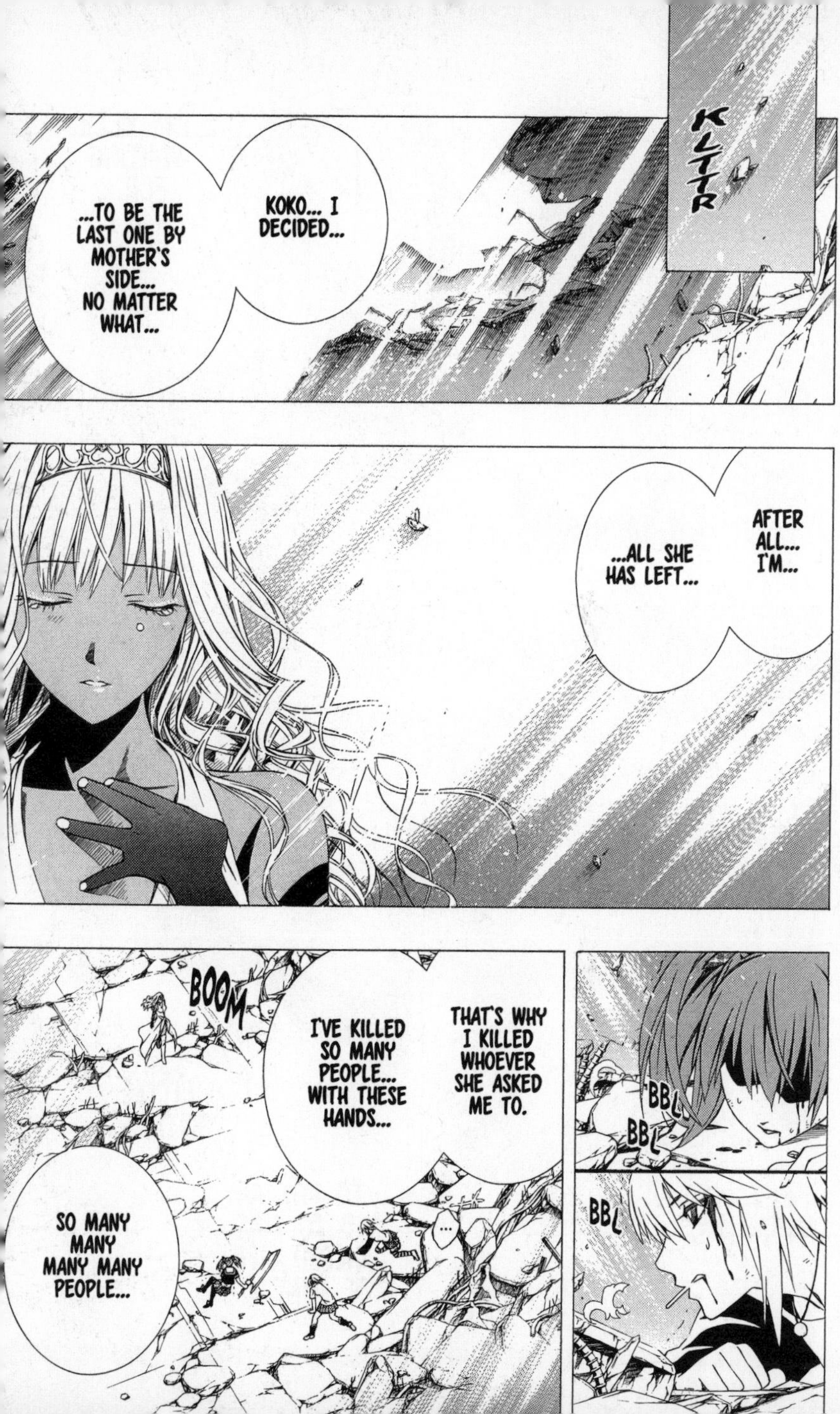
KLTTR
KOKO... I DECIDED...
...TO BE THE LAST ONE BY MOTHER'S SIDE... NO MATTER WHAT...
AFTER ALL... I'M...
...ALL SHE HAS LEFT...
BBL
BBL
BBL
THAT'S WHY I KILLED WHOEVER SHE ASKED ME TO.
I'VE KILLED SO MANY PEOPLE... WITH THESE HANDS...
BOOM
...
SO MANY MANY MANY MANY PEOPLE...

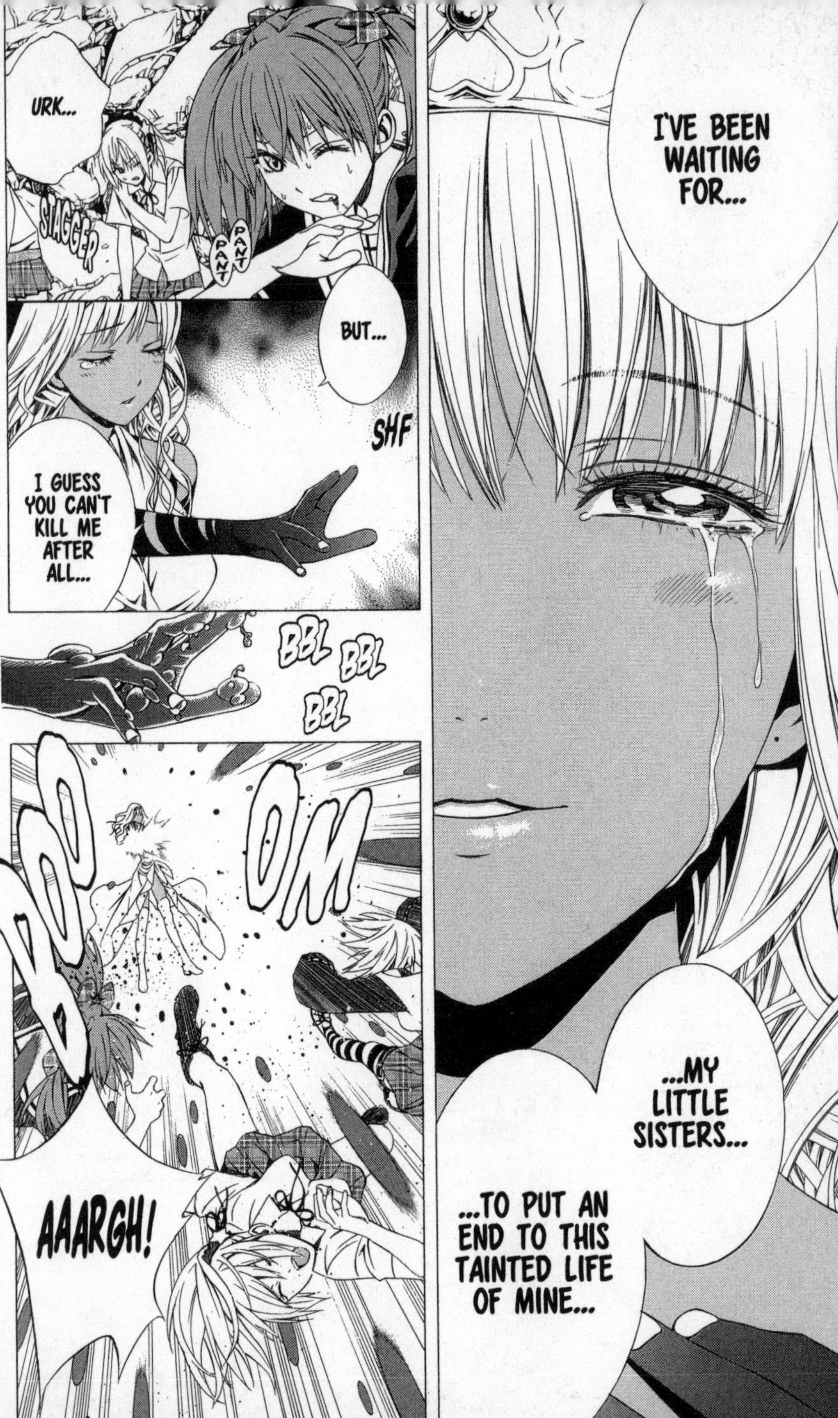
I'VE BEEN WAITING FOR...
...MY LITTLE SISTERS...
...TO PUT AN END TO THIS TAINTED LIFE OF MINE...
URK...
STAGGER
PANT PANT
BUT...
SHF
I GUESS YOU CAN'T KILL ME AFTER ALL...
BBL BBL BBL
OM
BOO
AAARGH!

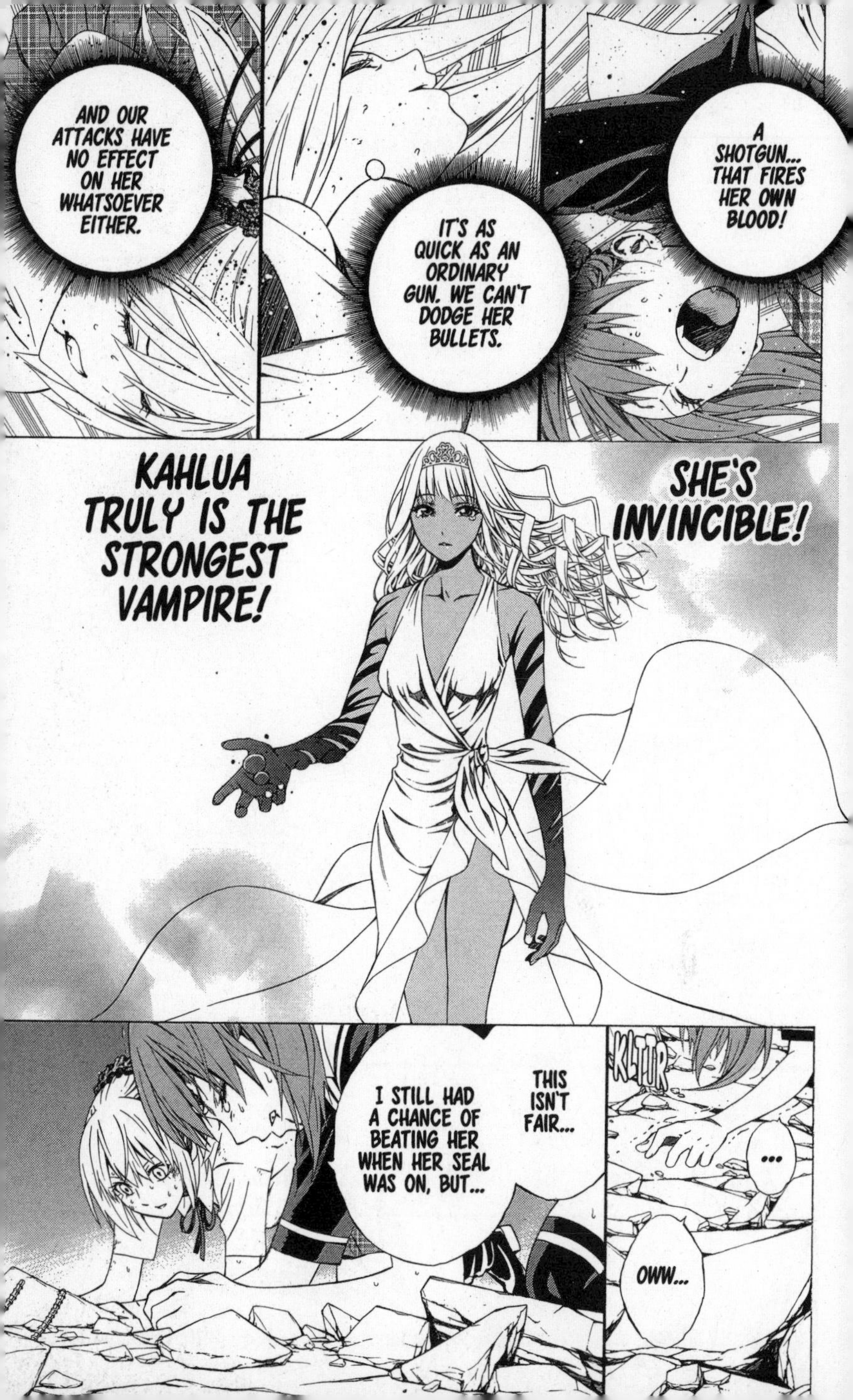
A SHOTGUN... THAT FIRES HER OWN BLOOD!
IT'S AS QUICK AS AN ORDINARY GUN. WE CAN'T DODGE HER BULLETS.
AND OUR ATTACKS HAVE NO EFFECT ON HER WHATSOEVER EITHER.
SHE'S INVINCIBLE!
KAHLUA TRULY IS THE STRONGEST VAMPIRE!
KLTTR
...
OWW...
THIS ISN'T FAIR...
I STILL HAD A CHANCE OF BEATING HER WHEN HER SEAL WAS ON, BUT...

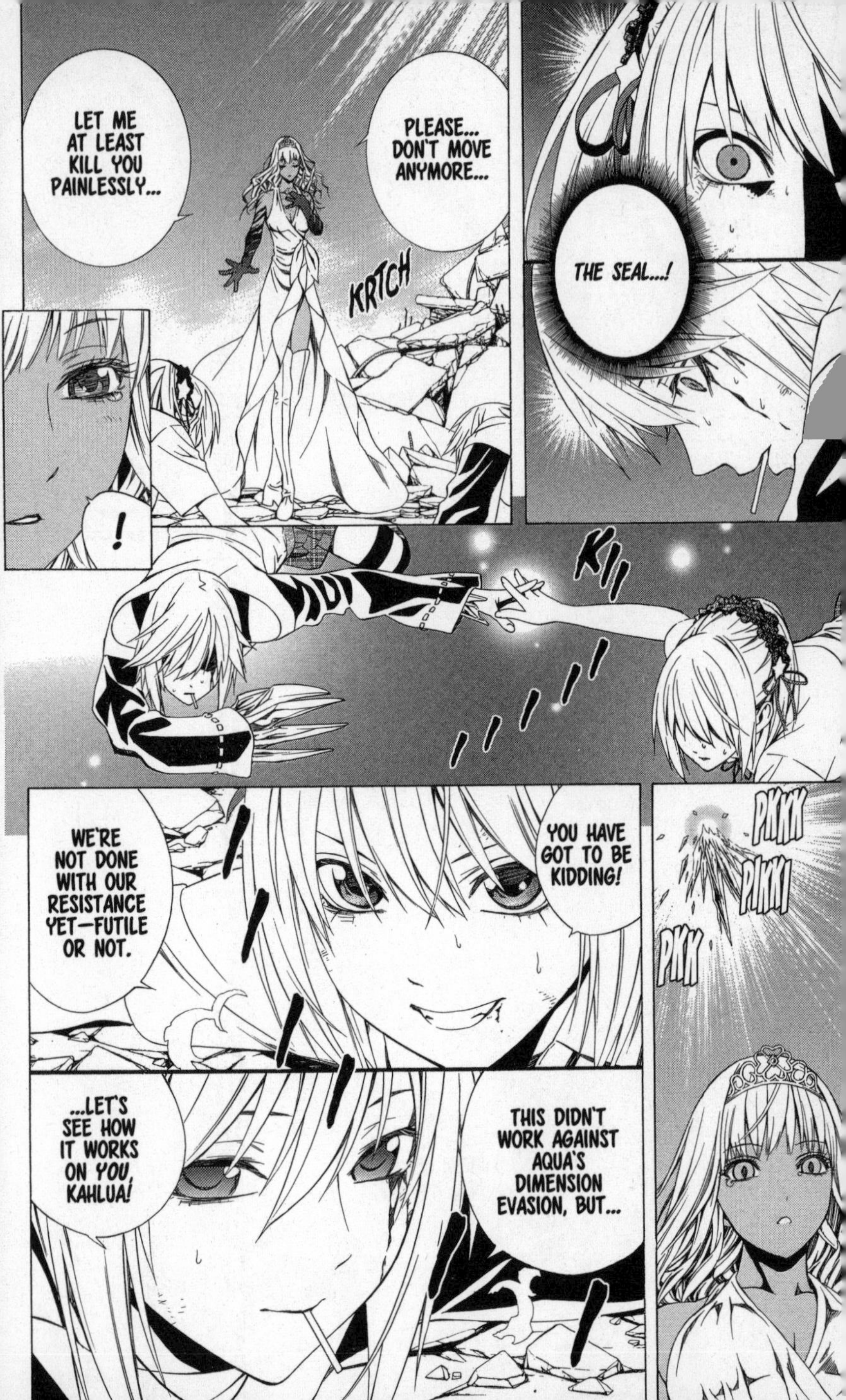
THE SEAL...!
PLEASE... DON'T MOVE ANYMORE...
LET ME AT LEAST KILL YOU PAINLESSLY...
KRTCH
!
KII
PKKK
PIKKI
PKK
YOU HAVE GOT TO BE KIDDING!
WE'RE NOT DONE WITH OUR RESISTANCE YET—FUTILE OR NOT.
THIS DIDN'T WORK AGAINST AQUA'S DIMENSION EVASION, BUT...
...LET'S SEE HOW IT WORKS ON *YOU*, KAHLUA!

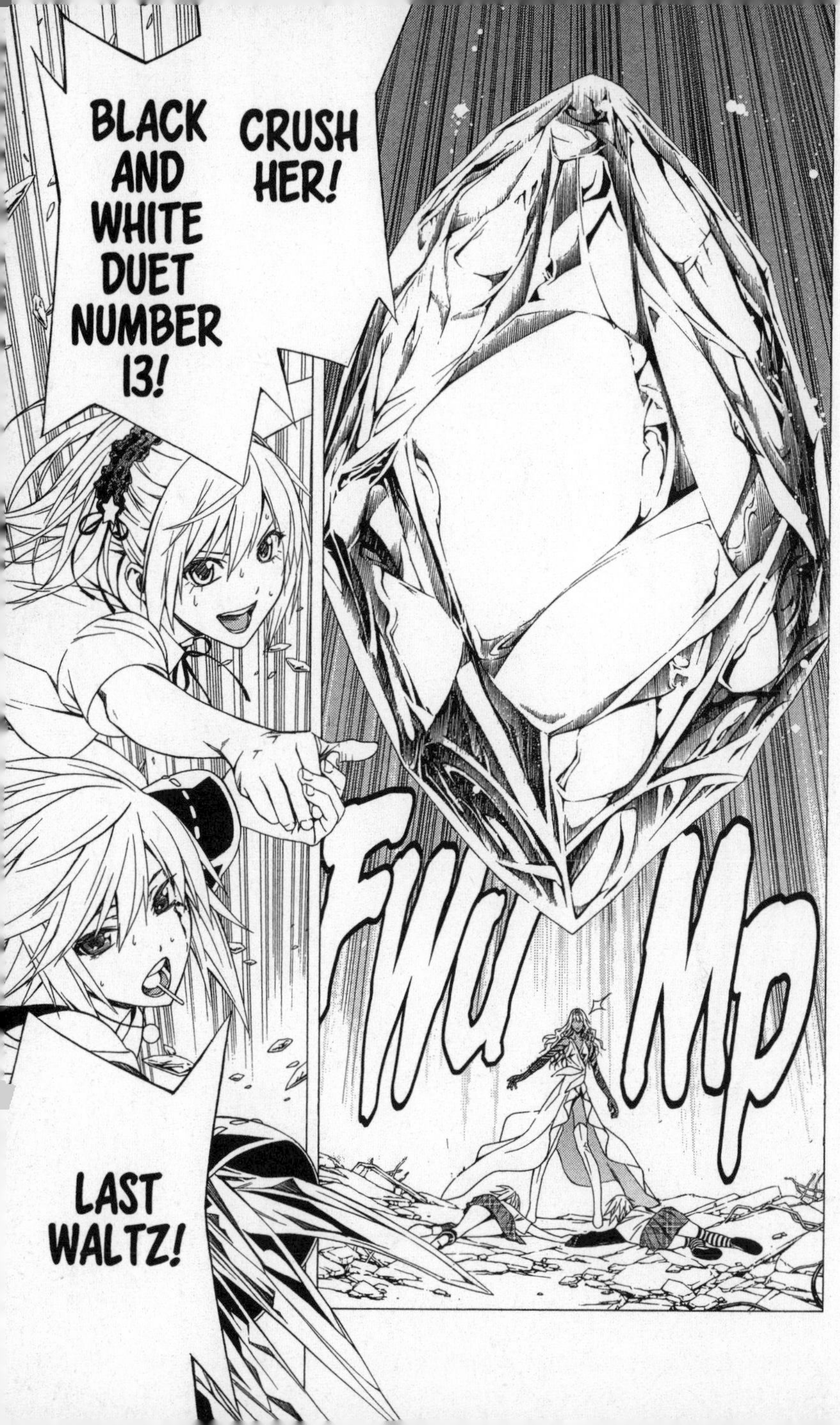
CRUSH HER!
BLACK AND WHITE DUET NUMBER 13!
LAST WALTZ!

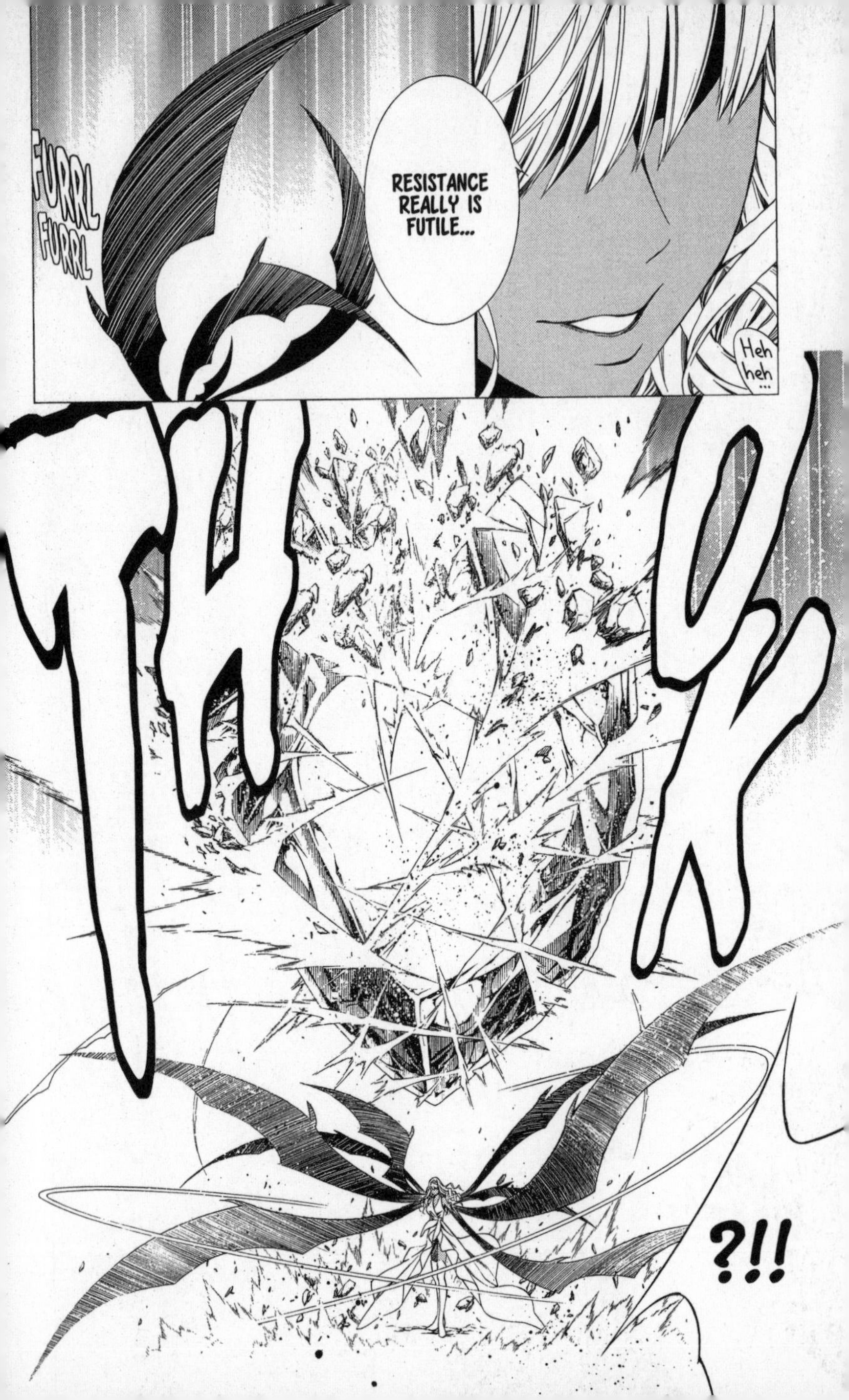
RESISTANCE REALLY IS FUTILE...
Heh heh...
FURRL FURRL
?!!

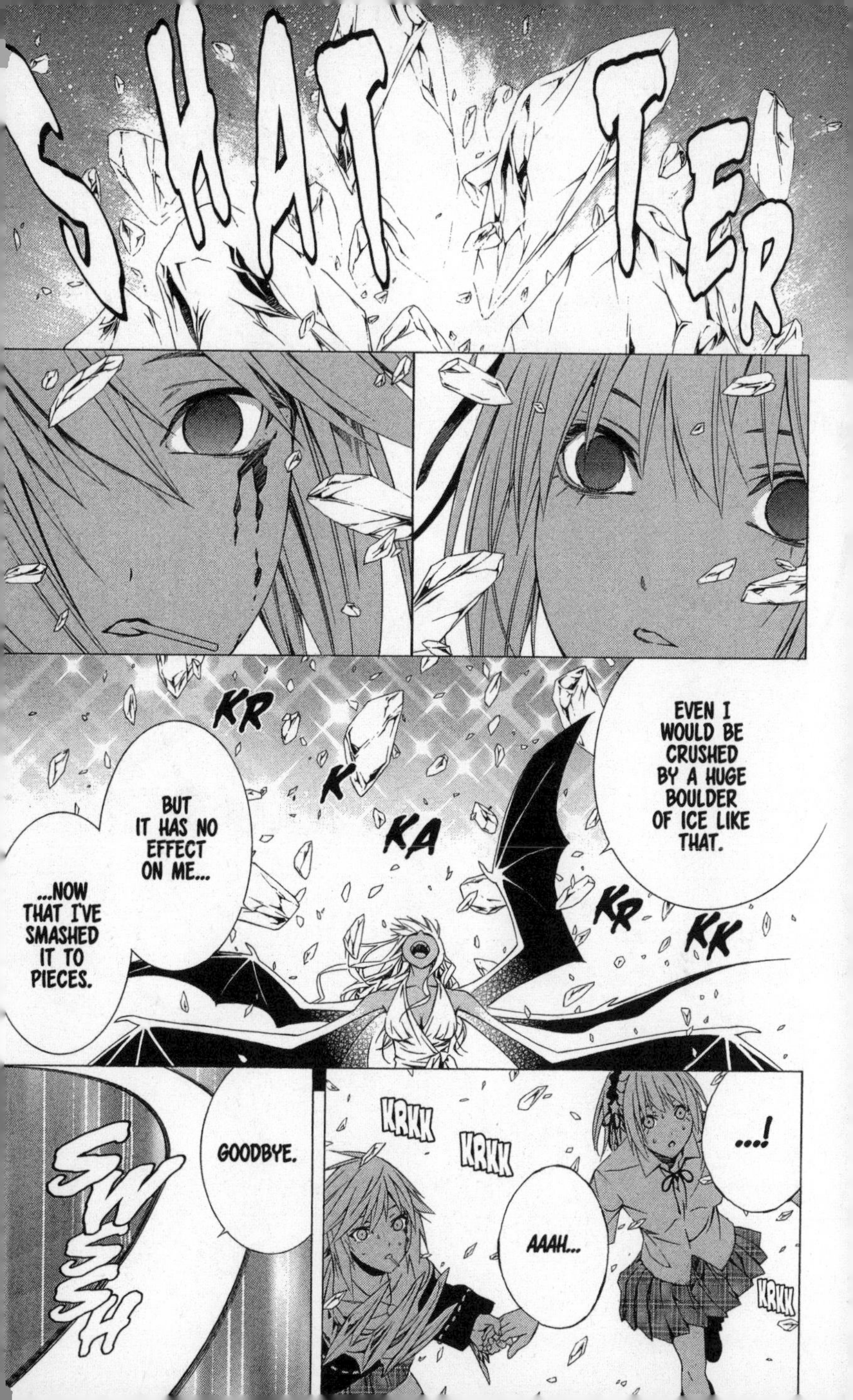
SHATTER
EVEN I WOULD BE CRUSHED BY A HUGE BOULDER OF ICE LIKE THAT.
KR
K
KA
KR
KK
BUT IT HAS NO EFFECT ON ME...
...NOW THAT I'VE SMASHED IT TO PIECES.
...!
KRKK
KRKK
AAAH...
KRKK
GOODBYE.
SWSSH

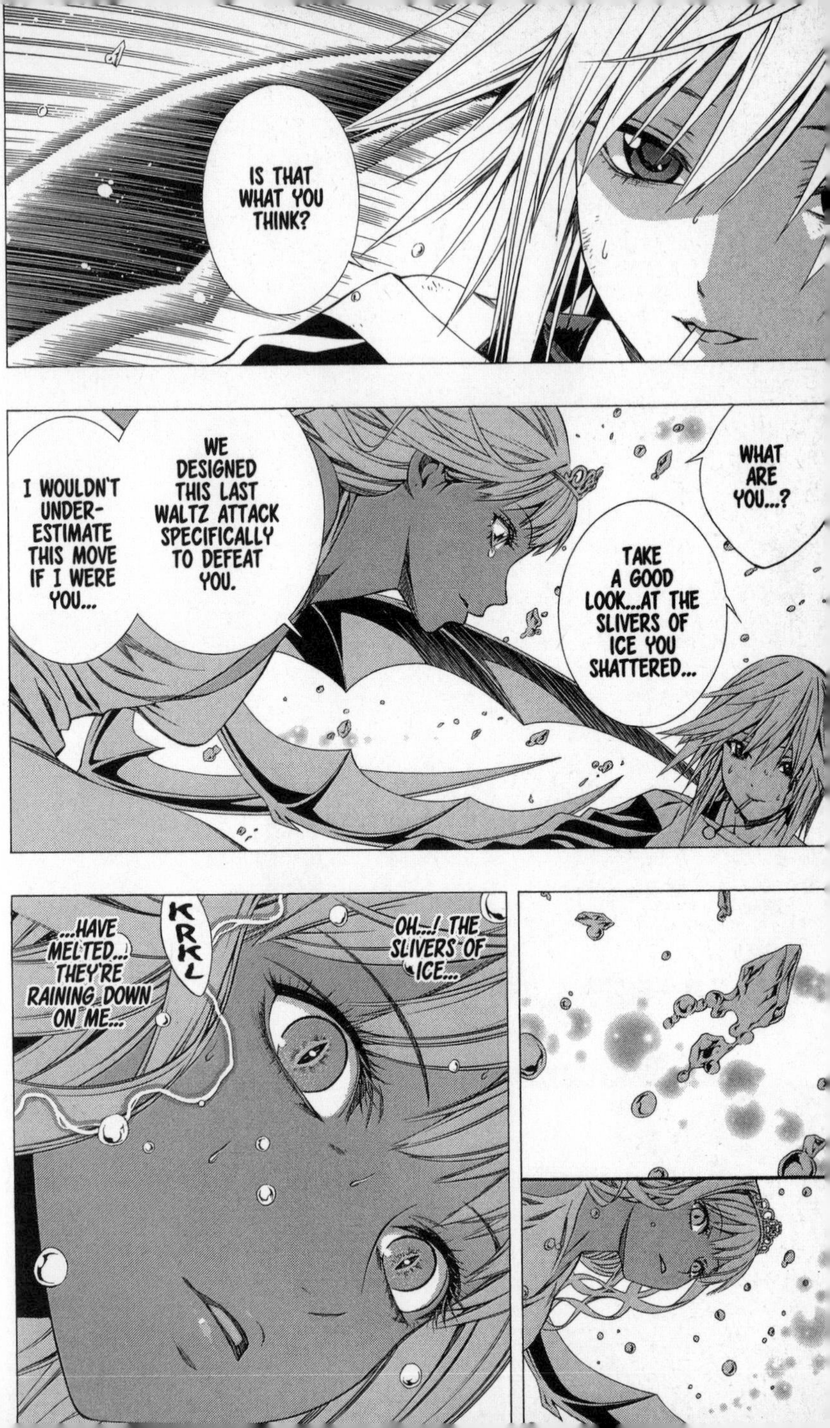
IS THAT WHAT YOU THINK?
WHAT ARE YOU...?
TAKE A GOOD LOOK...AT THE SLIVERS OF ICE YOU SHATTERED...
WE DESIGNED THIS LAST WALTZ ATTACK SPECIFICALLY TO DEFEAT YOU.
I WOULDN'T UNDER-ESTIMATE THIS MOVE IF I WERE YOU...
OH...! THE SLIVERS OF ICE...
KRKL
...HAVE MELTED... THEY'RE RAINING DOWN ON ME...

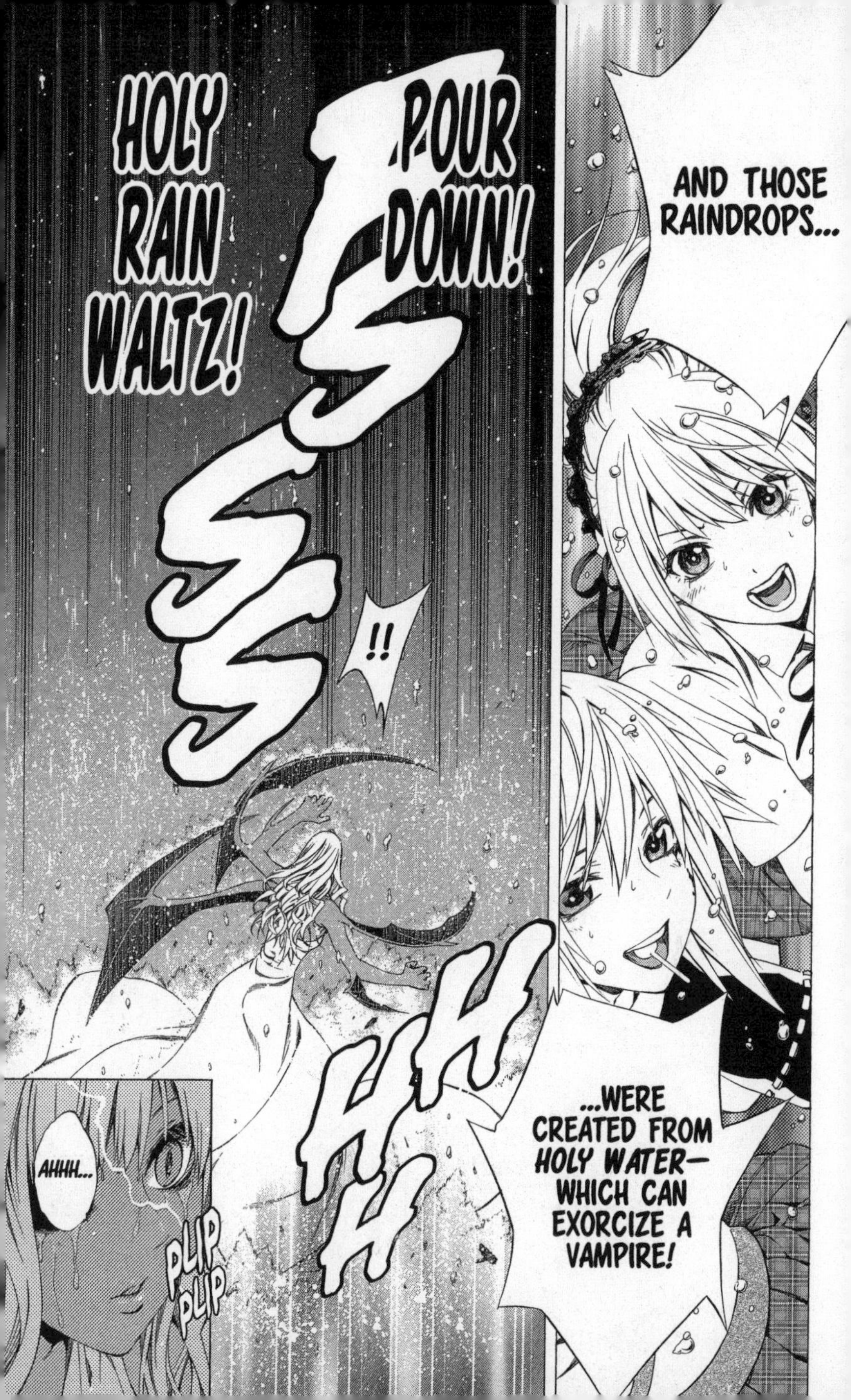
AND THOSE RAINDROPS...
...WERE CREATED FROM HOLY WATER— WHICH CAN EXORCIZE A VAMPIRE!
...POUR DOWN!
HOLY RAIN WALTZ!
SSSHH
!!
AHHH...
PLIP PLIP

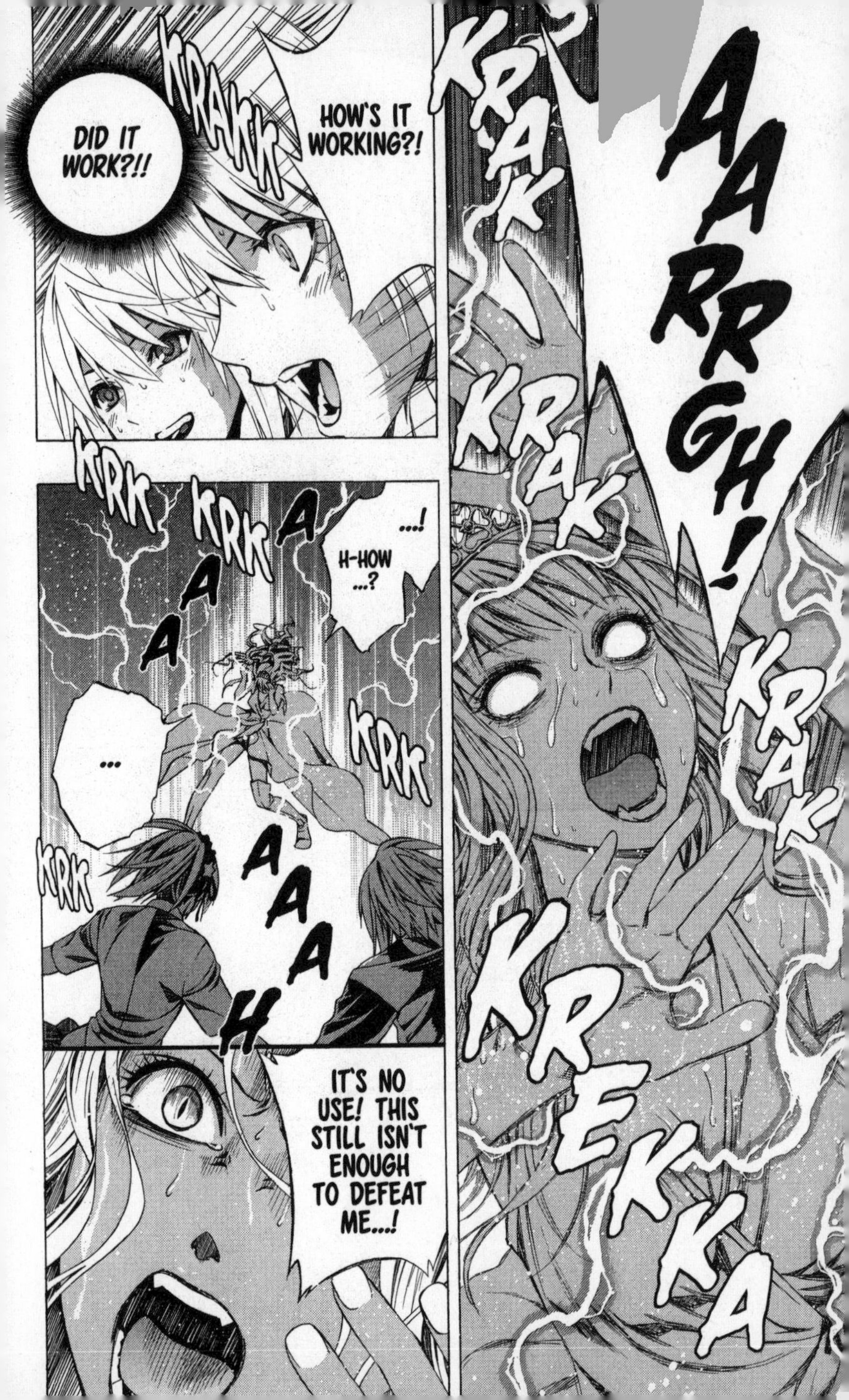
KRAK
AAARRGH!
KRAK
KRAK
KREKKA
HOW'S IT WORKING?!
KRAKK
DID IT WORK?!!
...!
H-HOW ...?
KRK
KRK
AAAAAAAH
KRK
...
KRK
IT'S NO USE! THIS STILL ISN'T ENOUGH TO DEFEAT ME...!

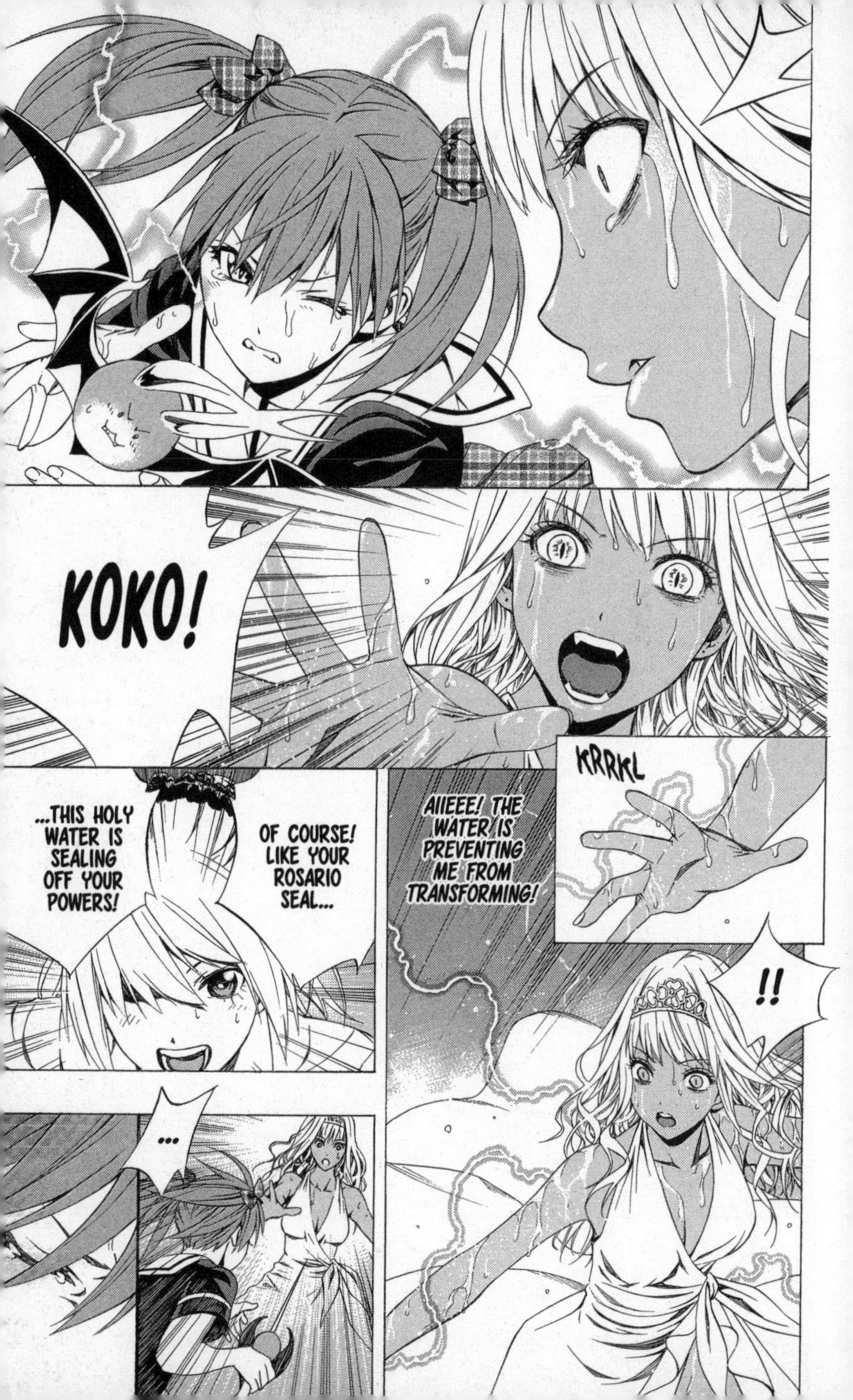
KOKO!
KRRKL
AIIEEE! THE WATER IS PREVENTING ME FROM TRANSFORMING!
!!
OF COURSE! LIKE YOUR ROSARIO SEAL...
...THIS HOLY WATER IS SEALING OFF YOUR POWERS!
...

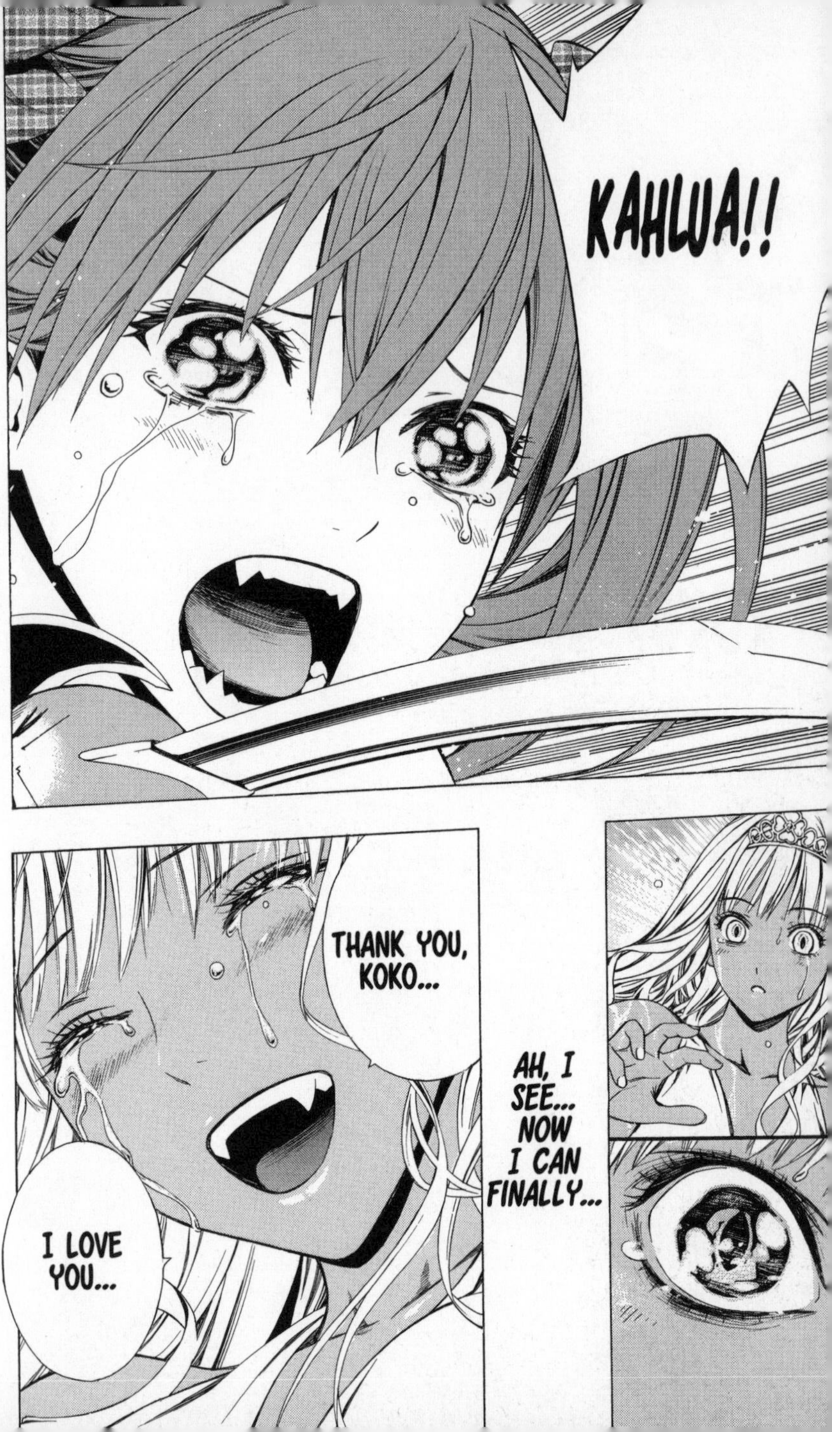
KAHLUA!!
AH, I SEE... NOW I CAN FINALLY...
THANK YOU, KOKO...
I LOVE YOU...

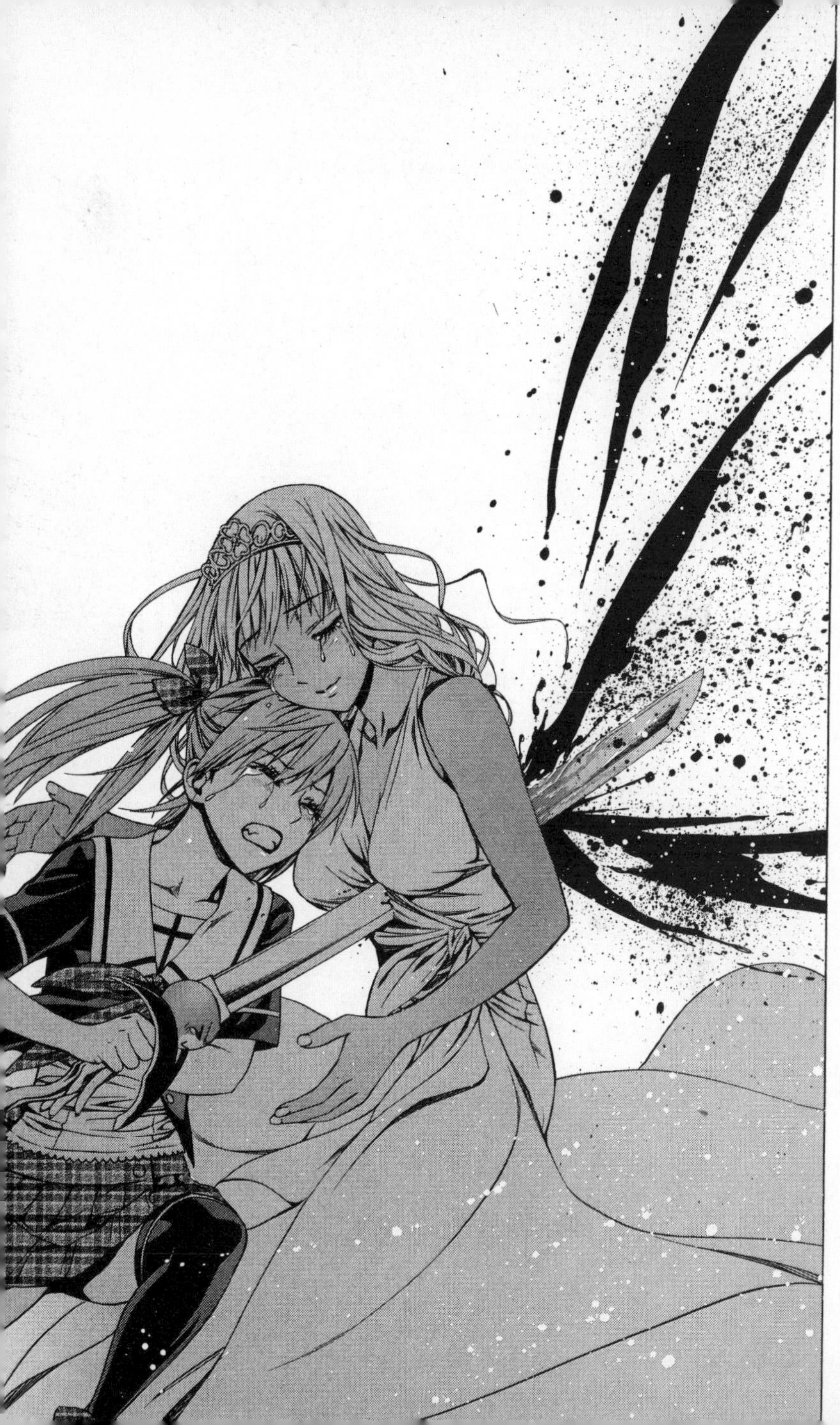

64: If Only We Could Start Over Again

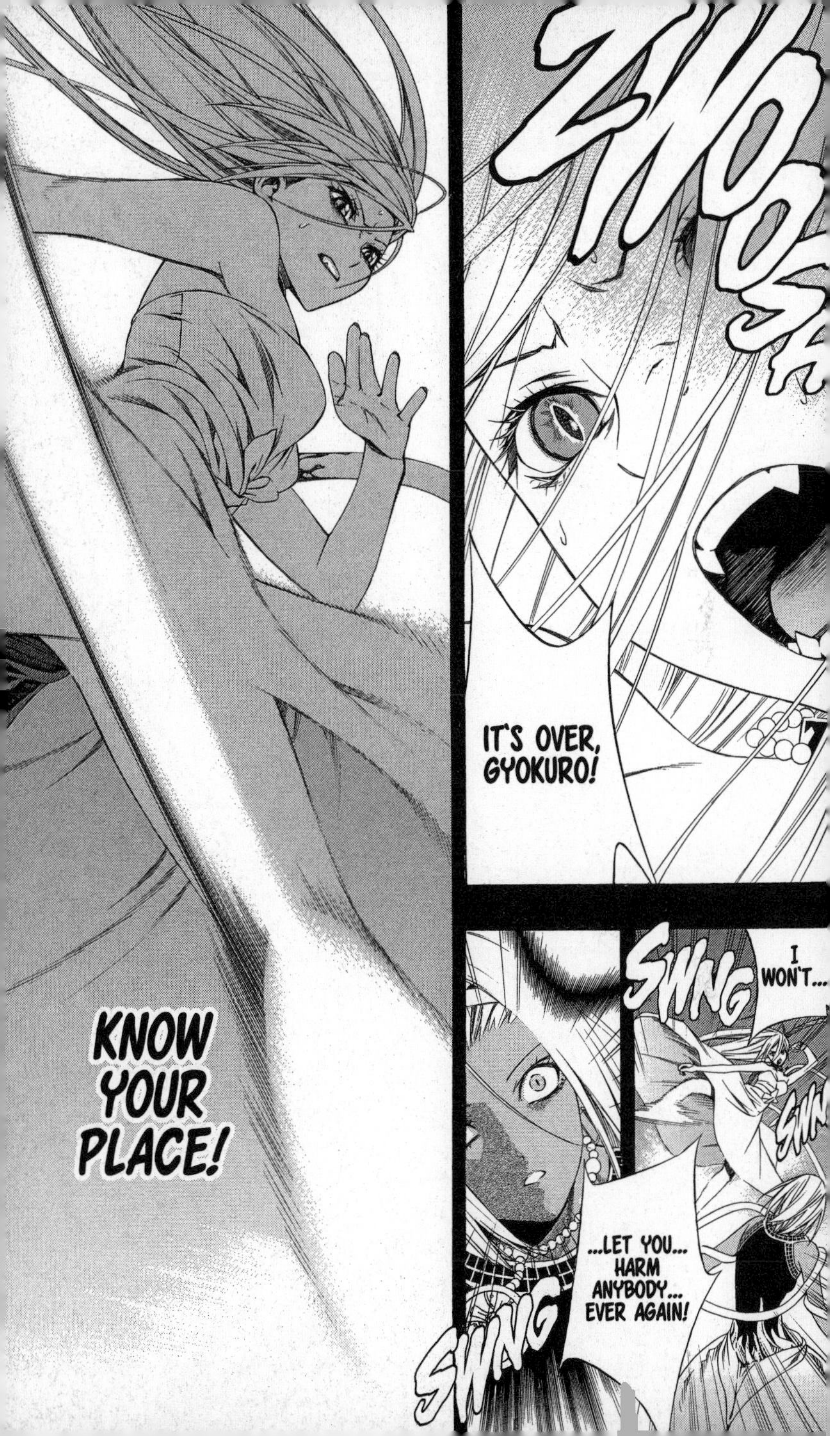
ZWOOSH
IT'S OVER, GYOKURO!
SWING
I WON'T...
...LET YOU... HARM ANYBODY... EVER AGAIN!
SWING
KNOW YOUR PLACE!

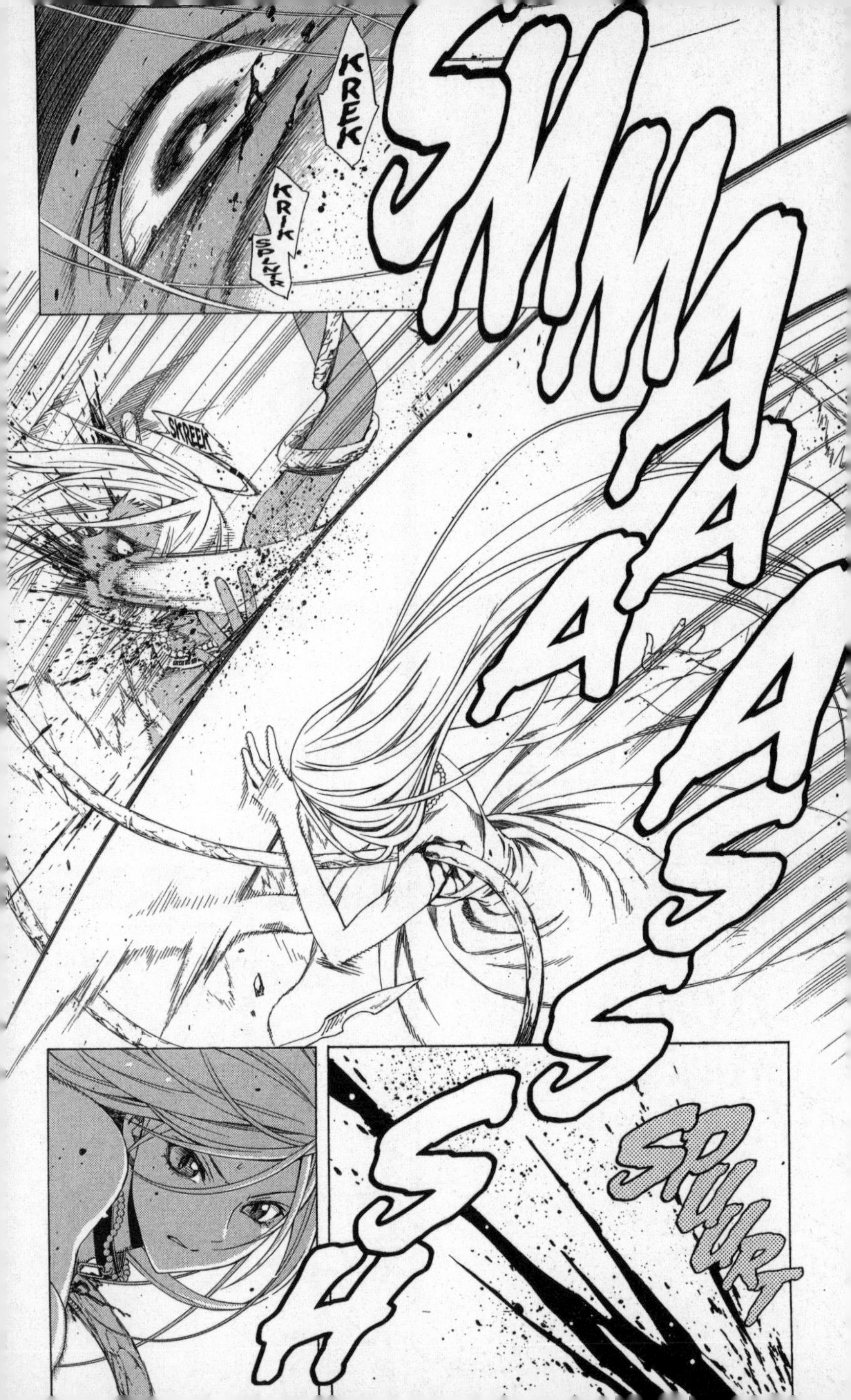
SHWAAAASSSH
KREK
KRIK
SPLNTR
SKREEK
SPLURT

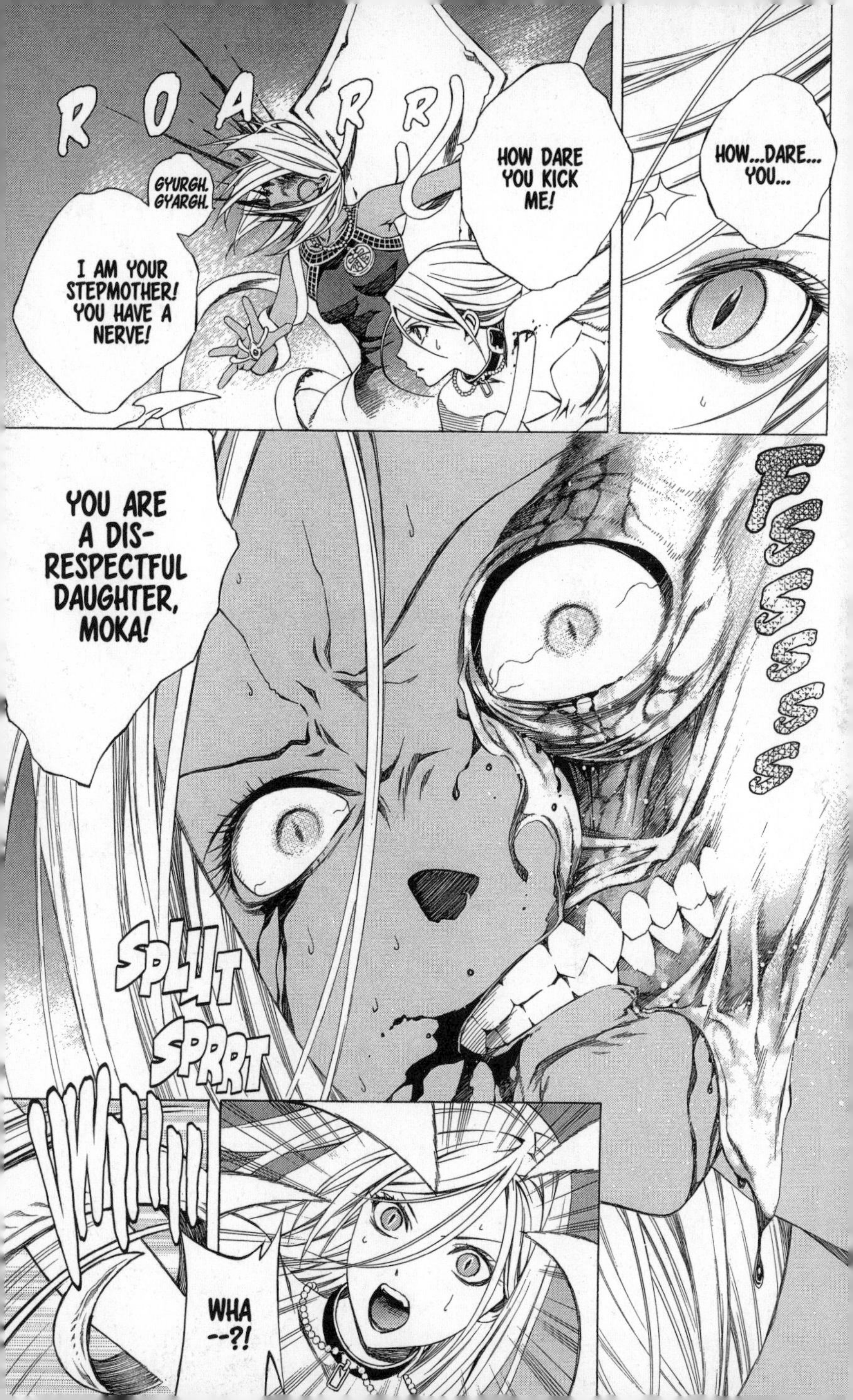
HOW...DARE... YOU...
HOW DARE YOU KICK ME!
ROARRR
GYURGH. GYARGH.
I AM YOUR STEPMOTHER! YOU HAVE A NERVE!
FSSSSS
YOU ARE A DIS-RESPECTFUL DAUGHTER, MOKA!
SPLUT
SPRRT
WHA --?!

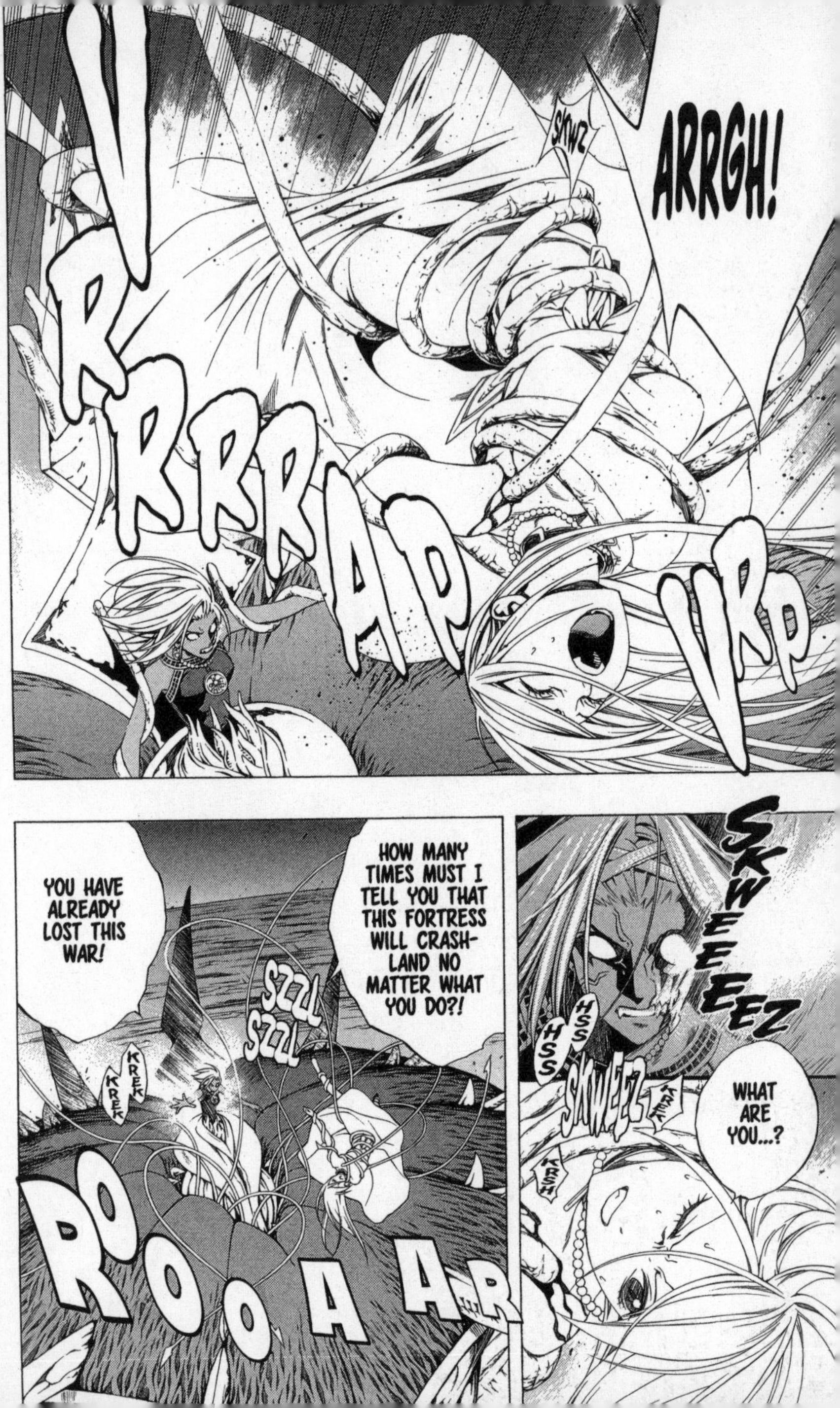
ARRGH!
SKWZ
RRRRAP
VRP
SKWEEEEEZ
HSS HSS
SKWEEZ
KREK
WHAT ARE YOU...?
KRSH
HOW MANY TIMES MUST I TELL YOU THAT THIS FORTRESS WILL CRASH-LAND NO MATTER WHAT YOU DO?!
YOU HAVE ALREADY LOST THIS WAR!
SZZL SZZL
KREK KREK
ROOAAR

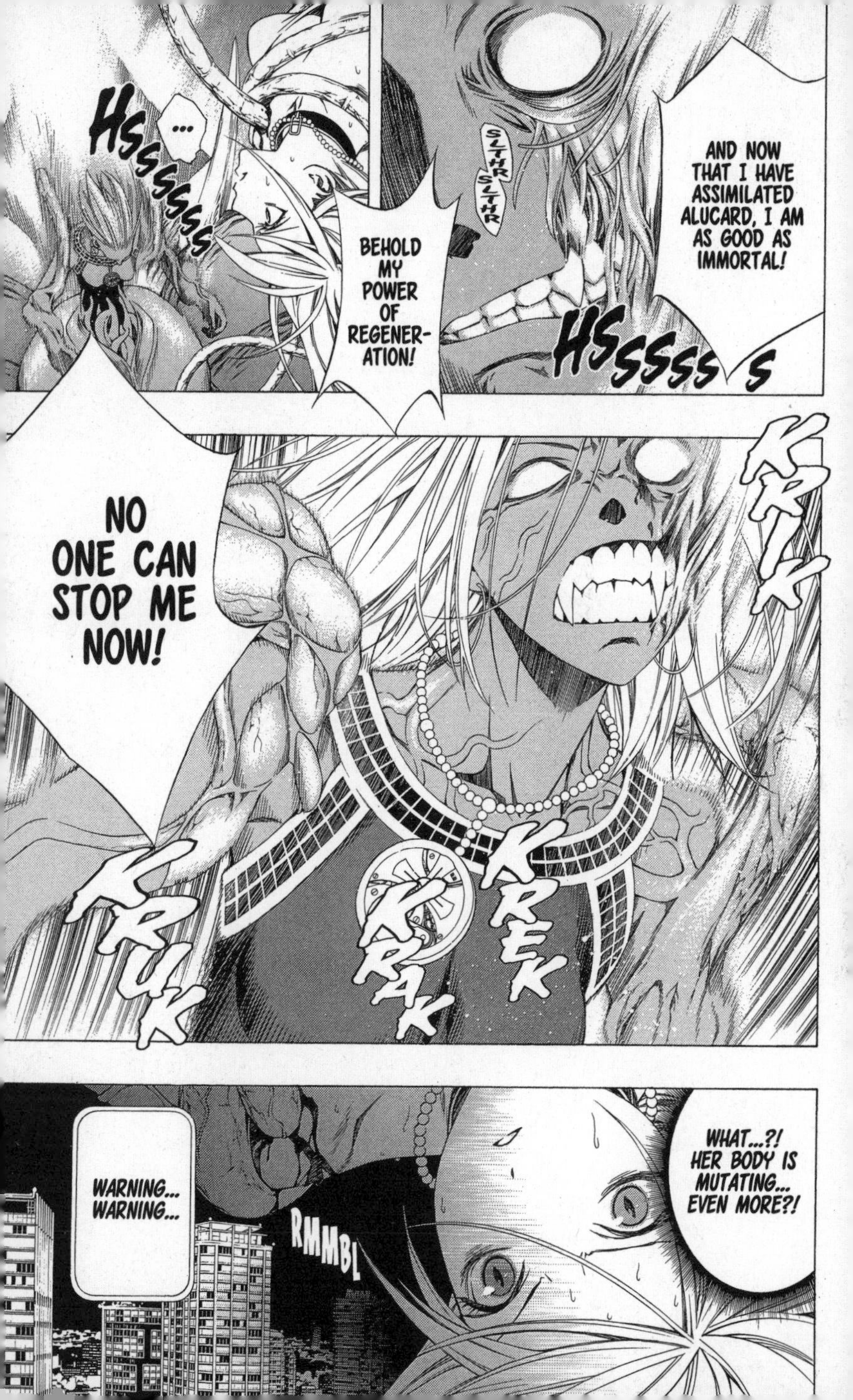
AND NOW THAT I HAVE ASSIMILATED ALUCARD, I AM AS GOOD AS IMMORTAL!
SLTHR SLTHR
BEHOLD MY POWER OF REGENER-ATION!
HSSSSS S
...
HSSSSSS
NO ONE CAN STOP ME NOW!
KRIK
KREK
KRAK
KRUK
WHAT...?! HER BODY IS MUTATING... EVEN MORE?!
WARNING... WARNING...
RMMBL

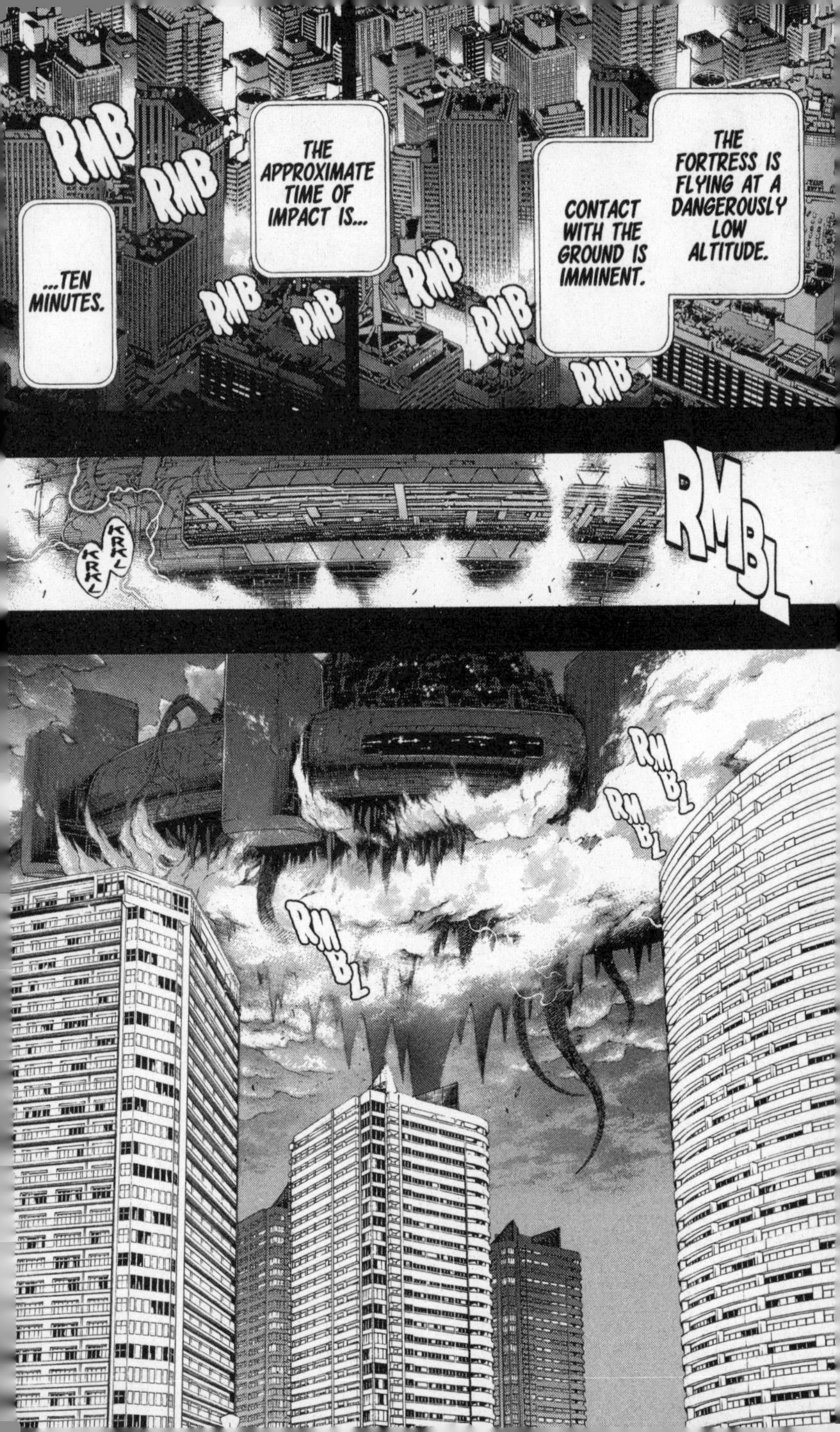
THE FORTRESS IS FLYING AT A DANGEROUSLY LOW ALTITUDE.
CONTACT WITH THE GROUND IS IMMINENT.
RMB
RMB
RMB
THE APPROXIMATE TIME OF IMPACT IS...
RMB
RMB
RMB
RMB
...TEN MINUTES.
RMBL
KRKL
KRKL
RMBL
RMBL
RMBL

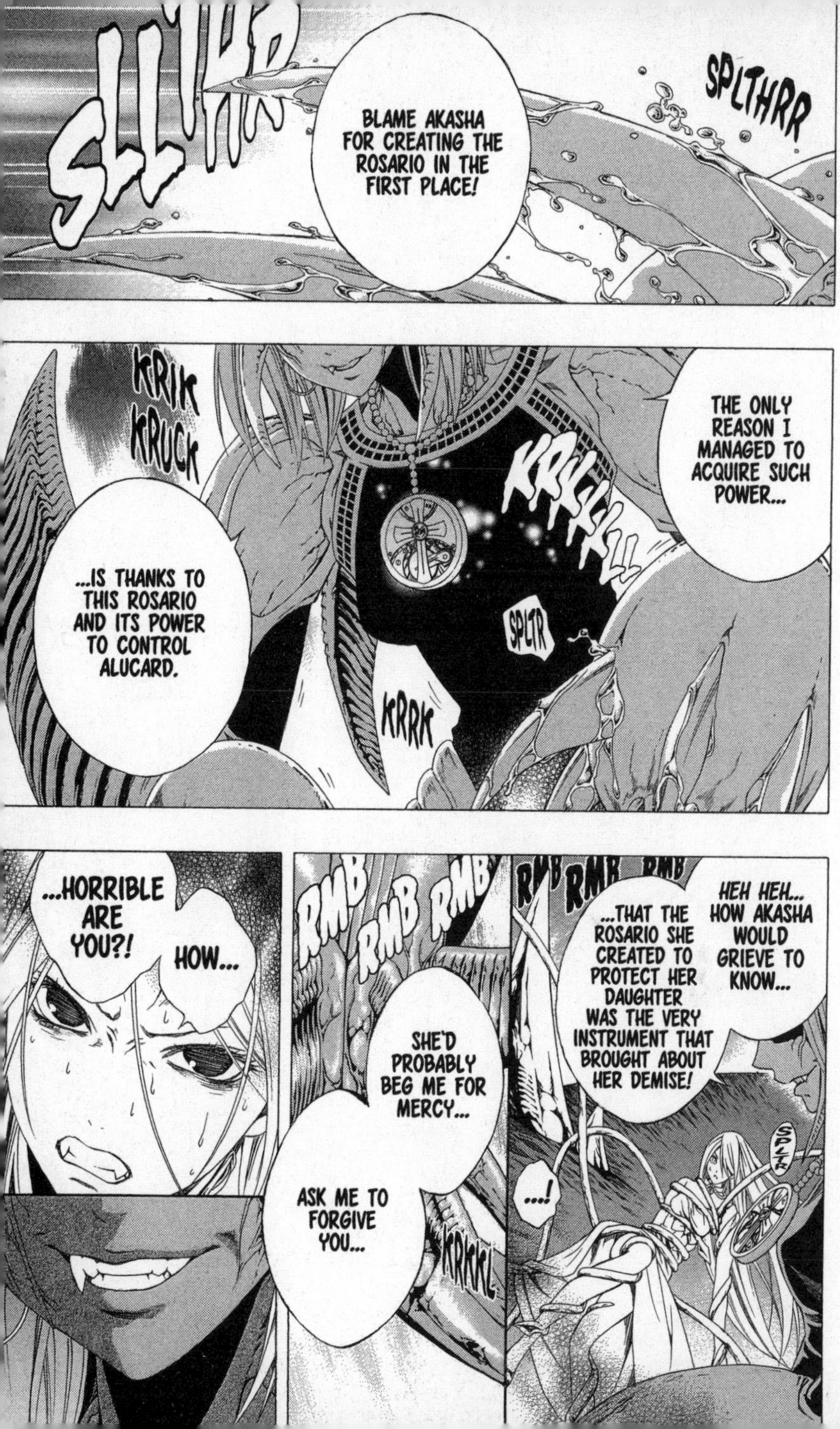
SPLTHRR
BLAME AKASHA FOR CREATING THE ROSARIO IN THE FIRST PLACE!
THE ONLY REASON I MANAGED TO ACQUIRE SUCH POWER...
SPLTR
KRIK KRUCK
...IS THANKS TO THIS ROSARIO AND ITS POWER TO CONTROL ALUCARD.
KRRK
HEH HEH... HOW AKASHA WOULD GRIEVE TO KNOW...
...THAT THE ROSARIO SHE CREATED TO PROTECT HER DAUGHTER WAS THE VERY INSTRUMENT THAT BROUGHT ABOUT HER DEMISE!
RMB RMB RMB
SPLTR
...!
RMB RMB RMB
SHE'D PROBABLY BEG ME FOR MERCY...
ASK ME TO FORGIVE YOU...
KRKKL
HOW...
...HORRIBLE ARE YOU?!

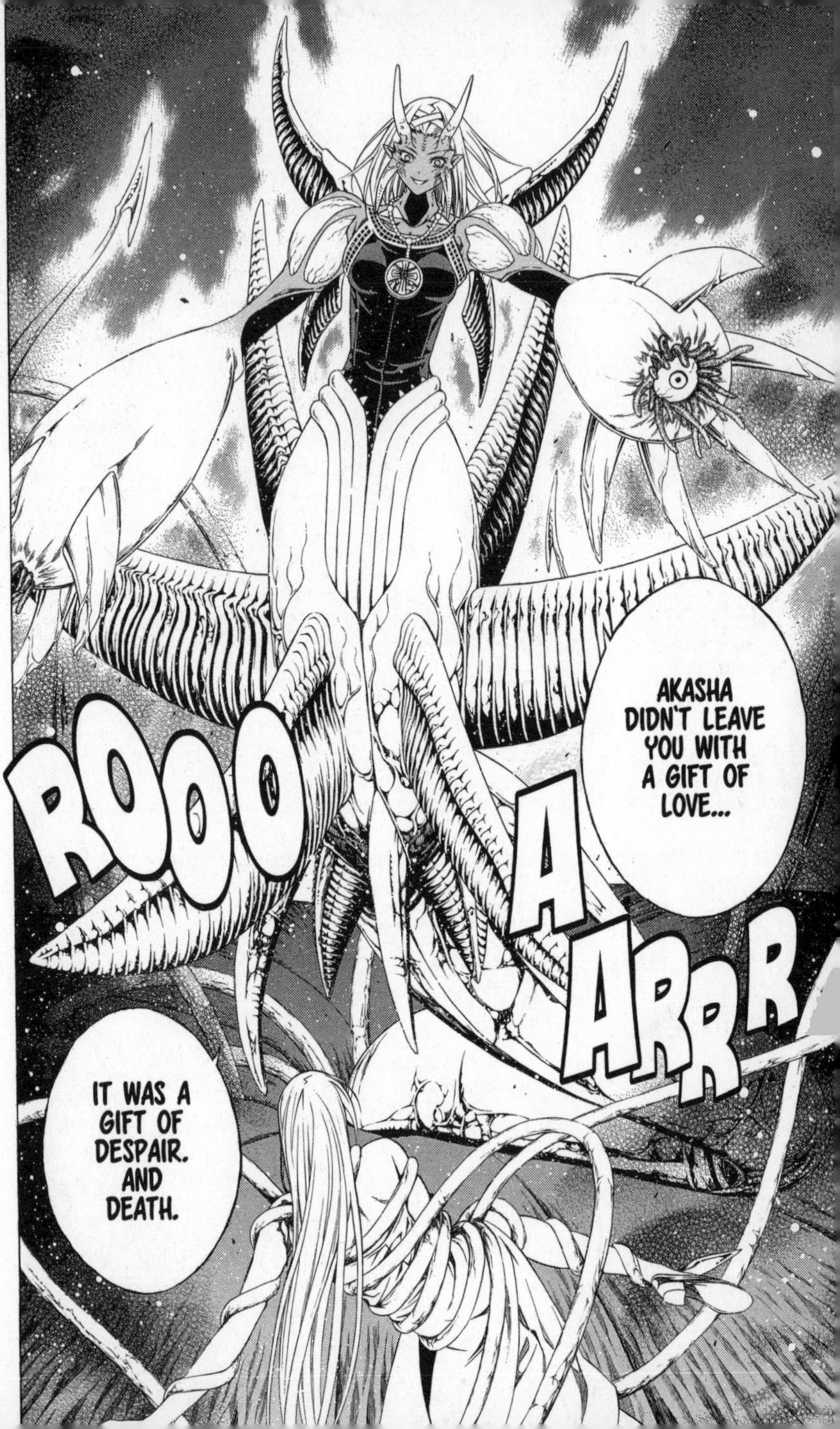
AKASHA DIDN'T LEAVE YOU WITH A GIFT OF LOVE...
ROOOAARRR
IT WAS A GIFT OF DESPAIR. AND DEATH.

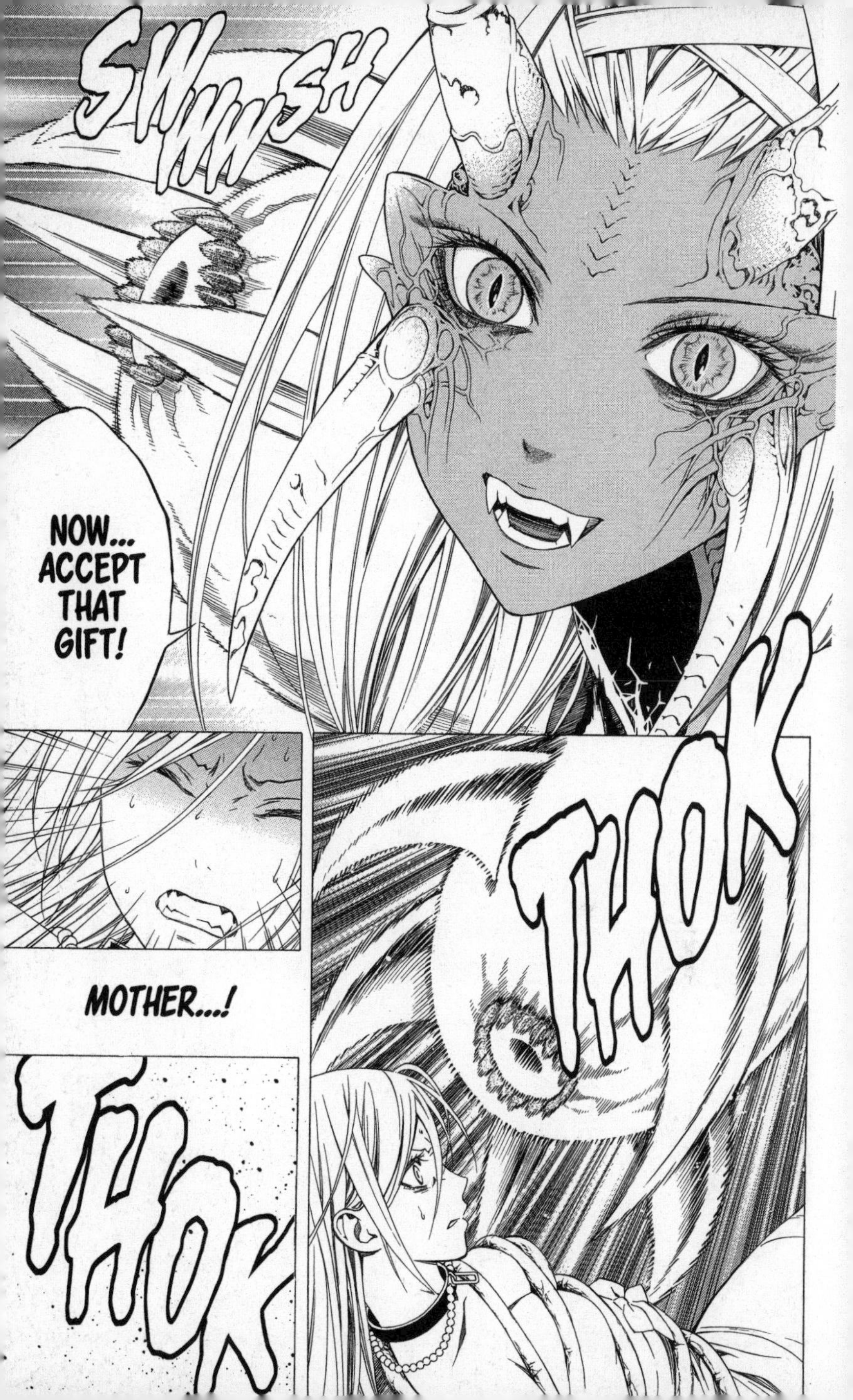
SWWWSH
NOW... ACCEPT THAT GIFT!
THOK
MOTHER...!
THOK

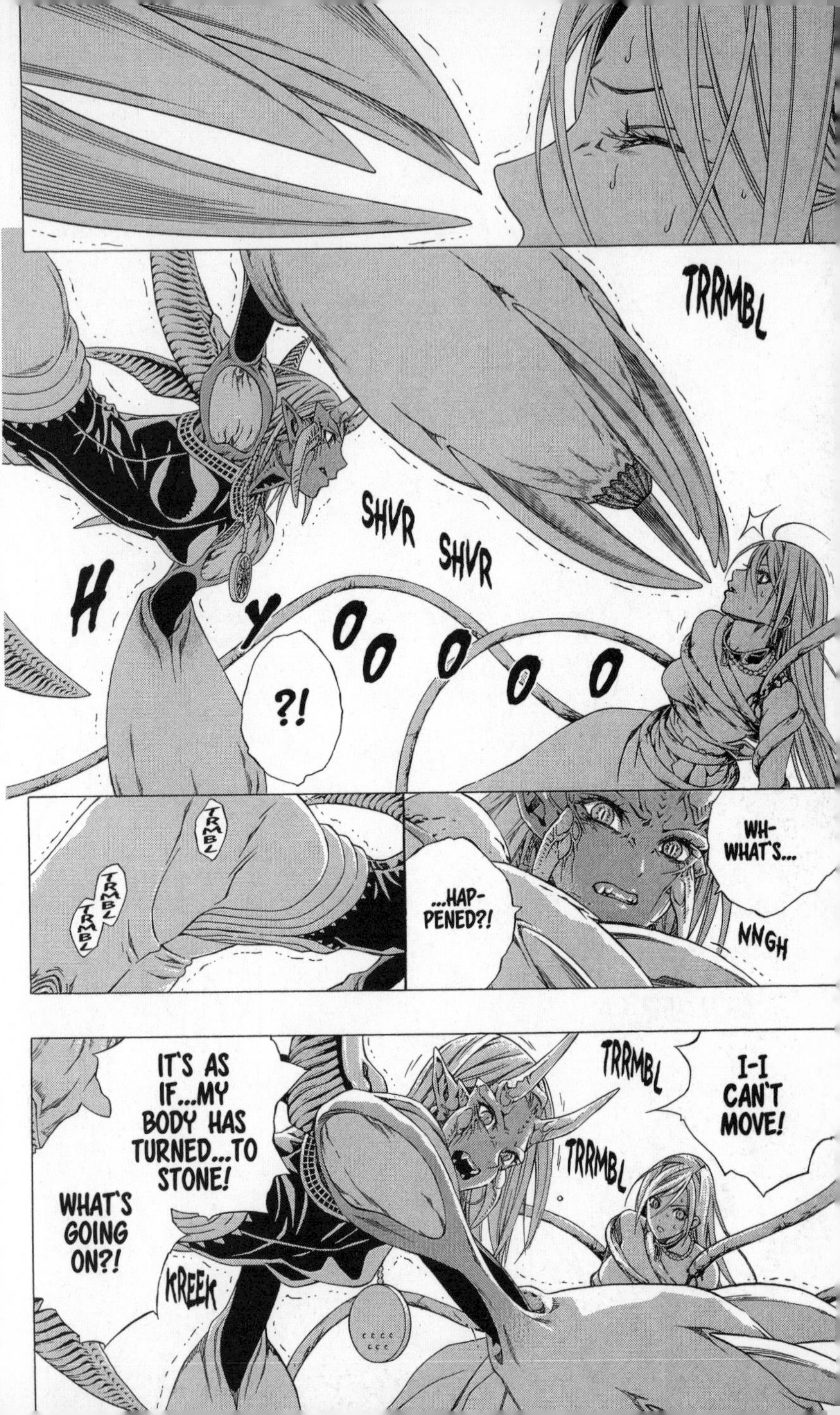
TRRMBL
SHVR SHVR
HYOOOOO
?!
WH- WHAT'S...
...HAP- PENED?!
NNGH
TRMBL
TRMBL
TRMBL
I-I CAN'T MOVE!
TRRMBL
TRRMBL
IT'S AS IF...MY BODY HAS TURNED...TO STONE!
WHAT'S GOING ON?!
KREEK
......

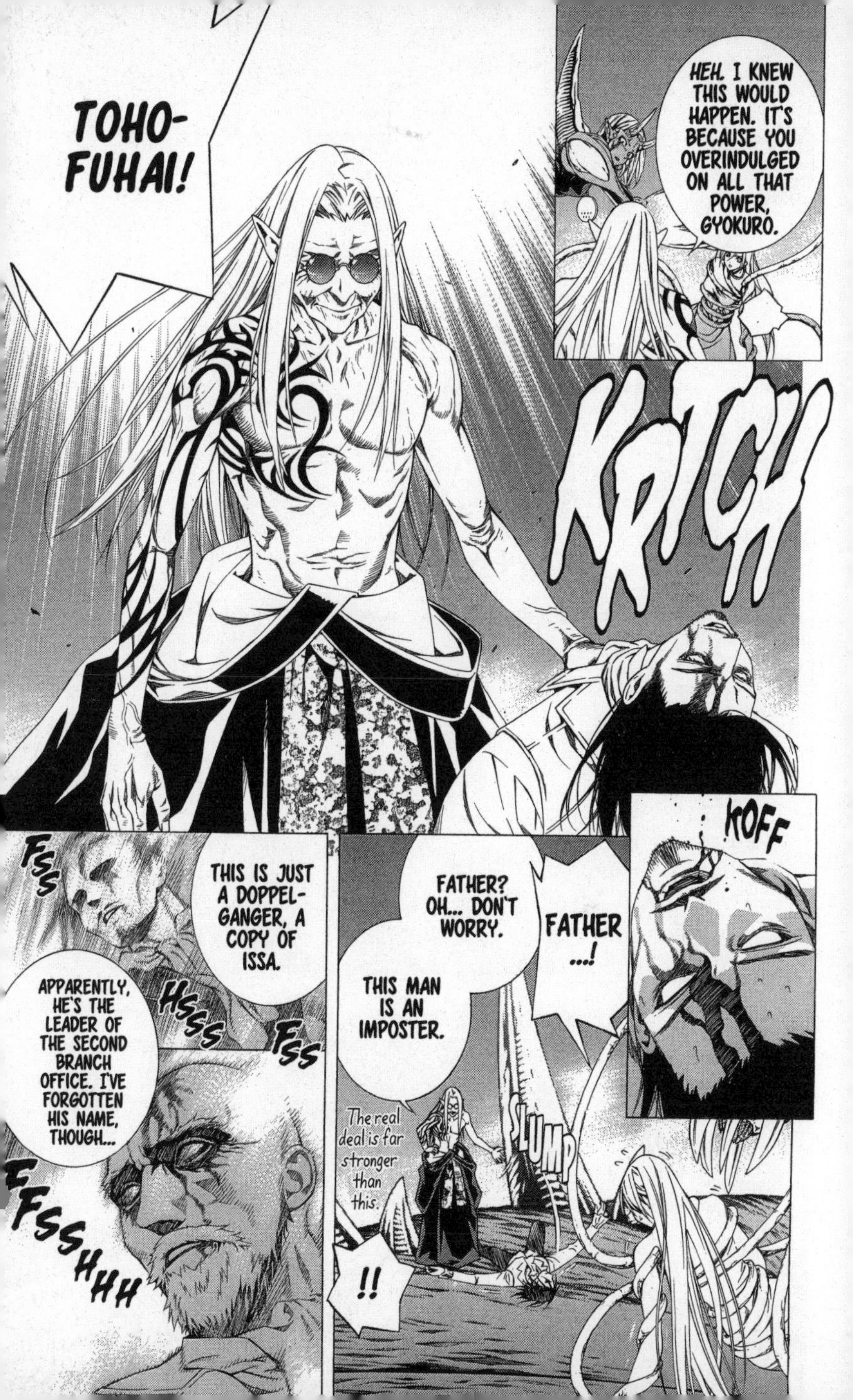
HEH. I KNEW THIS WOULD HAPPEN. IT'S BECAUSE YOU OVERINDULGED ON ALL THAT POWER, GYOKURO.
TOHO-FUHAI!
KRTCH
KOFF
FATHER...!
FATHER? OH... DON'T WORRY.
THIS MAN IS AN IMPOSTER.
The real deal is far stronger than this.
SLUMP
!!
FSS
THIS IS JUST A DOPPEL-GANGER, A COPY OF ISSA.
HSSS
FSS
APPARENTLY, HE'S THE LEADER OF THE SECOND BRANCH OFFICE. I'VE FORGOTTEN HIS NAME, THOUGH...
FFSSHHH

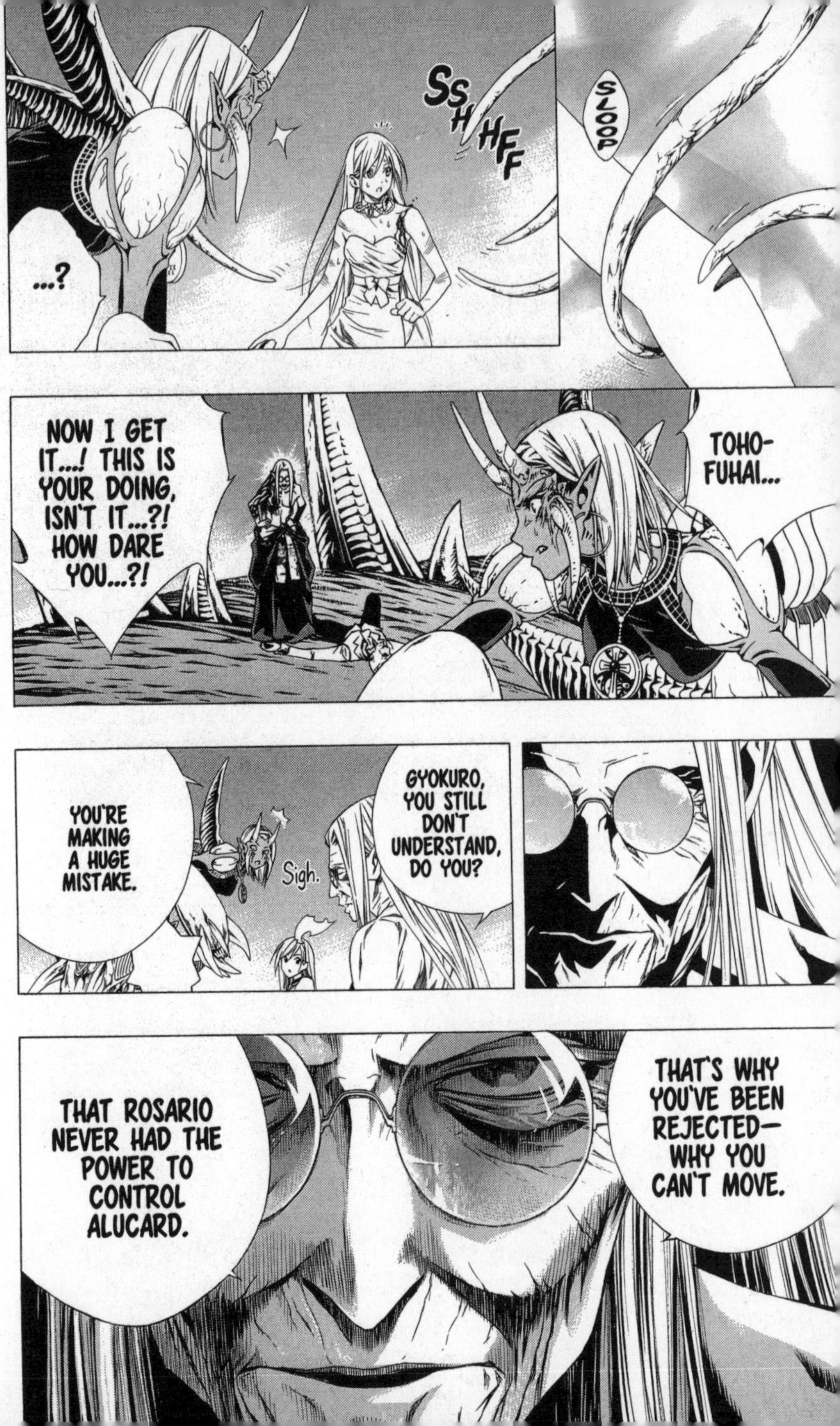
SLOOP
SSHHFF
...?
TOHO-FUHAI...
NOW I GET IT...! THIS IS YOUR DOING, ISN'T IT...?! HOW DARE YOU...?!
GYOKURO, YOU STILL DON'T UNDERSTAND, DO YOU?
Sigh.
YOU'RE MAKING A HUGE MISTAKE.
THAT'S WHY YOU'VE BEEN REJECTED— WHY YOU CAN'T MOVE.
THAT ROSARIO NEVER HAD THE POWER TO CONTROL ALUCARD.

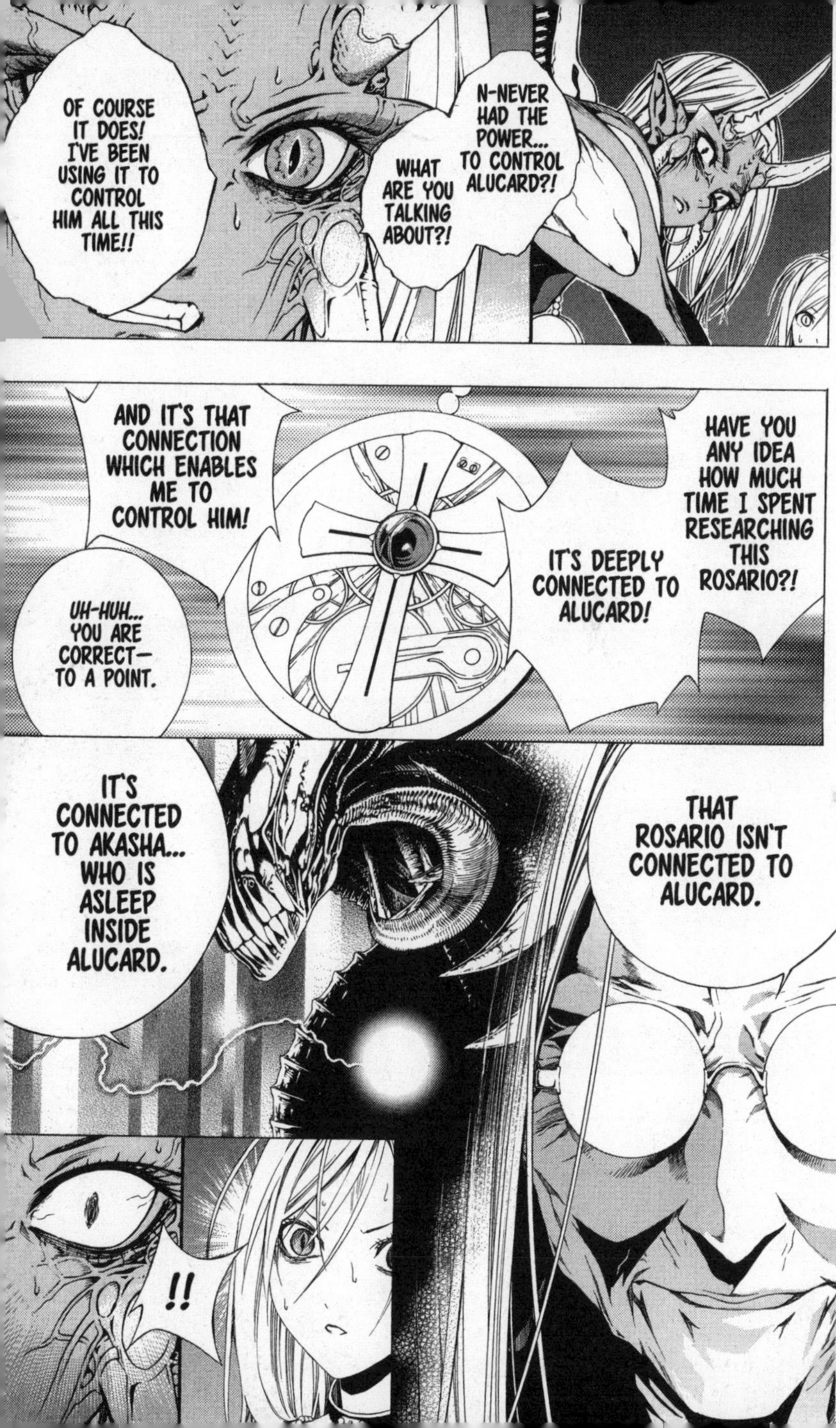
N-NEVER HAD THE POWER... TO CONTROL ALUCARD?!
WHAT ARE YOU TALKING ABOUT?!
OF COURSE IT DOES! I'VE BEEN USING IT TO CONTROL HIM ALL THIS TIME!!
HAVE YOU ANY IDEA HOW MUCH TIME I SPENT RESEARCHING THIS ROSARIO?!
IT'S DEEPLY CONNECTED TO ALUCARD!
AND IT'S THAT CONNECTION WHICH ENABLES ME TO CONTROL HIM!
UH-HUH... YOU ARE CORRECT— TO A POINT.
THAT ROSARIO ISN'T CONNECTED TO ALUCARD.
IT'S CONNECTED TO AKASHA... WHO IS ASLEEP INSIDE ALUCARD.
!!

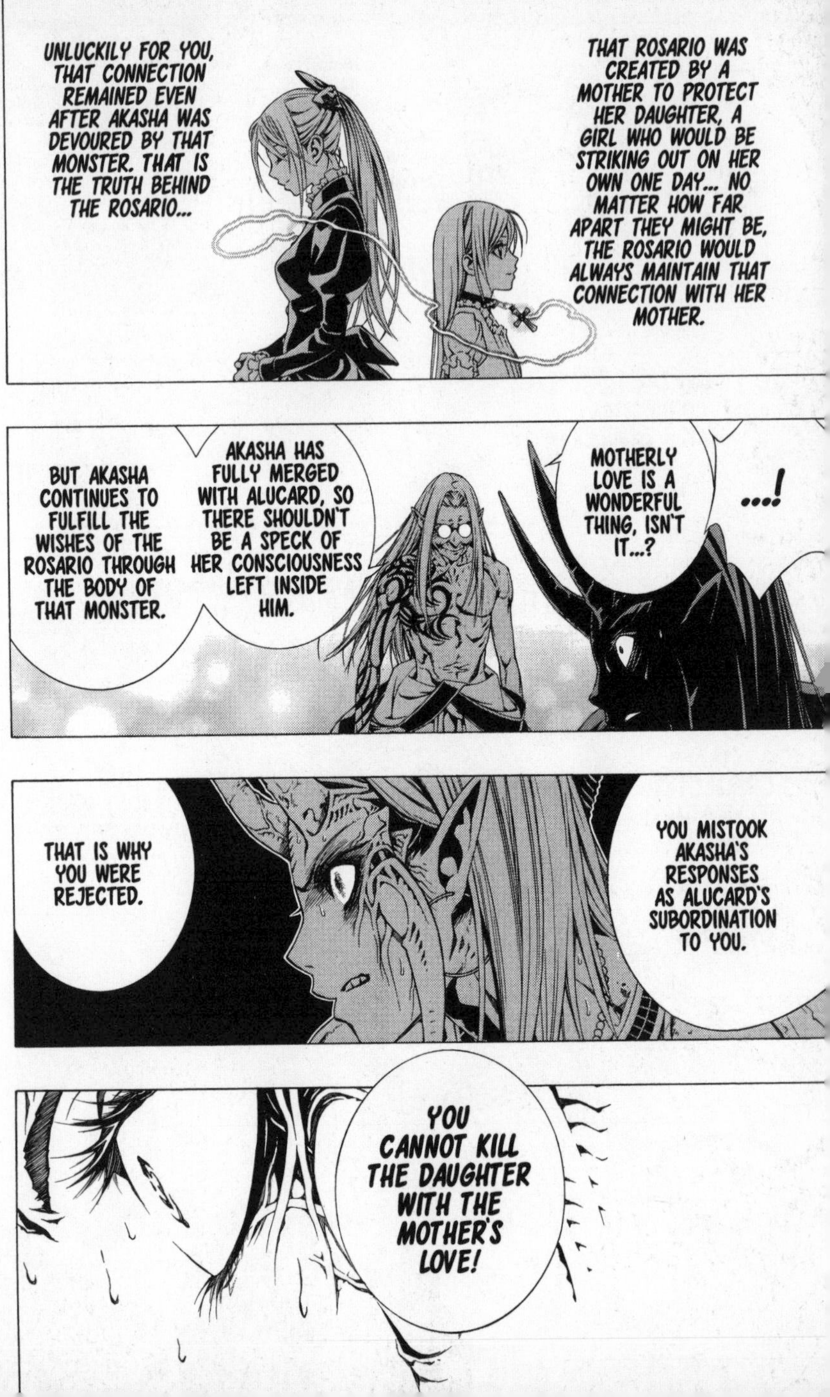
THAT ROSARIO WAS CREATED BY A MOTHER TO PROTECT HER DAUGHTER, A GIRL WHO WOULD BE STRIKING OUT ON HER OWN ONE DAY... NO MATTER HOW FAR APART THEY MIGHT BE, THE ROSARIO WOULD ALWAYS MAINTAIN THAT CONNECTION WITH HER MOTHER.
UNLUCKILY FOR YOU, THAT CONNECTION REMAINED EVEN AFTER AKASHA WAS DEVOURED BY THAT MONSTER. THAT IS THE TRUTH BEHIND THE ROSARIO...
MOTHERLY LOVE IS A WONDERFUL THING, ISN'T IT...?
...!
AKASHA HAS FULLY MERGED WITH ALUCARD, SO THERE SHOULDN'T BE A SPECK OF HER CONSCIOUSNESS LEFT INSIDE HIM.
BUT AKASHA CONTINUES TO FULFILL THE WISHES OF THE ROSARIO THROUGH THE BODY OF THAT MONSTER.
YOU MISTOOK AKASHA'S RESPONSES AS ALUCARD'S SUBORDINATION TO YOU.
THAT IS WHY YOU WERE REJECTED.
YOU CANNOT KILL THE DAUGHTER WITH THE MOTHER'S LOVE!

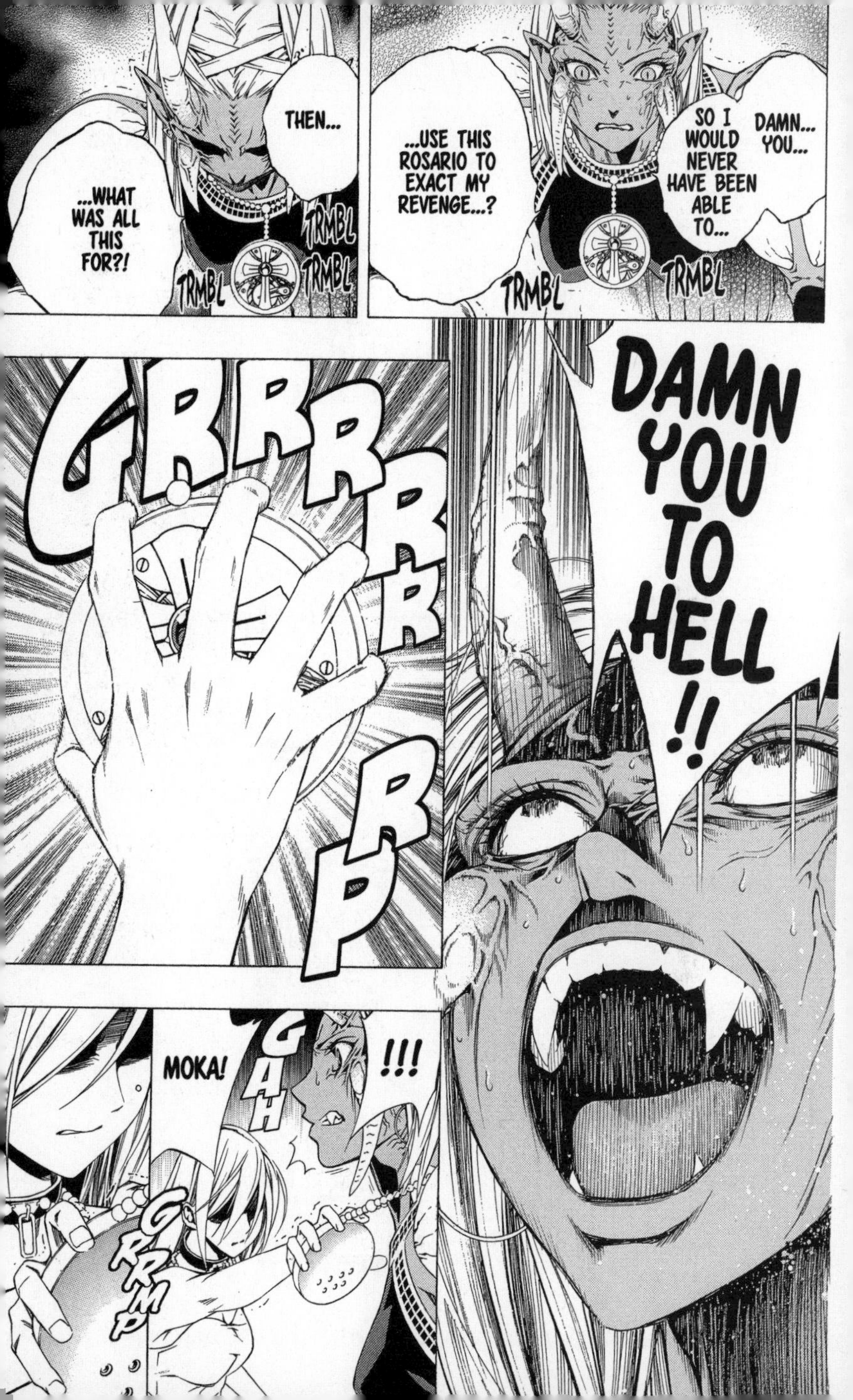
DAMN... YOU...
SO I WOULD NEVER HAVE BEEN ABLE TO...
...USE THIS ROSARIO TO EXACT MY REVENGE...?
TRMBL
TRMBL
THEN...
...WHAT WAS ALL THIS FOR?!
TRMBL
TRMBL
TRMBL
DAMN YOU TO HELL!!
GRRRRRRP
!!!
GAH
MOKA!
GRRMP

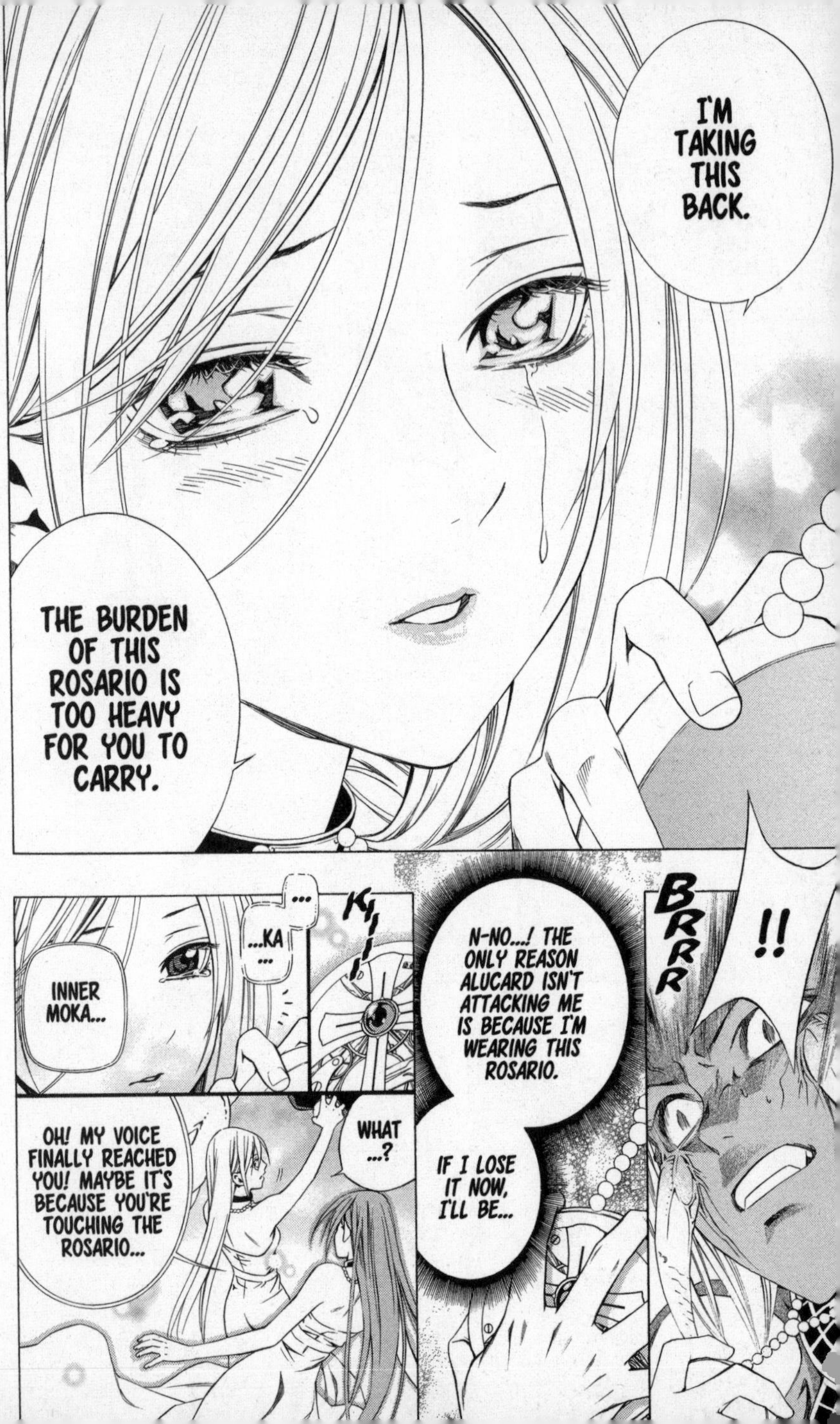

I'M TAKING THIS BACK.
THE BURDEN OF THIS ROSARIO IS TOO HEAVY FOR YOU TO CARRY.
BRRR
!!
N-NO...! THE ONLY REASON ALUCARD ISN'T ATTACKING ME IS BECAUSE I'M WEARING THIS ROSARIO.
IF I LOSE IT NOW, I'LL BE...
KYIII
...
...KA ...
INNER MOKA...
WHAT ...?
OH! MY VOICE FINALLY REACHED YOU! MAYBE IT'S BECAUSE YOU'RE TOUCHING THE ROSARIO...

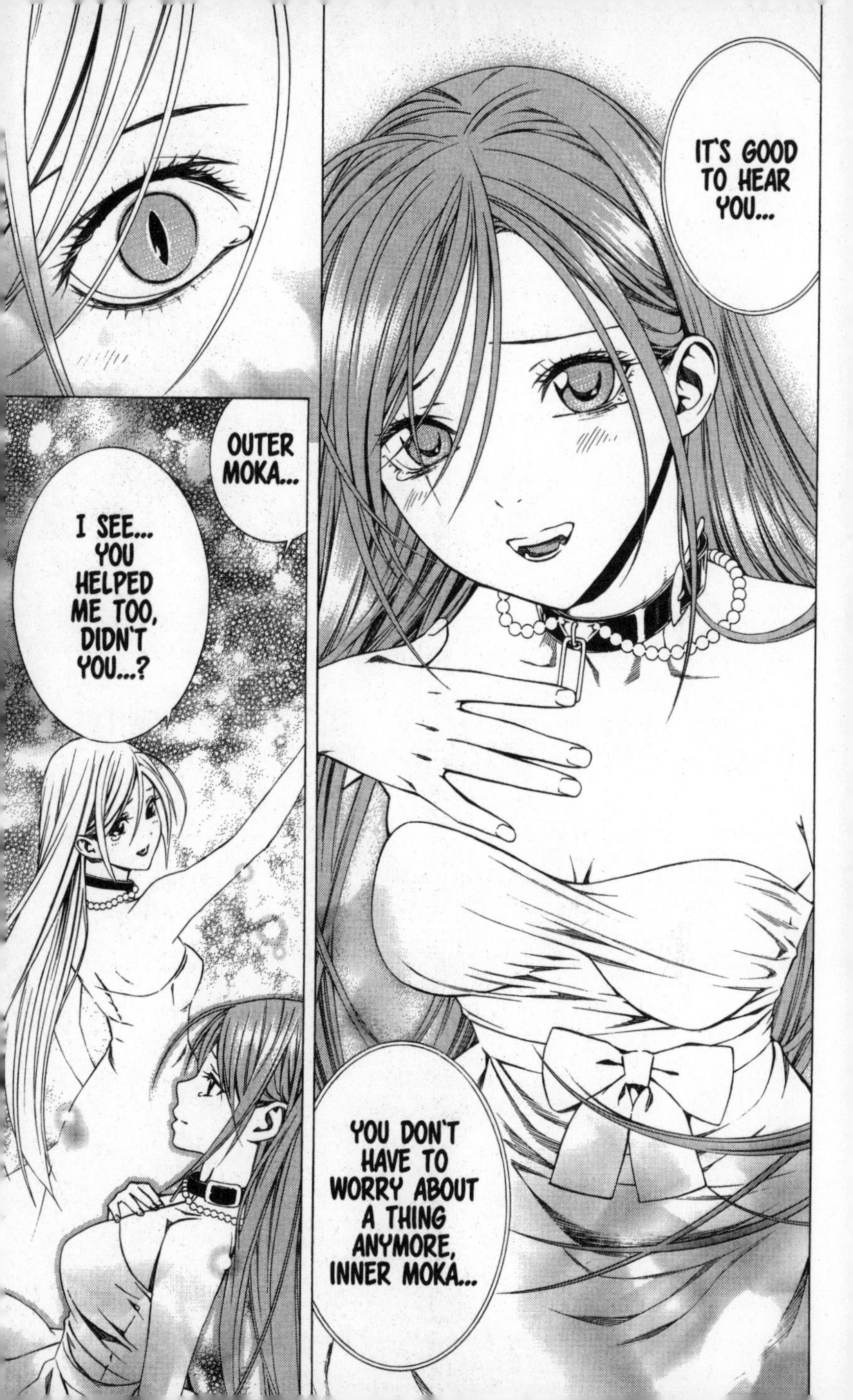
IT'S GOOD TO HEAR YOU...
YOU DON'T HAVE TO WORRY ABOUT A THING ANYMORE, INNER MOKA...
OUTER MOKA...
I SEE... YOU HELPED ME TOO, DIDN'T YOU...?

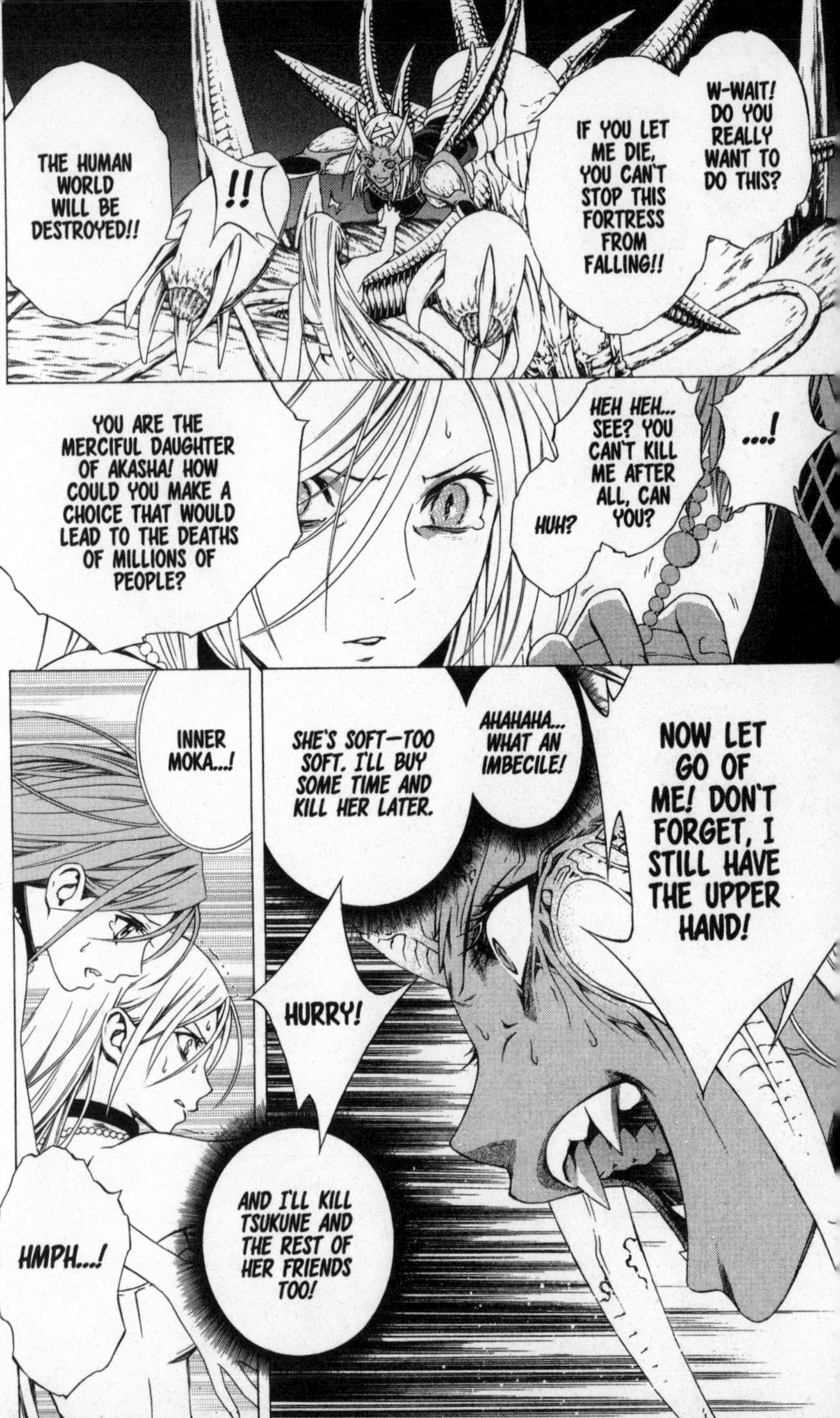
W-WAIT! DO YOU REALLY WANT TO DO THIS?
IF YOU LET ME DIE, YOU CAN'T STOP THIS FORTRESS FROM FALLING!!
!!
THE HUMAN WORLD WILL BE DESTROYED!!
...!
HEH HEH... SEE? YOU CAN'T KILL ME AFTER ALL, CAN YOU?
HUH?
YOU ARE THE MERCIFUL DAUGHTER OF AKASHA! HOW COULD YOU MAKE A CHOICE THAT WOULD LEAD TO THE DEATHS OF MILLIONS OF PEOPLE?
NOW LET GO OF ME! DON'T FORGET, I STILL HAVE THE UPPER HAND!
AHAHAHA... WHAT AN IMBECILE!
SHE'S SOFT—TOO SOFT. I'LL BUY SOME TIME AND KILL HER LATER.
HURRY!
AND I'LL KILL TSUKUNE AND THE REST OF HER FRIENDS TOO!
INNER MOKA...!
HMPH...!

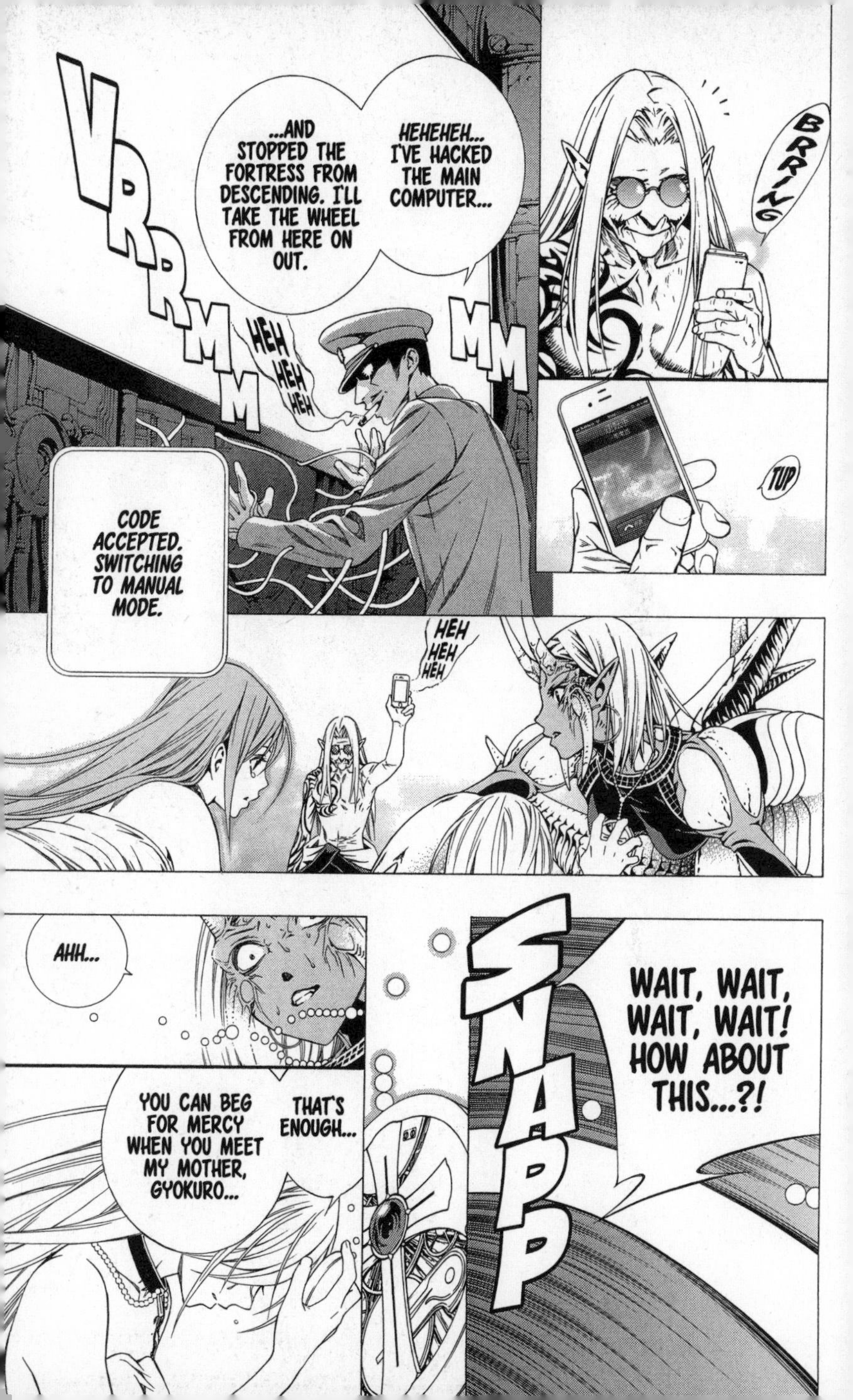
BRRING
TUP
VRRRMMMM
HEHEHEH... I'VE HACKED THE MAIN COMPUTER...
...AND STOPPED THE FORTRESS FROM DESCENDING. I'LL TAKE THE WHEEL FROM HERE ON OUT.
MM
HEH HEH HEH
CODE ACCEPTED. SWITCHING TO MANUAL MODE.
HEH HEH HEH
SNAPP
WAIT, WAIT, WAIT, WAIT! HOW ABOUT THIS...?!
AHH...
THAT'S ENOUGH...
YOU CAN BEG FOR MERCY WHEN YOU MEET MY MOTHER, GYOKURO...

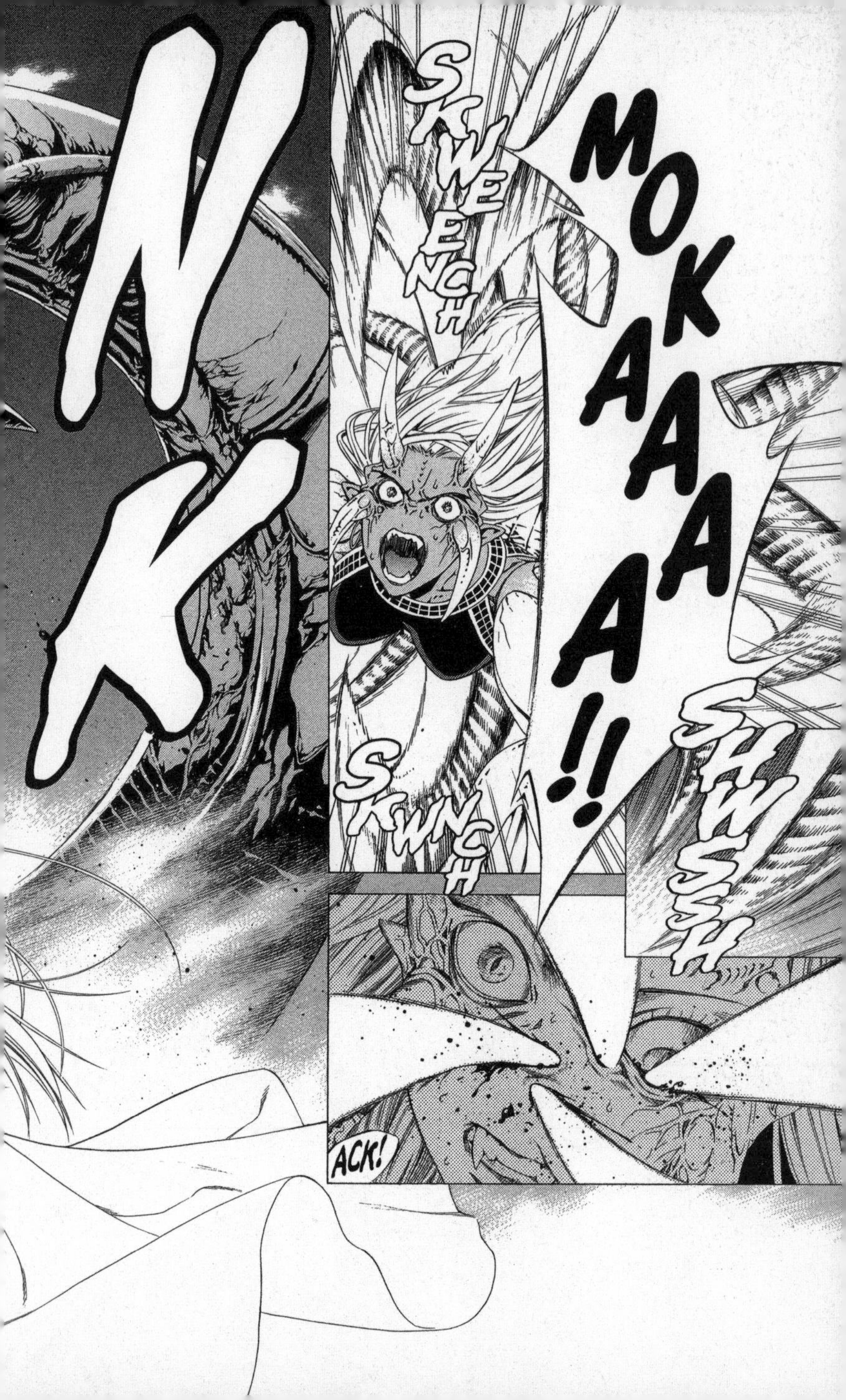
MOKAAAAA!!
SKWEENCH
SKWNCH
SHWSSH
ACK!
NK

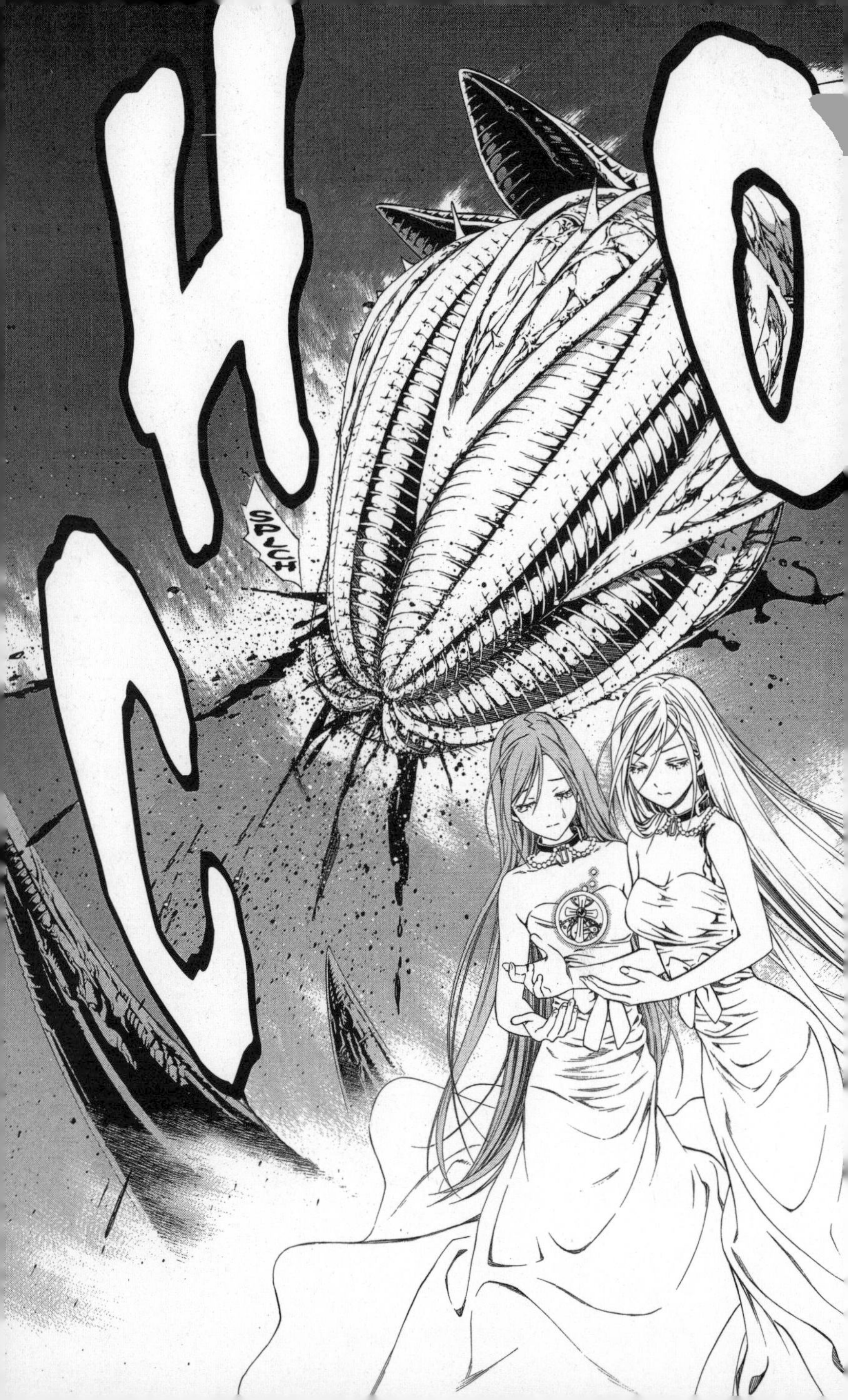
SPLCH

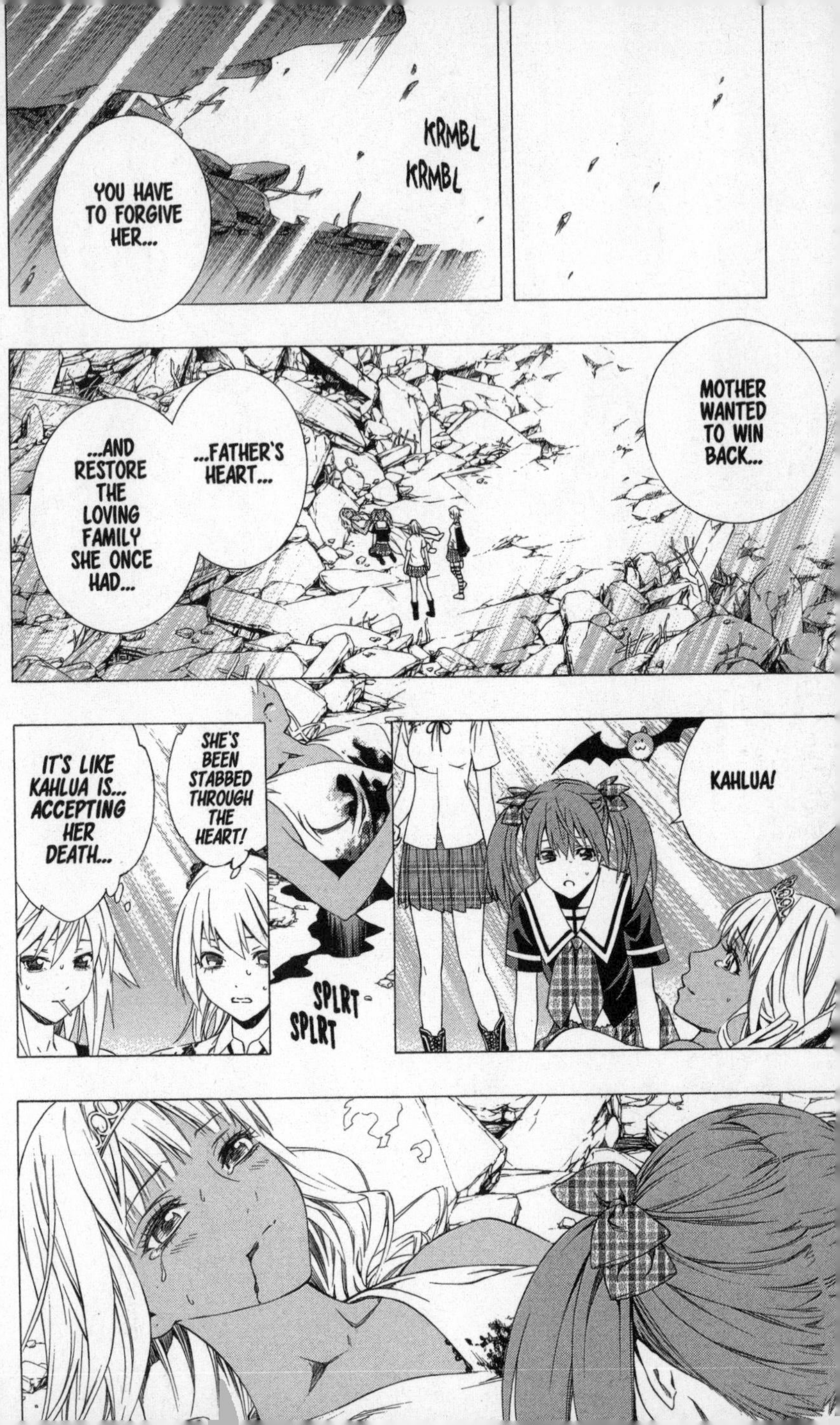
YOU HAVE TO FORGIVE HER...
KRMBL
KRMBL
MOTHER WANTED TO WIN BACK...
...FATHER'S HEART...
...AND RESTORE THE LOVING FAMILY SHE ONCE HAD...
KAHLUA!
SHE'S BEEN STABBED THROUGH THE HEART!
IT'S LIKE KAHLUA IS... ACCEPTING HER DEATH...
SPLRT
SPLRT

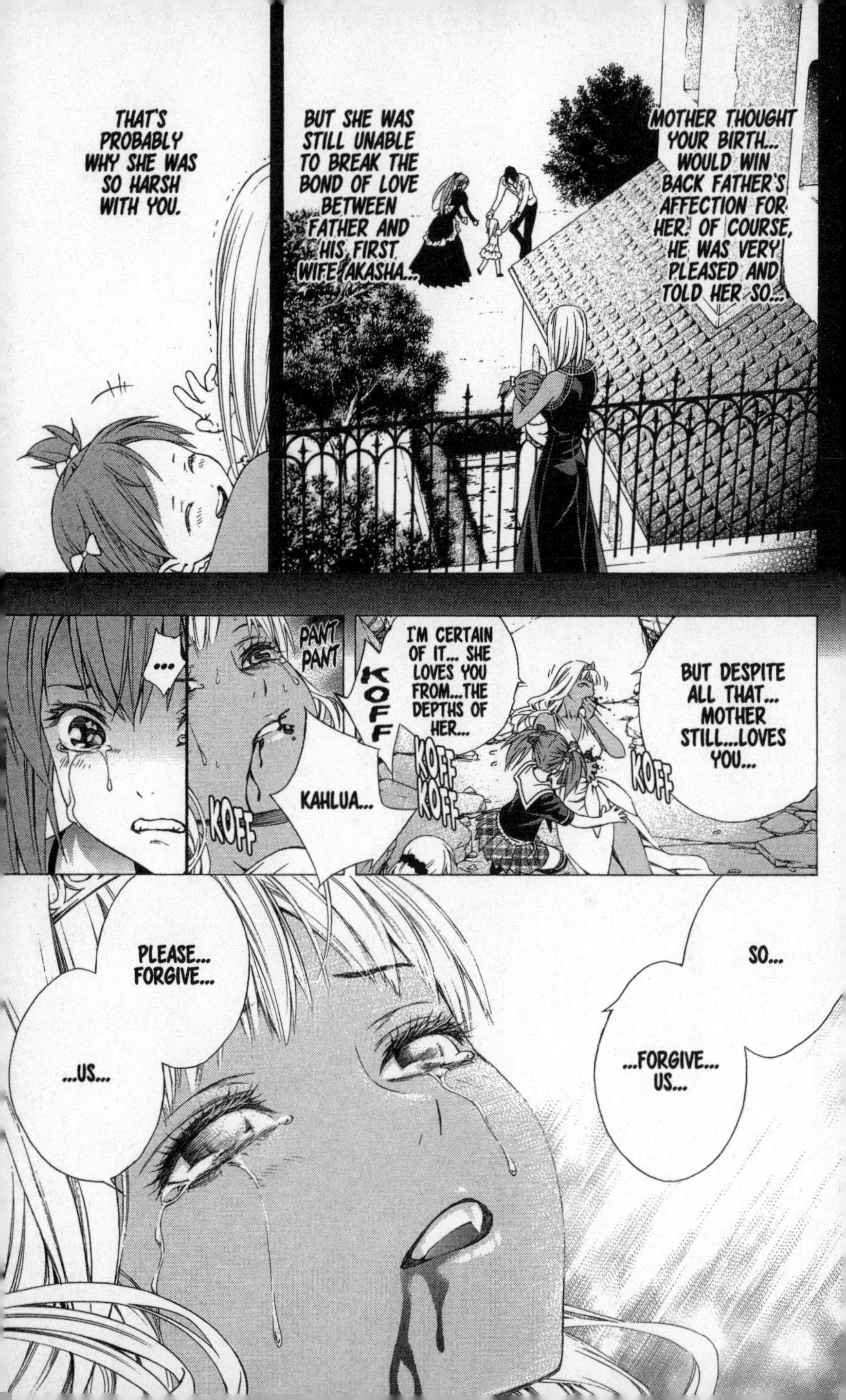

MOTHER THOUGHT YOUR BIRTH... WOULD WIN BACK FATHER'S AFFECTION FOR HER. OF COURSE, HE WAS VERY PLEASED AND TOLD HER SO...
BUT SHE WAS STILL UNABLE TO BREAK THE BOND OF LOVE BETWEEN FATHER AND HIS FIRST WIFE AKASHA...
THAT'S PROBABLY WHY SHE WAS SO HARSH WITH YOU.
BUT DESPITE ALL THAT... MOTHER STILL...LOVES YOU...
KOFF
KOFF KOFF
I'M CERTAIN OF IT... SHE LOVES YOU FROM...THE DEPTHS OF HER...
KOFF
PANT PANT
KAHLUA...
KOFF
...
SO...
...FORGIVE... US...
PLEASE... FORGIVE...
...US...

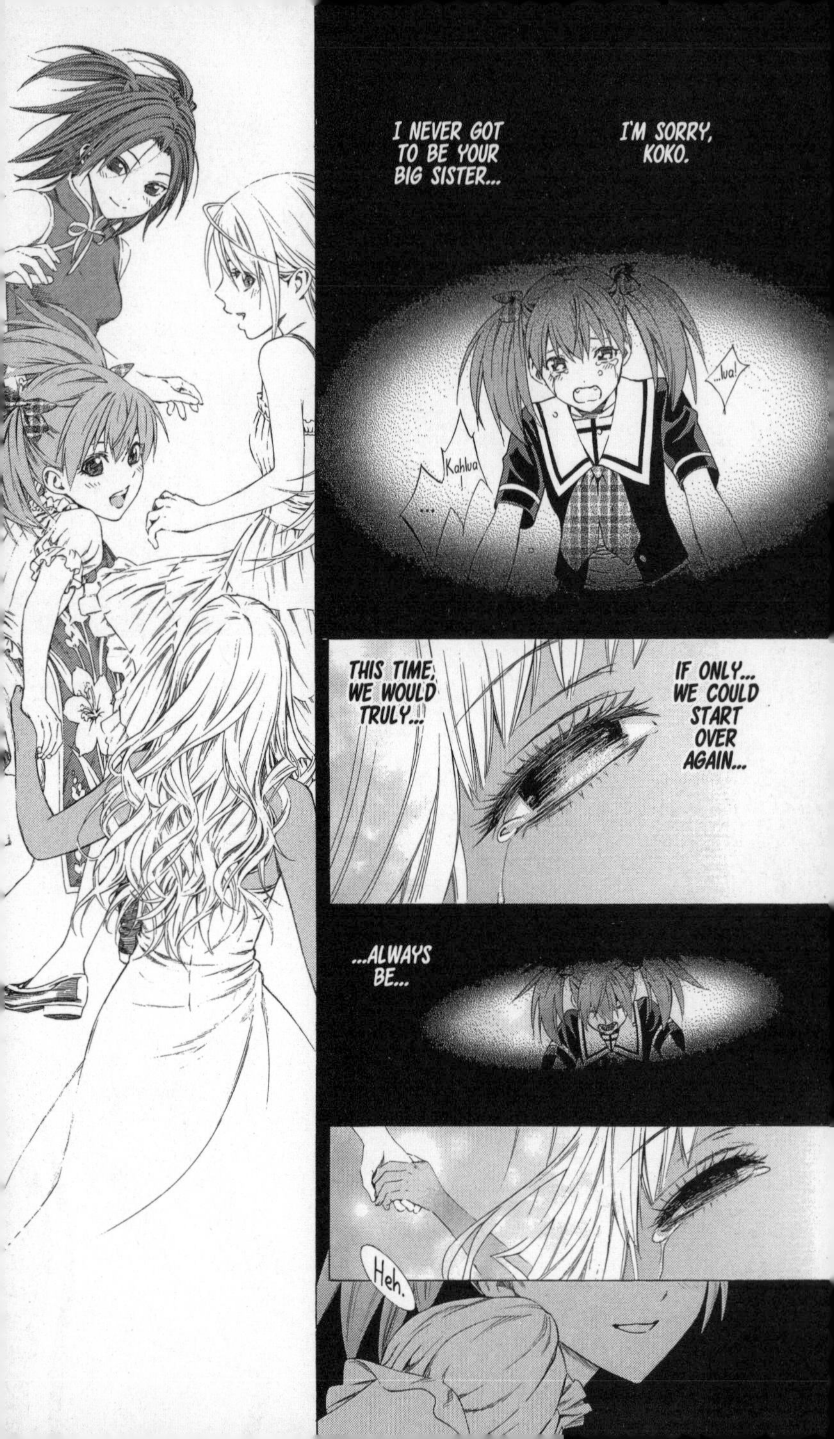
I'M SORRY, KOKO.
I NEVER GOT TO BE YOUR BIG SISTER...
...lua!
Kahlua!
...
IF ONLY... WE COULD START OVER AGAIN...
THIS TIME, WE WOULD TRULY...
...ALWAYS BE...
Heh.

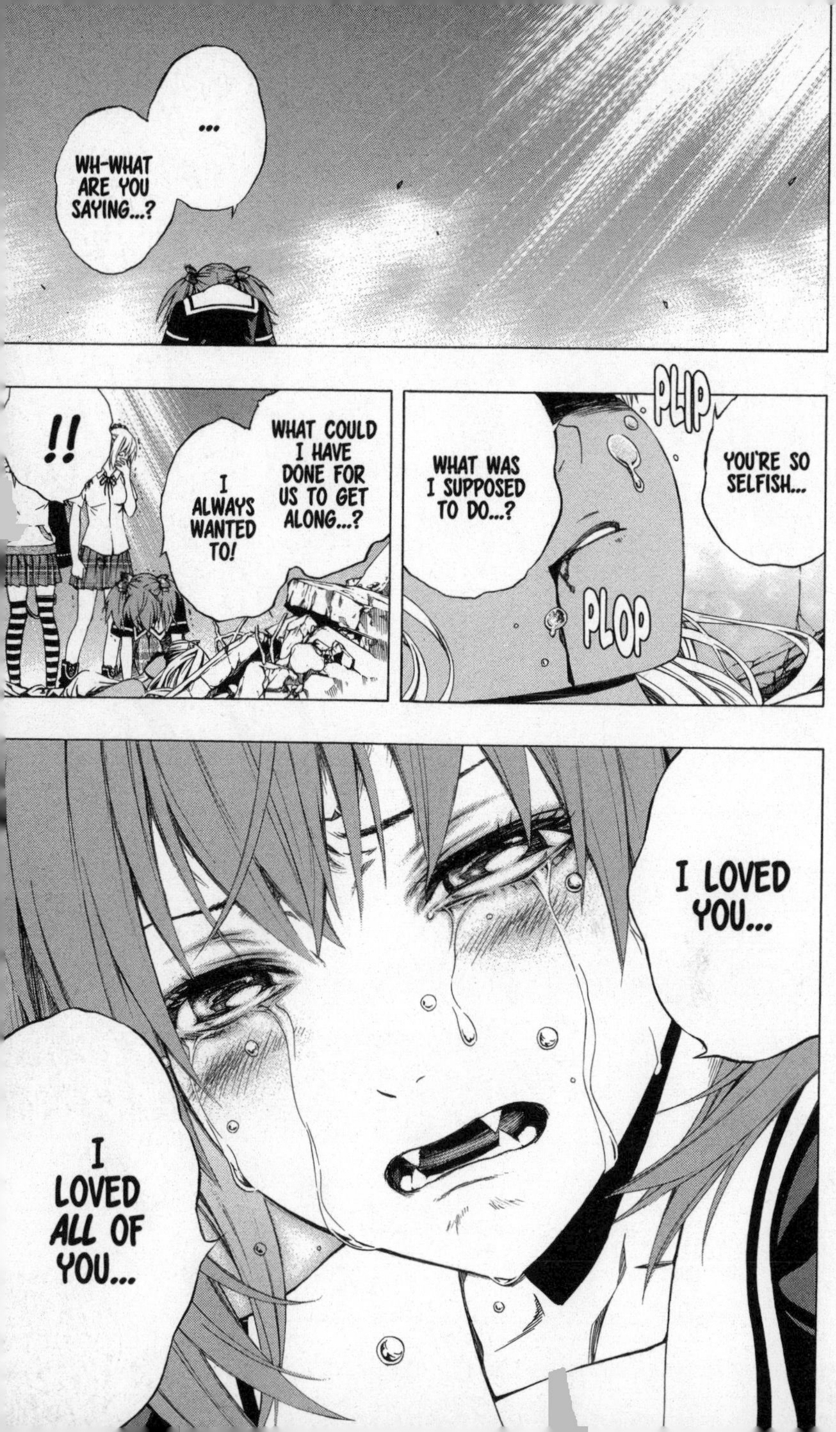
...
WH-WHAT ARE YOU SAYING...?
PLIP
YOU'RE SO SELFISH...
WHAT WAS I SUPPOSED TO DO...?
PLOP
WHAT COULD I HAVE DONE FOR US TO GET ALONG...?
I ALWAYS WANTED TO!
!!
I LOVED YOU...
I LOVED ALL OF YOU...

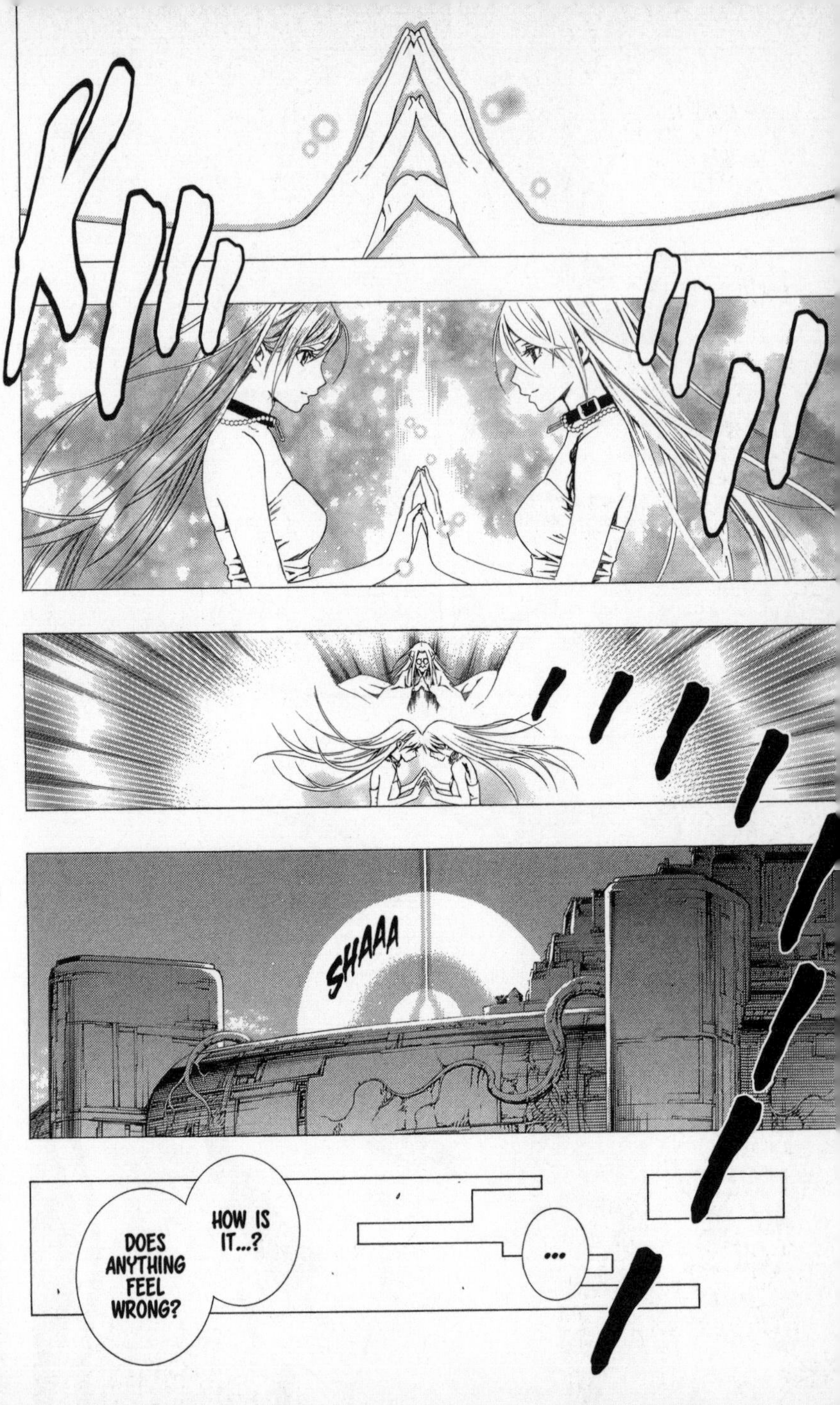
SHAAA
HOW IS IT...?
DOES ANYTHING FEEL WRONG?
...

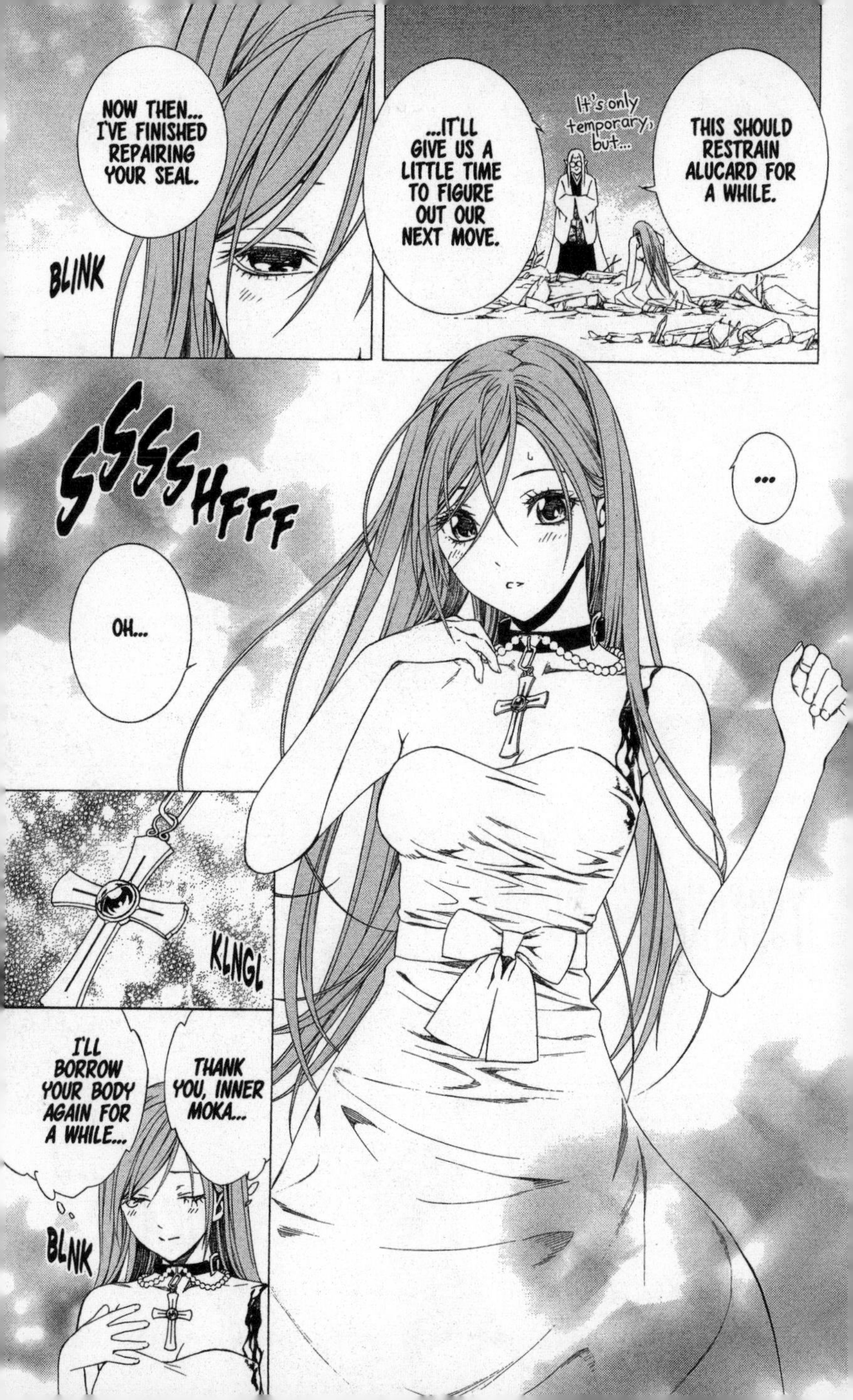
THIS SHOULD RESTRAIN ALUCARD FOR A WHILE.
It's only temporary, but...
...IT'LL GIVE US A LITTLE TIME TO FIGURE OUT OUR NEXT MOVE.
NOW THEN... I'VE FINISHED REPAIRING YOUR SEAL.
BLINK
...
SSSSHFFF
OH...
KLNGL
THANK YOU, INNER MOKA...
I'LL BORROW YOUR BODY AGAIN FOR A WHILE...
BLNK

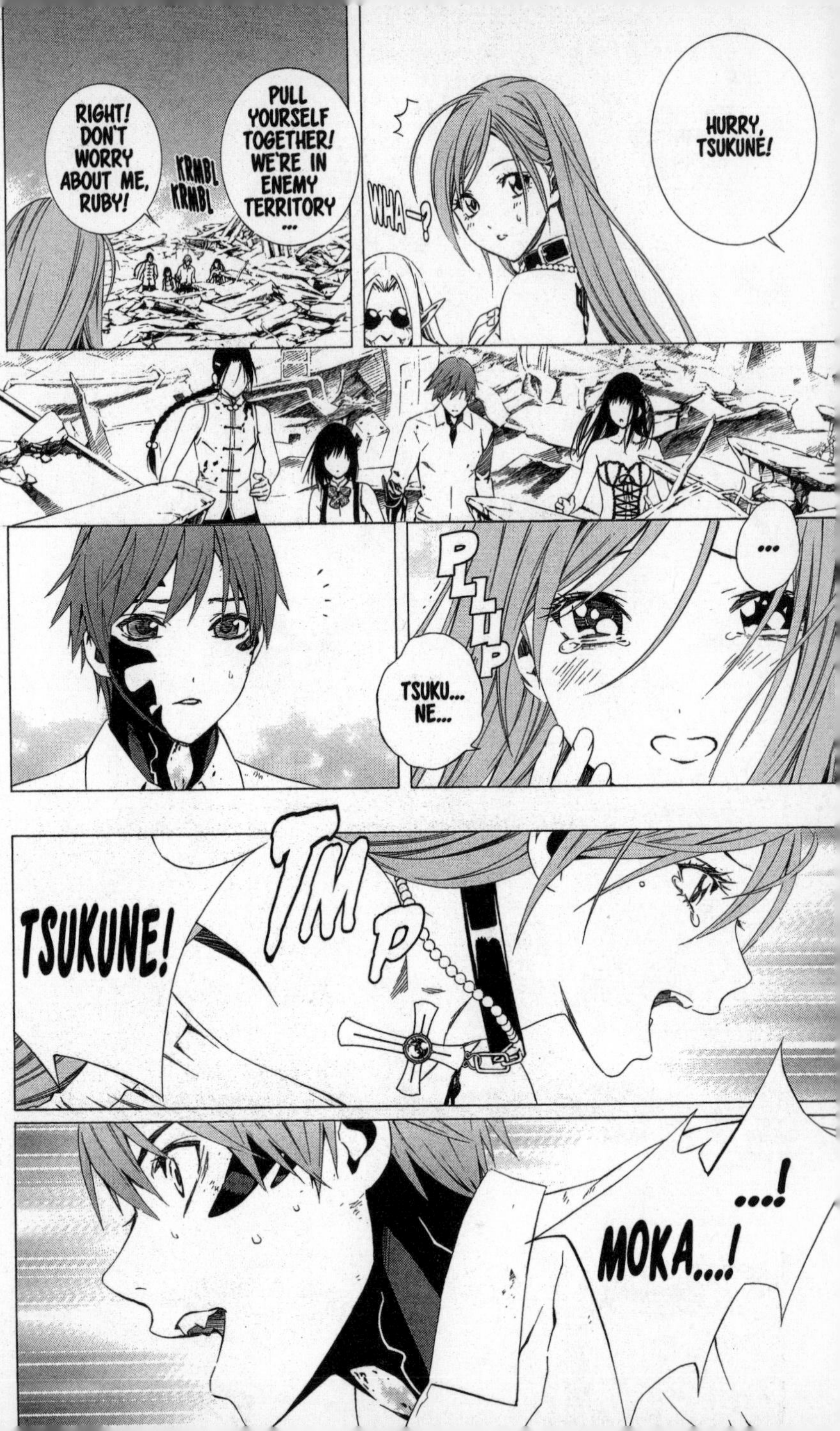
HURRY, TSUKUNE!
WHA--?
PULL YOURSELF TOGETHER! WE'RE IN ENEMY TERRITORY ...
KRMBL KRMBL
RIGHT! DON'T WORRY ABOUT ME, RUBY!
...
PLLUP
TSUKU... NE...
TMP
TSUKUNE!
...!
MOKA...!

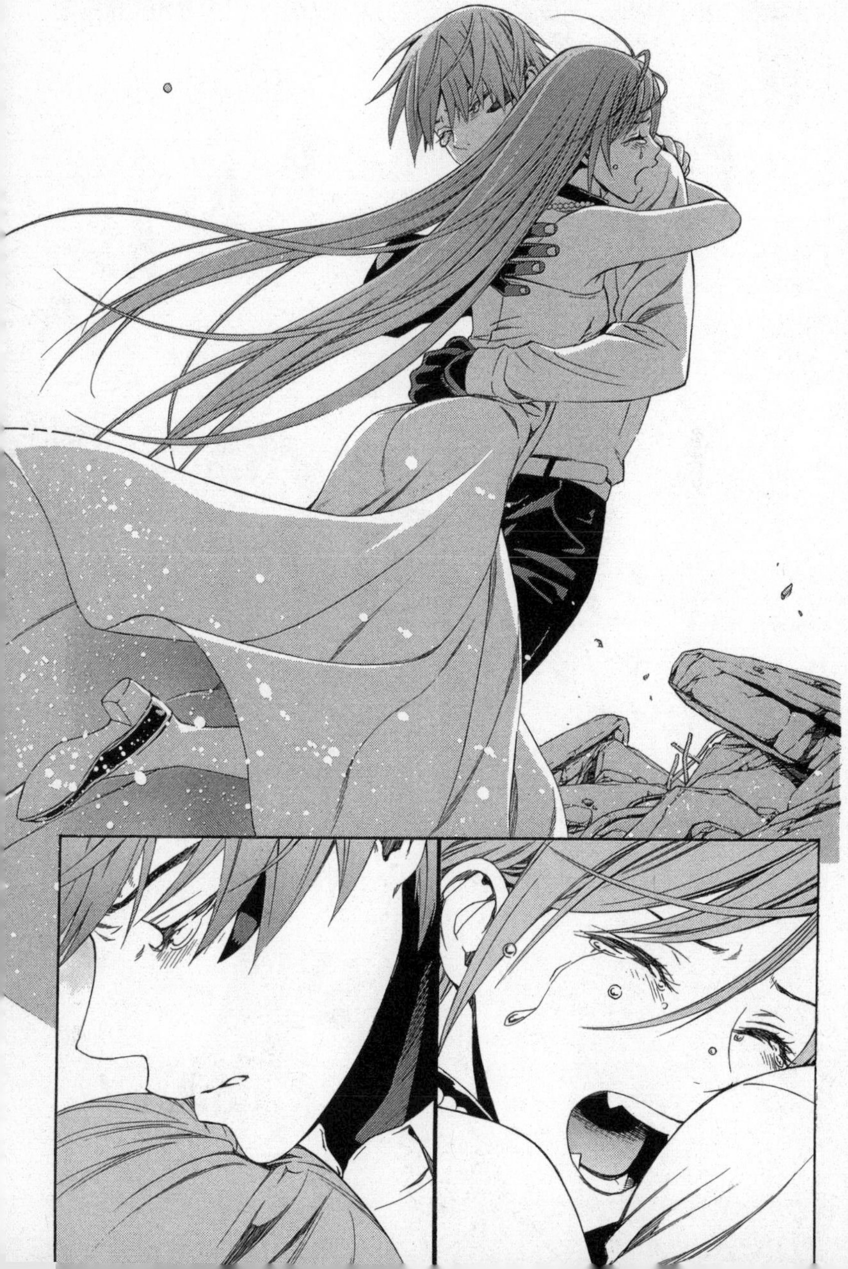

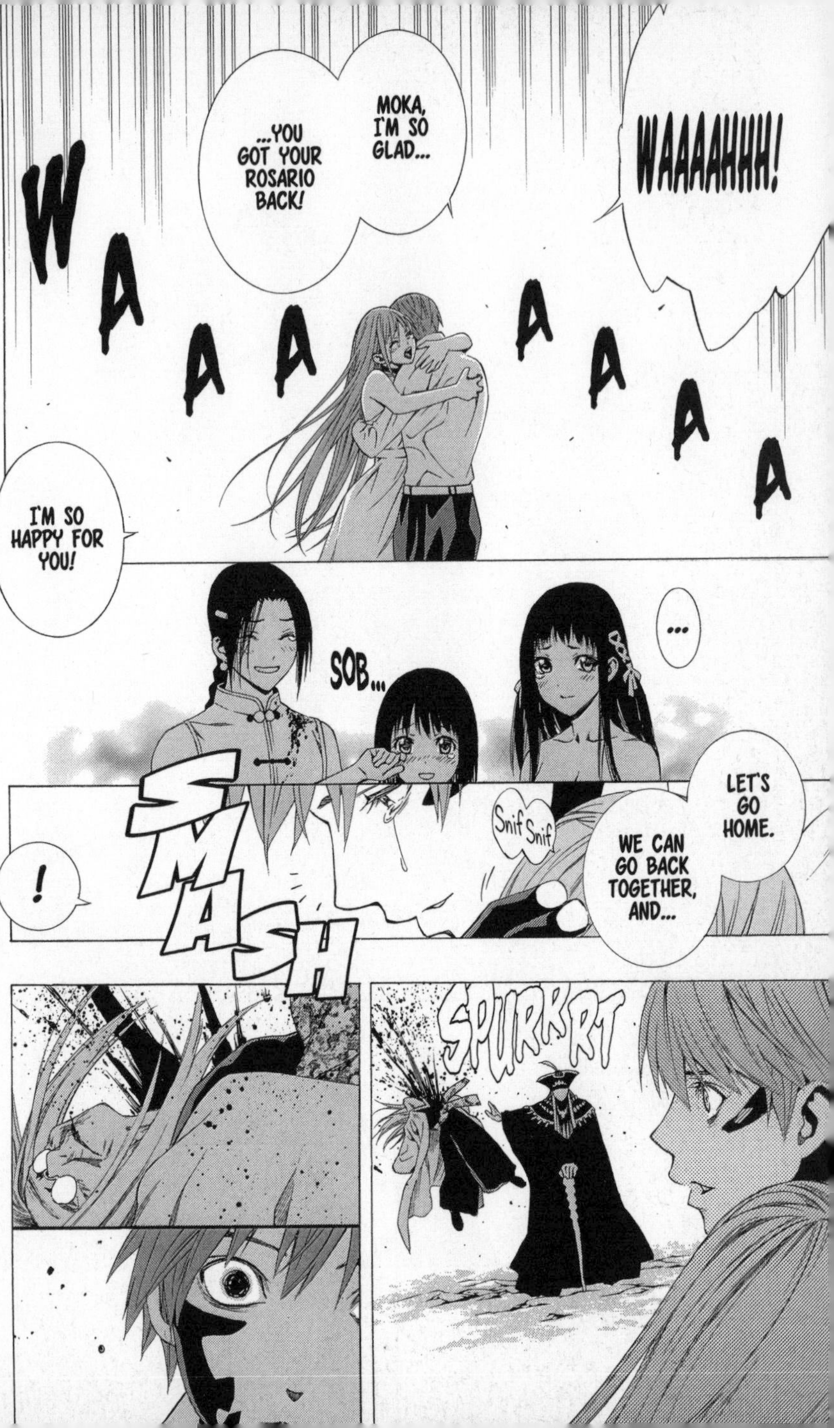
WAAAAHHH!
MOKA, I'M SO GLAD...
...YOU GOT YOUR ROSARIO BACK!
WAAAAAAA
I'M SO HAPPY FOR YOU!
...
SOB...
LET'S GO HOME.
WE CAN GO BACK TOGETHER, AND...
Snif Snif
SMASH
!
SPURRRT

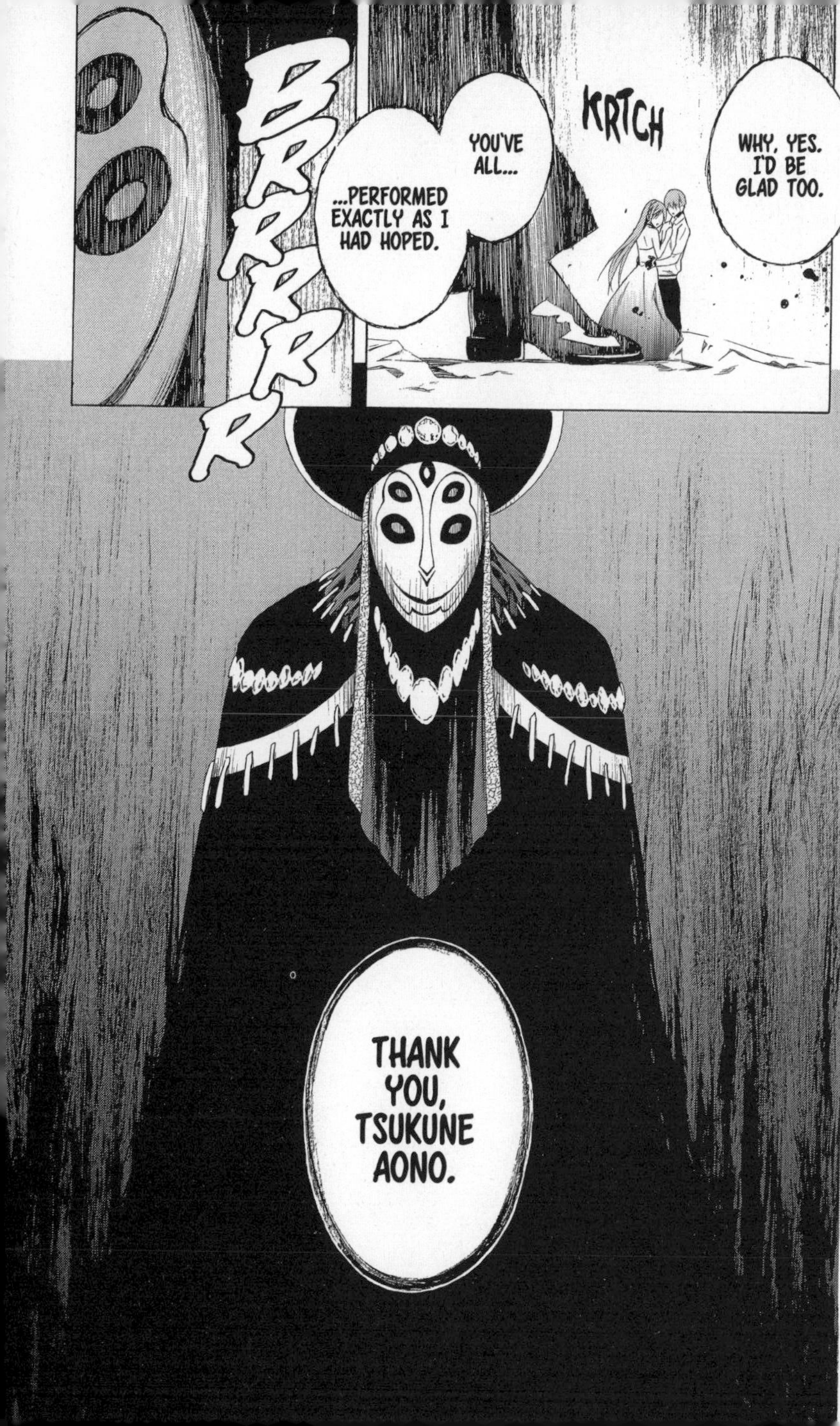
WHY, YES. I'D BE GLAD TOO.
KRTCH
YOU'VE ALL...
...PERFORMED EXACTLY AS I HAD HOPED.
BRRRRR
THANK YOU, TSUKUNE AONO.

65: The End of the World

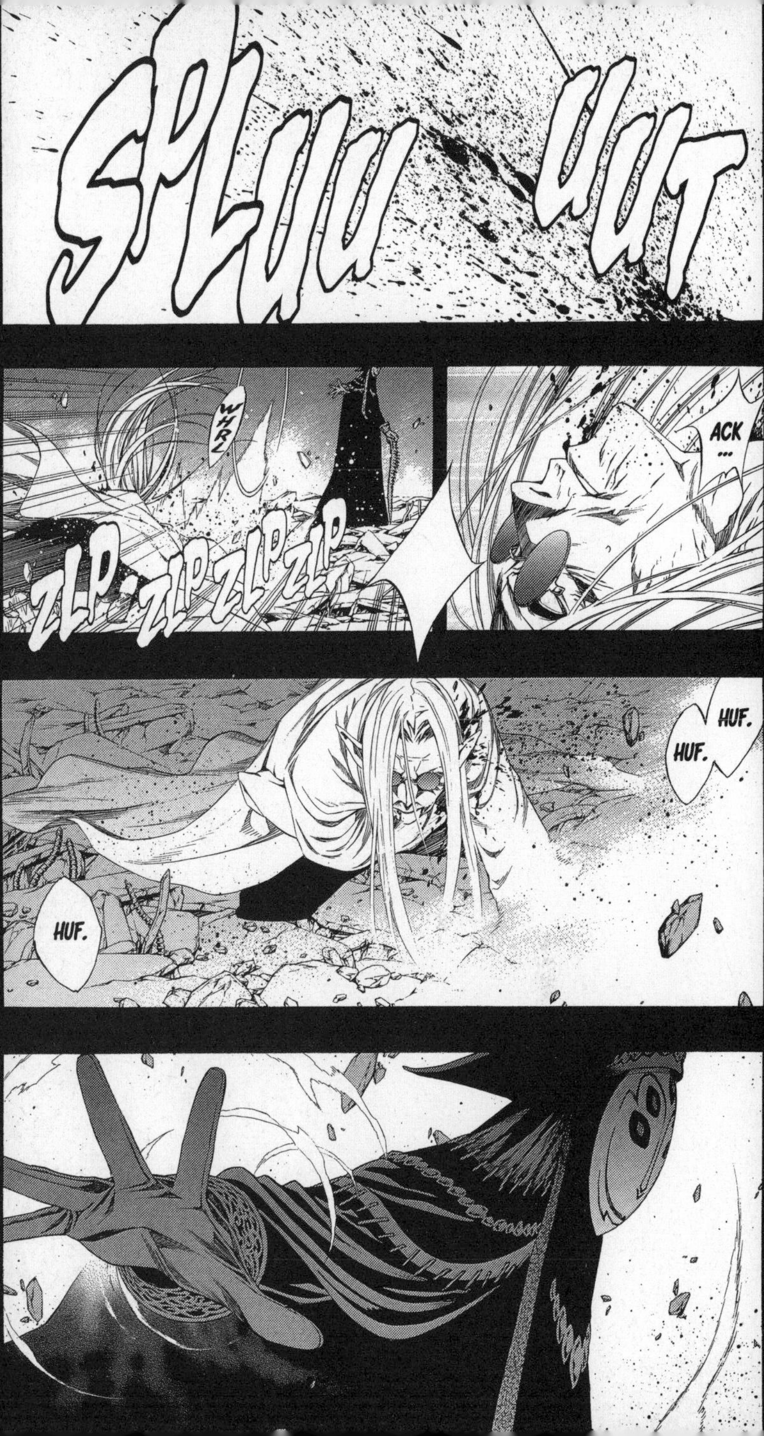
SPLUUUUUT
ACK...
WHRL
ZIP ZIP ZIP ZIP
HUF.
HUF.
HUF.

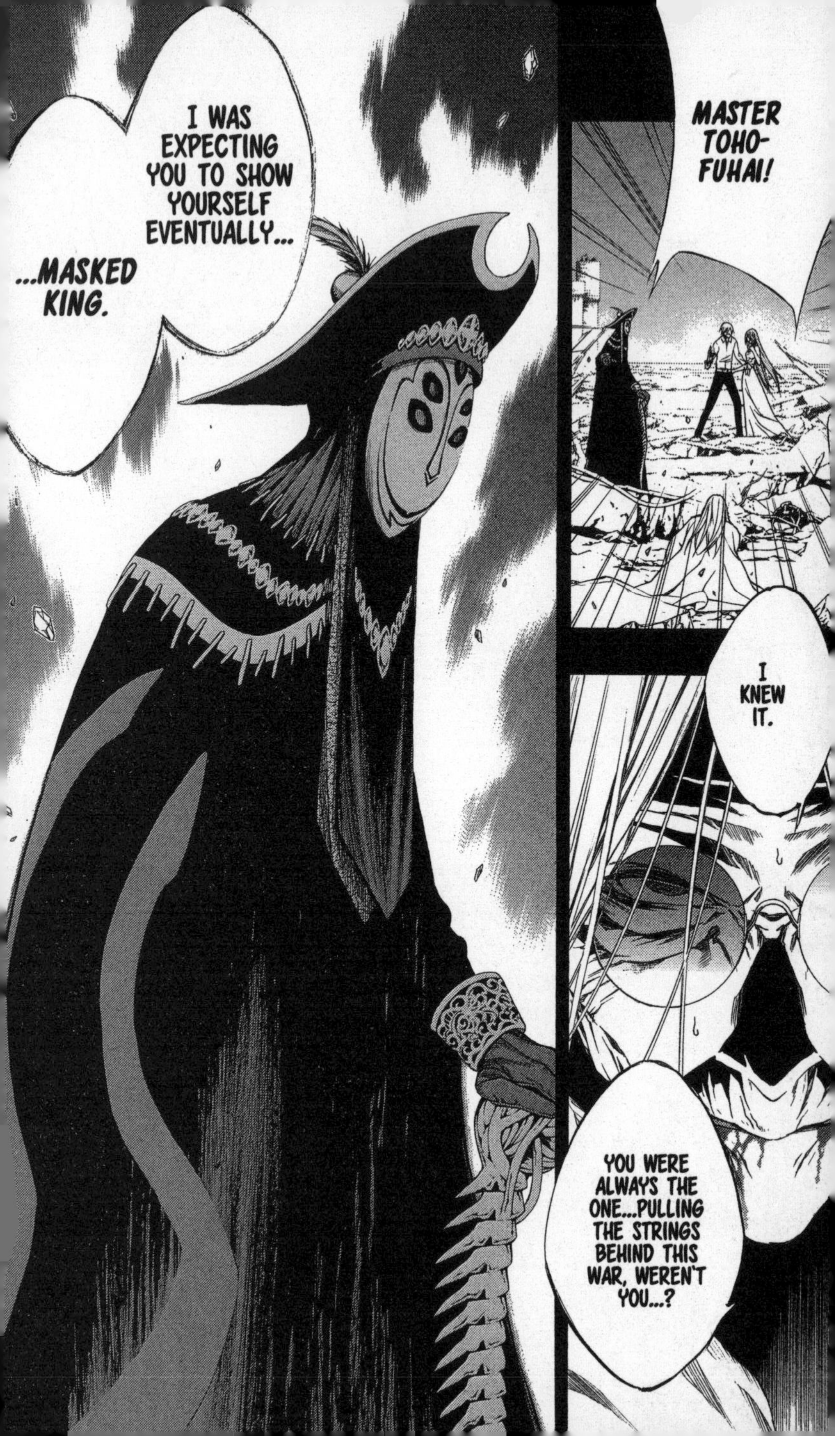
MASTER TOHO-FUHAI!
I KNEW IT.
YOU WERE ALWAYS THE ONE...PULLING THE STRINGS BEHIND THIS WAR, WEREN'T YOU...?
I WAS EXPECTING YOU TO SHOW YOURSELF EVENTUALLY...
...MASKED KING.

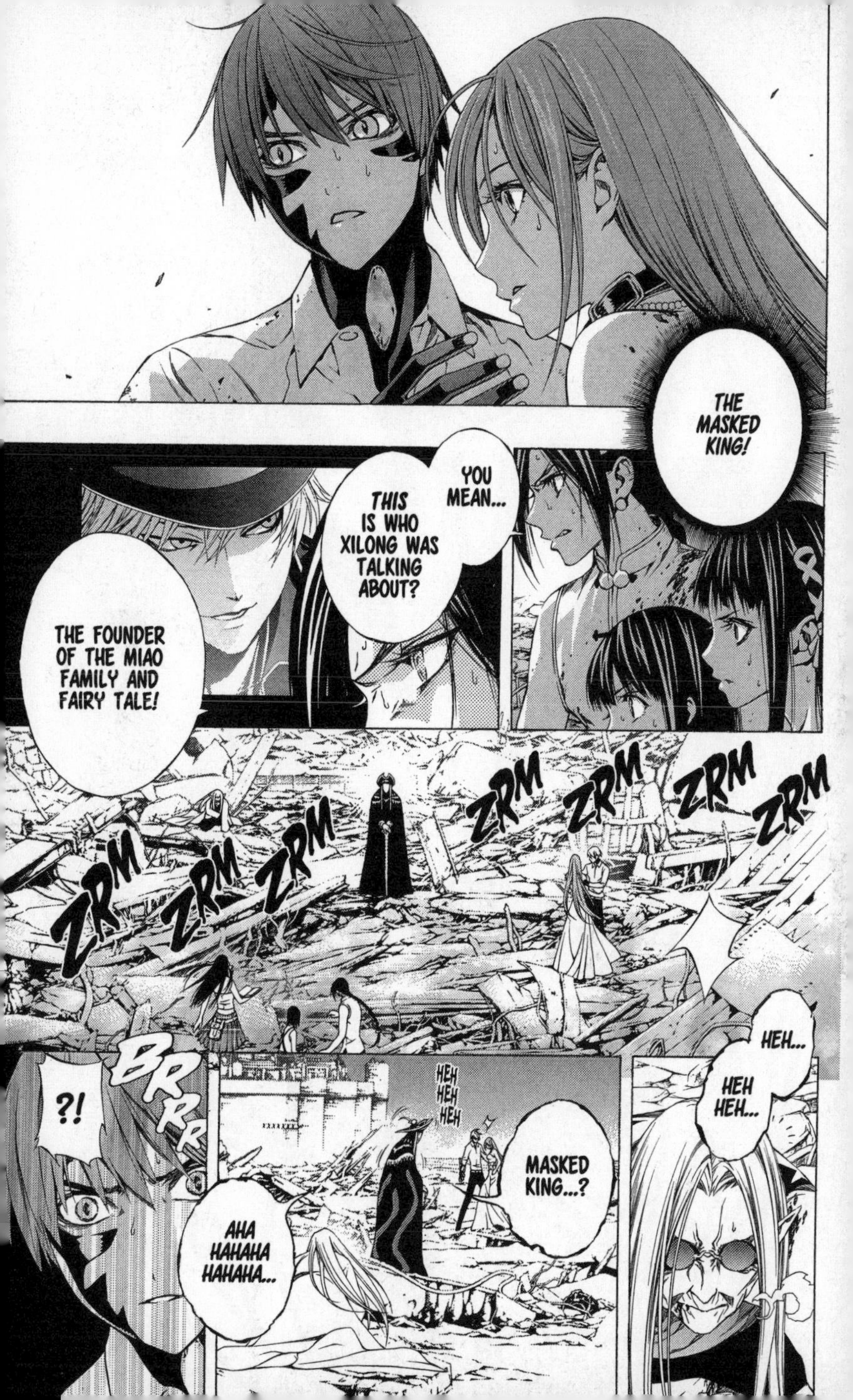
THE MASKED KING!
YOU MEAN...
THIS IS WHO XILONG WAS TALKING ABOUT?
THE FOUNDER OF THE MIAO FAMILY AND FAIRY TALE!
ZRM ZRM ZRM ZRM ZRM ZRM ZRM
HEH... HEH HEH...
HEH HEH HEH
MASKED KING...?
AHA HAHAHA HAHAHA...
BRRR
?!

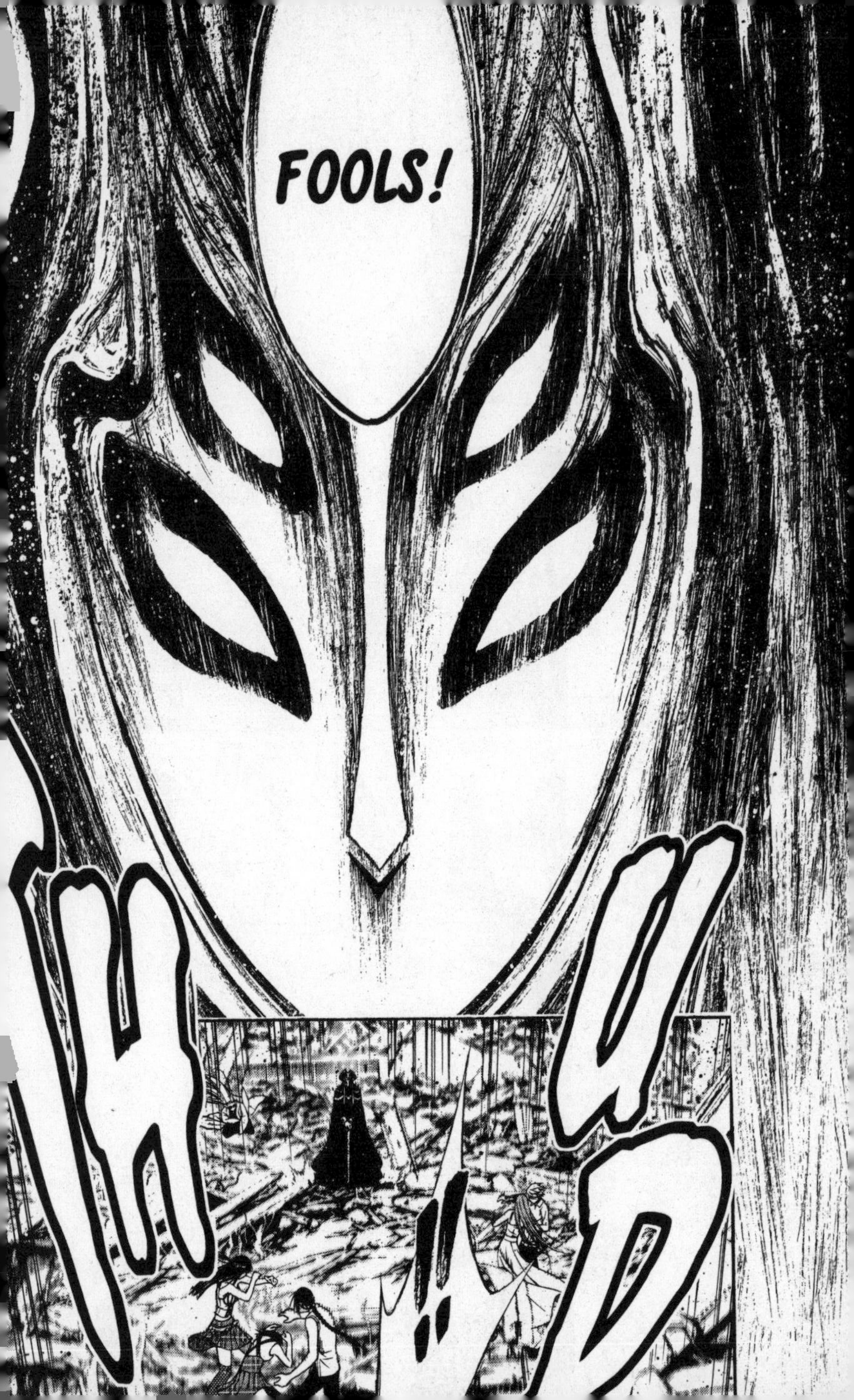
FOOLS!
HUD!!

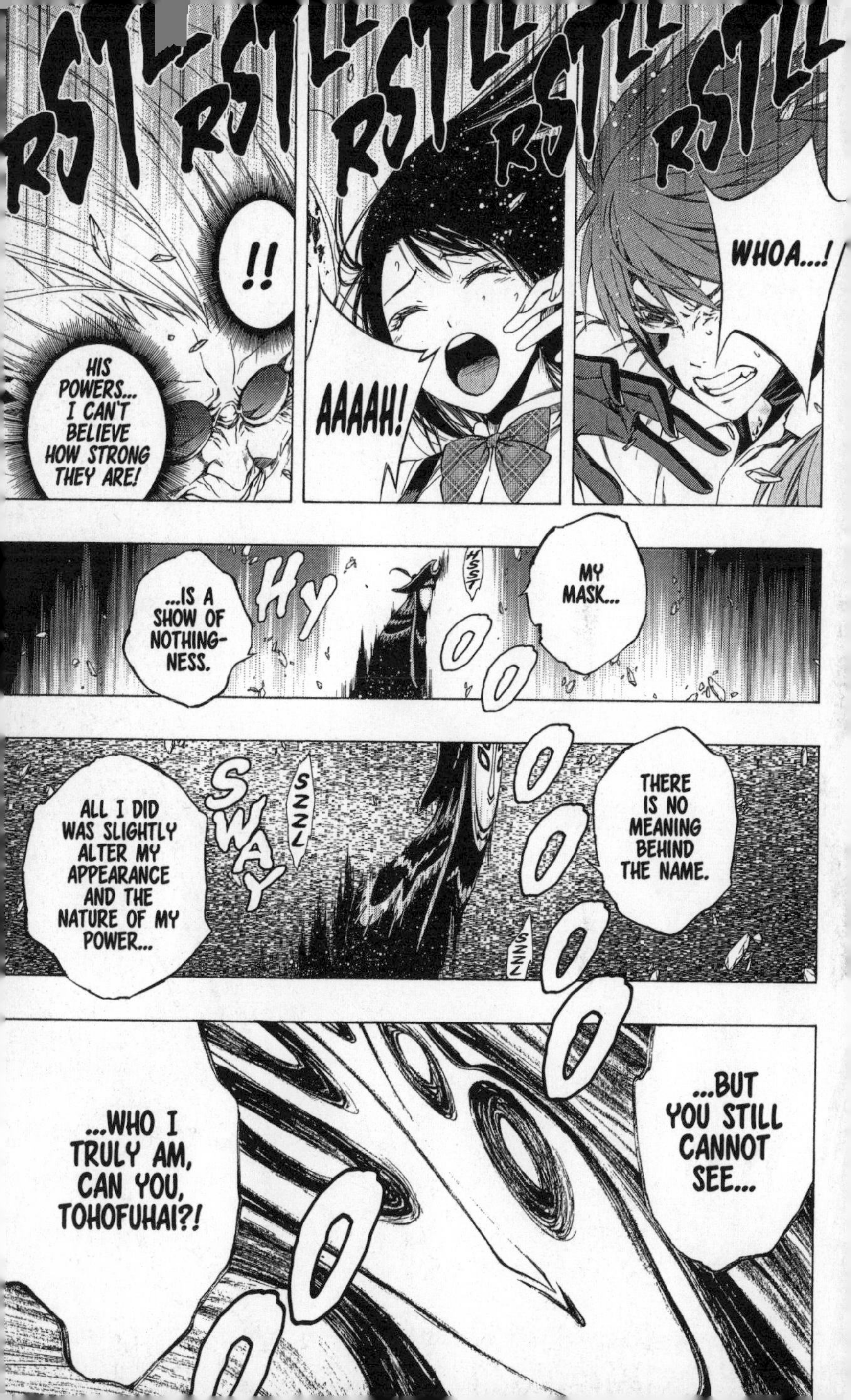
RSTLLL
RSTLLL
WHOA...!
RSTLLL
RSTLLL
AAAAH!
RSTLL-
RSTLL
!!
HIS POWERS... I CAN'T BELIEVE HOW STRONG THEY ARE!
MY MASK...
HSST
HYOOOOOOOOOO
...IS A SHOW OF NOTHINGNESS.
THERE IS NO MEANING BEHIND THE NAME.
SZZL
SZZL
SWAY
ALL I DID WAS SLIGHTLY ALTER MY APPEARANCE AND THE NATURE OF MY POWER...
...BUT YOU STILL CANNOT SEE...
...WHO I TRULY AM, CAN YOU, TOHOFUHAI?!

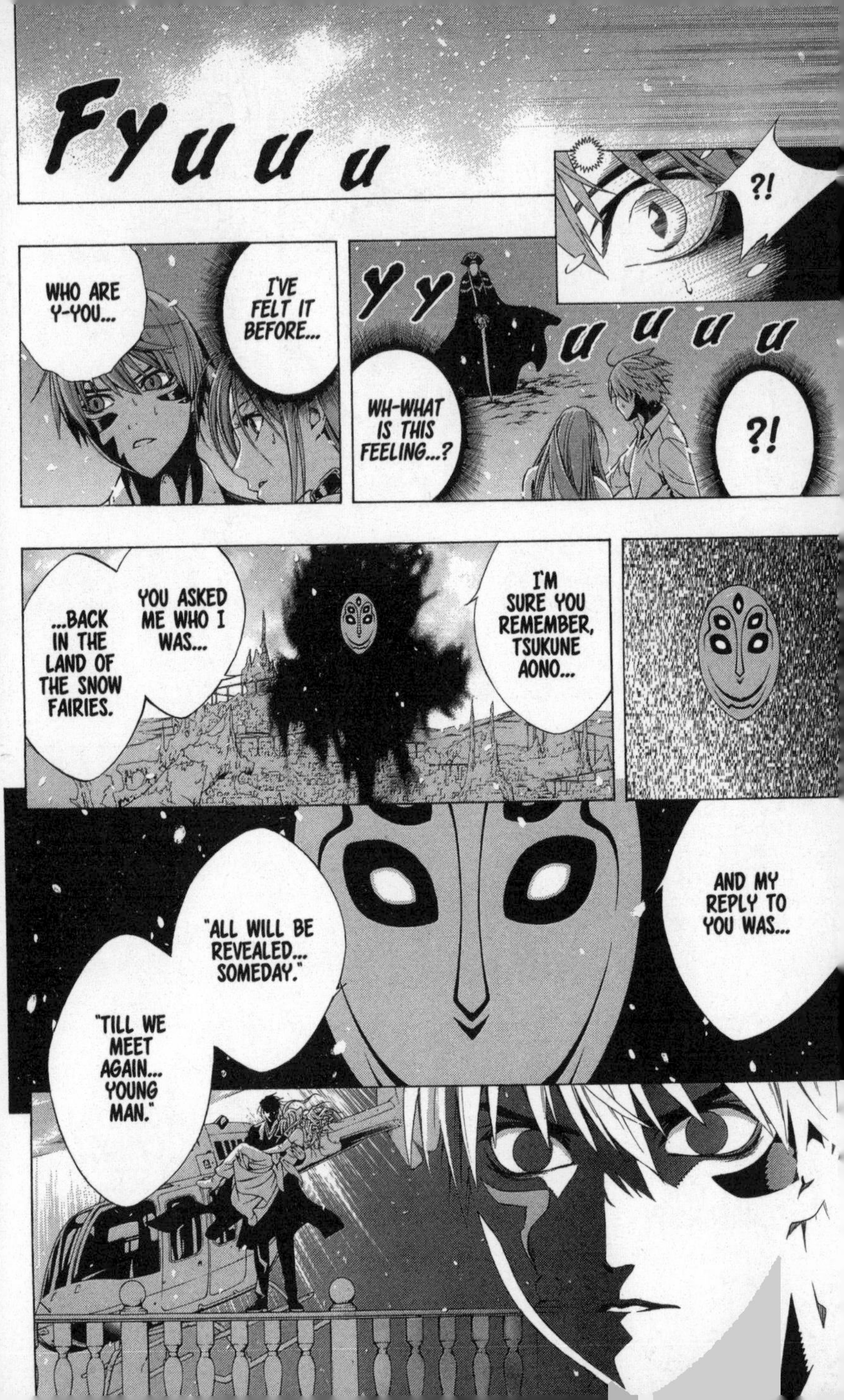
Fyuuuu
?!
yyuuuuu
?!
WH-WHAT IS THIS FEELING...?
I'VE FELT IT BEFORE...
WHO ARE Y-YOU...
I'M SURE YOU REMEMBER, TSUKUNE AONO...
YOU ASKED ME WHO I WAS...
...BACK IN THE LAND OF THE SNOW FAIRIES.
AND MY REPLY TO YOU WAS...
"ALL WILL BE REVEALED... SOMEDAY."
"TILL WE MEET AGAIN... YOUNG MAN."

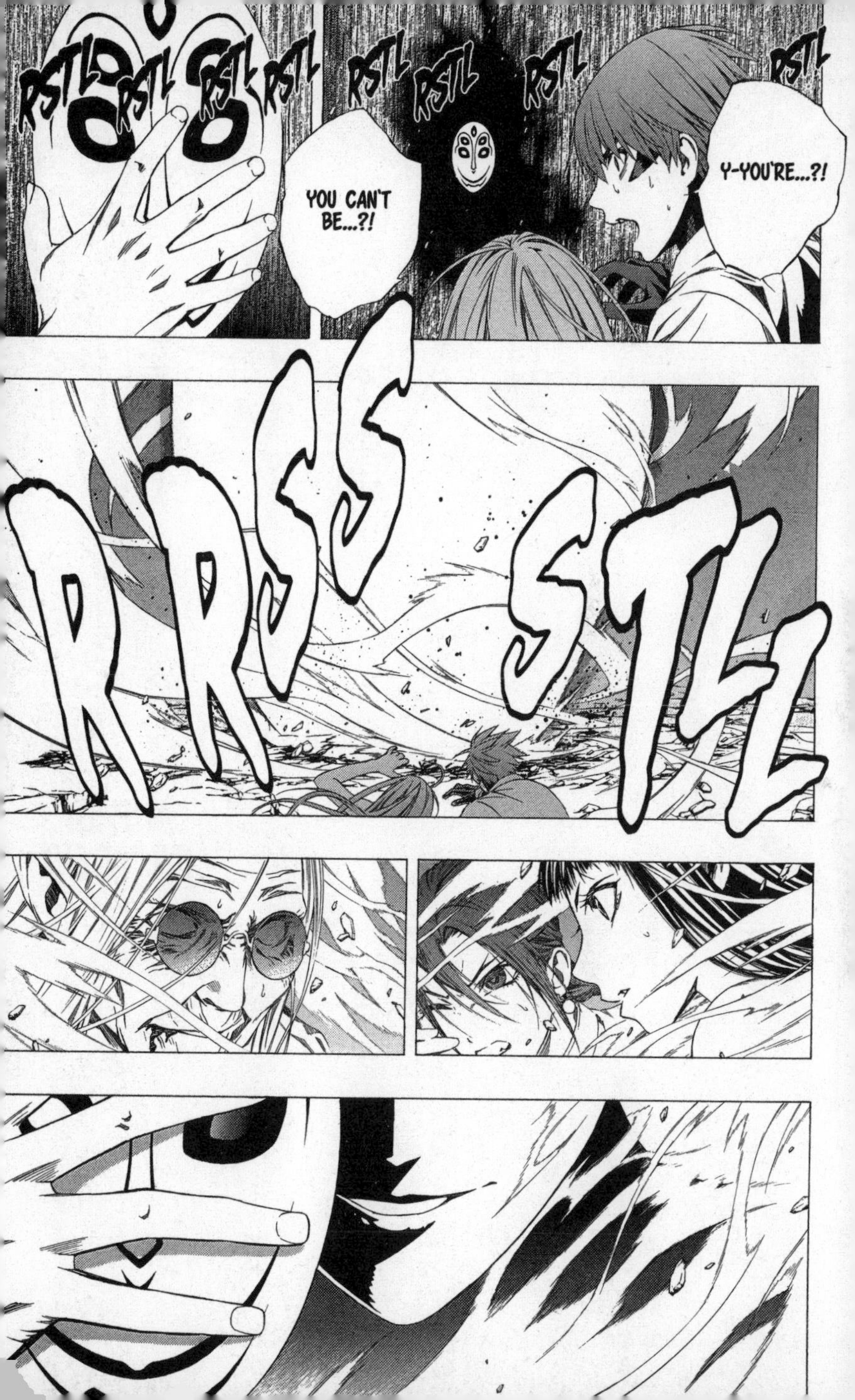
RSTL RSTL RSTL RSTL
Y-YOU'RE...?!
YOU CAN'T BE...?!
RSTL RSTL RSTL RSTL
RRSS STLL

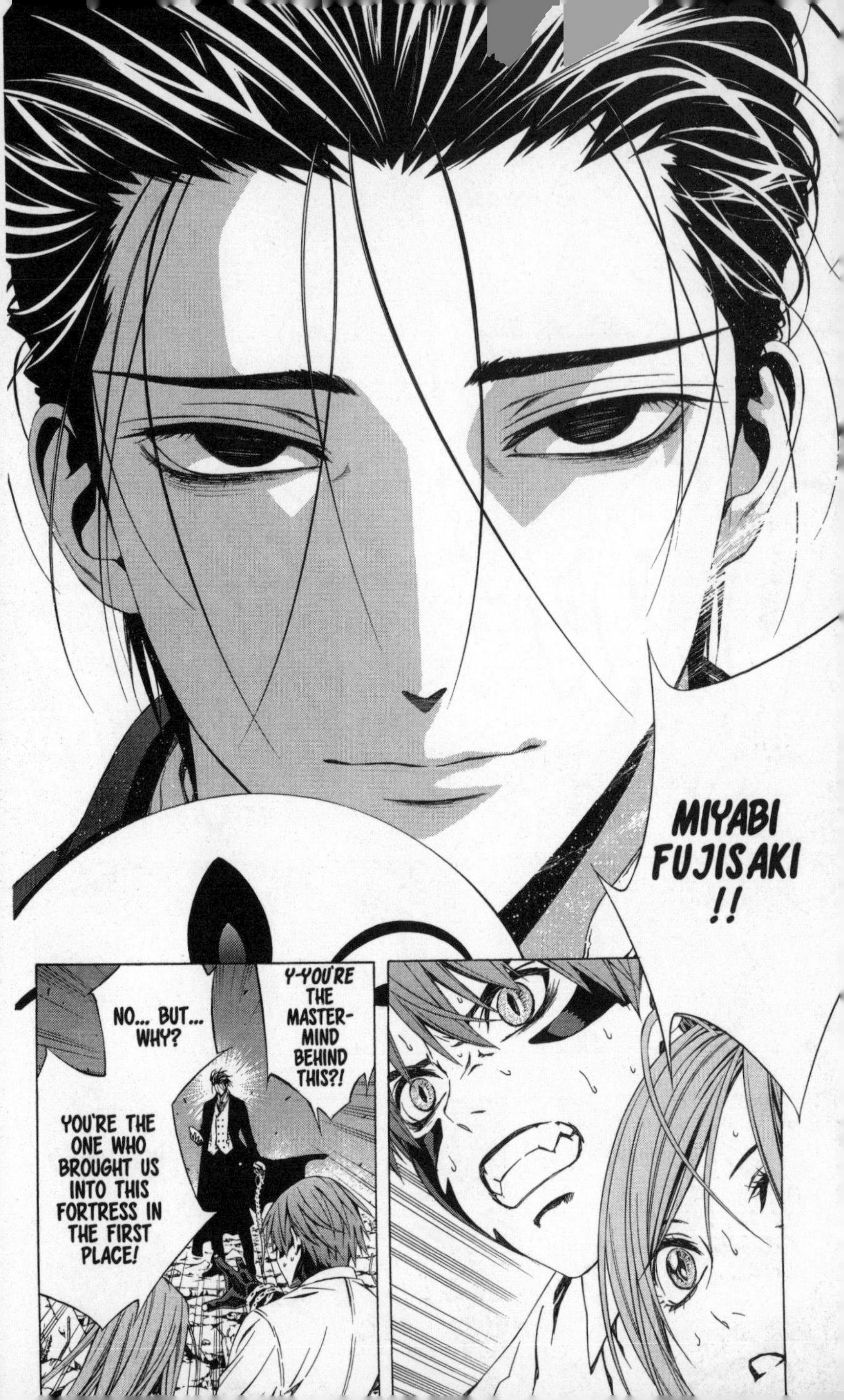
MIYABI FUJISAKI !!
Y-YOU'RE THE MASTER-MIND BEHIND THIS?!
NO... BUT... WHY?
YOU'RE THE ONE WHO BROUGHT US INTO THIS FORTRESS IN THE FIRST PLACE!

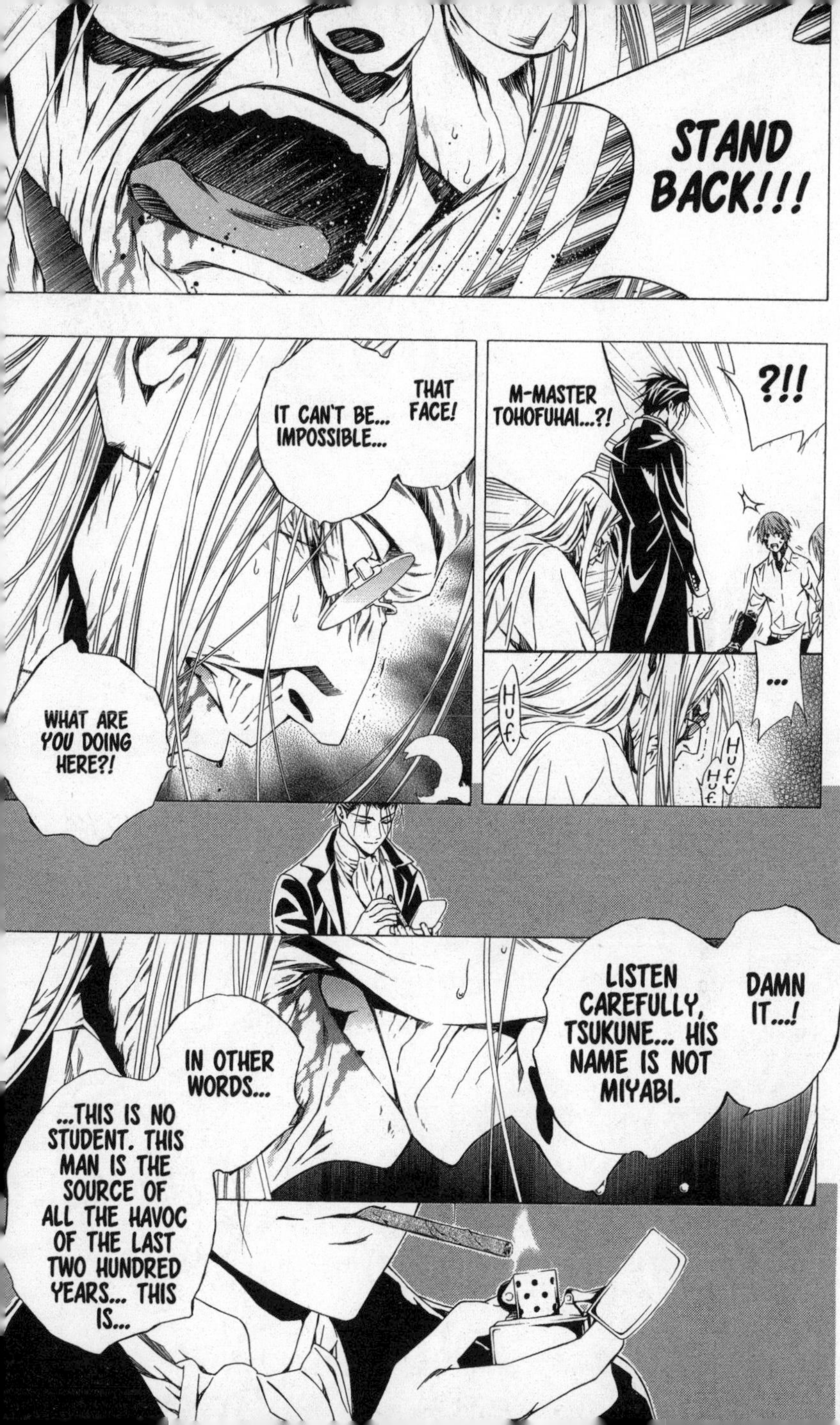
STAND BACK!!!
?!!
M-MASTER TOHOFUHAI...?!
...
Huf.
Huf.
Huf.
THAT FACE!
IT CAN'T BE... IMPOSSIBLE...
WHAT ARE YOU DOING HERE?!
DAMN IT...!
LISTEN CAREFULLY, TSUKUNE... HIS NAME IS NOT MIYABI.
IN OTHER WORDS...
...THIS IS NO STUDENT. THIS MAN IS THE SOURCE OF ALL THE HAVOC OF THE LAST TWO HUNDRED YEARS... THIS IS...

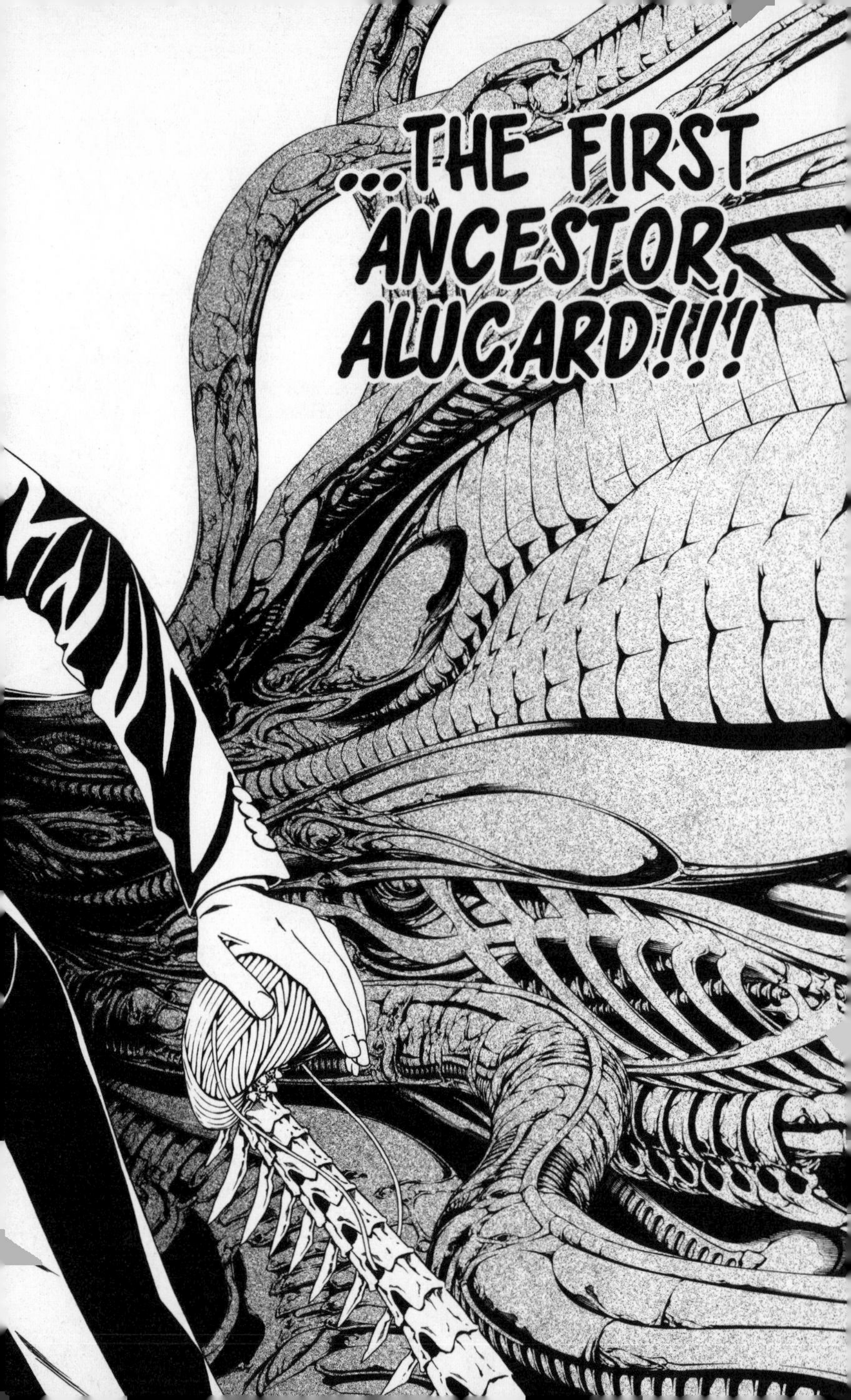
...THE FIRST ANCESTOR, ALUCARD!!!!

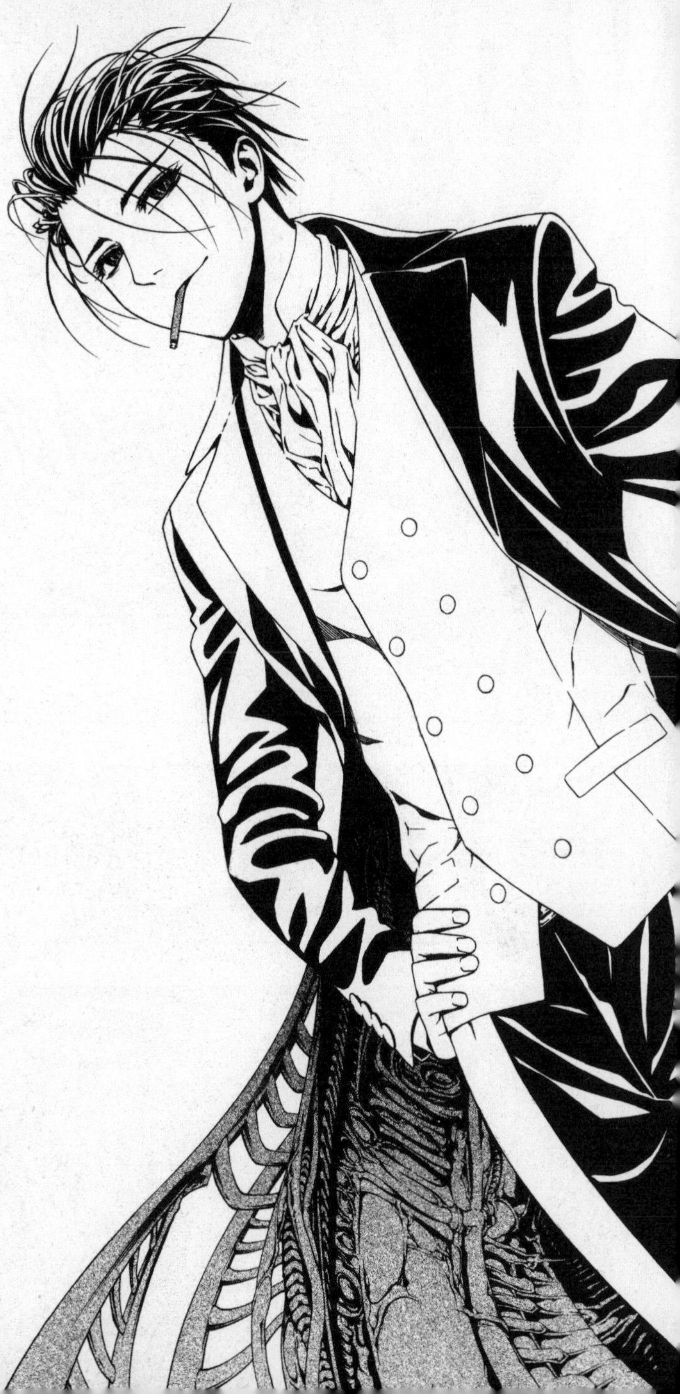

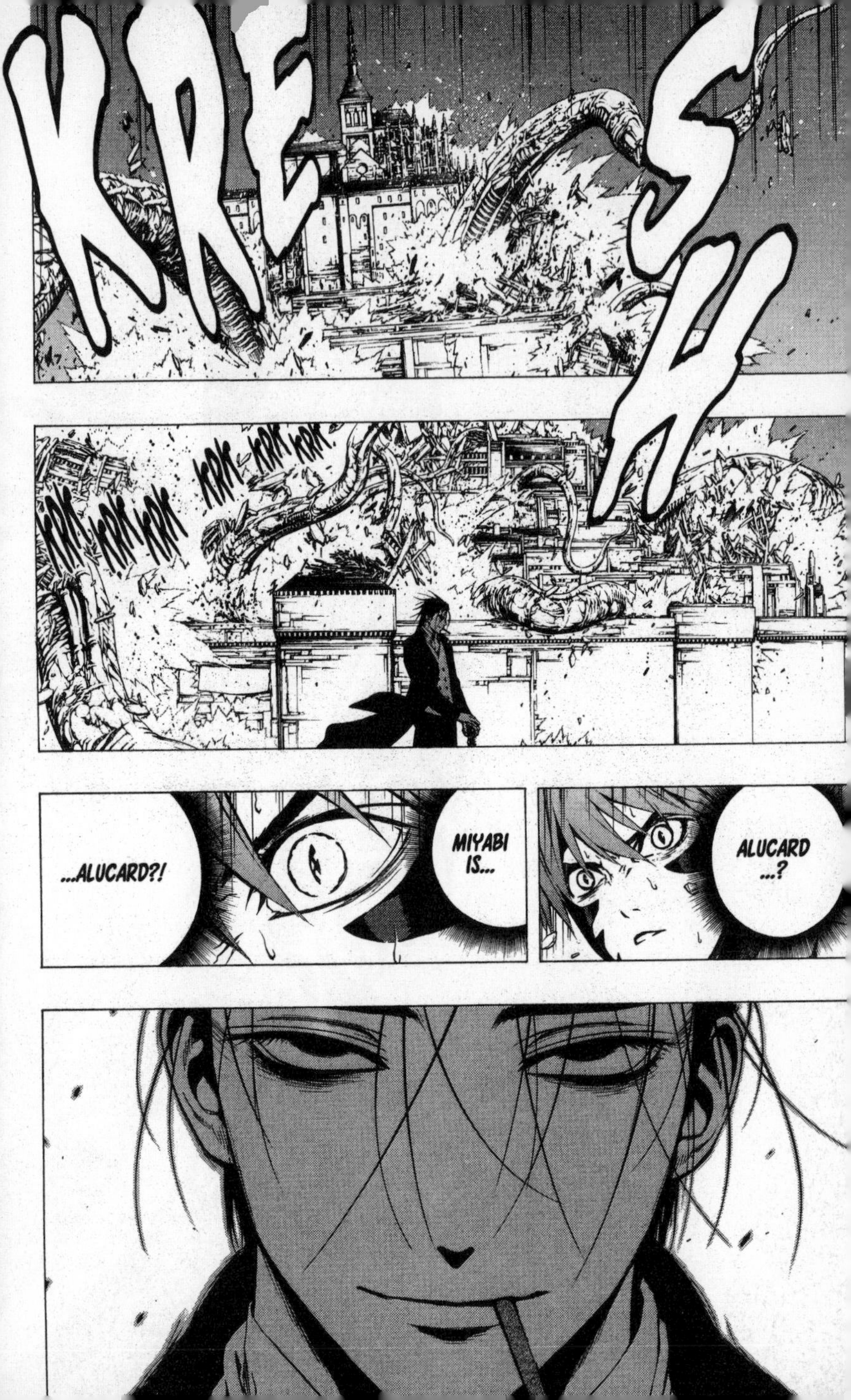
KRESH
KRK KRK KRK
KRK KRK KRK
ALUCARD ...?
MIYABI IS...
...ALUCARD?!

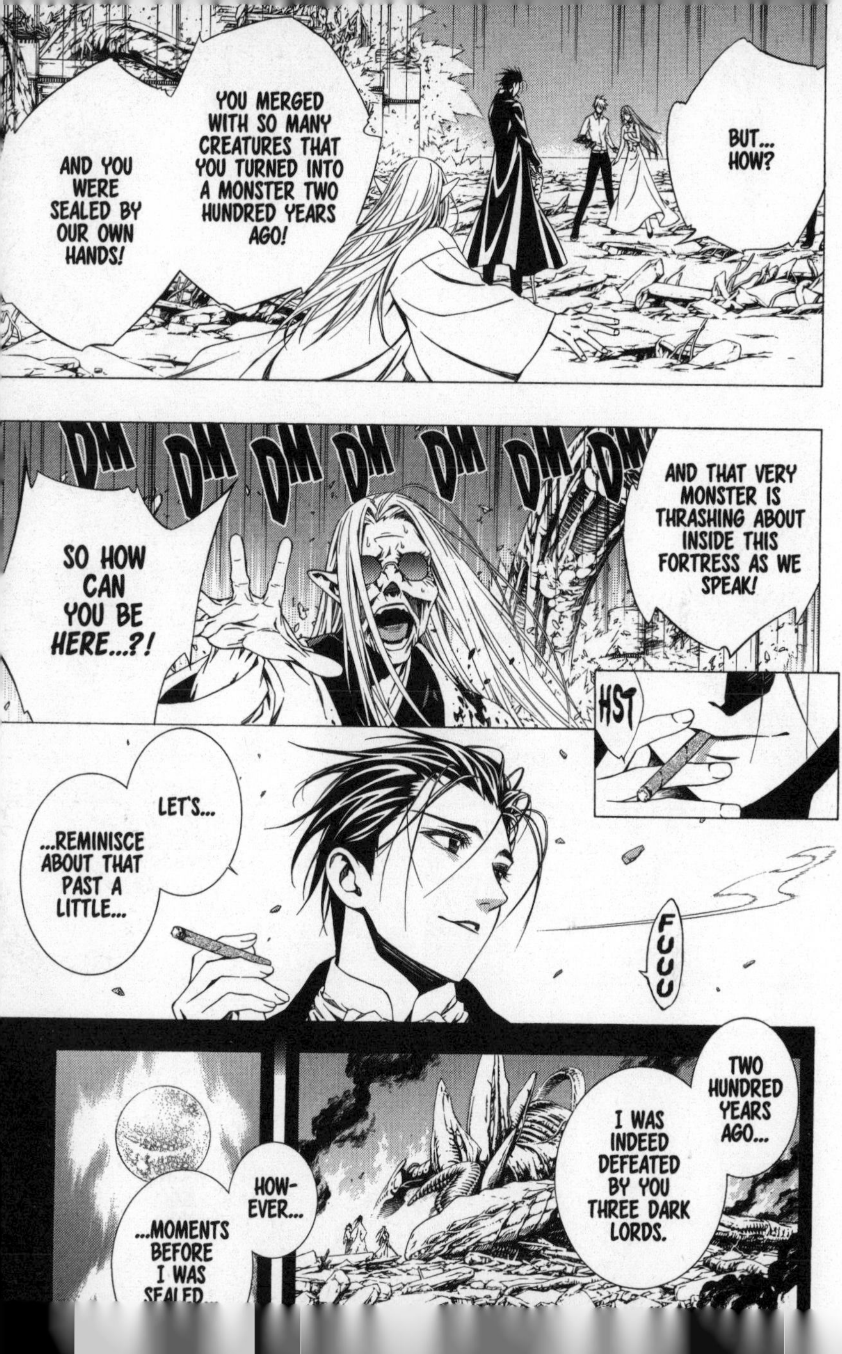
BUT... HOW?
YOU MERGED WITH SO MANY CREATURES THAT YOU TURNED INTO A MONSTER TWO HUNDRED YEARS AGO!
AND YOU WERE SEALED BY OUR OWN HANDS!
DM DM DM DM DM DM DM
AND THAT VERY MONSTER IS THRASHING ABOUT INSIDE THIS FORTRESS AS WE SPEAK!
SO HOW CAN YOU BE HERE...?!
HST
FUUU
LET'S...
...REMINISCE ABOUT THAT PAST A LITTLE...
TWO HUNDRED YEARS AGO...
I WAS INDEED DEFEATED BY YOU THREE DARK LORDS.
HOW-EVER...
...MOMENTS BEFORE I WAS SEALED...

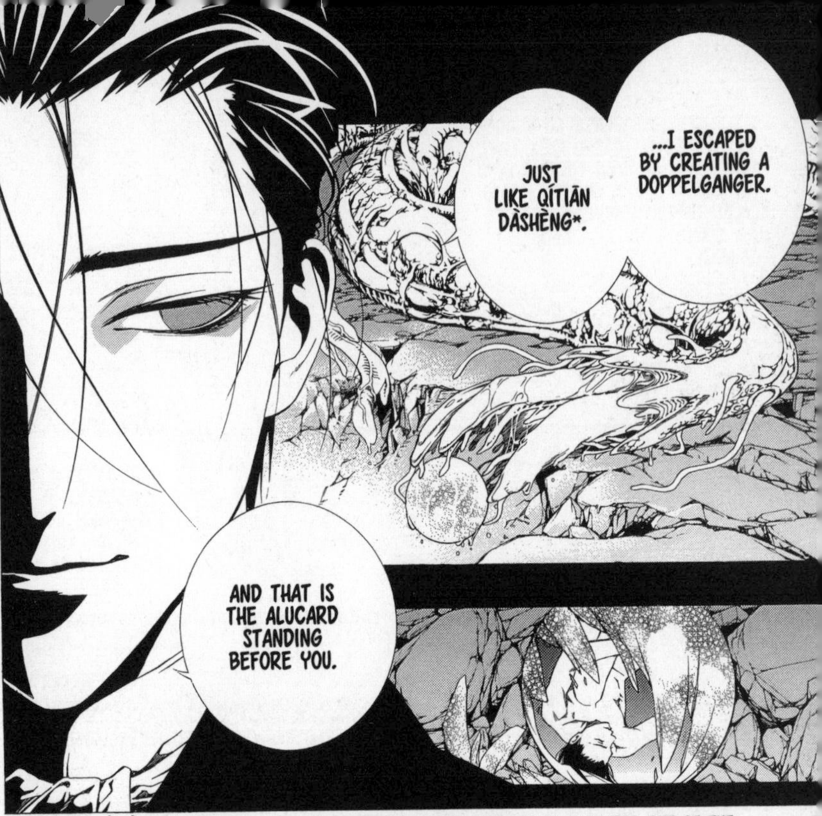
...I ESCAPED BY CREATING A DOPPELGANGER.
JUST LIKE QÍTIĀN DÀSHÈNG*.
AND THAT IS THE ALUCARD STANDING BEFORE YOU.

QÍTIĀN DÀSHÈNG: THE MONKEY KING WHO APPEARS IN THE JOURNEY TO THE WEST, ONE OF THE FOUR GREAT CLASSIC NOVELS OF CHINESE LITERATURE. HE IS OTHERWISE FAMOUSLY KNOWN AS "SUN WUKONG." HE HAS THE ABILITY TO CREATE NUMEROUS DOUBLES OUT OF HIS FUR.

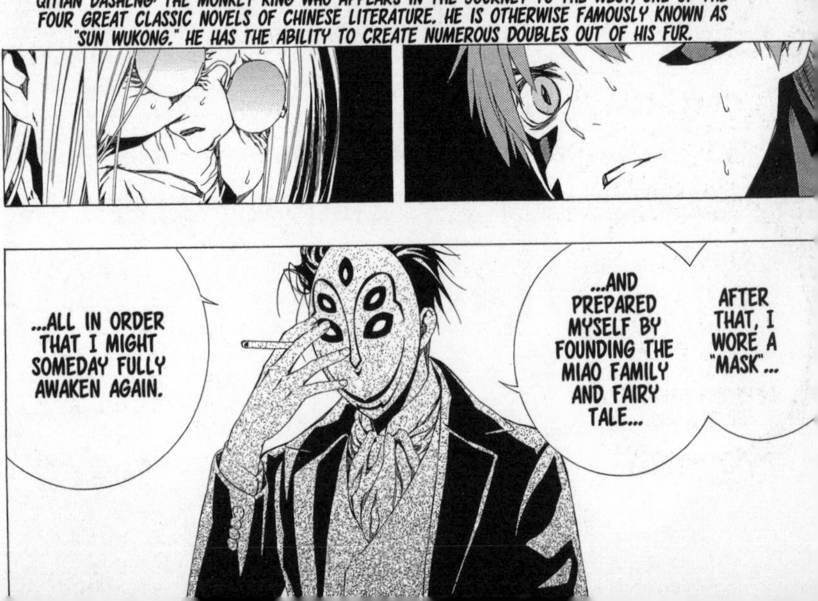
AFTER THAT, I WORE A "MASK"...
...AND PREPARED MYSELF BY FOUNDING THE MIAO FAMILY AND FAIRY TALE...
...ALL IN ORDER THAT I MIGHT SOMEDAY FULLY AWAKEN AGAIN.

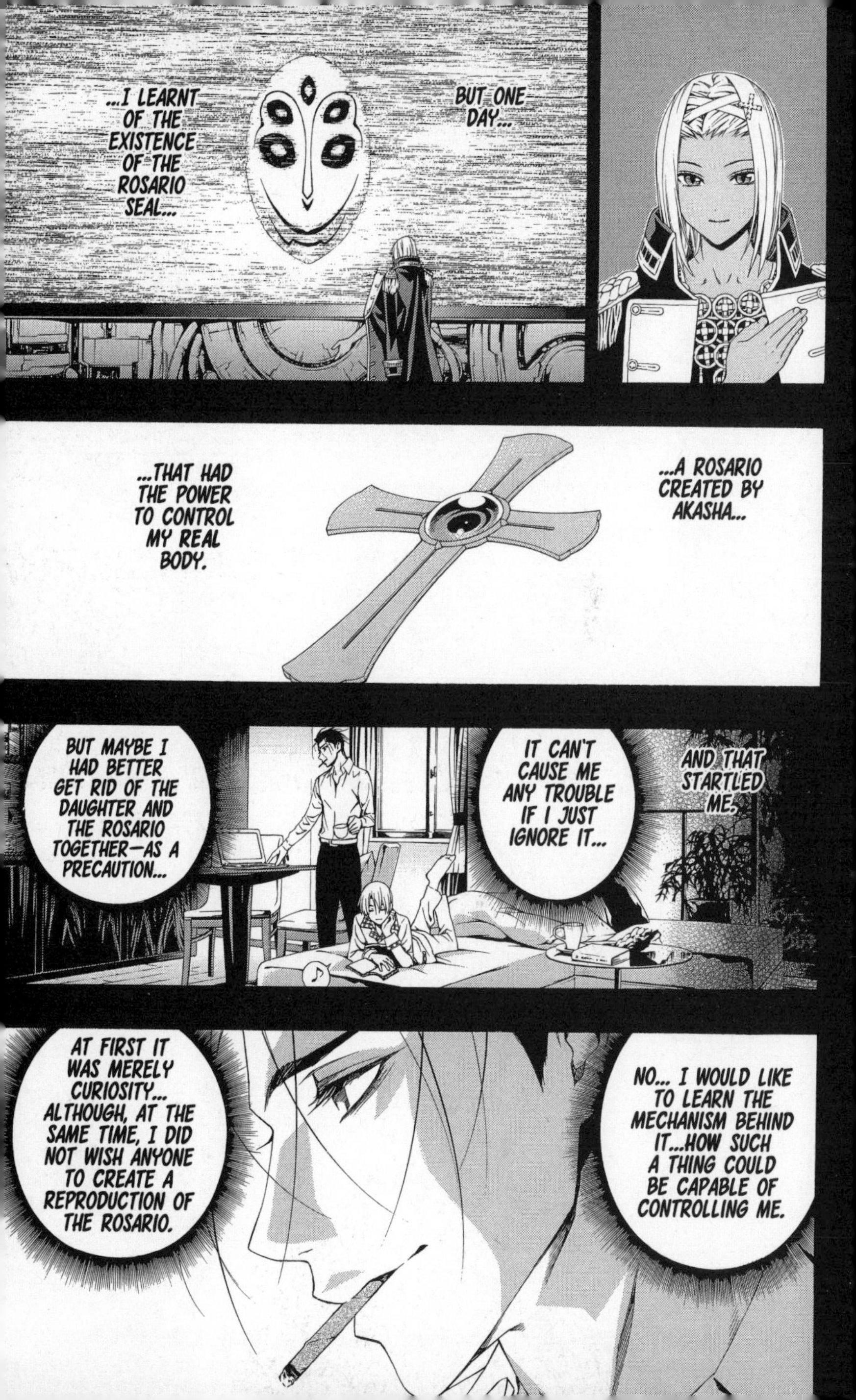
BUT ONE DAY...
...I LEARNT OF THE EXISTENCE OF THE ROSARIO SEAL...
...A ROSARIO CREATED BY AKASHA...
...THAT HAD THE POWER TO CONTROL MY REAL BODY.
AND THAT STARTLED ME.
IT CAN'T CAUSE ME ANY TROUBLE IF I JUST IGNORE IT...
BUT MAYBE I HAD BETTER GET RID OF THE DAUGHTER AND THE ROSARIO TOGETHER—AS A PRECAUTION...
NO... I WOULD LIKE TO LEARN THE MECHANISM BEHIND IT...HOW SUCH A THING COULD BE CAPABLE OF CONTROLLING ME.
AT FIRST IT WAS MERELY CURIOSITY... ALTHOUGH, AT THE SAME TIME, I DID NOT WISH ANYONE TO CREATE A REPRODUCTION OF THE ROSARIO.

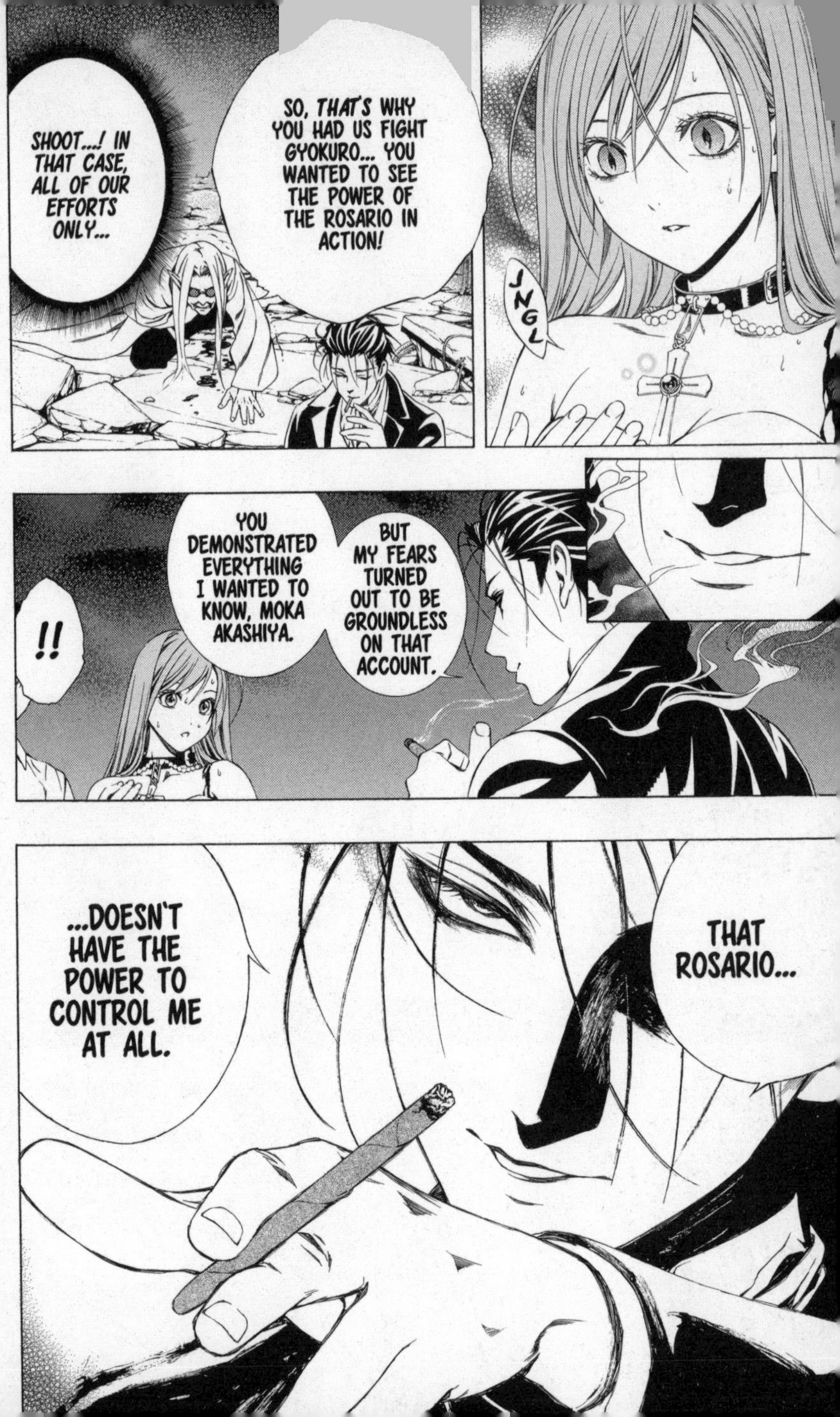
JNGL
SO, *THAT'S* WHY YOU HAD US FIGHT GYOKURO... YOU WANTED TO SEE THE POWER OF THE ROSARIO IN ACTION!
SHOOT...! IN THAT CASE, ALL OF OUR EFFORTS ONLY...
BUT MY FEARS TURNED OUT TO BE GROUNDLESS ON THAT ACCOUNT.
YOU DEMONSTRATED EVERYTHING I WANTED TO KNOW, MOKA AKASHIYA.
!!
THAT ROSARIO...
...DOESN'T HAVE THE POWER TO CONTROL ME AT ALL.

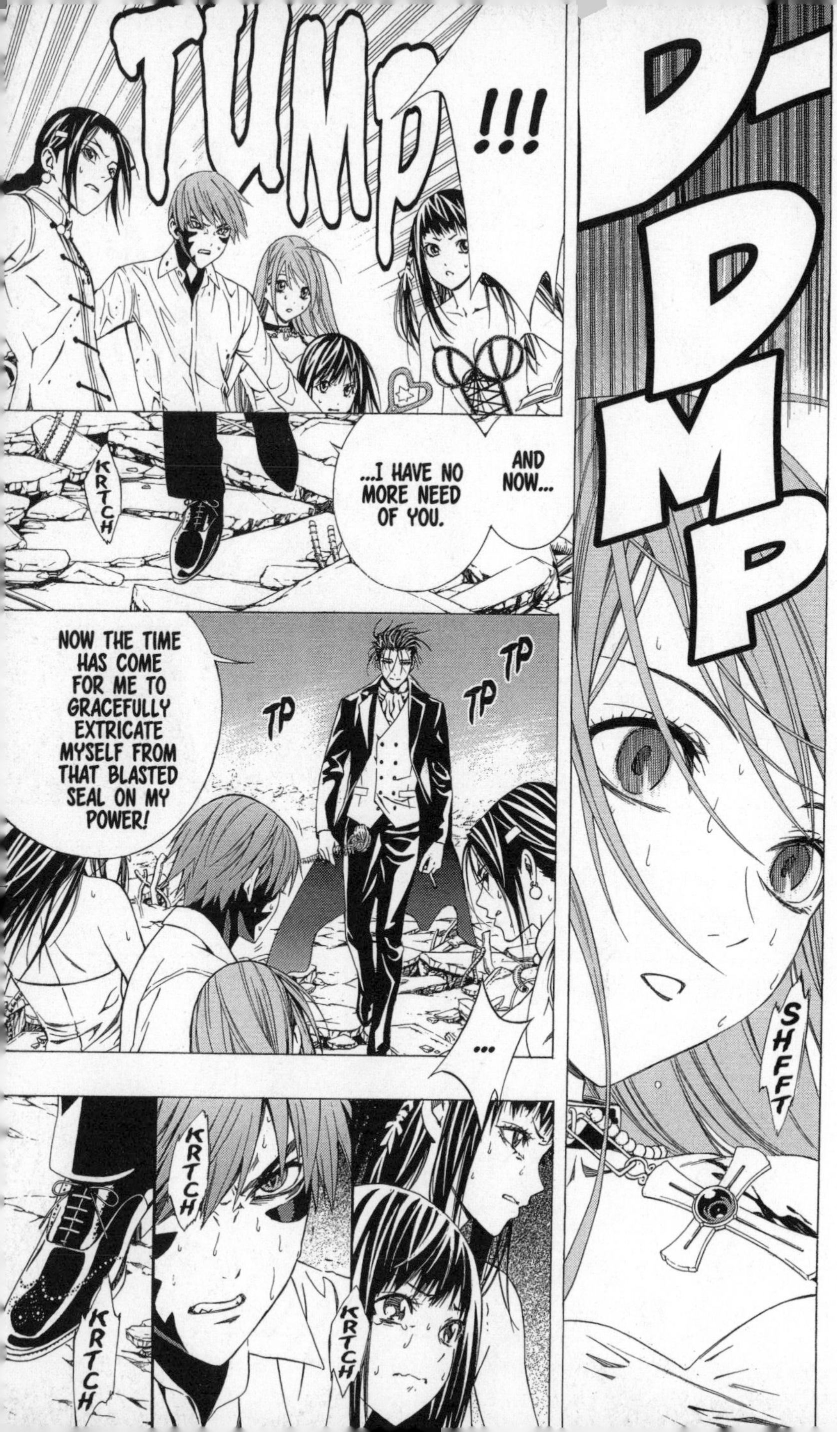

D-DMP
SHFFT
TUMP!!!
AND NOW...
...I HAVE NO MORE NEED OF YOU.
KRTCH
TP TP TP
NOW THE TIME HAS COME FOR ME TO GRACEFULLY EXTRICATE MYSELF FROM THAT BLASTED SEAL ON MY POWER!
TP
...
KRTCH
KRTCH
KRTCH

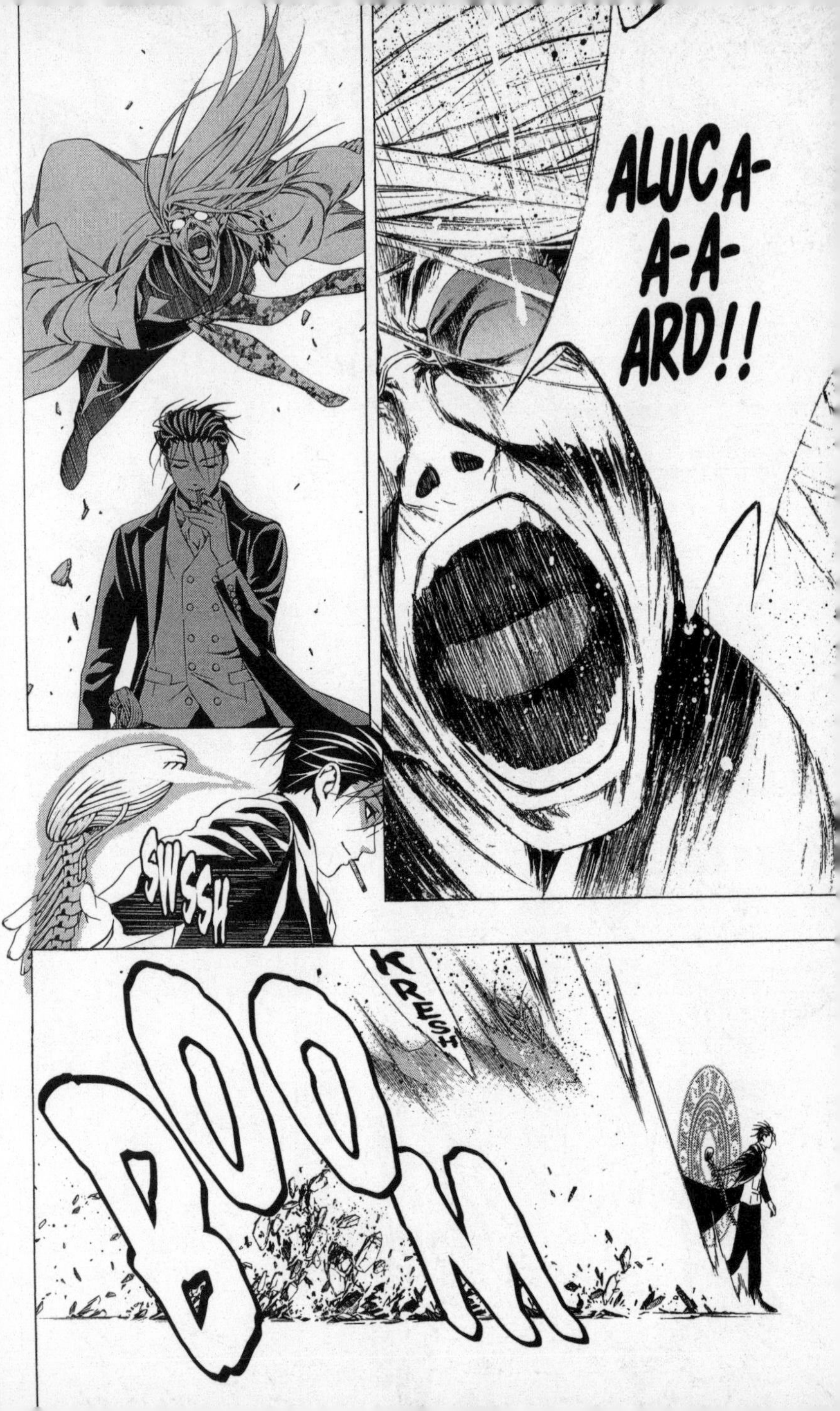
ALUCA-A-A-ARD!!
SWSSH
KRESH
BOOM

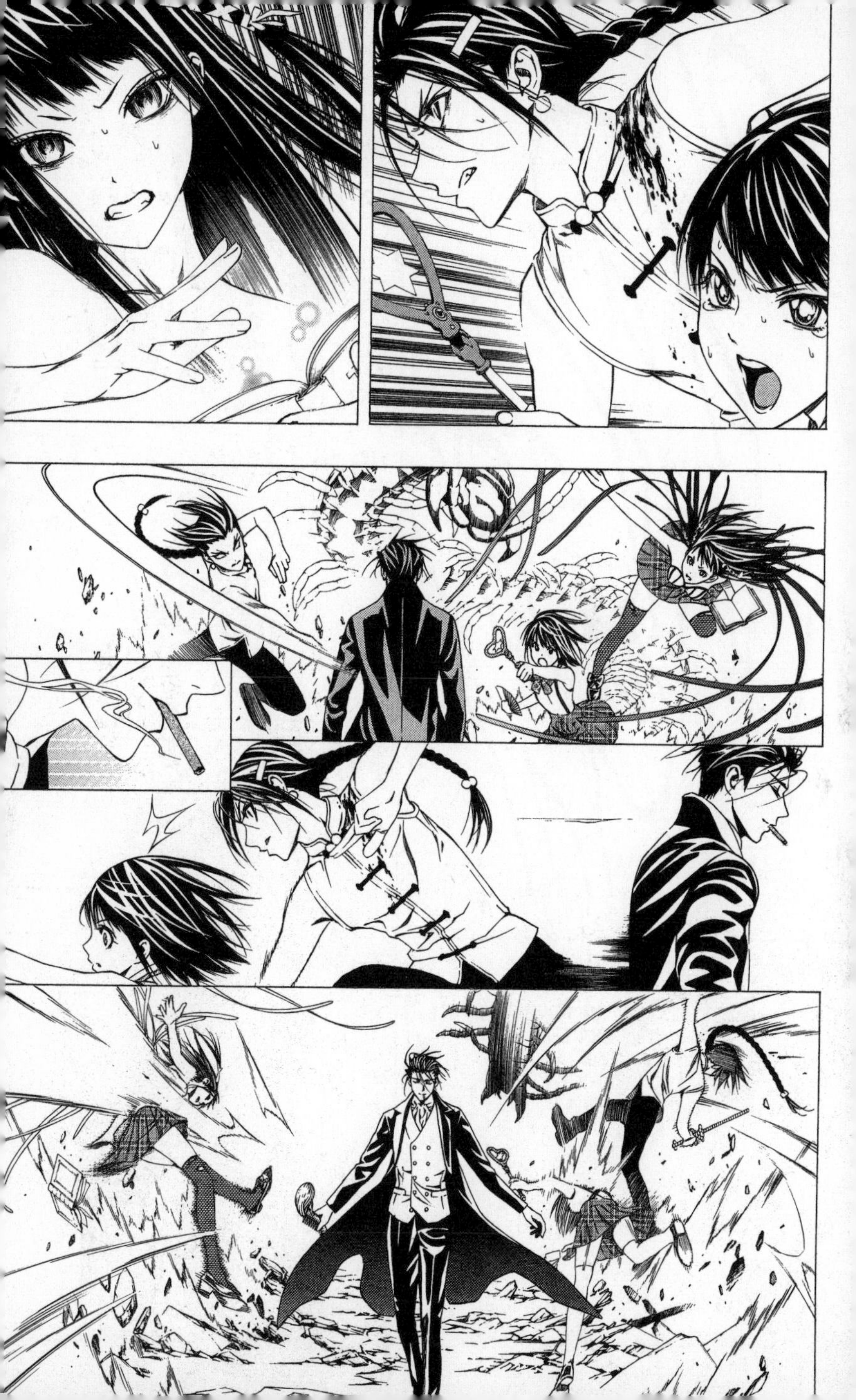

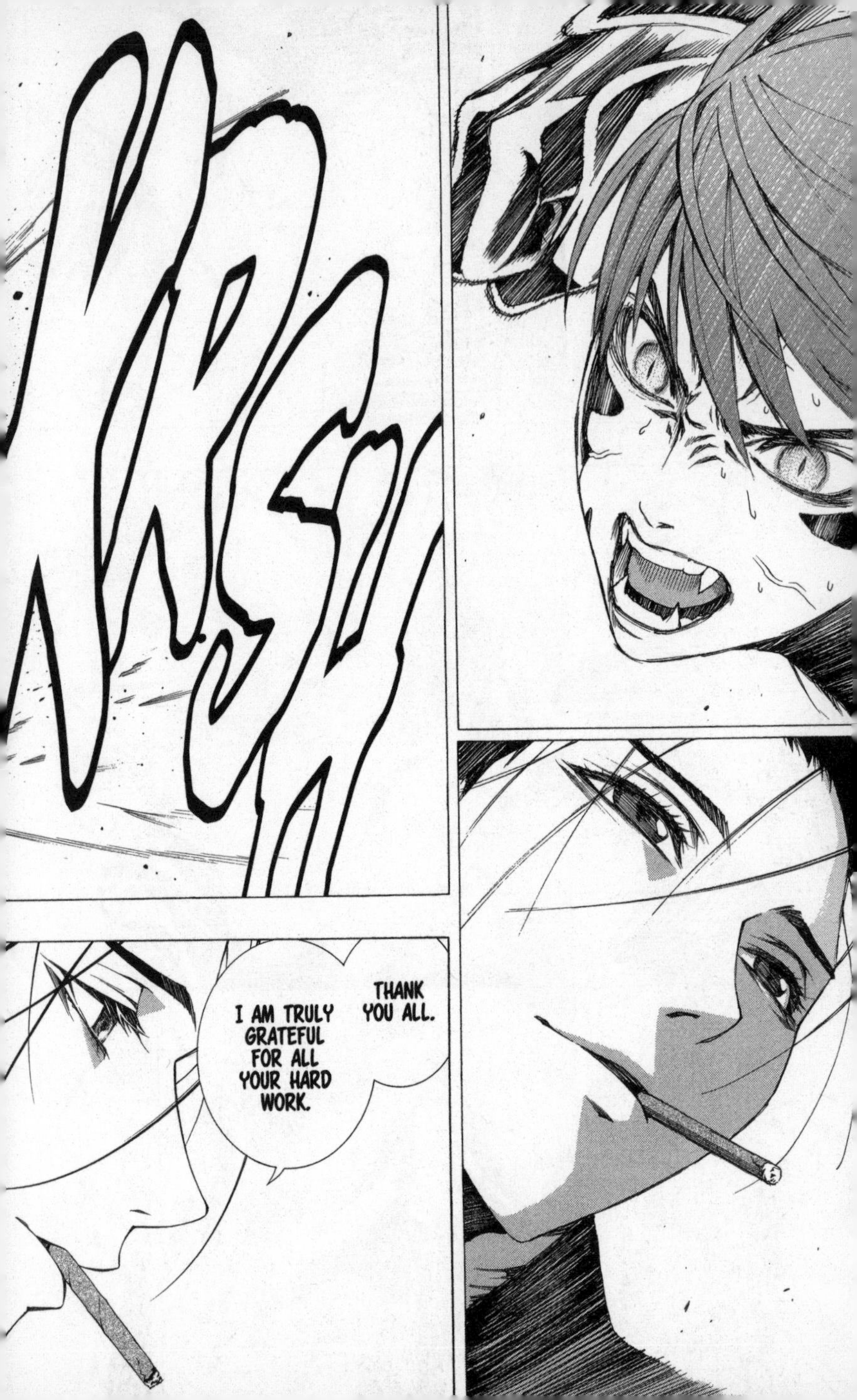
THANK YOU ALL.
I AM TRULY GRATEFUL FOR ALL YOUR HARD WORK.

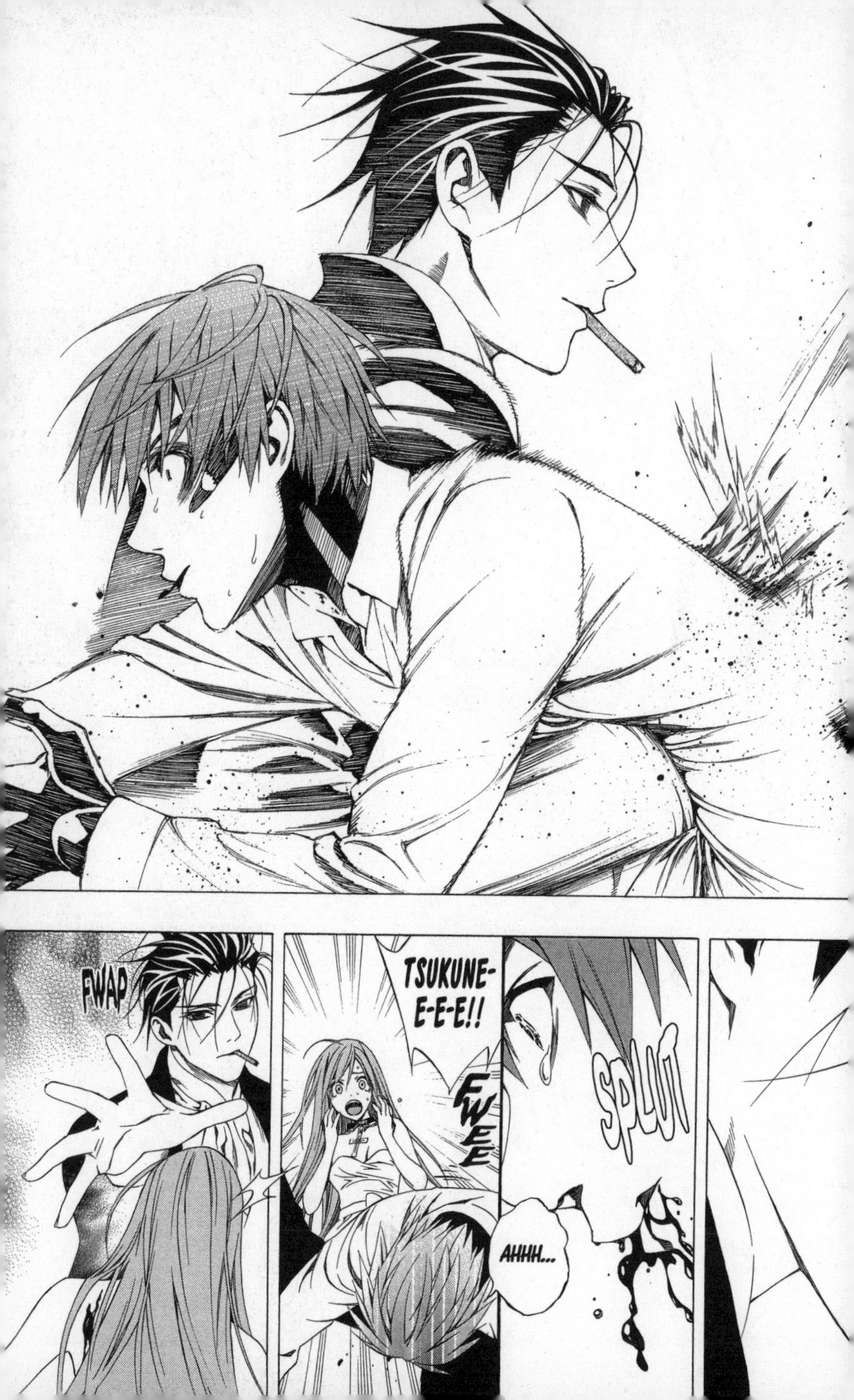
SPLUT
AHHH...
TSUKUNE-E-E-E!!
FWEE
FWAP

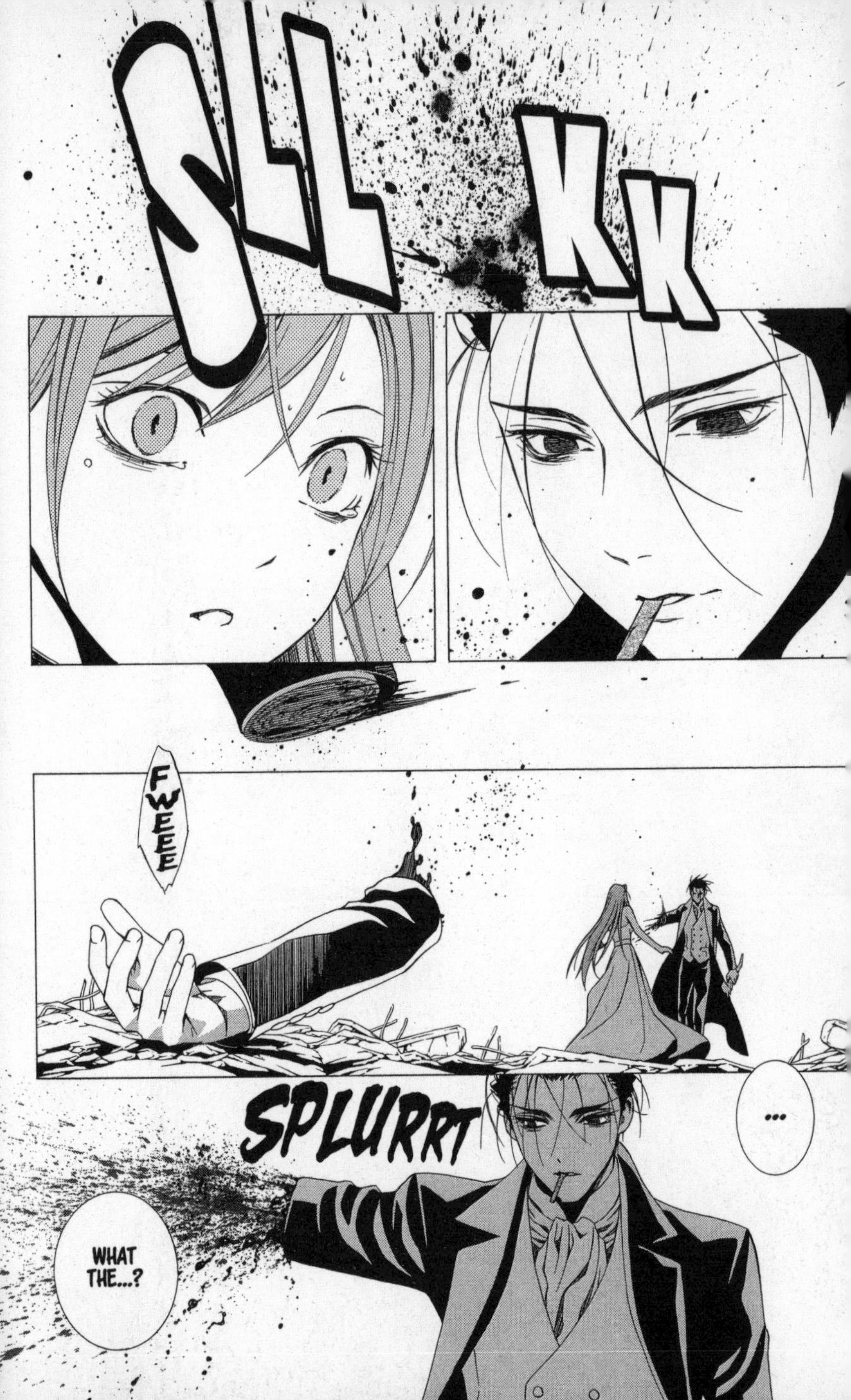
SLLKK
FWEEE
...
SPLURRT
WHAT THE...?

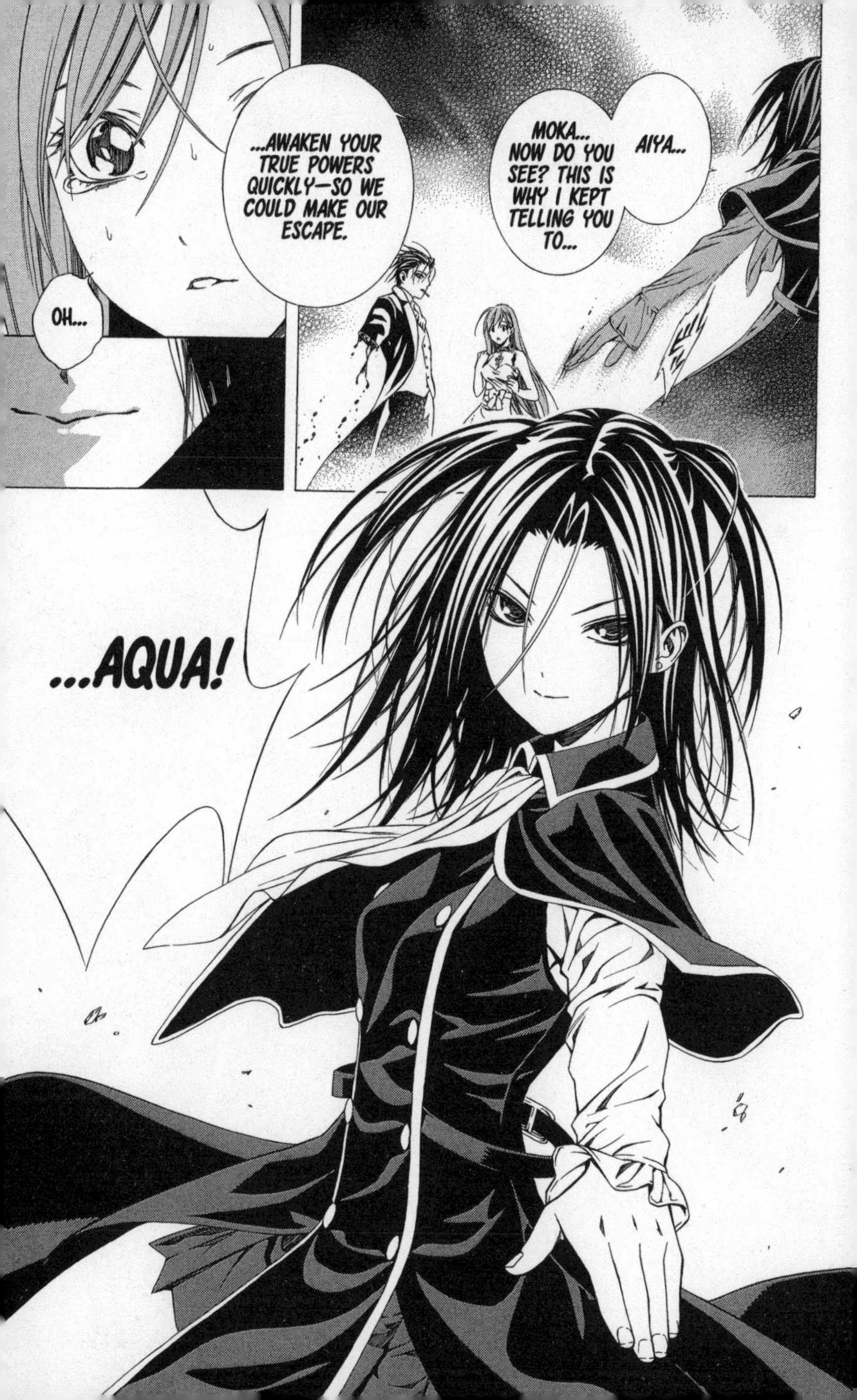
AIYA...
MOKA... NOW DO YOU SEE? THIS IS WHY I KEPT TELLING YOU TO...
...AWAKEN YOUR TRUE POWERS QUICKLY—SO WE COULD MAKE OUR ESCAPE.
OH...
...AQUA!

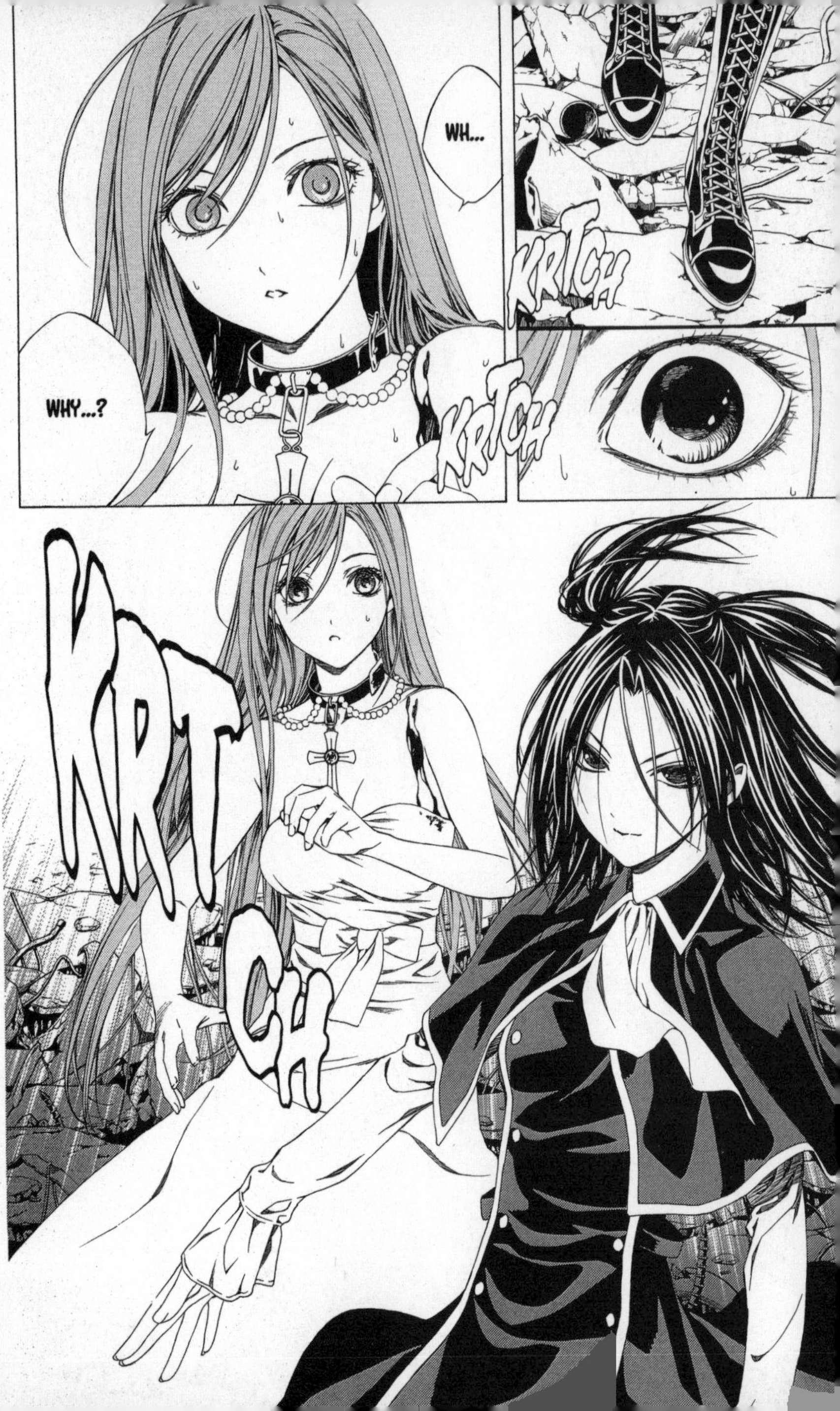
KRTCH
KRTCH
WH...
WHY...?
KRTCH

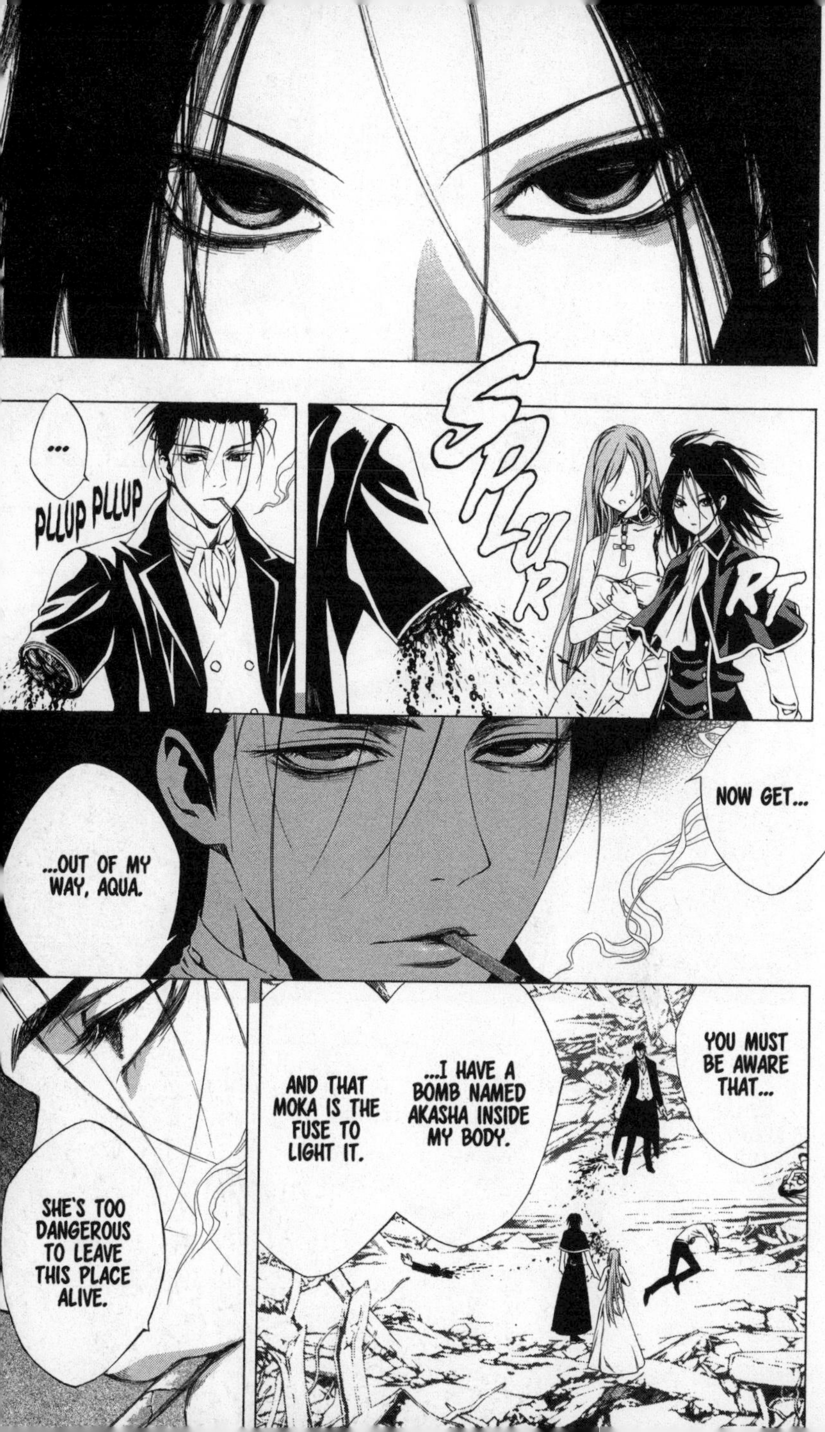
SPLURRT
...
PLLUP PLLUP
NOW GET...
...OUT OF MY WAY, AQUA.
YOU MUST BE AWARE THAT...
...I HAVE A BOMB NAMED AKASHA INSIDE MY BODY.
AND THAT MOKA IS THE FUSE TO LIGHT IT.
SHE'S TOO DANGEROUS TO LEAVE THIS PLACE ALIVE.

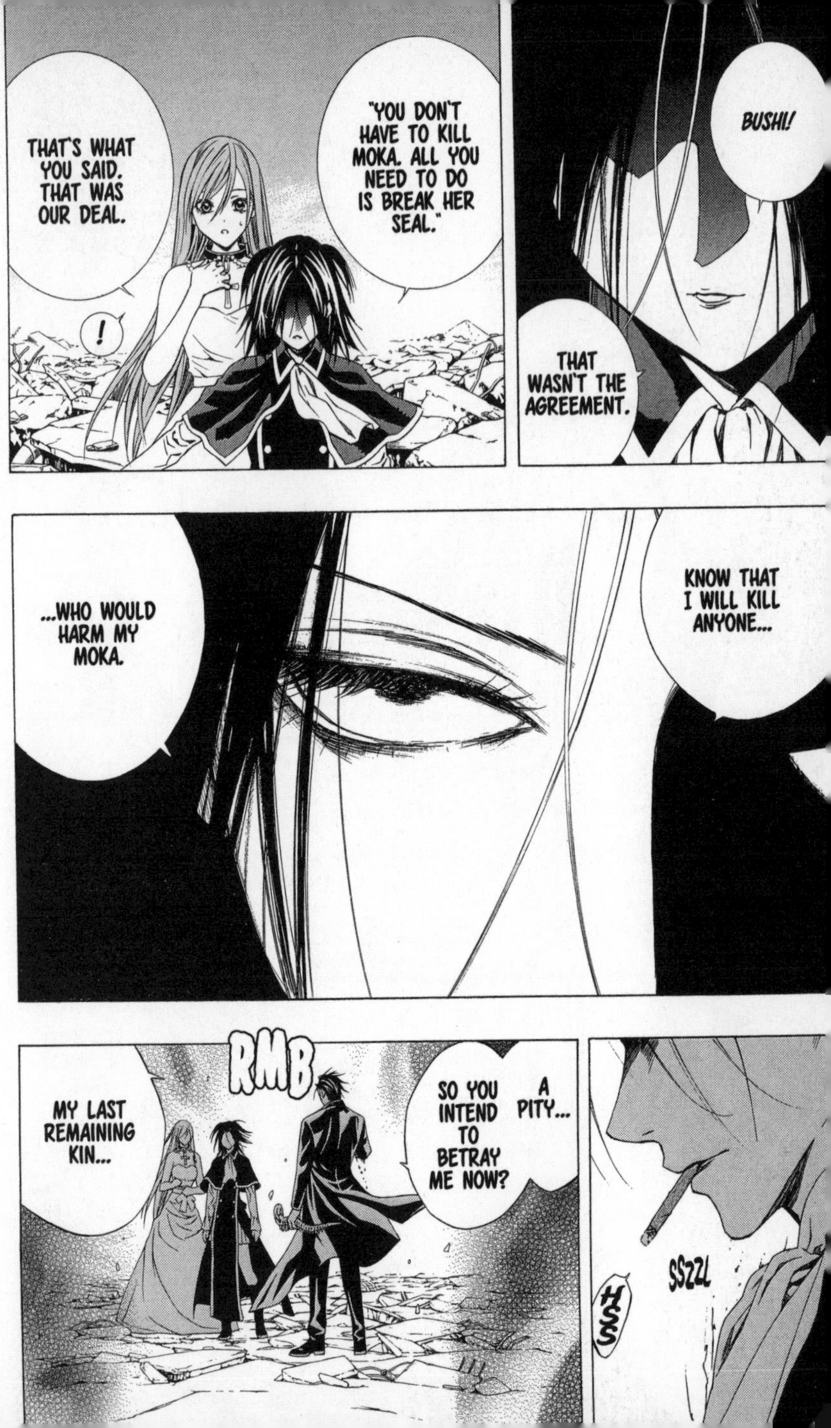
BUSHI!
THAT WASN'T THE AGREEMENT.
"YOU DON'T HAVE TO KILL MOKA. ALL YOU NEED TO DO IS BREAK HER SEAL."
THAT'S WHAT YOU SAID. THAT WAS OUR DEAL.
!
KNOW THAT I WILL KILL ANYONE...
...WHO WOULD HARM MY MOKA.
SSZZL
HSS
A PITY...
SO YOU INTEND TO BETRAY ME NOW?
RMB
MY LAST REMAINING KIN...

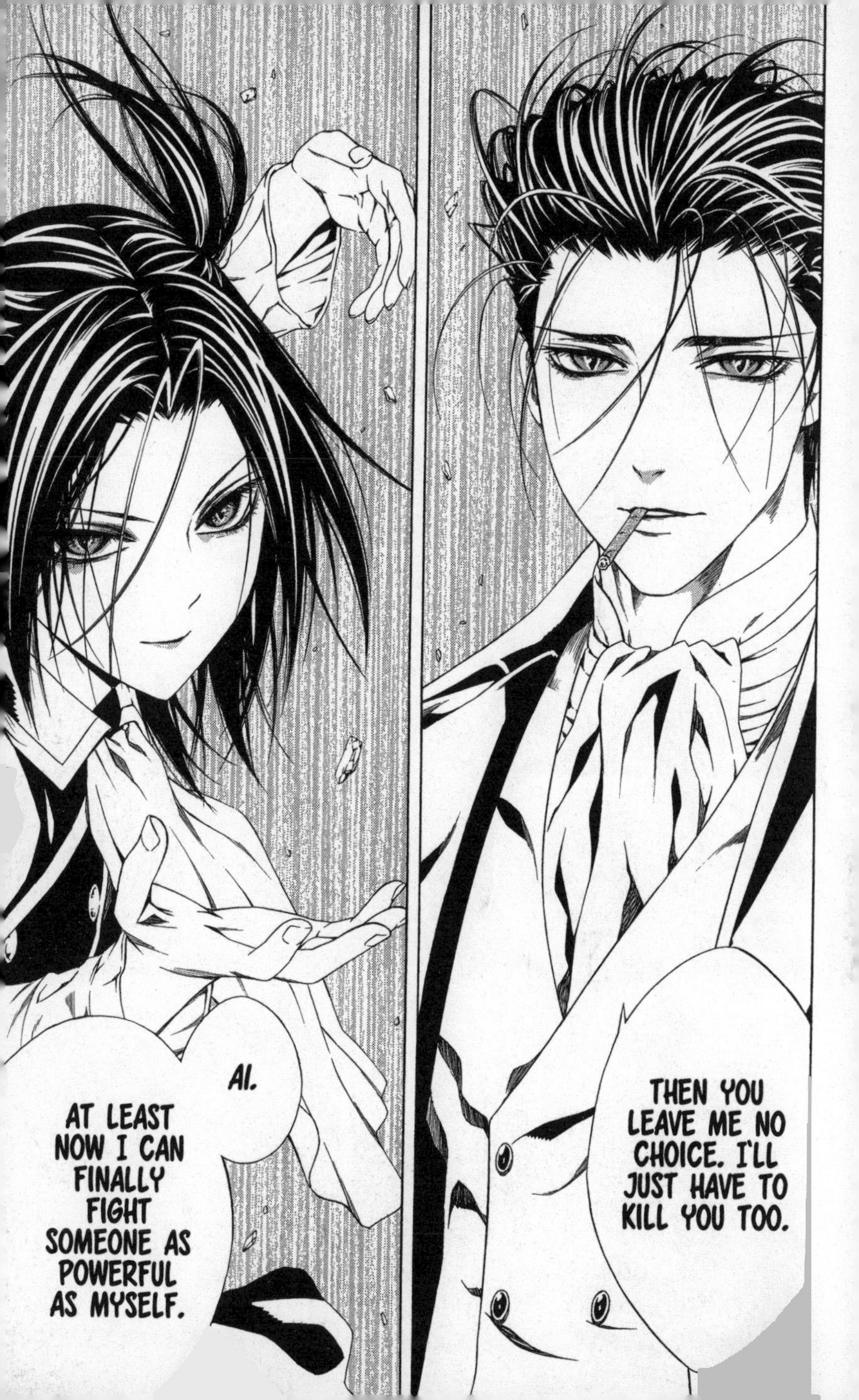
THEN YOU LEAVE ME NO CHOICE. I'LL JUST HAVE TO KILL YOU TOO.
AI.
AT LEAST NOW I CAN FINALLY FIGHT SOMEONE AS POWERFUL AS MYSELF.

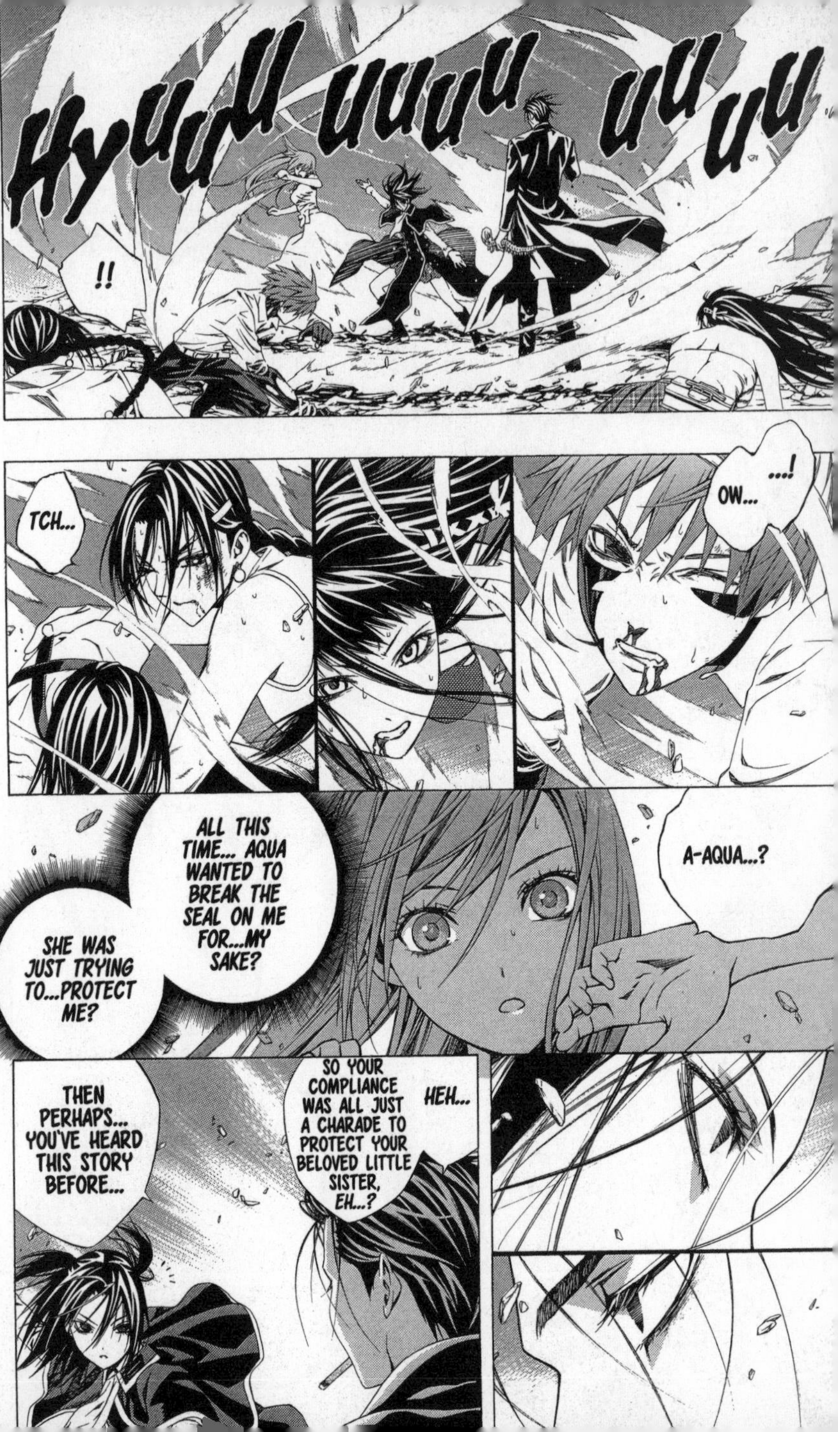
HYUUU UUUUU UUUU
!!
...!
OW...
TCH...
A-AQUA...?
ALL THIS TIME... AQUA WANTED TO BREAK THE SEAL ON ME FOR...MY SAKE?
SHE WAS JUST TRYING TO...PROTECT ME?
HEH...
SO YOUR COMPLIANCE WAS ALL JUST A CHARADE TO PROTECT YOUR BELOVED LITTLE SISTER, EH...?
THEN PERHAPS... YOU'VE HEARD THIS STORY BEFORE...

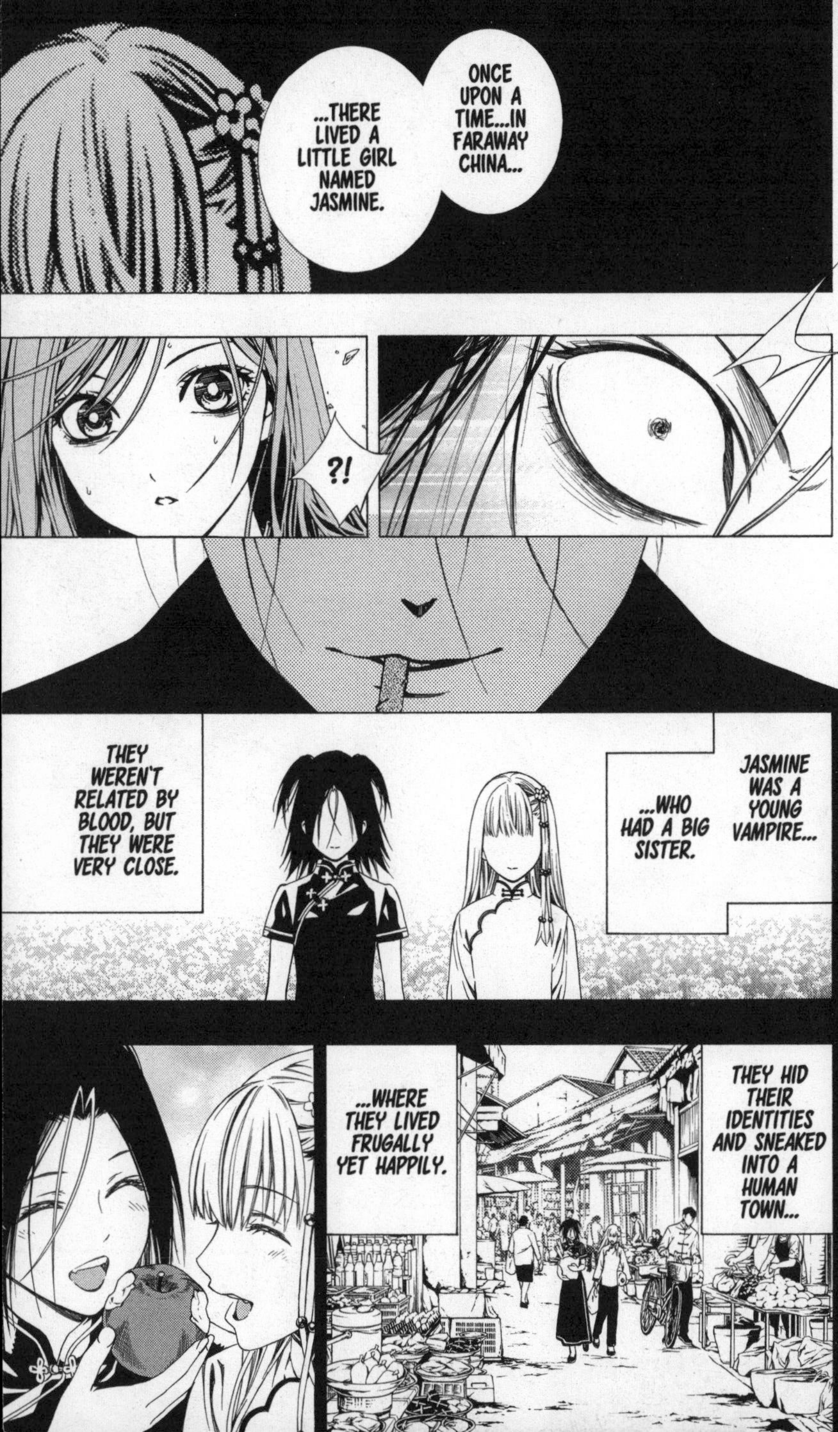
ONCE UPON A TIME...IN FARAWAY CHINA...
...THERE LIVED A LITTLE GIRL NAMED JASMINE.
?!
JASMINE WAS A YOUNG VAMPIRE...
...WHO HAD A BIG SISTER.
THEY WEREN'T RELATED BY BLOOD, BUT THEY WERE VERY CLOSE.
THEY HID THEIR IDENTITIES AND SNEAKED INTO A HUMAN TOWN...
...WHERE THEY LIVED FRUGALLY YET HAPPILY.

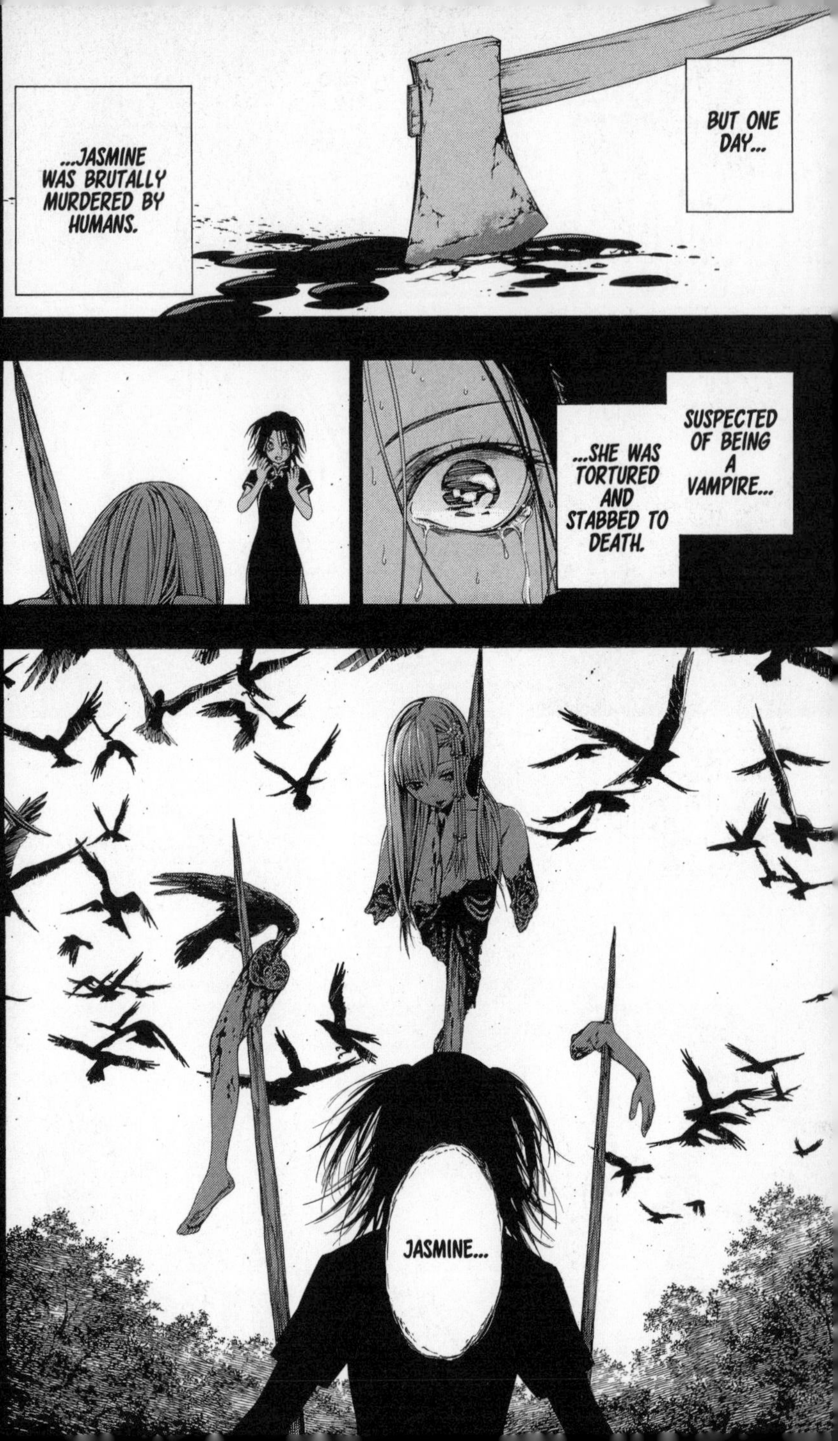
BUT ONE DAY...
...JASMINE WAS BRUTALLY MURDERED BY HUMANS.
SUSPECTED OF BEING A VAMPIRE...
...SHE WAS TORTURED AND STABBED TO DEATH.
JASMINE...

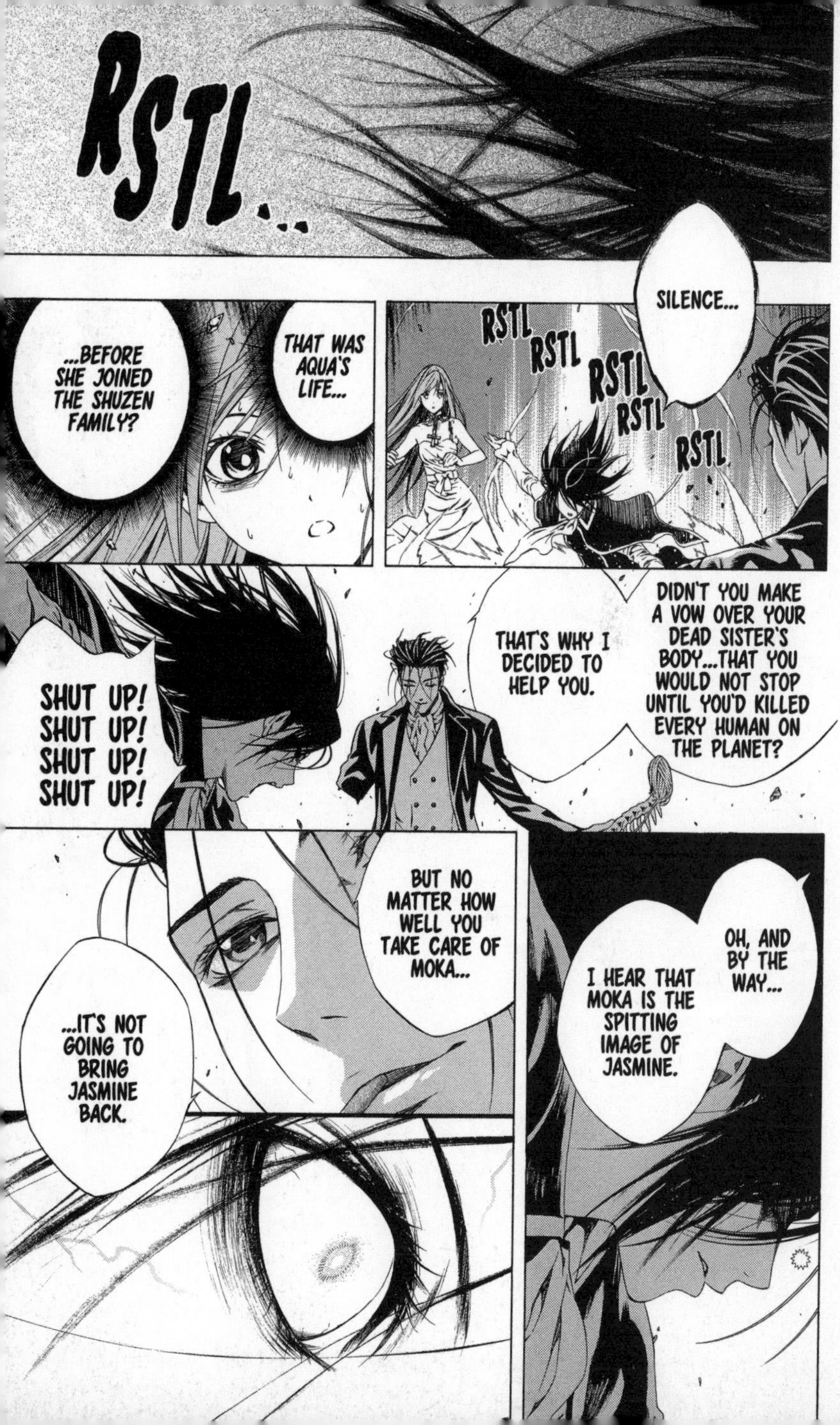
RSTL...
SILENCE...
RSTL
RSTL
RSTL
RSTL
RSTL
THAT WAS AQUA'S LIFE...
...BEFORE SHE JOINED THE SHUZEN FAMILY?
DIDN'T YOU MAKE A VOW OVER YOUR DEAD SISTER'S BODY...THAT YOU WOULD NOT STOP UNTIL YOU'D KILLED EVERY HUMAN ON THE PLANET?
THAT'S WHY I DECIDED TO HELP YOU.
SHUT UP! SHUT UP! SHUT UP! SHUT UP!
OH, AND BY THE WAY...
I HEAR THAT MOKA IS THE SPITTING IMAGE OF JASMINE.
BUT NO MATTER HOW WELL YOU TAKE CARE OF MOKA...
...IT'S NOT GOING TO BRING JASMINE BACK.

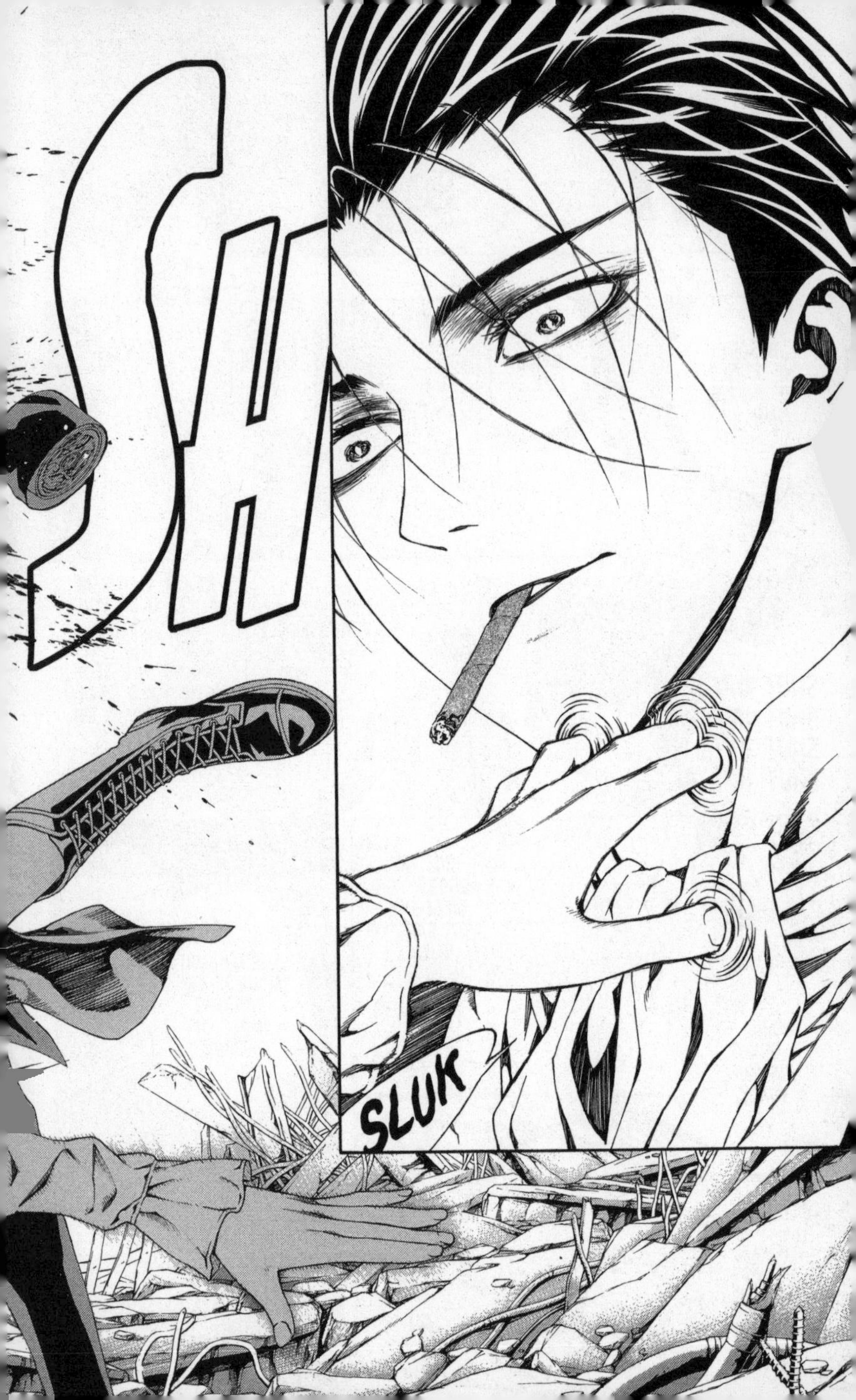
SH
SLUK

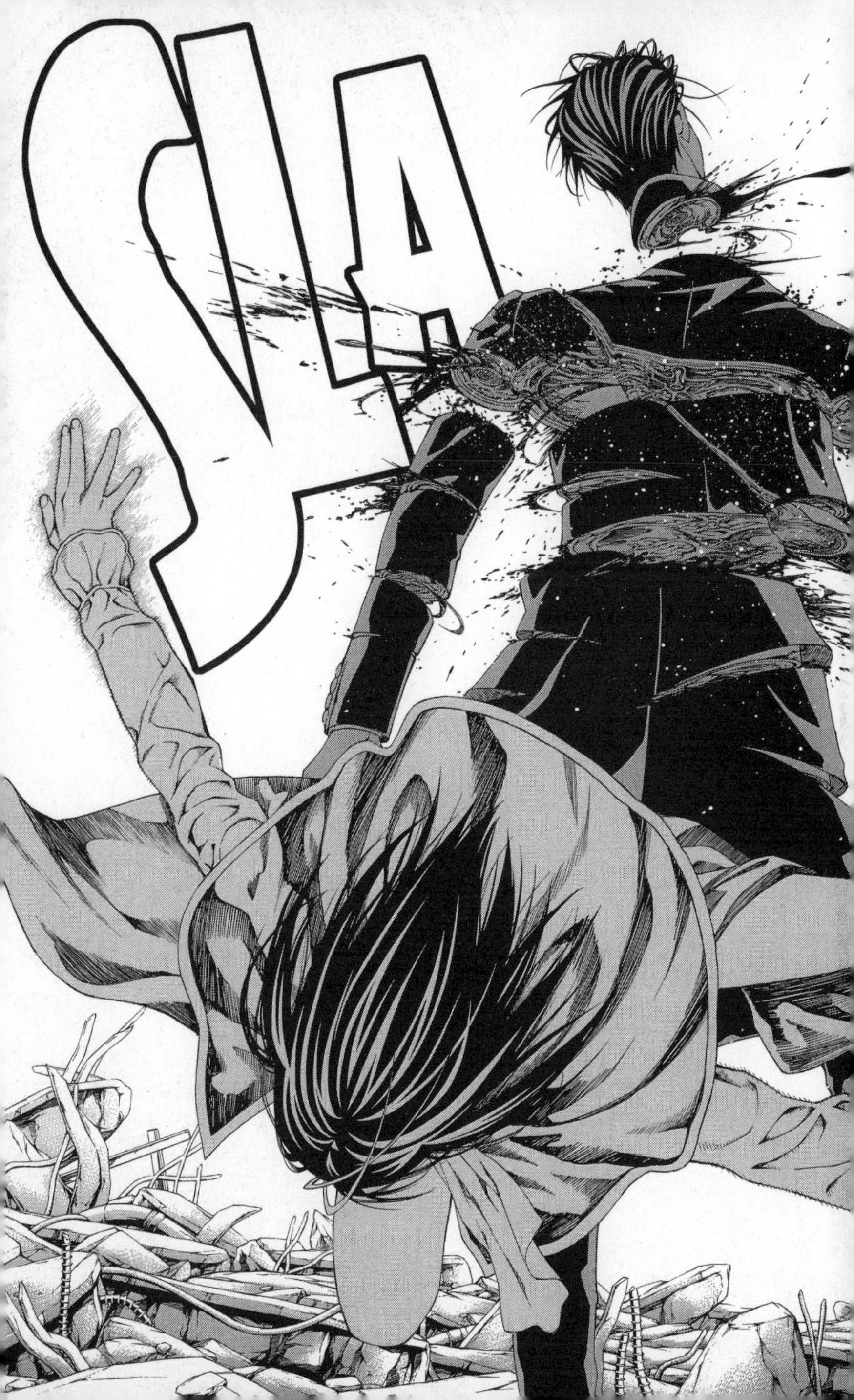

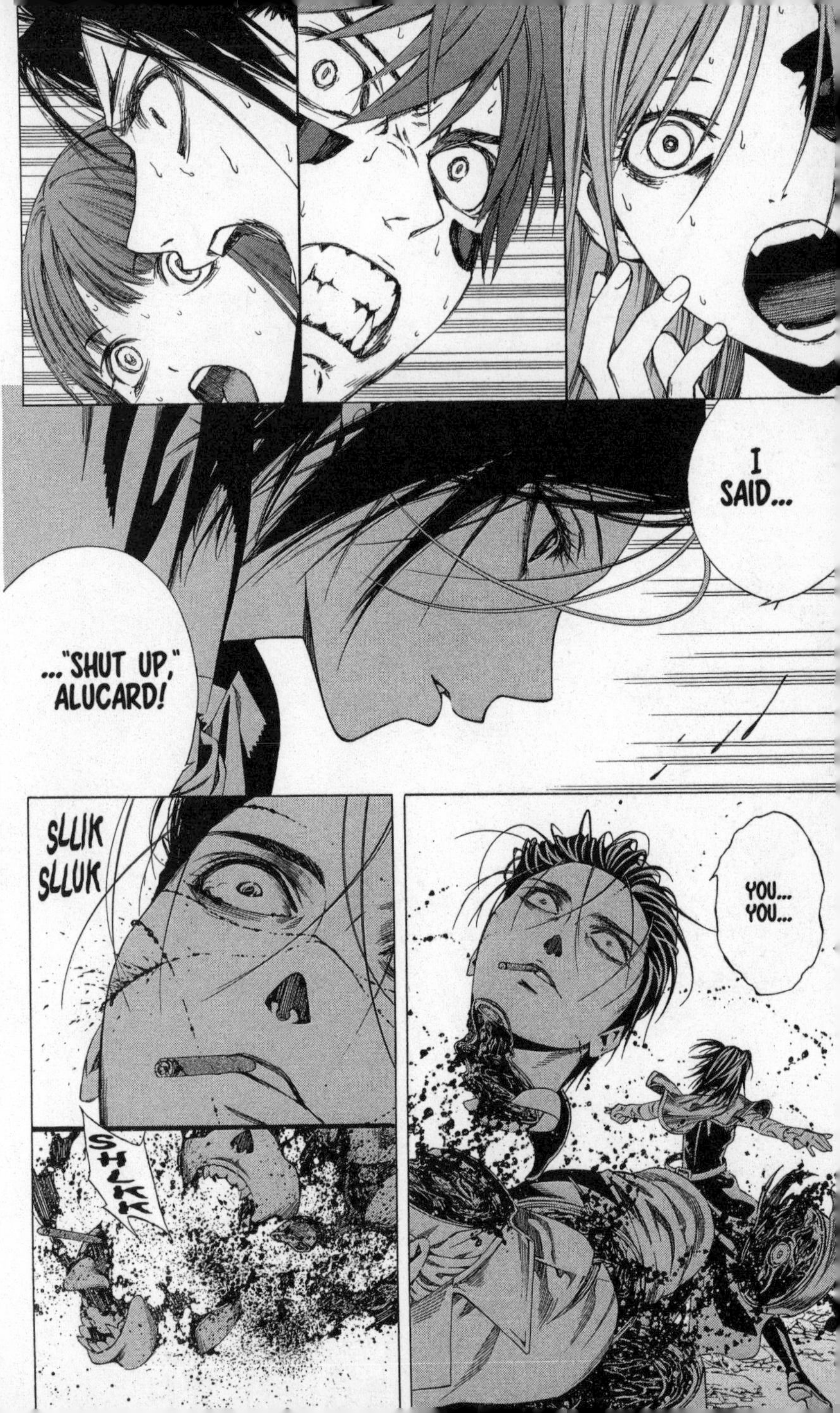
I SAID...
..."SHUT UP," ALUCARD!
YOU... YOU...
SLLIK SLLUK
SHLKK

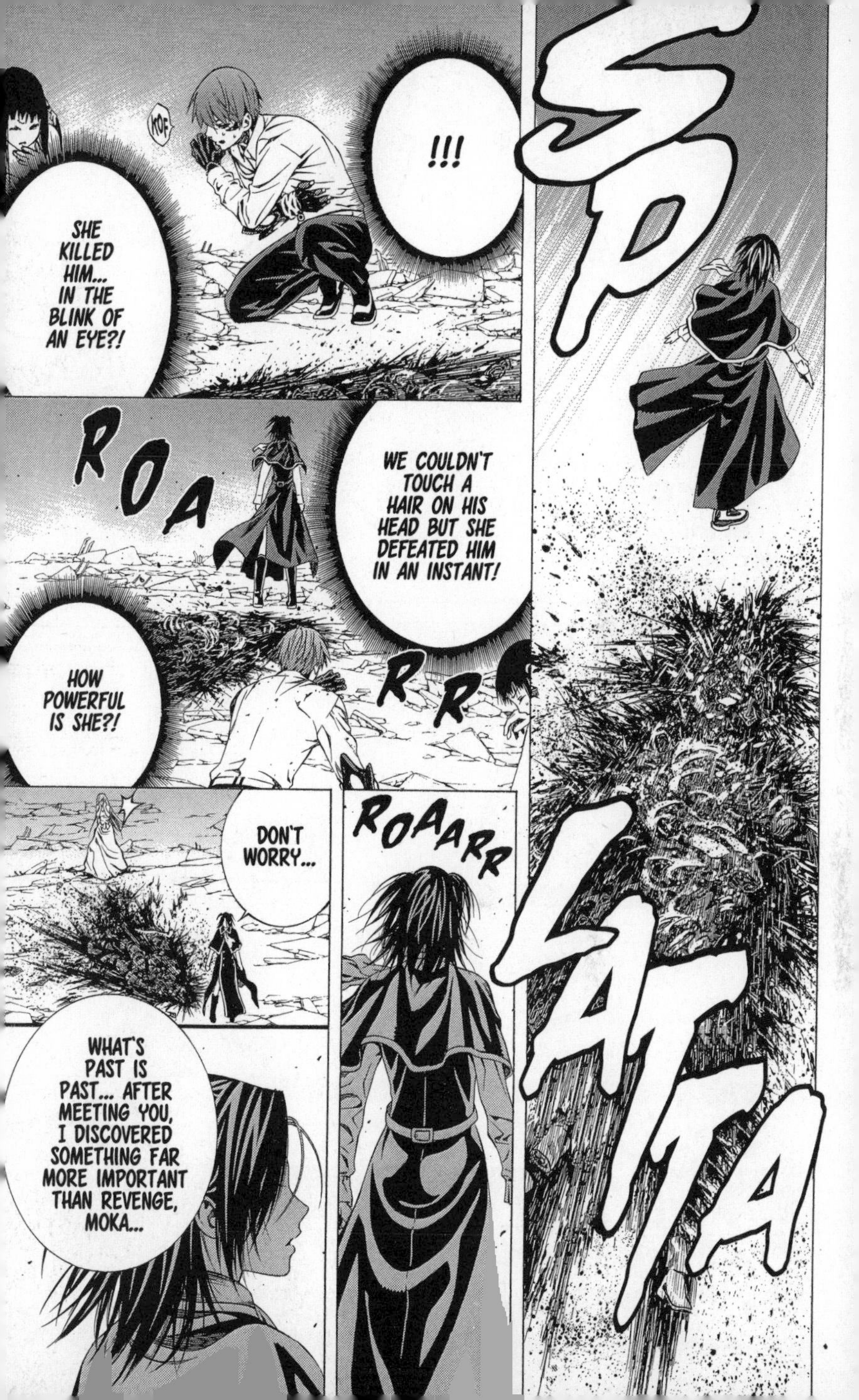
SPLATTA
!!!
KOF
SHE KILLED HIM... IN THE BLINK OF AN EYE?!
WE COULDN'T TOUCH A HAIR ON HIS HEAD BUT SHE DEFEATED HIM IN AN INSTANT!
ROARR
HOW POWERFUL IS SHE?!
ROAARR
DON'T WORRY...
WHAT'S PAST IS PAST... AFTER MEETING YOU, I DISCOVERED SOMETHING FAR MORE IMPORTANT THAN REVENGE, MOKA...

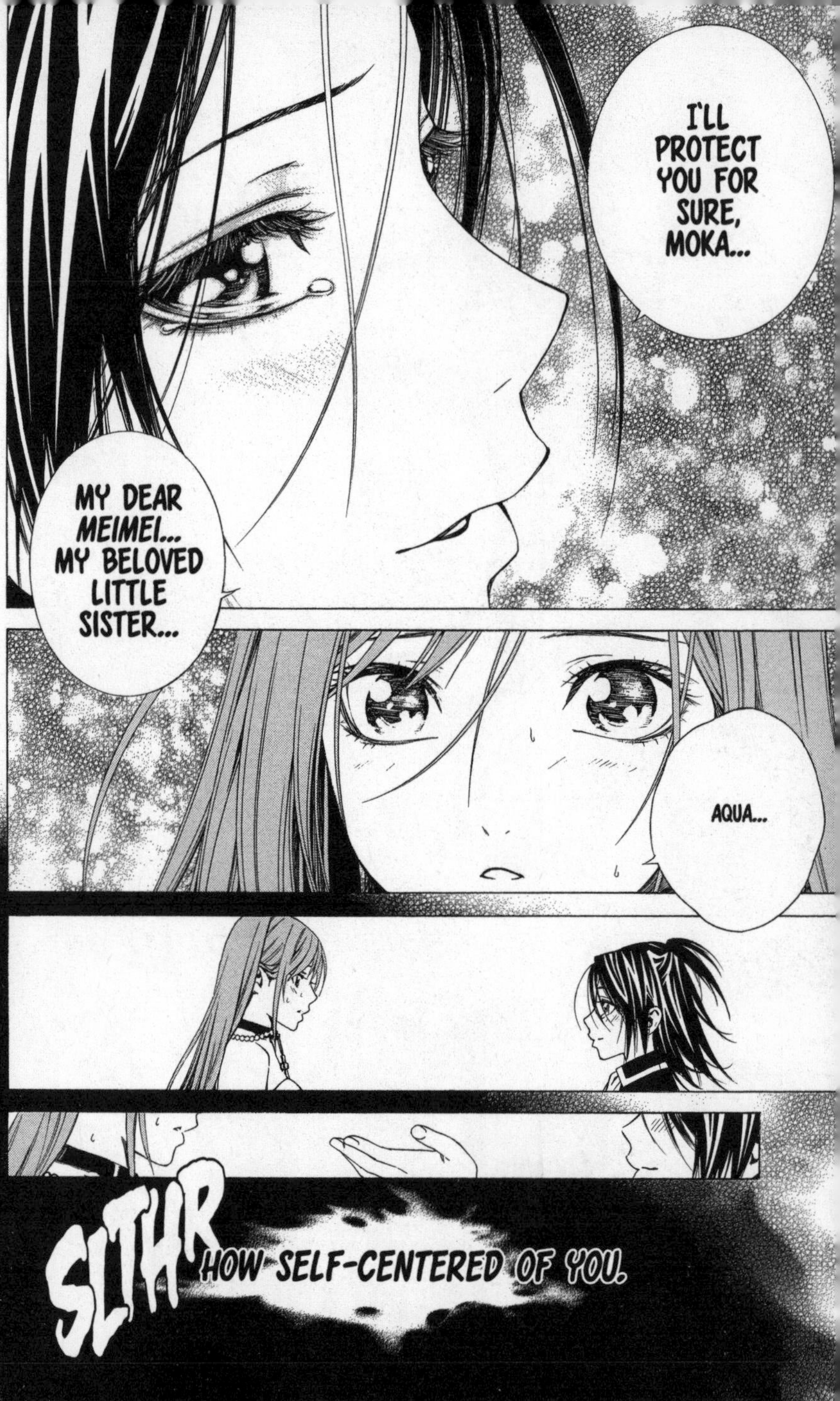
I'LL PROTECT YOU FOR SURE, MOKA...
MY DEAR MEIMEI... MY BELOVED LITTLE SISTER...
AQUA...
SLTHR
HOW SELF-CENTERED OF YOU.

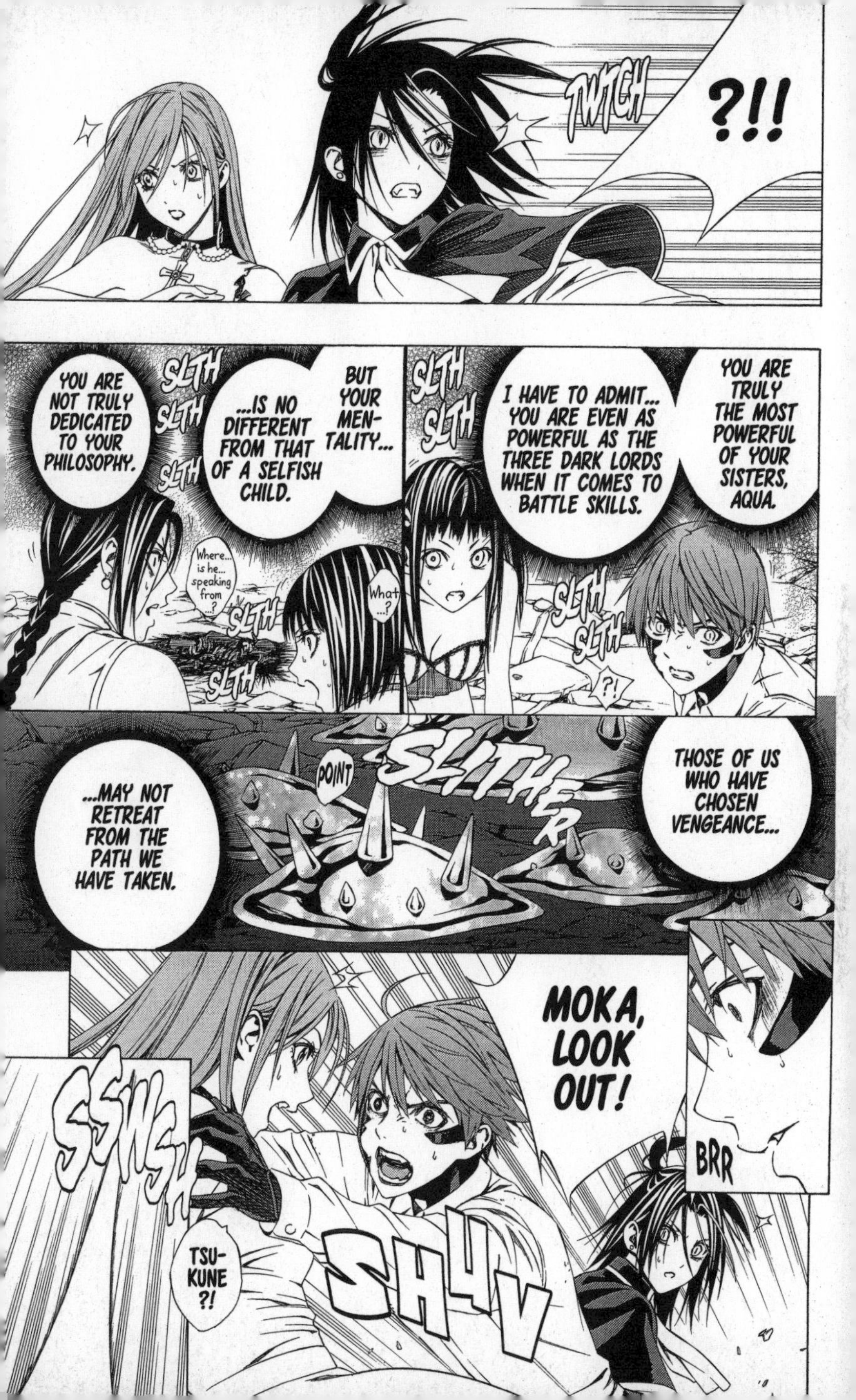
?!!
TWITCH
YOU ARE TRULY THE MOST POWERFUL OF YOUR SISTERS, AQUA.
I HAVE TO ADMIT... YOU ARE EVEN AS POWERFUL AS THE THREE DARK LORDS WHEN IT COMES TO BATTLE SKILLS.
SLTH SLTH
SLTH SLTH
?!
What ...?
BUT YOUR MEN-TALITY...
...IS NO DIFFERENT FROM THAT OF A SELFISH CHILD.
SLTH SLTH SLTH
YOU ARE NOT TRULY DEDICATED TO YOUR PHILOSOPHY.
Where... is he... speaking from ...?
SLTH
SLTH
THOSE OF US WHO HAVE CHOSEN VENGEANCE...
SLITHER
POINT
...MAY NOT RETREAT FROM THE PATH WE HAVE TAKEN.
BRR
MOKA, LOOK OUT!
SHUV
SSWSH
TSU-KUNE ?!

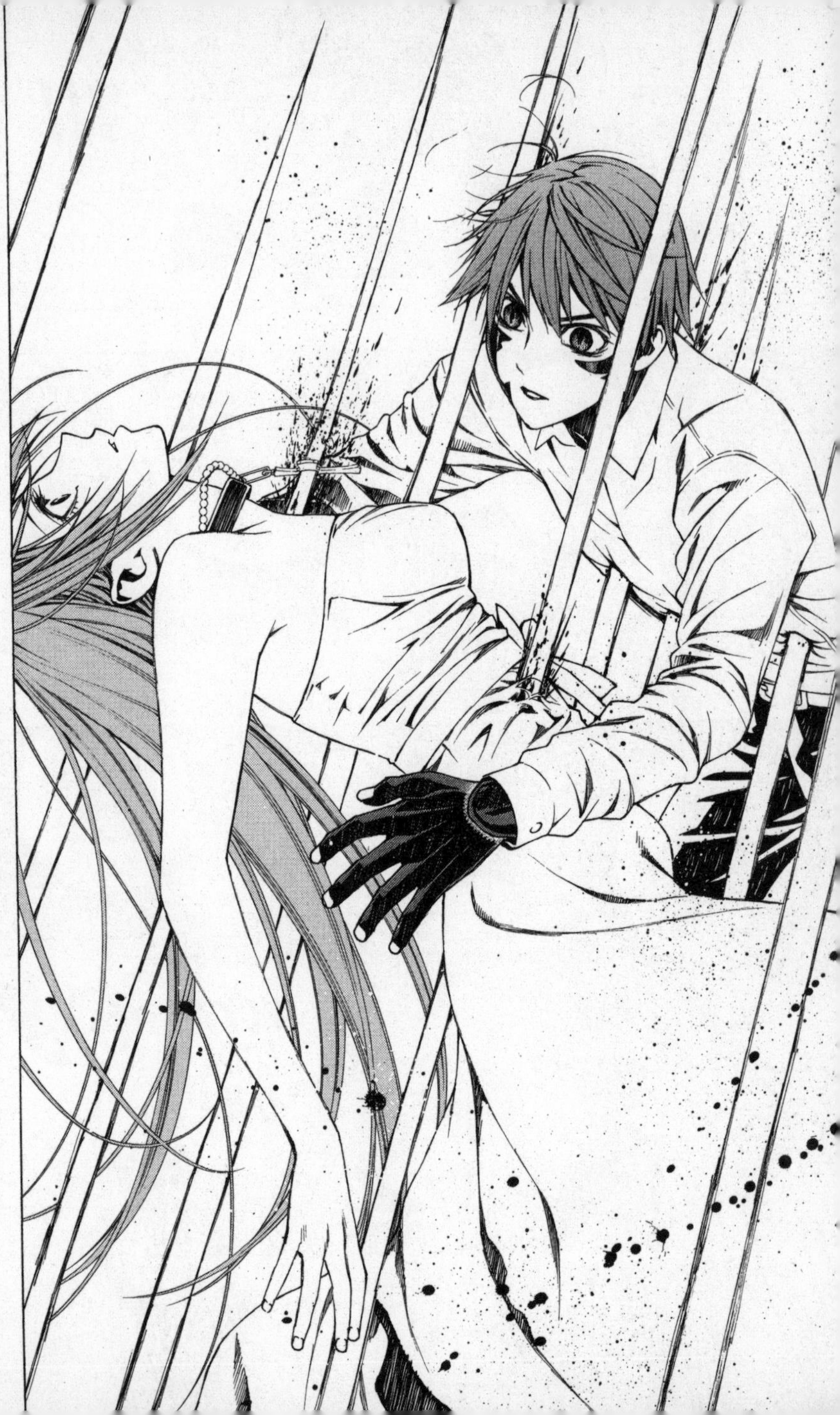

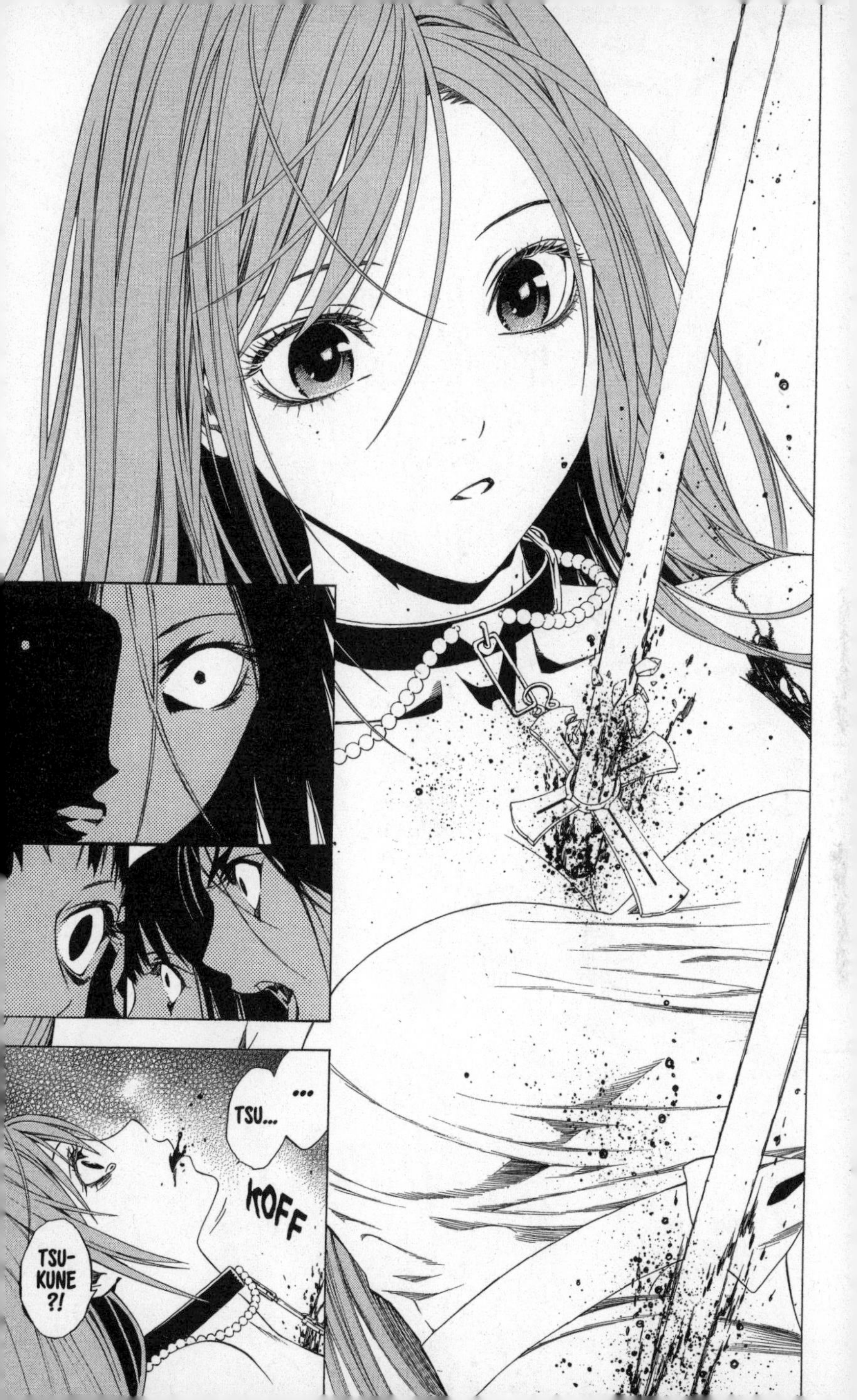
...
TSU...
KOFF
TSU-
KUNE
?!

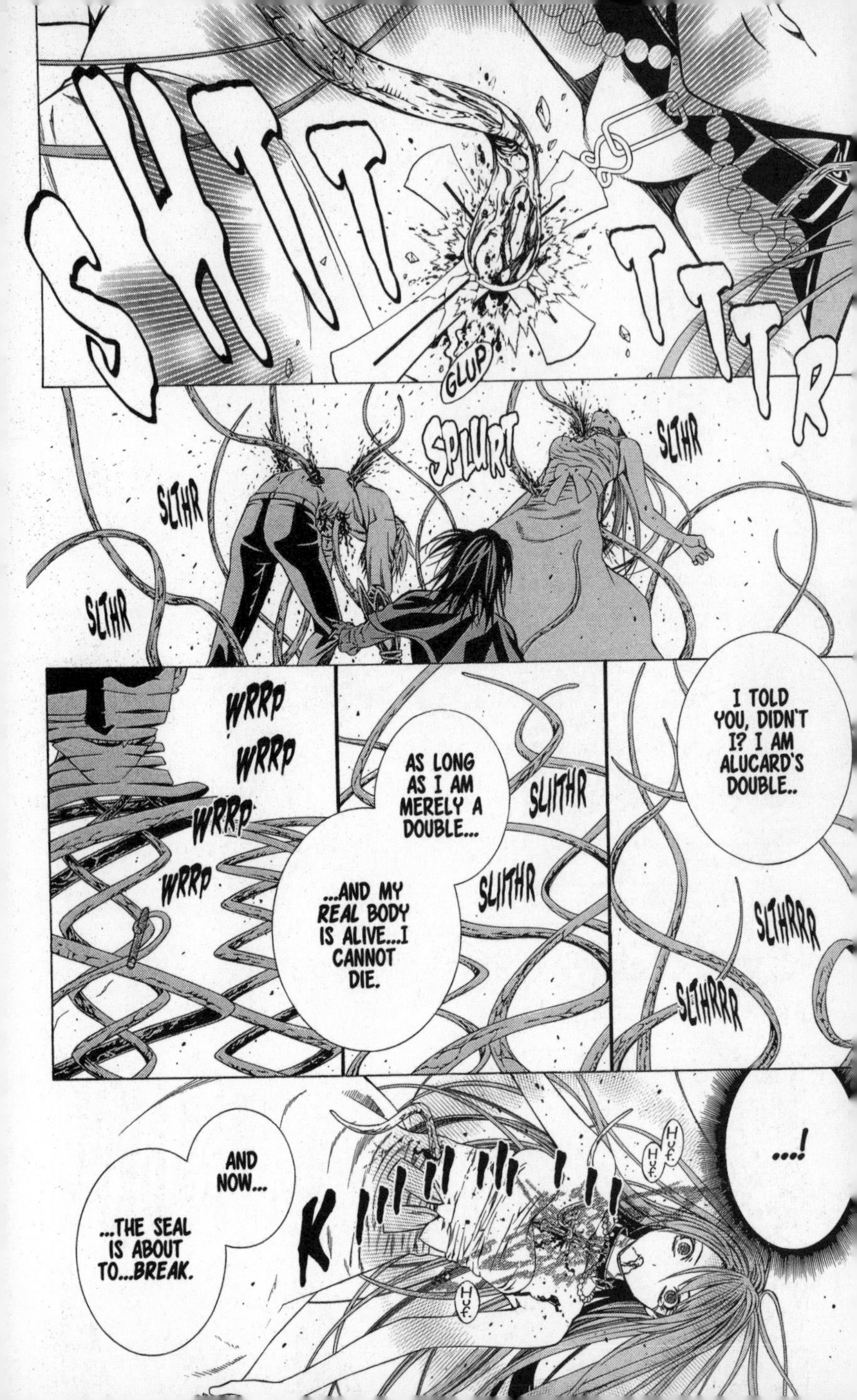
SHTIT
TTTR
GLUP
SPLURT
SLTHR
SLTHR
SLTHR
I TOLD YOU, DIDN'T I? I AM ALUCARD'S DOUBLE..
SLTHRRR
SLTHRRR
AS LONG AS I AM MERELY A DOUBLE...
...AND MY REAL BODY IS ALIVE...I CANNOT DIE.
SLIITHR
SLIITHR
WRRP
WRRP
WRRP
WRRP
...!
Huf.
Huf.
Huf.
KIIIIIII
AND NOW...
...THE SEAL IS ABOUT TO...BREAK.

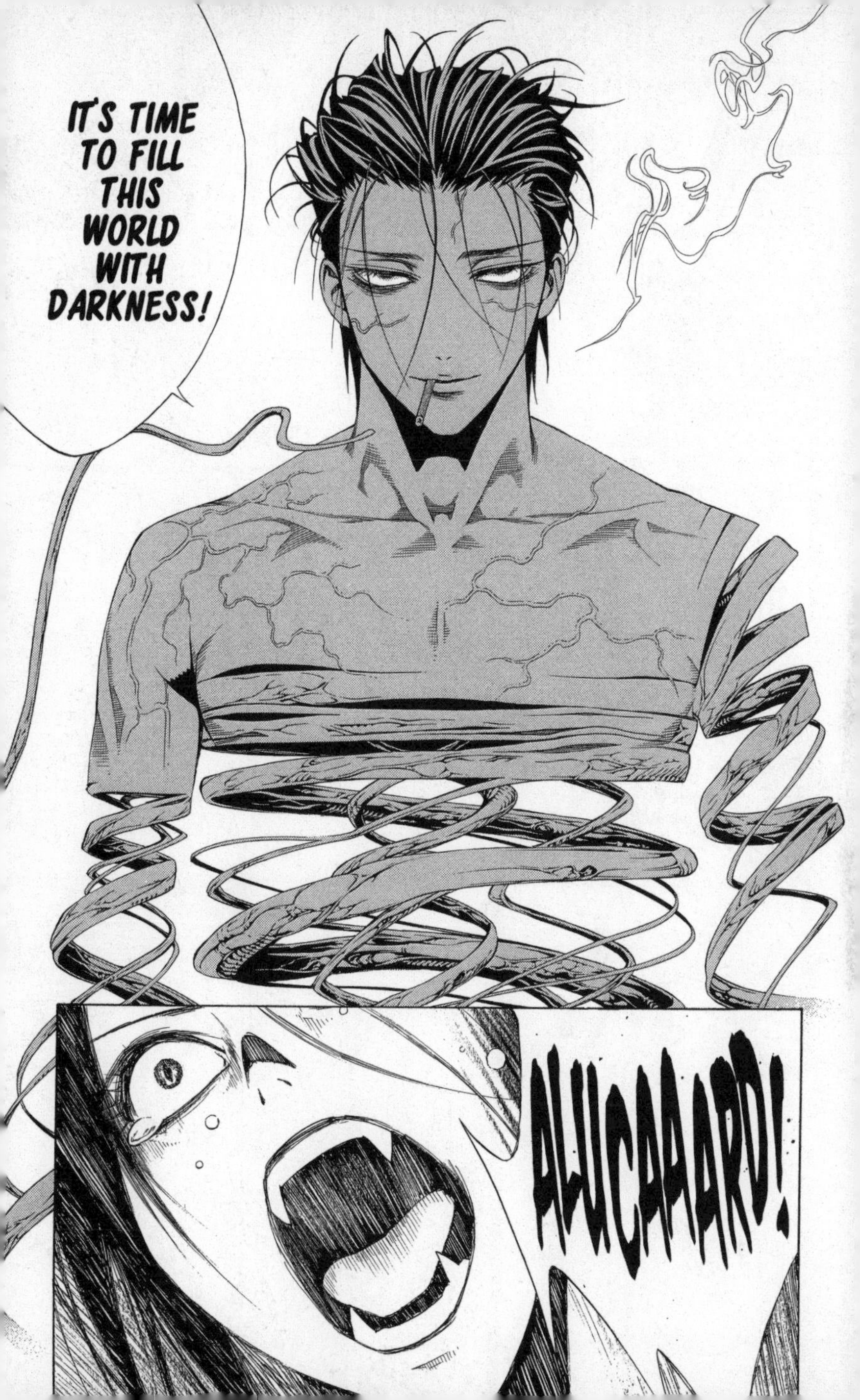
IT'S TIME TO FILL THIS WORLD WITH DARKNESS!
ALUCAAARD!

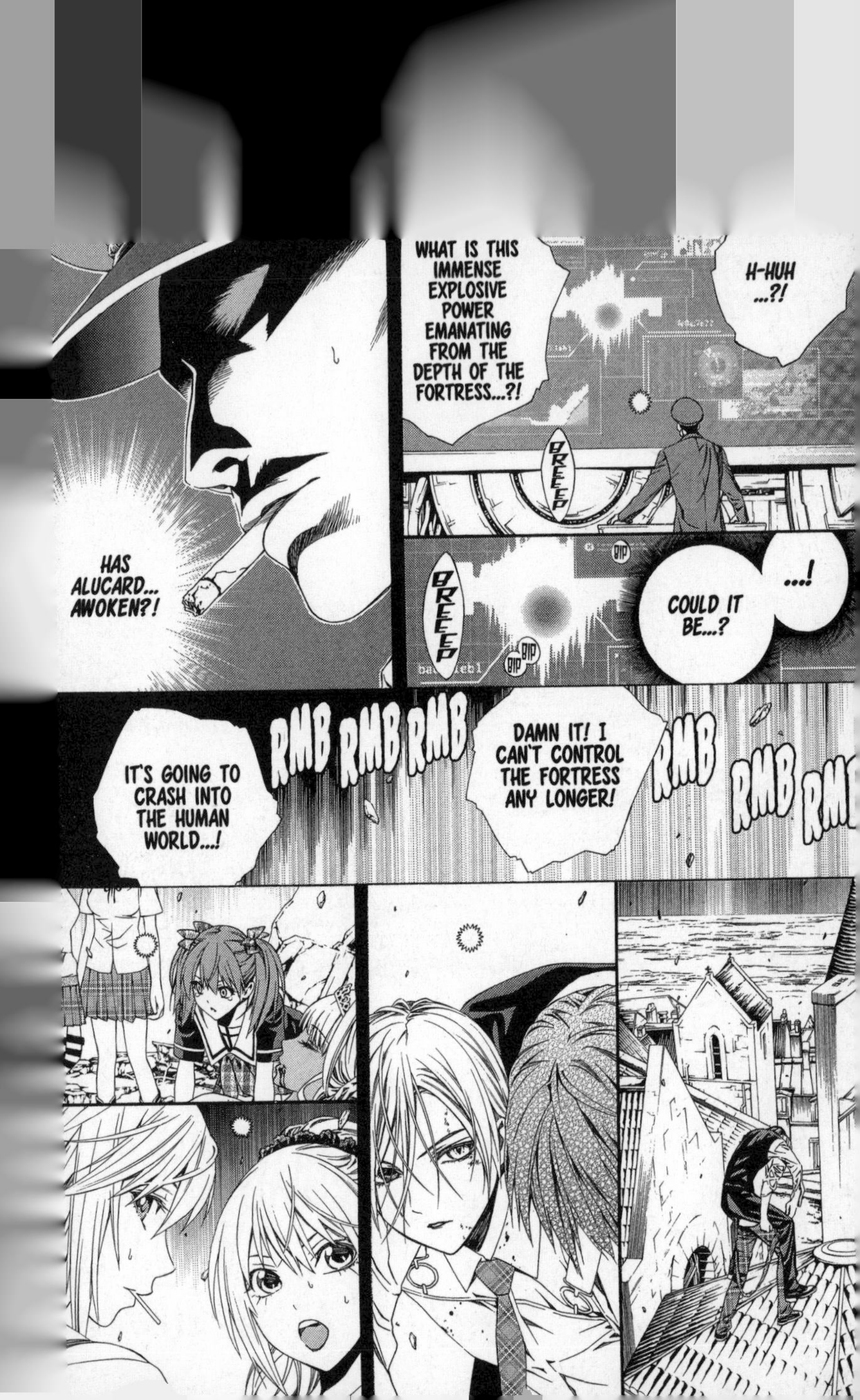

H-HUH ...?!
WHAT IS THIS IMMENSE EXPLOSIVE POWER EMANATING FROM THE DEPTH OF THE FORTRESS...?!
BREEEP
...!
COULD IT BE...?
BIP
BREEEP
BIP BIP
HAS ALUCARD... AWOKEN?!
RMB RMB RMB
DAMN IT! I CAN'T CONTROL THE FORTRESS ANY LONGER!
RMB RMB RMB
IT'S GOING TO CRASH INTO THE HUMAN WORLD...!

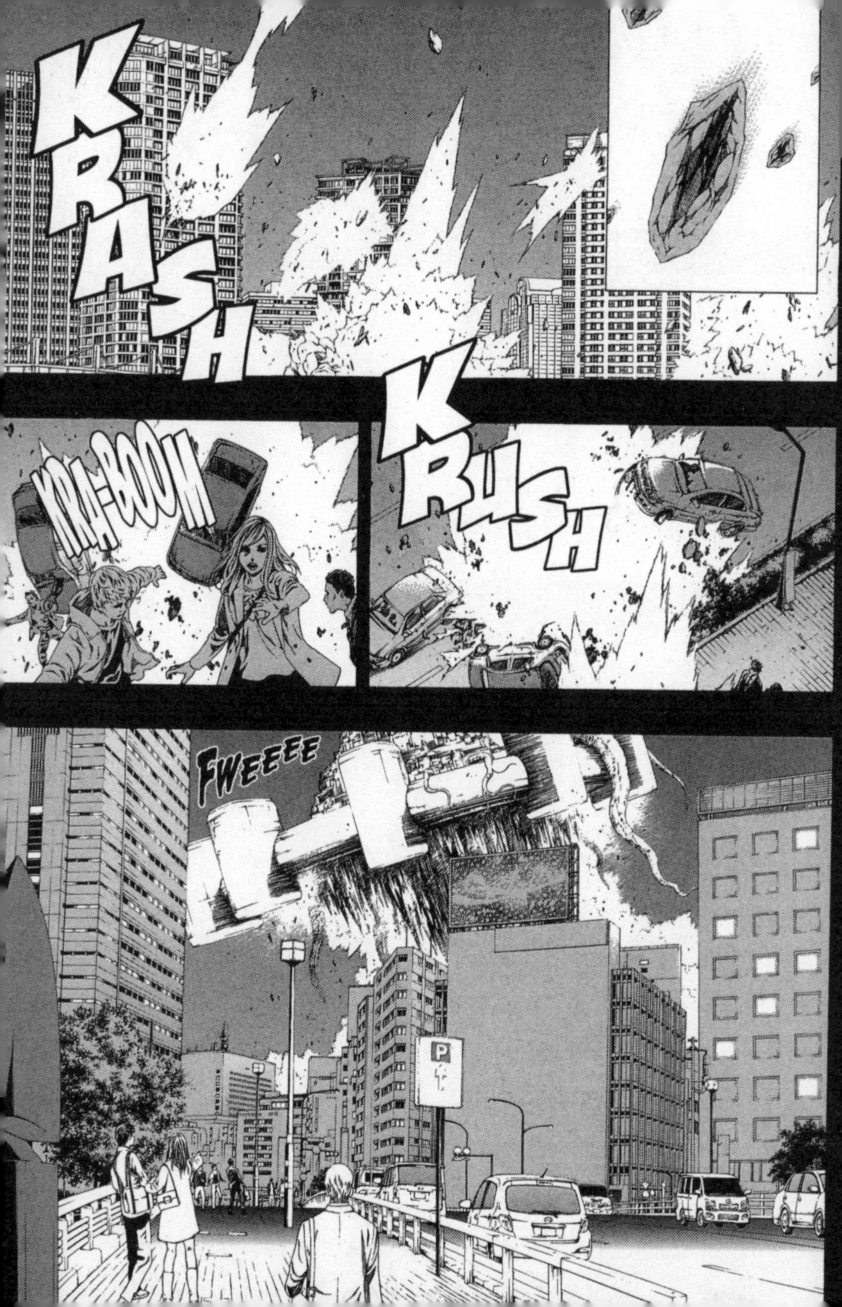
KRASH
KRUSH
KRA-BOOM
FWEEEE

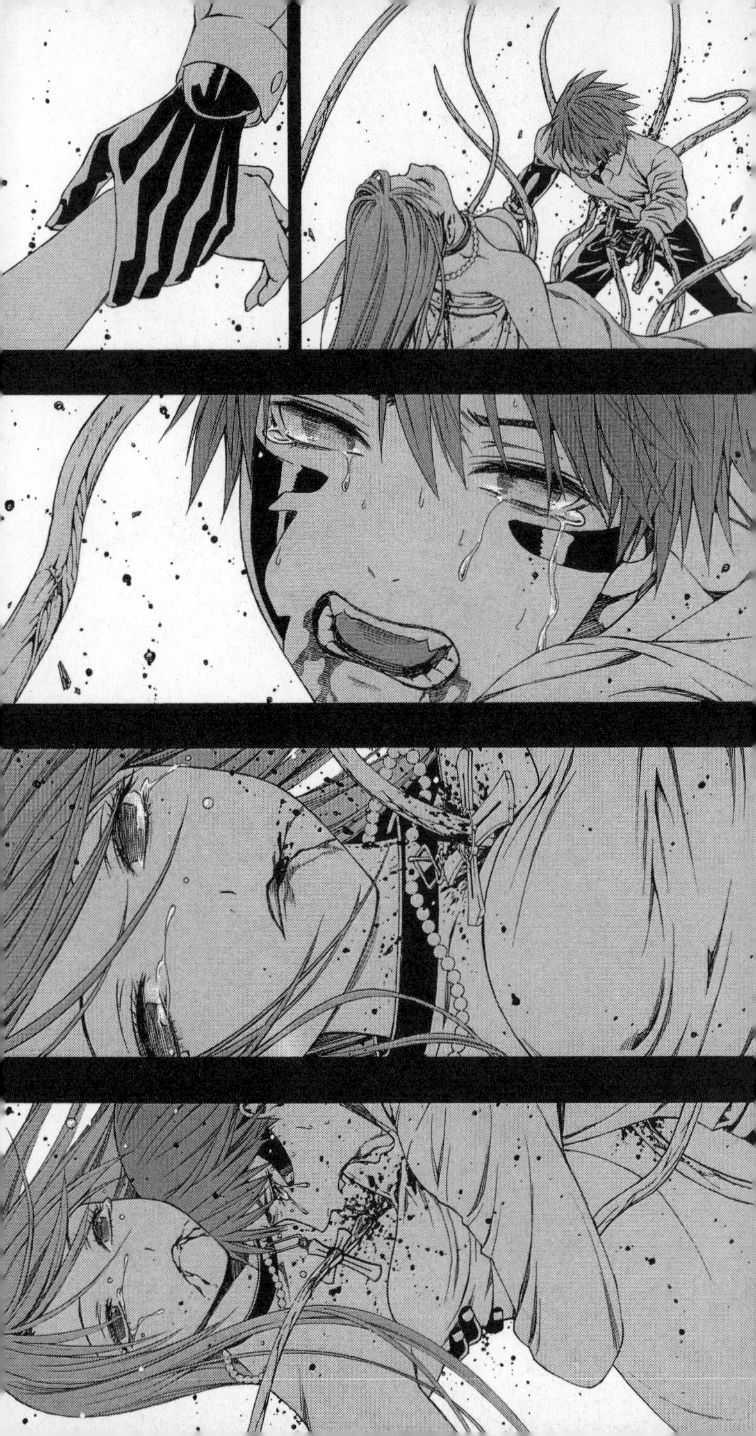

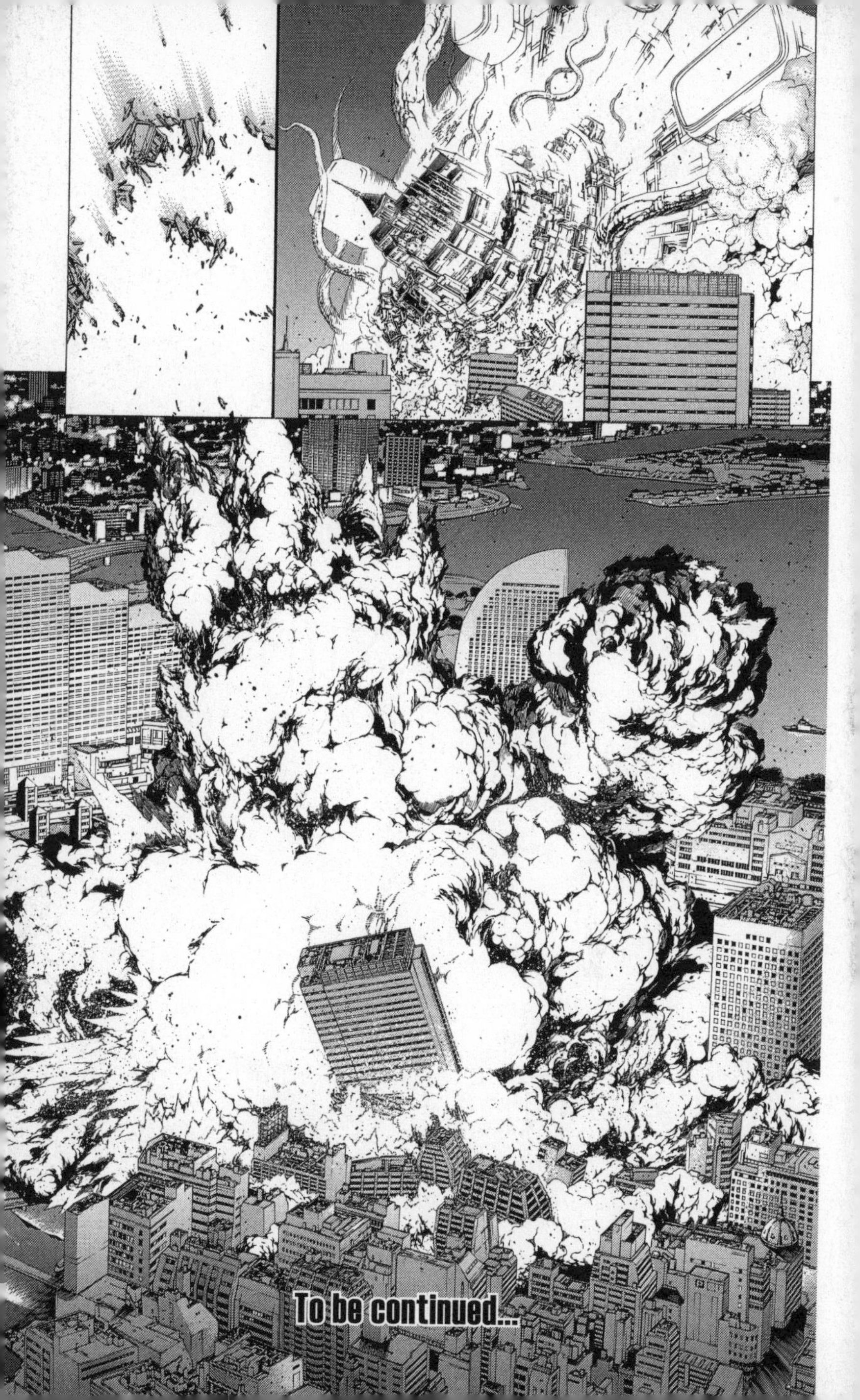
To be continued...

Meaningless End-of-Volume Theater

XIII

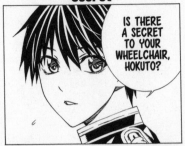

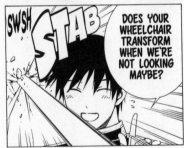

SKWEE

•Secret•

IS THERE A SECRET TO YOUR WHEELCHAIR, HOKUTO?
HOW DO YOU MEAN?
WELL...YOU DON'T HAVE A PROBLEM GOING OVER BUMPS...
...AND I SUSPECT YOU CAN EVEN CLIMB THESE STAIRS IN IT.
DOES YOUR WHEELCHAIR TRANSFORM WHEN WE'RE NOT LOOKING MAYBE?
STAB
SWSH
THAT'S RIDICULOUS! COME ON, WE HAVE TO HURRY!
STAB
PUSH
STAB
...

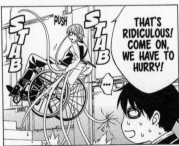

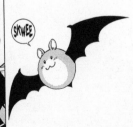

•A Man of Mystery•

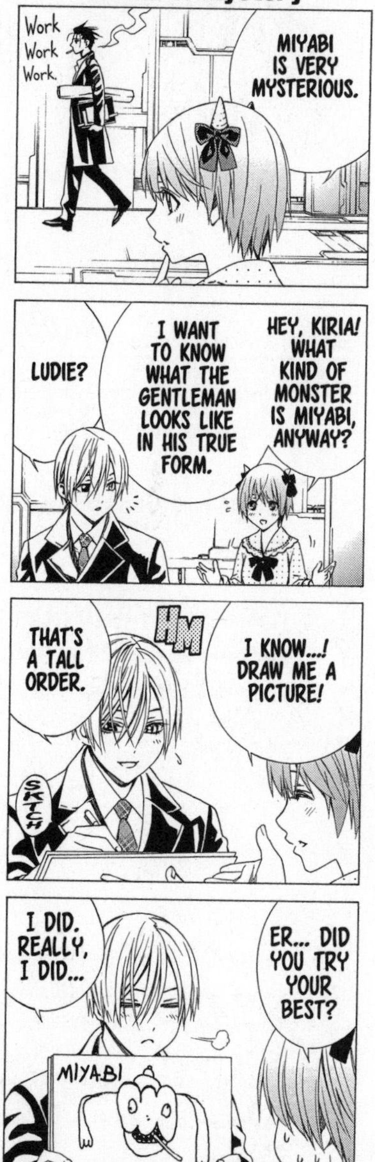
MIYABI IS VERY MYSTERIOUS.
Work Work Work.
HEY, KIRIA! WHAT KIND OF MONSTER IS MIYABI, ANYWAY?
I WANT TO KNOW WHAT THE GENTLEMAN LOOKS LIKE IN HIS TRUE FORM.
LUDIE?
I KNOW...! DRAW ME A PICTURE!
HM
THAT'S A TALL ORDER.
SKTCH
ER... DID YOU TRY YOUR BEST?
I DID. REALLY, I DID...
MIYABI

• More Mysteries of the Man of Mystery •

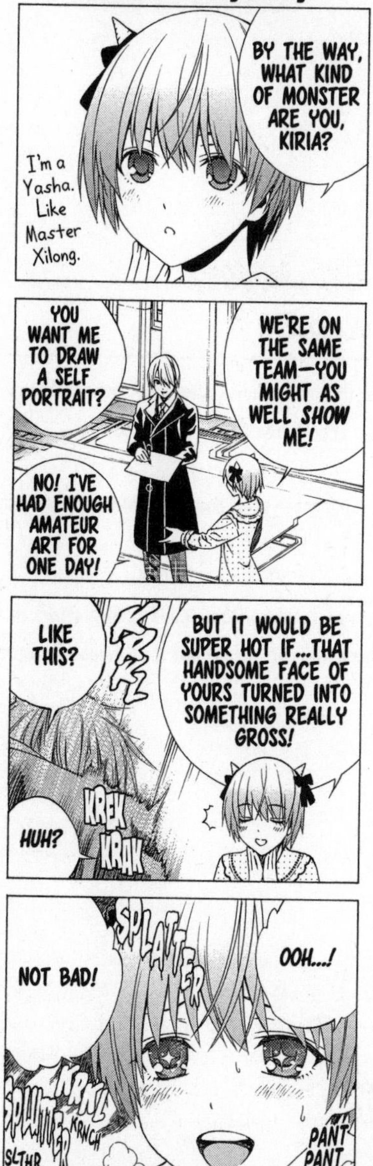
BY THE WAY, WHAT KIND OF MONSTER ARE YOU, KIRIA?
I'm a Yasha. Like Master Xilong.
WE'RE ON THE SAME TEAM—YOU MIGHT AS WELL SHOW ME!
YOU WANT ME TO DRAW A SELF PORTRAIT?
NO! I'VE HAD ENOUGH AMATEUR ART FOR ONE DAY!
BUT IT WOULD BE SUPER HOT IF...THAT HANDSOME FACE OF YOURS TURNED INTO SOMETHING REALLY GROSS!
KRKL
LIKE THIS?
KREK KRAK
HUH?
OOH...!
SPLATTER
NOT BAD!
PANT PANT
KRKL
KRNCH
SPLUTTER
SLTHR

Staff: Akihisa Ikeda, Makoto Saito, Nobuyuki Hayashi, Rika Shirota
Help: Yosuke Takeda, Osamu Nishi   Editor: Shuhei Watanabe   Comic: Kenju Noro

AKIHISA IKEDA

There's a line in the movie *The Wind Rises*, by director Hayao Miyazaki—whom I greatly respect—that goes, "The time limit on an artist's creativity is ten years."

Rosario + Vampire has been running for roughly ten years now. And the story has reached its climax.

I want to put everything I have into this work so I can hold my head up high after I've used up my ten years and say, "I became a manga artist to create this." Please continue to support me until the end.

Akihisa Ikeda was born in 1976 in Miyazaki. He debuted as a mangaka with the four-volume magical warrior fantasy series *Kiruto* in 2002, which was serialized in *Monthly Shonen Jump*. *Rosario+Vampire* debuted in *Monthly Shonen Jump* in March of 2004 and is continuing in the magazine *Jump Square (Jump SQ)* as *Rosario+Vampire: Season II*. In Japan, *Rosario+Vampire* is also available as a drama CD. In 2008, the story was released as an anime. Season II is also available as an anime now. And in Japan, there is a Nintendo DS game based on the series.

Ikeda has been a huge fan of vampires and monsters since he was a little kid. He says one of the perks of being a manga artist is being able to go for walks during the day when everybody else is stuck in the office.

ROSARIO+VAMPIRE: Season II
13
SHONEN JUMP ADVANCED Manga Edition

STORY & ART BY AKIHISA IKEDA

Translation/Tetsuichiro Miyaki
English Adaptation/Annette Roman
Touch-up Art & Lettering/Stephen Dutro
Cover & Interior Design/Ronnie Casson
Editor/Annette Roman

Printed in the U.S.A.

Published by VIZ Media, LLC
P.O. Box 77010
San Francisco, CA 94107

10 9 8 7 6 5 4 3 2 1
First printing, August 2014

www.viz.com

www.shonenjump.com

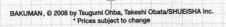

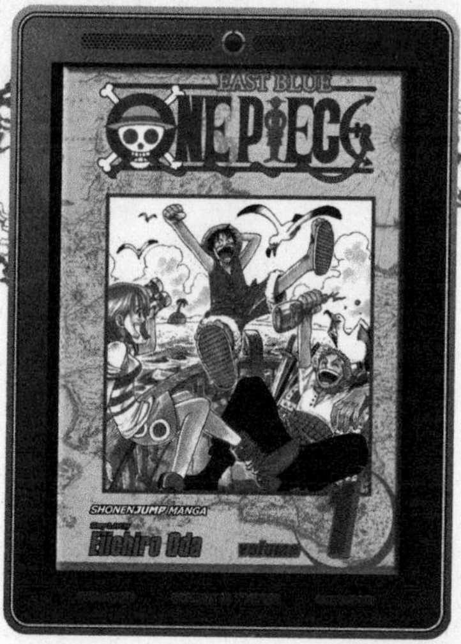
EAST BLUE
ONE PIECE
SHONEN JUMP MANGA
Eiichiro Oda
volume
1

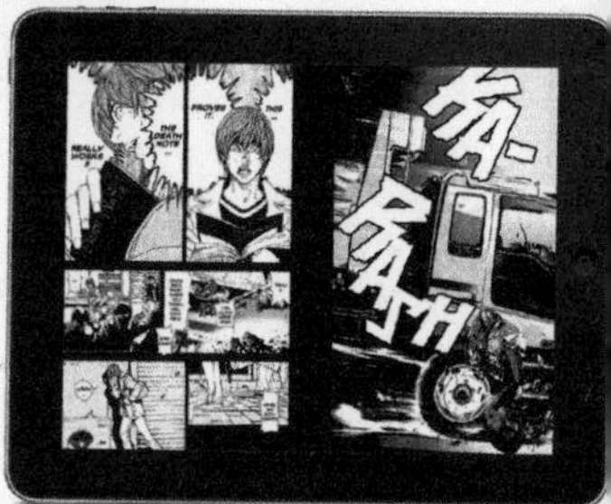

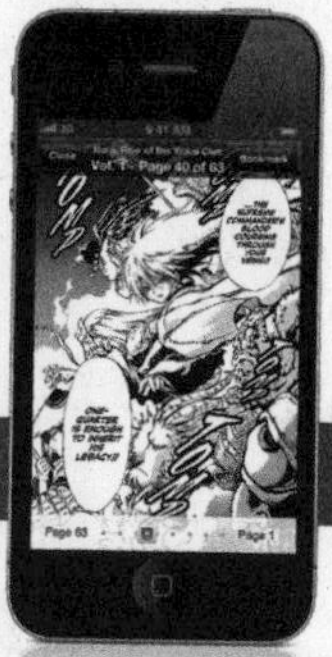

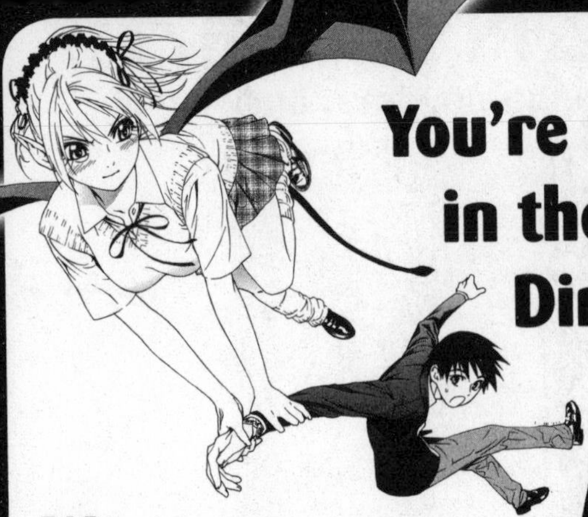

You're Reading in the Wrong Direction!!

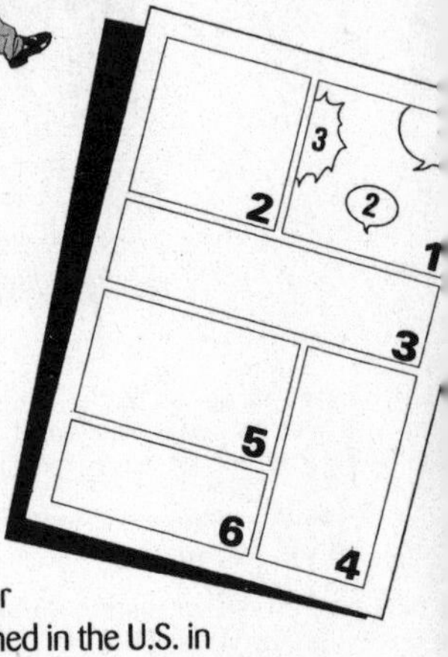

1
2
3
4
5
6

Whoops! Guess what? You're starting at the wrong end of the comic!

...It's true! In keeping with the original Japanese format, **Rosario+Vampire** is meant to be read from right to left, starting in the upper-right corner.

Unlike English, which is read from left to right, Japanese is read from right to left, meaning action, sound effects and word-balloon order are completely reversed... something which can make readers unfamiliar with Japanese feel pretty backwards themselves. For this reason, manga or Japanese comics published in the U.S. in English have sometimes been published "flopped"—that is, printed in exact reverse order, as though seen from the other side of a mirror.

By flopping pages, U.S. publishers can avoid confusing readers, but the compromise is not without its downside. For one thing, a character in a flopped manga series who once wore in the original Japanese version a T-shirt emblazoned with "M A Y" (as in "the merry month of") now wears one which reads "Y A M"! Additionally, many manga creators in Japan are themselves unhappy with the process, as some feel the mirror-imaging of their art skews their original intentions.

We are proud to bring you Akihisa Ikeda's **Rosario+Vampire** in the original unflopped format. For now, though, turn to the other side of the book and let the haunting begin...!

—Editor